UNBEARABLE WEIGHT

UNBEARABLE WEIGHT

FEMINISM,
WESTERN CULTURE,
AND THE BODY

Tenth Anniversary Edition

SUSAN BORDO

NEW PREFACE by the Author
NEW FOREWORD by Leslie Heywood

University of California Press
Berkeley · Los Angeles · London

University of California Press
Berkeley and Los Angeles, California

University of California Press, Ltd.
London, England

First Paperback Printing 1995
Tenth Anniversary Edition, 2003

Library of Congress Cataloging-in-Publication Data

Bordo, Susan, 1947–
 Unbearable weight : feminism, Western culture, and the body /
Susan Bordo ; with a new preface by the author ; new foreword
by Leslie Heywood. — 10th anniversary ed.
  p. cm.
 Originally published: c1993.
 Includes bibliographical references and index.
 ISBN 978-0-520-24054-4 (pbk. : alk. paper)
 1. Feminine beauty (Aesthetics)—United States.
2. Body, Human—Social aspects—United States.
3. Body image—United States. 4. Self-esteem in
women—United States. 5. Feminist criticism—
United States. I. Title.
HQ1220.U5B67 2004
305.42—dc21   2003055221

Printed in the United States of America

15 14 13 12 11 10 09
11 10 9 8 7 6 5

For Edward

Contents

Foreword: Reading Bordo

I first came upon Susan Bordo as a graduate student in an English department that specialized in critical theory. Its students were well versed in the languages of deconstruction and Lacanian psycho-analysis, as well as Foucauldian genealogies. Feeling a bit alienated, excluded, and desperate to prove our worth in that context, a group of students formed a feminist theory reading group that persisted for five years. Given our particular training in what counted as important and what didn't, the feminist theory we read was of a specific kind, often connected to the theorists named above. So it was that the summer of 1989 found us reading the essay collection *Feminism and Foucault: Reflections on Resistance,* which contained Bordo's early essay "Anorexia Nervosa: Psychopathology as the Crystallization of Culture."

What a difference an essay makes. Before reading Bordo, like many I was a driven, not particularly enthusiastic student. While I could churn out papers, I was detached from my work in a way that theory seemed to encourage, and I wrote in the highly abstract voice that was expected of graduate students at the time. I was not, as they say, *engaged.* But the afternoon I sat down to read Bordo's piece, my love of language, my sense of passionate connection to works I read, began to return with Bordo's words: "I take the psychopathologies that develop within a culture, far from being anomalies or aberrations, as characteristic expressions of that culture, as the crystallization, indeed, of much that is wrong with it."[1]

Reading Bordo that day was, as Conrad's Marlow says of Kurtz's famous proclamation in *Heart of Darkness,* "as if a veil had been rent." Indeed, her work functions much like the work of a great novelist in that it restores what is so often absent in the ordinary language of criticism: the sense of embodiment, of being there—the sense that what is being written about is pressingly real, that something is truly at stake, that we are, in some fundamental way, in the presence of a truth. The discussion we had in the reading group was substantively different that night. We all felt in some way like aberrations, women struggling to prove our worth as thinkers who were simultaneously members of an increasingly pervasive consumer culture that seemed in many ways to define us. But that night, reading Bordo, we didn't feel like outsiders struggling to speak a language foreign and even hostile to us. We felt included in the conversation. In refusing to stand outside the contemporary culture and administer criticisms from on high, Susan Bordo had given us both permission and a way to speak.

Unbearable Weight, itself the crystallization and development of that early piece, marked a milestone in the development of cultural criticism and gave to many within the academy and outside a substantive understanding of our culture. Truly interdisciplinary in its conceptualization and approach, it offered a whole new way of thinking and writing and living an intellectual life. Soon after its publication in 1993, it was nominated for a Pulitzer Prize. It helped generate a whole new genre in literary and cultural studies that now goes under the name of "body studies." It is cited as a foundational work in sociology, philosophy, English, gender studies, disability studies, psychology, and many others. New manuscripts repeatedly use Bordo as a theoretical framework to discuss everything from eating disorders to philosophers to Calvin Klein. *Unbearable Weight* is included on the "must read" list of websites dedicated to the interests of women, lesbians and gays, ethnicity, feminism, and pop culture. *Unbearable Weight* also became a kind of bible for a younger generation of scholars. While we reserved a kind of cool admiration and proper detachment for other theorists, our coolness when speaking of Susan would immediately thaw: "Susan Bordo?" we would say, "I *love* her! I mean, I really *love* her!!!" Though chronologically part of an earlier generation of scholars that is sometimes hostile to media culture and those who engage with it, she seemed to be simultaneously instructive and one of us. She spoke our language. She lived in our world. By extension, it seemed she loved and understood *us*.

To read Susan Bordo is to take a wild ride through the cultural images that form our daily lives, and to see them with a startling X-ray vision that reveals their blood and guts and bones, a vision that reveals us, finally, to ourselves. Vintage Bordo always articulates in a moment of clarity what we have on some level intuited but have been unable to put together into a coherent whole. Piece by piece, strand by careful strand, she shows the sources of our deepest anxieties in the history of philosophy, in gender and race ideologies and the way these get expressed in the cultural images that surround us, and, in some fundamental sense, constitute us. Bordo shows anyone the dominant culture defines as outside its margins of value the way toward the possession of a self, a way to break the historical links between subjectivity and self-denial. For *Unbearable Weight*, and indeed, all of Bordo's work, is, in its essence, a profound gift of insight, generosity, understanding. Though this edition marks the tenth anniversary of *Unbearable Weight*, these pages are as uncanny, insightful, and welcoming now as they were when they were first published. In the crazy, fast-moving world that is contemporary media culture, Susan Bordo is our guide, our companion, and our friend. Reading Bordo makes us grateful and stronger for the experience—this is her gift to us.

Leslie Heywood, 2003

NOTES

1. Susan Bordo, "Anorexia Nervosa: Psychopathology as the Crystallization of Culture," in *Feminism and Foucault: Reflections on Resistance*, ed. Irene Diamond and Lee Quinby (Boston: Northeastern University Press, 1988), p. 89.

In the Empire of Images:
Preface to the Tenth Anniversary Edition

For Cassie

In our Sunday news. With our morning coffee. On the bus, in the airport, at the checkout line. Sharing our day off from work, from school, illicit and delicious with us under the quilt. Or domestic company, out of the corner of the eye as we fold the laundry in front of the television. It may be a 5 A.M. addiction to the glittering promises of the infomercial: the latest in fat-dissolving pills, miracle hair restoration, make-up secrets of the stars. Or a glancing relationship while waiting at the dentist, trying to distract from the impending root canal. Or a luscious, shiny pile, a deliberate splurge, a can't-wait-to-get-home-with-you devotion. A teen magazine: tips on how to dress, how to wear your hair, how to make him want you. A movie seen at the theater, still large and magical in the dark. The endless commercials and advertisements we believe we pay no attention to.

Constant, everywhere, no big deal. Like the water in the goldfish bowl, barely noticed by inhabitants. Or noticed, but dismissed: "Eye Candy"—a harmless indulgence. They go down so easily, in and out, digested and forgotten. Hardly able anymore to rouse our indignation.

Just pictures.

"NO ONE GETS SICK FROM LOOKING AT A PICTURE": CROSS-CULTURAL SNAPSHOTS

The young girl stands in front of the mirror. Never fat to begin with, she's been on a no-fat diet for a couple of weeks and has reached her goal weight: 115 pounds, at 5-foot-4—exactly what she should weigh, according to her doctor's chart. But goddamnit, she still looks dumpy. She can't shake her mind free of the "Lady Marmalade" video from *Moulin Rouge*. Christina Aguilera, Pink, L'il Kim, and Mýa, each one perfect in her own way: every curve smooth and sleek, lean-sexy, nothing to spare. Self-hatred and shame start to burn in the girl, and other things too. When the video goes on, the singers' bodies are like magnets for her eyes; she feels like she's in love with them. But envy tears at her stomach, is enough to make her sick. She'll never look like them, no matter how much weight she loses. Look at that stomach of hers, see how it sticks out? Those thighs—they actually jiggle. Her butt is monstrous. She's fat, gross, a dough girl.

Frontline asked Alexandra Shulman, editor of British *Vogue,* if the fashion industry felt any responsibility for creating the impossible-to-achieve images that young girls measure themselves against. Shulman shrugged. "Not many people have actually said to me that they have looked at my magazine and decided to become anorexic."[1]

Is it possible that Shulman actually believes it works that way?

In Central Africa, ancient festivals still celebrate voluptuous women. In some regions, brides are sent to fattening farms, to be plumped and massaged into shape for their wedding night. In a country plagued by AIDS, the skinny body has meant—as it used to mean among Italian, Jewish, and Black Americans—poverty, sickness, death. "An African girl must have hips," says dress designer Frank Osodi. "We have hips. We have bums. We like flesh in Africa." For years, Nigeria sent its local version of beautiful to the Miss World Competition. The contestants did very poorly. Then a savvy entrepreneur went against local ideals and entered Agbani Darego, a light-skinned, hyper-skinny beauty. (He got his inspiration from M-Net, the South African network seen across Africa on satellite television, which broadcasts mostly American movies and television shows.) Agbani Darego won the Miss World Pageant, the first Black African to do so. Now, Nigerian teenagers fast and exercise, trying to become "lepa"—a popular slang phrase for the thin "it" girls that are all the rage. Said one: "People have realized that slim is beautiful."[2]

Brenda Richardson and Elane Rehr, authors of *101 Ways to Help Your Daughter Love Her Body,* tell the story of the newly arrived Russian immigrants Sasha, thirty-two, and her fourteen-year-old sister. Sasha, who immediately lost twenty pounds, became disgusted with her little sister's upper arms and thighs. "My little sis has fleshy arms and thighs ribboned with cellulite," she told Richardson, and complained that their mother was dressing her in short-sleeved dresses. When her mother did this, Sasha tried to stop her, telling her sister to "cover up her fat."[3]

Rent a Russian movie made before the doors to U.S. culture were flung open; look at the actresses' arms. You'll see just how extraordinary—and how illuminating—this one little anecdote is.[4]

I was intrigued when my articles on eating disorders began to be translated, over the past few years, into Japanese and Chinese. Among the members of audiences at my talks, Asian women had been among the most insistent that eating and body image weren't problems for their people, and indeed, my initial research showed that eating disorders were virtually unknown in Asia. But when, this year, a Korean translation of *Unbearable Weight* was published, I felt I needed to revisit the situation. I discovered multiple reports on dramatic increases in eating disorders in China, South Korea, and Japan. "As many Asian countries become Westernized and infused with the Western aesthetic of a tall, thin, lean body, a virtual tsunami of eating disorders has swamped Asian countries," writes Eunice Park in *Asian Week* magazine. Older people can still remember when it was very different. In China, for example, where revolutionary ideals once condemned any focus on appearance and there have been several disastrous famines, "little fatty" was a term of endearment for children. Now, with fast food on every corner, childhood obesity is on the rise, and the cultural meaning of fat and thin has changed. "When I was young," says Li Xiaojing, who manages a fitness center in Beijing, "people admired and were even jealous of fat people since they thought they had a better life. . . . But now, most of us see a fat person and think 'He looks awful.' "[5]

Because of their remote location, the Fiji islands did not have access to television until 1995, when a single station was introduced. It broadcasts programs from the United States, Great Britain, and Australia. Until that time, Fiji had no reported cases of eating disorders, and a study conducted by the anthropologist Anne Becker showed that most Fijian girls and women, no matter how large, were comfortable with their bodies. In 1998, just three years after the station began broadcasting, 11 percent of girls reported vomiting to control weight, and 62 percent of the girls surveyed reported dieting during the previous months.

Becker was surprised by the change; she had though that Fijian cultural traditions, which celebrate eating and favor voluptuous bodies, would "withstand" the influence of media images. Her explanation for the Fijians' vulnerability? They were not sophisticated enough about media to recognize that the television images were not "real."[6]

"REALITY" IN THE EMPIRE OF IMAGES

Are we sophisticated enough to recognize that the images are not "real"? Does it matter?

In the charming *L.A. Story*, Steve Martin asks Sarah Jessica Parker why her breasts feel so funny to the touch. "Oh, that's because they're real," she replies. It's funny. But it's also no longer a joke—because real breasts are the anomaly among actresses and models nowadays, with consequences that extend beyond the wacky culture of celebrity-bodies. Many young men can't get aroused by breasts that don't conform to Hollywood standards of size and firmness. Do they care that those centerfold breasts aren't "real"? No. Nor do the more than 215,000 women who purchased breast implants in 2001.[7] Breast enhancement is one of the most common surgical procedures for teenagers.[8] These girls are not superficial creatures who won't be satisfied unless they look like goddesses. More and more, girls who get implants feel that they need them in order to look normal in a culture in which "normal" is being radically redefined, not only by the images but by the surgeons. A cosmetic surgeon's ad in the *Lexington Herald Journal:* "Certainly, models and entertainers have breast augmentation, but the typical patients are women that you see every day. Your neighbors. Your co-workers. They could even be you."

In *Unbearable Weight,* I describe the postmodern body, increasingly fed on "fantasies of rearranging, transforming, and correcting, limitless improvement and change, defying the historicity, the mortality, and, indeed, the very materiality of the body. In place of that materiality, we now have cultural plastic."

When I wrote these words, the most recent statistics, from 1989, listed 681,000 surgical procedures performed.

In 2001, 8.5 million procedures were performed.[9]

They are cheaper than ever, safer than ever, and increasingly used, not for correcting major defects, but for "contouring" the face and body. Plastic surgeons seem to have no ethical problem with this. "I'm not here to play philosopher king," says Dr. Randal Haworth in a *Vogue* interview; "I don't have a problem with women who already look good who want to look perfect."[10] Perfect. When did "perfection" become applicable to a human body? The word suggests a Platonic form of timeless beauty—appropriate for marble, perhaps, but not for living flesh. We change, we age, we die. Learning to deal with this is part of the existential challenge—and richness—of mortal life. But nowadays, those who can afford to do so have traded the messiness and fragility of life, the vulnerability of intimacy, the comfort of human connection, for fantasies of limitless achievement, "triumphing" over everything that gets in the way, "going for the gold." The Greeks called it hubris. We call it our "right" to be all that we can be.[11]

What Haworth isn't saying, too, is that the bar of what we consider "perfection" is constantly being raised—by cultural imagery, by the surgeon's own recommendations, and by eyes that become habituated to interpreting every deviation as "defect." Ann, a prospective patient described in the same *Vogue* article, has a well-toned body of 105 pounds but is obsessed with what she sees as grotesque fat pockets on her inner thighs. "No matter how skinny I get, they get smaller but never go away," she complains. It's unlikely that Ann, whom Haworth considers a perfect candidate for liposuction, will stop there. "Plastic surgery sharpens your eyesight," admits a more honest surgeon, "You get something done, suddenly you're looking in the mirror every five minutes—at imperfections nobody else can see."[12]

Where did Ann get the idea that any vestige of fat must be banished from her body? Most likely, it wasn't from comparing herself to other real women, but to those computer-generated torsos—in ads for anti-cellulite cream and the like—whose hips and thighs and buttocks are smooth and seamless as gently sloping sand-dunes. No actual person has a body like that. But that doesn't matter—because our expectations, our desires, our judgments about bodies, are becoming dictated by the digital. When was the last time you actually saw a wrinkle—or cellulite—or a drooping jowl—or a pore or a pucker—in a magazine or video image? Ten years ago *Harper's* magazine printed the invoice *Esquire* had received for retouching a cover picture of Michelle Pfeiffer. The picture was accompanied by copy that read: "What Michelle Pfeiffer needs . . . is absolutely nothing." What Pfeiffer's picture alone needed to appear on that cover was actually $1,525 worth of chin trimming, complexion cleansing, neck softening, line removal, and other assorted touches.

That was then.

Now, in 2003, virtually every celebrity image you see—in the magazines, in the videos, and sometimes even in the movies—has been digitally modified. Virtually every image. Let that sink in. Don't just let your mind passively receive it. Confront its implications. This is not just a matter of deception—boring old stuff, which ads have traded in from their beginnings. This is perceptual pedagogy, How to Interpret Your Body 101. These images are teaching us how to see. Filtered, smoothed, polished, softened, sharpened, re-arranged. And passing. Digital creations, visual cyborgs, teaching us what to expect from flesh and blood. Training our perception in what's a defect and what is normal.

Are we sophisticated enough to know the images are not "real"? Does it matter? There are no disclaimers on the ads: "Warning: This body is generated by a computer. Don't expect your thighs to look this way." Would it matter to Ann if there were? Who cares about reality when beauty, love, acceptance beckon? Does sophistication have anything to do with it?

A SAD CONFIRMATION

When I wrote *Unbearable Weight,* it was widely believed that privileged white girls had the monopoly on eating and body-image problems. The presumption was a relic of the old medical models, which accepted the "profile" presented by the typical recipient of therapy—who was indeed largely white and upper middle class—as definitive, and which failed to recognize the central role of media imagery in "spreading" eating and body-image problems across race and class (and sexual orientation). Like the Black Africans and the Fijians and the Russians (and lesbians and Latins and every other "subculture" boasting a history of regard for fleshy women), African Americans were believed "protected" by their alternative cultural values. And so, many young girls were left feeling stranded and alone, dealing with feelings about their bodies that they weren't "supposed" to have, as they struggled, along with their white peers, with unprecedented pressure to achieve, and watched Janet Jackson and Halle Berry shrink before their eyes.

Many medical professionals, too, were trapped in what I'd call the "anorexic paradigm." They hadn't yet understood that eating problems take many different forms and inhabit bodies of many different sizes and shapes. Binge eating—a chronic problem among many African American women—is no less a disordered relation to food than habitual purging, and large women who don't or won't diet are not necessarily comfortable with their bodies. Exercise addiction is rarely listed among the criteria for eating problems, but it has become the weight control of choice among a generation emulating Jennifer Lopez's round, tight buns rather than Kate Moss's skeletal collarbones. Just because a teenager looks healthy and fit does not mean that she is not living her life on a treadmill—metaphorically as well as literally—which she dare not step off lest food and fat overtake her body.

Until recently, most clinicians were not receptive to the arguments of feminists like Susie Ohrbach (and later, myself) that "body image disturbance syndrome," binge/purge cycling, "bulimic thinking," and all the rest needed to be understood as much more culturally normative than generally recognized. They wanted to draw a sharp dividing line between pathology and normality—a line that can be very blurry when it comes to eating and body-image problems in this culture. And while they acknowledged that images "play a role," they clung to the notion that only girls with a "predisposing vulnerability" get into trouble. Trained in a medical model which seeks the cause of disorder in individual and family pathology, they hadn't yet understood just how powerful, ubiquitous, and invasive the demands of culture are on our bodies and souls.

Families matter, of course, and so do racial and ethnic traditions. But families exist in cultural time and space—and so do racial groups. Thus, no one lives in a bubble of self-generated "dysfunction" or permanent immunity—especially today, as mass media culture increasingly has provided the dominant "public education" in our children's lives. The "profile" of girls with eating problems is dynamic, not static; heterogeneous, not uniform. Therapists now report treating the anorexic daughters of anorexics, and are coming to realize the role parents play, not just in being "over-controlling" or overly demanding of their children, but in modeling obedience to cultural norms. And the old generalizations about race and "fat acceptance," while perhaps valid for older generations of Black Americans, do not begin to adequately describe the complex and often conflicted attitudes of younger people, many of whom are aware of traditional values but constantly feel the pull of contemporary demands. While working on *Unbearable Weight*, I called up organizations devoted to Black women's health issues, asking for statistics and clinical anecdotes, and was told: "That's a white girl's thing. African American women are comfortable with their bodies." For twenty-something Tenisha Williamson, who suffers from anorexia, such notions are almost as oppressive as her eating disorder: "From an African American standpoint," she writes, "we as a people are encouraged to 'embrace our big, voluptuous bodies.' This makes me feel terrible because I don't want a big, voluptuous body! I don't ever want to be fat—ever, and I don't ever want to gain weight. I would rather die from starvation than gain a single pound. [This makes me feel like] the proverbial Judas of my race . . . and so incredibly shallow."[13]

In fact, the starving white girls were just the forward guard, the miners' canaries warning of how poisonous the air was becoming for everyone. I could see it in the magazines, the videos, and in my students' journals. I could see it, as I write in "Material Girl," in the transformations of Madonna and other performers of Italian, Jewish, and African American descent who seemed, at the start of their careers, to represent resistance to the waifs and willows but who just couldn't hold out against what, indeed, had begun to look like a tsunami, a cultural tidal wave of obsession with achieving a disciplined, normalized body.

It became a central argument of *Unbearable Weight* that eating disorders, analyzed as a social formation rather than personal pathology, represented a "crystallization" of particular currents, some historical and some contemporary, within Western culture. Western philosophy and religion, to begin with, have a long history of anxiety about the body as a source of hungers, needs, and physical vulnerabilities always threatening to spin out of control. But maintaining some zone of comfort with the body's needs is especially difficult in our own time. Consumer culture continually excites and encourages us to "let go," indulge in our desires—for sugar, fat, sex, mindless entertainment. But at the same time, burgeoning industries centered on diet, exercise, and body enhancement glamorize self-discipline and code fat as a symbol of laziness and lack of willpower. It's hard to find a place of moderation and stability in all this, easy to fall into disorder. For girls and women, the tensions of consumer capitalism are layered, additionally, with the contradictions of being female in our time. These contradictions, I argued, are succinctly embodied in the slenderness ideal. On the one hand, the lean body represents a rejection of the fifties ideal of cuddly, reproductive womanhood, and an assertion of a post-feminist, non-domestic identity. On the other hand, the steadily shrinking space permitted the female body seemed expressive of discomfort with greater female power and presence.

One of the hardest challenges I faced, in presenting these ideas at conferences and public lectures, was getting medical professionals and academics to take cultural imagery seriously. Most clinicians, unaccustomed to viewing images as anything other than "mere fashion," saw cultural interpretation as somehow minimizing the seriousness of eating disorders. I insisted—an argument I laid out explicitly in a later book, *Twilight Zones*—that images of slenderness are never "just pictures," as the fashion magazines continually maintain (disingenuously) in their own defense. Not only are the artfully arranged bodies in the ads and videos and fashion spreads powerful lessons in how to see (and evaluate) bodies, but also they offer fantasies of safety, self-containment, acceptance, immunity from pain and hurt. They speak to young people not just about how to be beautiful but about how to become what the dominant culture admires, how to be cool, how to "get it together." To girls who have been abused they may speak of transcendence or armoring of too-vulnerable female flesh. For racial and ethnic groups whose bodies have been marked as foreign, earthy, and primitive, or considered unattractive by Anglo-Saxon norms, they may cast the lure of assimilation, of becoming (metaphorically speaking) "white."

Academics, on their part, were not hostile to interpretation but to what they saw as my suppression of racial and ethnic "difference." As I saw my argument, I was calling attention to a discernable historical development—the spread of normalizing imagery across race and nationality. "Difference" was being effaced, indeed. But it was mass popular culture that was effacing it, not me. Today, the evidence of this is indisputable. There is no denying that there are still racial differences in attitudes toward eating, dieting, body aesthetics. But even more dramatic are the generational differences, which show that "comfort with the body" is fast becoming a relic of another era, irrespective of race or nationality.[14] The mythology persists, of course; it's a big ingredient in a certain kind of ethnic pride. So, Jennifer Lopez and Beyoncé Knowles insist they are happy with their bodies, bragging about their bodacious bottoms. "Us sisters have padding back there," says Beyoncé. "Being bootylycious is about being comfortable with your body." But sexy booty is okay, apparently, only if it's high and hard, and if other body-parts are held firmly in check. Beyoncé is comfortable with her body because she works on it constantly. On the road, she does five hundred sit-ups a night, and Jennifer ("One of the most driven people I've ever seen," according to her personal trainer) does ninety minutes of hard training "at least" four times a week.[15] Her truly voluptuous *Selena* body is a thing of the distant past. J.Lo and Beyoncé are "full-figured" only if Lara Flynn Boyle is your yardstick.

And then there are the men and boys, who once seemed so immune. If ever there was confirmation that eating and body image problems are products of culture, they are surely it. Women, studies always showed, are chronically dissatisfied with themselves. But ten years ago men tended, if anything, to see themselves as better looking than they (perhaps) actually were. Straight guys were proud of their beer bellies. "Do I look like I care?" was the manly way to be. Body-sculpting? Very sexually suspect. Dieting? The average, white, heterosexual guy would no more be seen at Weight Watchers than in a feather boa. The "one" in "Pepsi One" was created to sell men a diet drink without having to call it that.

And then, as I chronicle in *The Male Body*, the diet industries, the cosmetics manufacturers, and the plastic surgeons "discovered" the male body. With so much money to be made, why did it take so long? Arguably, manufacturers and advertisers feared that anxiety about being seen as gay would prevent heterosexual men from showing too obvious an interest in their bodies. African American athletic superstars like Michael Jordan and hip-hop performers like Puff Daddy (Sean P. Diddy) Combs did a lot to change that. They made jewelry, high fashion, strutting one's stuff into a macho thing. But designer Calvin Klein broke the biggest barrier. He brought the sinuous, sculpted male body out of the closet, and made everyone, gay and straight, male and female, succumb to its classic, masculine beauty. I remember the first time I saw one of his underwear ads. No male waif, the model's body projected strength, solidity. But his finely muscled chest was not so overdeveloped as to suggest a sexuality immobilized—like Schwarzenegger's, say—by the thick matter of the body. He didn't stare at the viewer challengingly, belligerently ("Yeah, this is an underwear ad and I'm half-naked. But I'm still the one in charge here. Who's gonna look away first?"). No, this model's languid body-posture, eyes downcast but not closed, offered itself nonaggressively to the gaze of another. Feast on me; I'm here to be looked at.

Today, men no longer think of personal care or taking pleasure in one's clothing, one's body, one's beauty in the eyes of another as feminine things. But basking in the admiration of the gaze, as men are finding out, requires committed bodily upkeep. This is consumer culture, after all. It can never have too much of a good thing. It thrives on our capacity for excess; it wants us to not be able to stop. Today, the athletic, muscular male body that Calvin first plastered all over buildings, magazines, and subway stops has become an aesthetic requirement, for straights as well as gays. "No pecs, no sex," is how the trendy David Barton gym sells itself: "My motto is not 'Be healthy'; it's 'Look better naked,'" Barton says.[16]

And now, young guys are looking in their mirrors, finding themselves soft and ill defined, no matter how muscular they are. Now they are developing the eating and body image disorders that we once thought only girls had. Now they are abusing steroids, measuring their own muscularity against the oiled and perfected images of professional athletes, bodybuilders, *Men's Health* models. Now the industries in body enhancement—cosmetic surgeons, manufacturers of anti-aging creams, spas and salons—are making huge bucks off men, too.

Now, too, that boys and men are developing body-image problems, feminist cultural arguments—unacknowledged—seem to have finally won the day. Psychologists are producing pictures demonstrating the increasing lean, muscular proportions of toys like G.I. Joe, illustrating their studies with photos of "steroided" centerfolds, and reassuring readers that even the most "well-adjusted men" are at risk. Say the authors of *The Adonis Complex* (all medical professionals): "Men could be relieved of much suffering if they could only be liberated from society's unrealistic ideals of what they should look like."[17]

I agree, of course. But I can't help but think of all the guilt and shame that girls, women, and their families have suffered, as our body disorders have been trivialized and pathologized over the years. It's time we made it decisively clear that "well-adjusted" girls and women are at risk, too. That no racial or ethnic group is invulnerable. That body insecurity can be exported, imported, and marketed across the globe—just like any other profitable commodity.

AGING IN THE EMPIRE OF IMAGES

They carded me until I was thirty-five. Even when I was forty-five, people were shocked to hear my age. Young men flirted with me, even at fifty. Having hated my face as a child—bushy red hair, freckles, Jewish nose—I was surprised to find myself fairly pleased with it as an adult. Then, suddenly, it all changed. The women at the make-up counter no longer compliment me on my skin. Men don't catch my eye with playful promise in theirs.

I'm fifty-six. The magazines tell me that at this age, a woman can still be beautiful. But they don't mean me. They mean Cher, Goldie, Faye, Candace. Women whose jowls have disappeared as they've aged, whose eyes have become less droopy, lips grown plumper, foreheads smoother with the passing years. They mean Susan Sarandon, who looked older in 1991's *Thelma and Louise* than she does in her movies today. "Aging beautifully" used to mean wearing one's years with style, confidence, and vitality. Today, it means not appearing to age at all. And—like breasts that defy gravity—it's becoming a new bodily norm.

Greta Van Susterin: former CNN legal analyst, forty-seven years old. When she had a face-lift, it was a real escalation in the stakes for ordinary women. She had a signature style: no bullshit, down-to-earth lack of pretense. (During the O.J. trial, she was the only white reporter many Blacks trusted.) Always stylishly dressed and coiffed, she wasn't really pretty. No one could argue that her career was built on her looks. Perhaps quite the opposite. She sent out a subversive message: brains and personality still count, even on television.

When Greta had her face lifted, another source of inspiration and hope bit the dust. The story was on the cover of *People*, and folks tuned in to her new show on Fox just to see the change—which was significant. But at least she was open about it. The beauties never admit they've had "work." Or if they do, it's vague, nonspecific, minimizing of the extent. Cher: "If I'd had as much plastic surgery as people say, there'd be another whole person left over!"[18] Okay, so how much have you had? The interviewers accept the silences and evasions. They even embellish the lie. How many interviews have you read which began: "She came into the restaurant looking at least twenty years younger than she is, fresh and relaxed without a speck of make-up."

This collusion, this myth, that Cher or Goldie or Faye Dunaway, unaltered, is "what fifty-something looks like today" has altered my face, however—and without benefit of surgery. By comparison with theirs, it has become much older than it is.

My expression now appears more serious, too (just what a feminist needs), thanks to the widespread use of botox. "It's now rare in certain social circles," a *New York Times* reporter observed, "to see a woman over the age of 35 with the ability to look angry."[19] This has frustrated some film directors, like Baz Luhrman (who did *Moulin Rouge*). "Their faces can't really move properly," Luhrman complained.[20] Last week I saw a sign in the beauty parlor where I get my hair cut. "Botox Party! Sign Up!" So my fifty-six-year-old forehead will now be judged against my neighbor's, not just Goldie's, Cher's, and Faye's. On television, a commercial describes the product (which really is a toxin, a dilution of botulism) as "botox cosmetic." No different from mascara and blush, it's just stuck in with a needle and makes your forehead numb.

To add insult to injury, the rhetoric of feminism has been picked up to help advance and justify the industries in anti-aging and body alteration. Face-lifts, implants, and liposuction are advertised as empowerment, "taking charge" of one's life. "I'm doing it for me"—the mantra of the talk shows. "Defy your age!"—Melanie Griffith, for Revlon. We're making a revolution, girls. Get your injection and pick up a sign!

Am I immune? Of course not. My bathroom shelves are cluttered with the ridiculously expensive age-defying lotions and potions that constantly beckon to me at the Lancome and Dior counters. I want my lines, bags, and sags to disappear, and so do the women who can only afford to buy their alpha-hydroxies at K-Mart. There's a limit, though, to what fruit acids can do. As surgeons develop ever more extensive and fine-tuned procedures to correct gravity and erase history from the faces of their patients, the difference between the cosmetically altered and the rest of us grows more and more dramatic.

"The rest of us" includes not only those who resist or are afraid of surgery but the many people who cannot afford basic health care, let alone aesthetic tinkering—not even of the K-Mart variety. As celebrity faces become increasingly more surreal in their wide-eyed, ever-bright agelessness, as *Time* and *Newsweek* (and *Discover* and *Psychology Today*) proclaim that we can now all "stay young forever," the poor continue to sag and wrinkle and lose their teeth.[21] But in the empire of images, where even people in the news for stock scandals or producing septuplets are given instant digital dental work for magazine covers,[22] this is a well-guarded secret. The celebrity testimonials, the advertisements, the beauty columns all participate in the fiction that the required time, money, and technologies are available to all.[23]

GROWING UP FEMALE IN THE EMPIRE OF IMAGES

Here's how I can tell the ages of audience members at the talks I give: My generation (and older) still refers to "air-brushing." Many still believe it is possible to "just turn off the television." They are scornful, disdainful, sure of their own immunity to the world I talk about. No one really believes the ads, do they? Don't we all know these are just images, designed to sell products? Scholars in the audience may trot out theory about cultural resistance and "agency." Men may insist that they love fleshy women.

Fifteen years ago, I felt very alone when my own generation said these things; it seemed that they were living in a different world from the one I was tracking and that there was little hope of bridging the gap. Now, I simply catch the eye of a twenty-year-old in the audience. They know. They understand that you can be as cynical as you want about the ads—and many of them are—and still feel powerless to resist their messages. They know, no matter what their parents, teachers, and clergy are telling them, that "inner beauty" is a big laugh in this culture.

In their world, there is a size zero, and it's a status symbol. The chronic dieters have been at it since they were eight and nine years old. "Epidemic of eating disorders" is old stuff; being preached to about it turns them right off. Their world is one in which the anorexics swap starvation diet tips on the Internet, participate in group fasts, offer advice on how to hide your "ana" from family members, and share inspirational photos of emaciated models. But full-blown anorexia has never been the norm among teenage girls; the real epidemic is among the girls with seemingly healthy eating habits, seemingly healthy bodies, who vomit or work their butts off as a regular form of anti-fat maintenance. These girls not only look "normal" but consider themselves normal. The new criterion circulating among teenage girls: If you get rid of it through exercise rather than purging or laxatives, you don't have a problem. Theirs is a world in which groups of dorm girls will plough voraciously through pizzas, chewing and then spitting out each mouthful. Do they have a disorder? Of course not—look, they're eating pizza.

Generations raised in the empire of images are both vulnerable and savvy. They snort when magazines periodically proclaim (about once every six months, the same frequency with which they run cover stories about "Starving Stars") that in the "new Hollywood" one can be "Sexy at Any Size." They are literati, connoisseurs of the images; they pay close attention to the pounds coming and going—on J.Lo, on Reese, on Thora, on Christina Aguilera, on Beyoncé. They know that Kate Winslett—whom director James Cameron called "Kate Weighs-a-lot" on the set of *Titanic*—was described by the tabloids as "packing on," "ballooning to," "swelling to," "shooting up

to," "tipping the scales at" a "walloping," "staggering" weight—of
135. That slender Courtney Thorne Smith, who played Calista Flock-
hart's friend/rival on *Ally McBeal*, quit the show because she could
no longer keep up with the pressure to remain as thin as David
Kelly wanted them to be. That Missy Elliot and Queen Latifah are
not on diets just for reasons of health.

I track the culture of young girls today with particular concern,
because I'm a mother now. My four-year-old daughter is a superb
athlete with supreme confidence in her body, who prides herself on
being able to do anything the boys can do—and better. When I see
young girls being diminished and harassed by the culture it feels
even more personal to me now. I'm grateful that there's a whole new
generation of female athletes to provide inspiration and support for
girls like Cassie. That our icons are no longer just tiny gymnasts,
but powerful soccer, softball, and tennis players, broad-shouldered
track stars. Mia Hamm, Sarah Walden, Serena Williams, Marion
Jones.[24] During a recent visit to a high school, I see how the eyes of
a fourteen-year-old athlete shine as she talks about what Marion
Jones means to her. In this young girl I see my own daughter, ten
years from now, and I'm filled with hope.

But then, I accidentally tune in to the *Maury* (Povich) show, and
my heart is torn in two. The topic of the day is "back-to-girl"
makeovers. One by one, five beautiful twelve-, thirteen-, and fourteen-year-old "tomboys" (as Maury called them) are "brought back
to their feminine side" (Maury again) through a fashion makeover.
We first see them in sweatshirts and caps, insisting that they are as
strong as any boy, that they want to dress for comfort, that they're
tired of being badgered to look like girls. Why, then, are they submitting to this one-time, on-air transformation? To please their
moms. And indeed, as each one is brought back on stage, in full
make-up and glamour outfit, hair swinging (and in the case of the
Black girls, straightened), striking vampy supermodel "power"
poses, their mothers sob as if they had just learned their daughters'
cancers were in remission. The moms are so overwhelmed they
don't need more, but Maury is clearly bent on complete conversion:
"Do you know how pretty you are?" "Look how gorgeous you
look!" "That guy in the audience—he's on the floor!" "Are you going to dress like this more often?" Most of the girls, unsurprisingly,
say yes. It's been a frontal assault; there's no room for escape.

As jaded as I am, this *Maury* show really got to me. I want to fold each one of the girls in my arms and get her out of there. Of course, what I really fear is that I won't be able to protect Cassie from the assault. It's happening already. I watch public television kids' shows with her, and can rarely find fault with the gender-neutral world they portray. We go to Disney movies and see resourceful, spirited heroines. Some of them, like the Hawaiian girls in *Lilo and Stitch*, even have thick legs and solid bodies. But then, on the way home from the movies, we stop at MacDonald's for a Happy Meal, and—despite the fact that Cassie insists she's a boy and wants the boy's toy, a hot wheels car—she is given a box with a little mini-Barbie in it. Illustrating the box is Barbie's room, and my daughter is given the challenging task of finding all the matching pairs of shoes on the floor.

Later that day, I open a Pottery Barn catalogue, browsing for ideas for Cassie's room. The designated boy's room is all in primary colors, the bedspread dotted with balls, bats, catching mitts. The caption reads: "I play so many sports that it's hard to pick my favorites." Sounds like my daughter. On the opposite page, the girls' room is pictured, a pastel planetary design. The caption reads: "I like stars because they are shiny." That, too, sounds like my daughter. But Pottery Barn doesn't think a child can inhabit both worlds. If their catalogues were as segregated and stereotyped racially as they are by gender, people would boycott.

I rent a video—*Jimmy Neutron, Boy Genius*—for Cassie. It's marketed as a kids' movie; it's on that wall at Blockbuster. And the movie is okay, for the most part. But then we get to the music video, which follows the movie, unaccompanied by any warnings. It's a group I've never heard of, singing a song called "Kids in America." Two of the girls are thirteen. Two are fifteen and one is sixteen. I know this because their ages are emblazoned across the screen, as each makes her appearance. They are all in full vixen attire, with professionally undulating bodies, professionally made-up, come-hither eyes.

Why are we told their ages, I wonder? Are we supposed to be amazed at the illusion of womanhood created by their performance? Or is their youth actually supposed to make it all right to show this to little kids? A way of saying "It's only make believe, only a dress-up game"? How long ago was it that an entire culture was outraged over clips of Jon Benet Ramsey, performing femininity in children's beauty pageants? In 2002, toddler versions of Britney Spears were walking the streets on Halloween night. Can it really be that we now think dressing our daughters up like tiny prostitutes is cute? That's what Sharon Lamb, author of *The Secret Lives of Girls*, thinks. She advises mothers to chill out if their nine-year-old girls "play lovely little games in high heels, strip teasing, flouncing, and jutting their chests out," to relax if their eleven-year-olds go out with "thick blue eye shadow, spaghetti straps and bra straps intertwined, long and leggy with short black dresses." They are "silly and adorable, sexy and marvelous all at once," she tells us, as they "celebrate their objectification," "playing out male fantasies . . . but without risk."[25]

Without risk? I have nothing against dress-up. But flouncing is one thing; stripteasing is another. Thick blue eye shadow in mommy's bathroom is fine; an eleven-year-old night on the town is not. Reading those words "without risk," I want to remind Sharon Lamb that 22 to 29 percent of all rapes against girls occur when they are eleven and younger.[26] We might like to think that these rapes are the work of deranged madmen, so disconnected from reality as to be oblivious to the culture around them. Putting vast media energy into a so-called epidemic of girl-snatching, such as we witnessed during the summer of 2002, helps sustain that myth and lets us believe that we are doing all we need to do to protect our daughters if we simply teach them not to take candy or go into cars with strangers.

The reality is, however, that young girls are much more likely to be raped by friends and family members than by strangers and that very few men, whether strangers or acquaintances, are unaffected by having a visual culture of nymphets prancing before their eyes, exuding a sexual knowledge and experience that preteens don't really have. Feminists used to call this "rape culture." We never hear that phrase anymore, do we?

HOPE AND FEAR

Still, progressive forces are not entirely asleep in the empire of images. I think of *YM* teen magazine, for example. After conducting a survey which revealed that 86 percent of its young readers were dissatisfied with the way their bodies looked, *YM* openly declared war on eating disorders and body-image problems, instituting an editorial policy against the publishing of diet pieces and deliberately seeking out full-size models—without "marking" them as such—for all its fashion spreads.[27] I like to think this resistance to the hegemony of the fat-free body may have something to do with the fact that the editors are young enough to have studied feminism and cultural studies while they got their B.A.'s in English and journalism.[28]

Most progressive developments in the media, of course, are driven by market considerations rather than social conscience. So, for example, the fact that 49 million women are size twelve or over is clearly the motive behind new, flesh-normalizing campaigns created by "Just My Size" and Lane Bryant.[29] These campaigns proudly show off unclothed *zaftig* bodies and, unlike older marketing to "plus-size" women, refuse to use that term, insisting (accurately) that what has been called "plus size" is in fact average. It's a great strategy for making profits (I know they've got my ten bucks), but a species of resistance nonetheless. "I won't allow myself to be invisible anymore," these ads proclaim, on our behalf. "But I won't be made visible as a cultural oddity or a joke, either, because I'm not. I'm the norm."

The amorality of consumer capitalism, in its restless search for new markets, new ways to generate and feed desire, has also created a world of racial representations that are far more diverse now than when I wrote *Unbearable Weight*. This is another issue that has acquired special meaning for me, because my daughter is biracial, and I am acutely aware of the world that she sees and what it is telling her about herself. Leafing through current magazines, noting the variety of skin tones, noses, mouths depicted there, I'm glad, for the moment, that Cassie is growing up today rather than in the seventies, when Cheryl Tiegs ruled. It's always possible, of course, to find things that are still "wrong" with these representations; racist codes and aesthetics die hard. The Jezebels and geishas are still with us, and although Black male models and toddlers are allowed to have locks and "naturals," straight hair—straighter nowadays than I ever thought it was possible for anyone's hair to be—seems almost a mandatory aesthetic for young Black women.[30]

It's easy, too, to be cynical. Today's fashionable diversity is brought to us, after all, by the same people who brought us the hegemony of the blue-eyed blonde and who've made wrinkles and cellulite into diseases. It's easy to dismiss fashion's current love affair with full lips and biracial children as ethnic chic, fetishes of the month. To see it all as a shameless attempt to exploit ethnic niches and white beauty–tourism. Having a child, however, has given me another perspective, as I try to imagine how it looks through her eyes. Cassie knows nothing about the motives of the people who've produced the images. At her age, she can only take them at face value. And at face value, they present a world which includes her, celebrates her, as the world that I grew up in did not include and celebrate me. For all my anger and cynicism and frustration with our empire of images, I cannot help but be grateful for this.

On good days, I feel heartened by what is happening in the teen magazines and in the Lane Bryant and "Just My Size" ads. Perhaps advertisers are discovering that making people feel bad about themselves, then offering products which promise to make it all better, is not the only way to make a buck. As racial representations have shown, diversity is marketable. Perhaps, as Lane Bryant and others are hoping, encouraging people to feel okay about their bodies can sell products too. Sometimes, surveying the plastic, digitalized world of bodies that are the norm now, I am convinced that our present state of enchantment is just a moment away from revulsion, or perhaps simply boredom. I see a twenty-something woman dancing at a local outdoor swing party, her tummy softly protruding over the thick leather belt on her low-rider jeans. Not taut, not toned, not artfully camouflaged like some unsightly deformity, but proudly, sensuously displayed, reminding me of Madonna in the days before she became the sinewy dominatrix. Is it possible that we are beginning to rebel against the manufactured look of celebrity bodies, beginning to be repelled by their armored "perfection"?

These hopeful moments, I have to admit, are fleeting. Usually, I feel horrified—and afraid for my daughter. I am sharply aware that expressing this horror openly nowadays is to run the risk of being thought a preachy prude, relic of an outmoded feminism. At talks to young audiences, I try to lighten my touch, celebrate the positive, make sure that my criticisms of our culture are not confused with being anti-beauty, anti-fitness, or anti-sex. But I also know that when parents and teachers become fully one with the culture, children are abandoned to it. I don't tell them to love their bodies or turn off the television—useless admonitions today, and ones I cannot obey myself. But I do try to provide a disruption, if only temporary, of their everyday immersion in the culture. For just an hour or so, I won't let it pass itself off simply as "normalcy."

The lights go down, the slides go up. Much bigger than they appear in the magazines, but also, oddly brought down to size. For just a moment, we confront how bizarre, how impossible, how contradictory the images are. We laugh together over Oprah's head digitally grafted to another women's body, at the ad for breast implants in which the boobs stick straight up in the air. We gasp together as the before and after photos of Jennifer Lopez are placed side by side. We cheer for Marion Jones's shoulders, boo the fact that WNBA Barbie is just the same old Barbie, but with a basketball in her hand. For just a moment, we are in charge of the impact the faked images of "perfect" bodies have on us.

We look at them together and share—just for a moment—outrage.

ACKNOWLEDGMENTS

I am especially indebted to my sister, Binnie Klein, who collaborated with me on research and brain-storming for *Size Fourteen,* a book that we've yet to write but that informs much of this preface. Binnie also provided detailed comments on several drafts, as did Althea Webb and Leslie Heywood; their suggestions, insights, and support were invaluable. Leslie, Binnie, and Althea, along with my husband, Edward Lee, have been my constant companions in the fascinating, challenging—and often infuriating—business of trying to understand and make one's way in this culture. Thanks also to Ellen Rosenman and Lara Baker Sedlaczek for extremely helpful suggestions, to Lara for fabulous assistance in gathering international studies and other research materials, to Virginia Blum for conversations about cosmetic surgery that began many years ago and continue today, and to the faculty and students at Babson College, Indiana University, Vanderbilt University, Moorehead State College, College of Saint Rose, University of Kentucky, and Emma Willard School for discussions following my talk "Beauty 2002: An Illustrated Journey through the Innovations, Oddities, and Obsessions of Our Culture."

NOTES

1. PBS *Frontline* show "Fat." Online discussion at http://pbs.org/wgbh/pages/frontline/shows/fat/etc/press.html.

2. Norimitsu Onishi, "Globalization of Beauty Makes Slimness Trendy," *New York Times*, Oct. 3, 2002 (http://www.nytimes.com/2002/10/03/international/africa/03NIGE.html). For more on the spread of eating and body-image disorders in Africa, see Suzan Chala, "Dying to Stay Thin," *The Teacher* (http://www.teacher.co.za/cms/article_2002_04_29_0257.html); Mark Stuart Ellison, "Anorexia and Women of Color," *Suite101.com* (http://www.suite101.com/article.cfm/anorexia/45443); "Eating Disorders Rise in Zulu Women," BBC News, Nov. 4, 2002 (http://news.bbc.co.uk/2/low/africa/2381161.stm); "Anorexia Found in Rural Africa," BBC News, July 5, 2000 (http://news.bbc.co.uk/2/hi/health/818725.stm).

3. Brenda Lane Richardson and Elane Rehr, *101 Ways to Help Your Daughter Love Her Body* (New York: Harper and Row, 2001), p. xx.

4. For more on eating and body-image disorders among immigrants, see Emily Wax, "Immigrant Girls Suffer from Anorexia," *Washington Post*, Mar. 12, 2000 (http://www.detnews.com/2000/nation/0003/12/A14–14421.htm); "Immigrant Girls Are Starving to Be American," *Tulsa World*, Sept. 16, 2002; "Immigrant Women and Eating Disorders," Colours of Ana website (http://www.coloursofana.com/r4.asp). This website provides a great deal of information on eating disorders and many different racial and ethnic groups, as well as compelling and illuminating personal stories.

5. Reported in Elizabeth Rosenthal, "Beijing Journal: China's Chic Waistline: Convex to Concave," *New York Times*, Dec. 9, 1999. For more on eating and body-image disorders among Asians and Asian Americans, see Eunice Park, "Starving in Silence," *Asian Week*, June 15–21, 2000; "Anorexia, Bulimia Rates Have Soared in Japan," *Reuters Health*, Sept. 25, 2001; "Asian Women and Eating Disorders," Colours of Ana website (http://www.coloursofana.com/r2.asp); Ellen Kim, "Asian Americans and Eating Disorders: A Silent Struggle," *Seattle Post-Intelligencer*, Jan. 28, 2003; Sing Lee, Y. Y. Lydia Chan, and L. K. George Hsu, "The Intermediate-Term Outcome of Chinese Patients with Anorexia Nervosa in Hong Kong," *American Journal of Psychiatry* 160 (May 2003): 967–972.

6. Reported in Nancy Snyderman, *The Girl in the Mirror* (New York: Hyperion, 2002), p. 84.

7. "Women and Cosmetic Surgery," Women's Health Project (http://www.nowfoundation.org/issues/health/whp/whp_fact1.html).

8. Richardson and Rehr, *101 Ways*, p. 223.

9. Galina Espinoza and Mike Neil, "About Face," *People Magazine*, Oct. 28, 2002, p. 53.

10. Sarah Brown, "Addicted to Lipo," *Vogue*, Oct. 2002, pp. 368, 370.

11. See "*Braveheart, Babe*, and the Contemporary Body," in Susan Bordo, *Twilight Zones: The Hidden Life of Cultural Images from Plato to O.J.*

(Berkeley and Los Angeles: University of California Press, 1997), for elaboration of these ideas.

12. Bordo, *Twilight Zones*, p. 45.

13. From the Colours of Ana website (http://www.coloursofana .com/ss8.asp). For more on African Americans and eating and body-image disorders, see Marian Fitzgibbon and Melinda Stolley, "Minority Women: The Untold Story," Nova Online, http://www.pbs.org/wgbh/nova/thin/ minorities.html; Liz Dittrich, "About-Face Facts on Socioeconomic Status, Ethnicity, and the Thin Ideal," About Face Online, http://dev.about-face .org/r/facts/ses.html; Mashadi Mataban, "Invisible Women, Silent Suffering," *Diversity or Division? Race, Class and America at the Millennium* (http://journalism.nyu.edu/pubzone/race_class/eating.htm); Ruth Striegel-Moore et al., "Eating Disorders in White and Black Women," *American Journal of Psychiatry* 160 (July 2003): 1326–1331.

14. Studies demonstrating this include research on Hawaiians, Hispanics, Native Americans, Jewish Americans, Indians, Argentineans, Mexican Americans, Alaskan natives, and Russians, in addition to the studies specifically cited above on Asians and Asian Americans, Africans, African Americans, immigrant populations, and Fijians.

15. Reported by Andrea Sattinger, "The Bod Squad," *Teen People,* Nov. 2002, pp. 108–116.

16. Reported in Dan Shaw, "Mirror, Mirror," *New York Times,* May 29, 1994, p. 6. See Susan Bordo, *The Male Body: A New Look at Men in Public and in Private* (New York: Farrar, Straus and Giroux, 1999), especially "Beauty Rediscovers the Male Body," for extended discussion of these developments.

17. Harrison Pope, Katharine Phillips, and Roberto Olivardia, *The Adonis Complex: The Secret Crisis of Male Body Obsession* (New York: The Free Press, 2000), p. 149.

18. Reported in Liz Smith, "What Cher Wants," *Good Housekeeping,* Nov. 2002, p. 112.

19. Alex Kuczynski, "Frowns Are Victims of Progress in Quest for Wrinkle-Free Look," *New York Times,* Feb. 7, 2002, p. A1.

20. Ibid., p. A26.

21. Fitness is class-biased, too, of course. Oprah presents each new diet and exercise program she embarks on as an inspiration for her fans. But how many of them have the money for a gym membership, let alone a personal trainer? How many even have the *time* to go to the gym? Magazines engage in debates about high-protein versus low-fat diets, as though our nation's "epidemic of obesity" can be solved by nutritional science. But high-quality, low-fat protein is expensive. So are fresh fruits and vegetables, and, unless you have the time to shop frequently, they are highly perishable. Millions of Americans exist on fatty, fried, carb-loaded fast food because it's the cheapest way to feed their families.

22. For those who were attentive, an unintentional visual exposé was provided when *Newsweek* decided to "fix" the crooked teeth of Bobbi

McCaughey (mother of the McCaughey septuplets) for their cover—while *Time* neglected to.

23. See *"Braveheart, Babe,* and the Contemporary Body," in Bordo, *Twilight Zones,* for extended discussions of cosmetic surgery and other forms of body alteration.

24. See Leslie Heywood and Shari Dworkin, *Built to Win: The Female Athlete as Cultural Icon* (Minneapolis: University of Minnesota Press, 2003), for the definitive work on these developments.

25. Sharon Lamb, *The Secret Lives of Girls* (New York: The Free Press, 2001), pp. 42, 43.

26. Cited in Rosalind Wiseman, *Queen Bees and Wannabees* (New York: Crown, 2002), p. 285.

27. *Teen People* and *Seventeen* have followed suit.

28. Thanks to Julie Childers for suggesting this explanation to me.

29. The average sixteen-year-old girl is 5-foot-4 and 135 pounds, and she wears a size ten to fourteen. See Kari Haskell, "Sizing Up Teenagers," *New York Times,* Oct. 13, 2002.

30. Many people, of course, no longer find this "politically" problematic. With a pre-schooler who is already finding fault with her hair, I worry.

Acknowledgments

It is extremely difficult for those of us at small colleges to find, in our heavy teaching schedules, time for writing. I have been both fortunate and highly privileged in having been given that time, in the form of more than generous institutional support from a variety of sources. Two residential fellowships, one to spend the spring semester of 1985 in Alison Jaggar's Laurie seminar at Douglass College and the second in 1987–88 as a Rockefeller Humanist in Residence at the Duke University/University of North Carolina Center for Research on Women, provided not only time to think and write but wonderful intellectual environments to stimulate the process. An American Council of Learned Societies/Ford Foundation Fellowship, awarded for the same period as the Rockefeller, made it possible for me to continue working on this project the following year, when I was generously granted early sabbatical leave by Le Moyne College. It is to Le Moyne that I owe my greatest debt—for several faculty research grants and course reductions in the past, for the open, diverse, and warm intellectual home that it has provided for me, and for its courageous decision to name a feminist scholar to its first endowed chair, the Joseph C. Georg Professorship. From my perspective, the award could not have been timelier; announced in 1991 just as I was entering the final stages of work on this book, it has provided me with needed time for revisions, financial resources for preparation of the manuscript and illustrations, and a boost of encouragement to see me through to the culmination of what has been a long and taxing—although absorbing and gratifying—project.

Because this book is made up of essays written over a period of years, many different people have contributed to it in different ways. I have tried to acknowledge those contributions in an opening note for each essay; I apologize for any that have gone unmentioned out of forgetfulness. What are not represented in those notes, however, are the intellectual conversations and emotional support informally provided at various stages of this project by friends and colleagues such as Linda Alcoff, Sandra Bartky, Susan Behuniak-Long, Jonathan Bennett, Janet Bogdan, Robert Bogdan, Celeste Brusati, Jack Carlson, Janet Coy, Sandra Harding, Erica Harth, Alison Jaggar, Ynestra King, Ted Koditschek, Drew Leder, Janice McLane, Paul Mattick, Mario Moussa, Jean O'Barr, Robert O'Brien, Linda Robertson, Sarah Ruddick, Jonathan Schonsheck, Maxine Sheets-Johnstone, R. J. Sidmore, Cynthia Willett, Bruce Wilshire, Donna Wilshire, Iris Young, and my sisters, Binnie Klein and Marilyn Silverman. I also thank Naomi Schneider, my editor at the University of California Press, for her encouragement and patience, Carol Miller for her reassuring expertise and professionalism in the computer preparation of the manuscript, and Jane-Ellen Long for her astute and clarifying copy-editing.

It is impossible to measure the contributions of Lynne Arnault and LeeAnn Whites or adequately to express my gratitude for the intellectual and emotional sustenance their friendship has provided for me. Finally, I thank Edward Lee for all our years of wonderful conversation, for his integrity and individuality, for his insights, his humor, and his kindness, and for the haven of our life together.

Introduction: Feminism, Western Culture, and the Body

THE HEAVY BEAR

"the withness of the body"
Whitehead

The heavy bear who goes with me,
A manifold honey to smear his face,
Clumsy and lumbering here and there,
The central ton of every place,
The hungry beating brutish one
In love with candy, anger, and sleep,
Crazy factotum, disheveling all,
Climbs the building, kicks the football,
Boxes his brother in the hate-ridden city.

Breathing at my side, that heavy animal,
That heavy bear who sleeps with me,
Howls in his sleep for a world of sugar,
A sweetness intimate as the water's clasp,
Howls in his sleep because the tight-rope
Trembles and shows the darkness beneath.
—The strutting show-off is terrified,
Dressed in his dress-suit, bulging his pants,
Trembles to think that his quivering meat
Must finally wince to nothing at all.

That inescapable animal walks with me,
He's followed me since the black womb held,
Moves where I move, distorting my gesture,
A caricature, a swollen shadow,
A stupid clown of the spirit's motive,
Perplexes and affronts with his own darkness,
The secret life of belly and bone,
Opaque, too near, my private, yet unknown,
Stretches to embrace the very dear
With whom I would walk without him near,

1

Touches her grossly, although a word
Would bare my heart and make me clear,
Stumbles, flounders, and strives to be fed
Dragging me with him in his mouthing care,
Amid the hundred million of his kind,
The scrimmage of appetite everywhere.

Delmore Schwartz

CULTURAL EXPRESSIONS OF MIND-BODY DUALISM

Through his metaphor of the body as "heavy bear," Delmore
Schwartz vividly captures both the dualism that has been characteristic of Western philosophy and theology and its agonistic,
unstable nature. Whitehead's epigraph sets out the dominating,
double-edged construction, the one that contains and regulates all
the others—that of disjunction and connection, separateness and
intimacy. "The withness of the body": the body as not "me" but
"*with*" me is at the same time the body that is *inescapably* "with me."
Like a Siamese twin, neither one with me nor separable from me,
my body has "followed me since the black womb held," moving
where I move, accompanying my every act. Even in sleep, "he" is
"breathing at my side." Yet, while I cannot rid myself of this creature, while I am forced to lived with "him" in intimacy, he remains
a strange, foreign presence to me: "private," "near," yet "opaque."

The body is a *bear*—a brute, capable of random, chaotic violence
and aggression ("disheveling all . . . kicks the football / Boxes his
brother in the hate-ridden city"), but not of calculated evil. For that
would require intelligence and forethought, and the bear is above
all else a creature of instinct, of primitive need. Ruled by orality, by
hunger, blindly "mouthing" experience, seeking honey and sugar,
he is "in love"—delicate, romantic sentiment—but with the most
basic, infantile desires: to be soothed by sweet things, to discharge
his anger, to fall exhausted into stupor. Even in that stupor he
hungers, he craves, he howls for a repletion dimly remembered
from life in the womb, when need and fulfillment occupied the same
moment, when frustration (and desire) was unknown.

The bear who is the body is clumsy, gross, disgusting, a lumbering fool who trips me up in all my efforts to express myself

clearly, to communicate love. Stupidly, unconsciously, dominated by appetite, he continually misrepresents my "spirit's motive," my finer, clearer self; like an image-maker from the darkness of Plato's cave, he casts a false image of me before the world, a swollen, stupid caricature of my "inner" being. I would be a sensitive, caring lover, I would tell my love my innermost feelings, but *he* only "touches her grossly," he only desires crude, physical release. I would face death bravely, but *he* is terrified, and in his terror, seeking comfort, petting, food to numb him to that knowledge, he is ridiculous, a silly clown performing tricks on a tightrope from which he must inevitably fall.

The bear who is my body is *heavy*, "dragging me with him." "The central ton of every place," he exerts a downward pull—toward the earth, and toward death. "Beneath" the tightrope on which he performs his stunts is the awful truth that one day the bear will become mere, lifeless *matter*, "meat" for worms. And he, "that inescapable animal," will drag *me* to that destiny; for it is he, not I, who is in control, pulling me with him into the "scrimmage of appetite," the Hobbesian scramble of instinct and aggression that is, in Schwartz's vision, the human condition.

The body as animal, as appetite, as deceiver, as prison of the soul and confounder of its projects: these are common images within Western philosophy. This is not to say that a negative construction of the body has ruled without historical challenge, or that it has taken only one form, for the imaginal shape of the body has been historically variable. For example, although Schwartz employs Platonic imagery in evoking the distortions of the body, his complaint about the body is quite different from Plato's. Plato imagines the body as an *epistemological* deceiver, its unreliable senses and volatile passions continually tricking us into mistaking the transient and illusory for the permanent and the real. For Schwartz, the body and its passions are obstacles to expression of the "inner" life; his characteristically modern frustration over the isolation of the self and longing for "authenticity" would seem very foreign to Plato.

Plato, arguably (and as another example of the historical range of Western images of the body), had a mixed and complicated attitude toward the sexual aspect of bodily life. In the *Phaedo* passion distracts the philosopher from the pursuit of knowledge, but in the *Symposium* it motivates that pursuit: love of the body is the essential first step on the spiritual ladder that culminates in recognition of the eternal form of Beauty. For Christian thought, on the other hand, the sexual body becomes much more unequivocally the gross, instinctual "bear" imagined by Schwartz, the animal, appetitive side of our nature. But even within the "same" dominating metaphor of the body as animal, *animality* can mean very different things. For Augustine, the animal side of human nature—symbolized for him by the rebelliously tumescent penis, insisting on its "law of lust" against the attempts of the spiritual will to gain control—inclines us toward sin and needs to be tamed. For the mechanistic science and philosophy of the seventeenth century, on the other hand, the body as animal is still a site of instinct but not primarily a site of *sin*. Rather, the instinctual nature of the body means that it is a purely mechanical, biologically programmed system that can be fully quantified and (in theory) controlled.

At different historical moments, out of the pressure of cultural, social, and material change new images and associations emerge. In the sixteenth century the epistemological body begins to be imagined not only as deceiving the philosopher through the untrustworthy senses (a Platonic theme) but also as the site of our *locatedness* in space and time, and thus as an impediment to objectivity.[1] Because we are embodied, our thought is perspectival; the only way for the mind to comprehend things as "they really are" is by attainment of a dis-embodied view from nowhere. In our own time (as another example of the emergence of new meanings), the "heaviness" of the bear has assumed a concrete meaning which it probably did not have for Schwartz, who uses it as a metaphor for the burdensome drag the body exerts on "the self"; my students, interpreting the poem, understood it as describing the sufferings of an overweight man. For Schwartz, the hunger for food is just one of the body's appetites; for my female students, it is *the* most insistent craving and the preeminent source of their anger and frustration with the body, indeed, of their *terror* of it.

Not all historical conceptions view the body as equally "inescapable." The Greeks viewed soul and body as inseparable except through death. Descartes, however, believed that with the right philosophical method we can transcend the epistemological limitations of the body. And contemporary culture, technologically armed, seems bent on defying aging, our various biological "clocks," and even death itself. But what remains the constant element throughout historical variation is the *construction* of body as something apart from the true self (whether conceived as soul, mind, spirit, will, creativity, freedom . . .) and as undermining the best efforts of that self. That which is not-body is the highest, the best, the noblest, the closest to God; that which is body is the albatross, the heavy drag on self-realization.[2]

WOMAN AS BODY

What is the relation of gender to this dualism? As feminists have shown, the scheme is frequently gendered, with woman cast in the role of the body, "weighed down," in Beauvoir's words, "by everything peculiar to it." In contrast, man casts himself as the "inevitable, like a pure idea, like the One, the All, the Absolute Spirit."[3] According to Dinnerstein, as a consequence of our infantile experience of woman as caretaker of our bodies, "the mucky, humbling limitations of the flesh" become the province of the female; on the other side stands "an innocent and dignified 'he' . . . to represent the part of the person that wants to stand clear of the flesh, to maintain perspective on it: 'I'ness wholly free of the chaotic, carnal atmosphere of infancy, uncontaminated humanness, is reserved for man."[4] The cost of such projections to women is obvious. For if, whatever the specific historical content of the duality, *the body* is the negative term, and if woman *is* the body, then women *are* that negativity, whatever it may be: distraction from knowledge, seduction away from God, capitulation to sexual desire, violence or aggression, failure of will, even death.

Although Schwartz's conception of the body is indeed gendered, it is not guilty of such projections. The "heavy bear" is clearly imaged and coded as male (and, arguably, racially and class-inflected as well). King Kong is evoked ("climbs the building"), as is male gang warfare ("boxes his brother in the hate-ridden city"), and one of the most striking metaphors of the poem is that of state of nature as football game ("the scrimmage of appetite"). It is not a maternal or feminine primitivity that is constructed, but a lumbering, rough, physically aggressive and emotionally helpless male animality. The feminine presence in the poem consists in the nostalgic memory of womb-life (the "water's clasp") and the present beloved, the "very dear" with whom he yearns for relations un-befouled by the crude instincts of the bear. Woman exists in this poem as a wrenching reminder both of past bliss and of present longing, but a reminder that is experienced without rancor, resentment, or anger at the object of desire. Schwartz, while projecting everything troubling onto the body, does not perform the additional projection of the body's troubles onto the figure of woman. He owns those troubles, albeit painfully and in estrangement, through the "bear" that is his body.

In his ownership of the instinctual, infantile body, Schwartz distinguishes himself from most of the Christian tradition and the deeply sedimented images and ideology that it has bequeathed to Western culture, from classical images of the woman as temptress (Eve, Salome, Delilah) to contemporary secular versions in such films as *Fatal Attraction* and *Presumed Innocent*. On television soap operas, the sexual temptress is a standard type. No show can earn big ratings without a Lucy Coe or Erica Kane; the Soap Opera Awards Show even has a category for Best Villainess. These depictions of women as continually and actively luring men to arousal (and, often, evil) work to disclaim male ownership of the body and its desires. The arousal of those desires is the result of female manipulation and therefore is the woman's fault. This construction is so powerful that rapists and child abusers have been believed when they have claimed that five-year-old female children "led them on."

Conscious intention, however, is not a requisite for females to be seen as responsible for the bodily responses of men, aggressive as well as sexual. One justification given for the exclusion of women from the priesthood is that their mere presence will arouse impure thoughts. Frequently, even when women are silent (or verbalizing exactly the opposite), their bodies are seen as "speaking" a language of provocation (Figure 1). When female bodies do not efface their femaleness, they may be seen as inviting, "flaunting": just two years ago, a man was acquitted of rape in Georgia on the defense that his victim had worn a miniskirt. When these inviting female bodies are inaccessible or unresponsive to male overtures, this may be interpreted as teasing, taunting, mocking. In Timothy Beneke's *Men on Rape*, several personal accounts demonstrate this interpretation. For example:

FIGURE 1

> Let's say I see a woman and she looks really pretty and really clean and sexy, and she's giving off very feminine, sexy vibes. I think, "Wow, I would love to make love to her," but I know she's not really interested. It's a tease. A lot of times a woman knows that she's looking really good and she'll use that and flaunt it, and it makes me feel like she's laughing at me and I feel *degraded*.[5]

In numerous "slasher" movies, female sexual independence is represented as an enticement to brutal murder, and chronic wife-batterers often claim that their wives "made them" beat them up, by looking at them the wrong way, by projecting too much cheek, or by some other (often very minor) bodily gesture of autonomy.

My point here, if it requires saying, is not to accuse all men of being potential rapists and wife-batterers; this would be to indulge in a cultural mythology about men as pernicious as the sexual-temptress myths about women. Rather, my aim is to demonstrate the continuing historical power and pervasiveness of certain cultural images and ideology to which not just men but also women (since we live in this culture, too) are vulnerable. Women and girls frequently internalize this ideology, holding themselves to blame for unwanted advances and sexual assaults. This guilt festers into unease with our femaleness, shame over our bodies, and self-loathing. For example, anorexia nervosa, which often manifests itself after an episode of sexual abuse or humiliation, can be seen as at least in part a defense against the "femaleness" of the body and a punishment of its desires. Those desires (as I argue in "Hunger as Ideology") have frequently been culturally represented through the metaphor of female appetite. The extremes to which the anorectic takes the denial of appetite (that is, to the point of starvation) suggest the dualistic nature of her construction of reality: either she transcends body totally, becoming pure "male" will, *or* she capitulates utterly to the degraded female body and its disgusting hungers. She sees no other possibilities, no middle ground.

Women may be quite ready, too, to believe the cultural mythology about some other woman or women, as responses to the Patricia Bowman/William Kennedy Smith rape trial demonstrated ("Why did she go home with him?" "Why did she let him kiss her?" "Why, if she only wanted to spend the evening with her girlfriends, did they go out to a bar?"). More striking, given the numbers of women who had had similar experiences, was female skepticism about Anita Hill's sexual-harassment charges against then-prospective Supreme Court Justice Clarence Thomas ("Why did she follow him to the EEOC?" "Why did she call him on the telephone?" "Why did she drive him to the airport?"). Generally, such questions were raised to attack Hill's credibility rather than to suggest that she had initiated a sexual relationship with Thomas. But it seemed clear to me that underlying the specifics of the attack was a generalized condemnation of Hill's behavior as inappropriate, insufficiently cautious, overly ambitious, and "asking for" *whatever* it was that happened. The intensity and even venom with which some women engaged in such attacks is suggestive of powerful projections at work, projections which may serve to protect women against their own self-doubts. "Why did she wait so long to tell? If what she says happened to her had happened to *me*, *I'd* never let him get away with it!" Thus, at Hill's expense, women shored up belief in the robustness of their own self-respect, self-confidence, and "purity."

For African American critics of Anita Hill—male and female—the situation was more complicated than this, of course. In the face of pervasive ideology that stereotypes black males as oversexed animals, many felt that to support Hill was to lend credence to racist mythologies. Some African American women, while believing Hill's charges, were furious at her for publicly exposing a black man as she did. Leaving aside the question of to what degree these criticisms were just (I discuss the Hill/Thomas hearings in more detail in "Feminism, Postmodernism, and Gender Skepticism"), what they seem to overlook (and what was certainly ignored by the white, male senators and in the media coverage of the hearings) is the fact that the racist ideology and imagery that construct non-European "races" as "primitive," "savage," sexually animalistic, and indeed more *bodily* than the white "races"[6] extends to black women as well as black men.

Corresponding to notions that all black men are potential rapists by nature are stereotypes of black women as amoral Jezebels who can never truly be raped, because *rape* implies the invasion of a personal space of modesty and reserve that the black woman has not been imagined as having. Corresponding to the popular sexual myth that black men are genitally over-endowed are notions, harking back to the early nineteenth century, that African women's sexual organs are more highly developed than (and configured differently from) those of European women, explaining (according to J. J. Virey's study of race) their greater "voluptuousness" and "lascivity."[7] "Scientific" representations of the black woman's body, like evolutionists' comparisons of the skull shapes of African males and orangutans, exaggerated (and often created) relations of similarity to animals, particularly monkeys. The "Hottentot Venus," a South African woman who was exhibited in London and Paris at the end of the eighteenth century, was presented as a "living ethnographic specimen" of the animal-like nature of the black woman.[8] Several commissioned portraits depict her with grotesquely disproportionate buttocks, as though she were in a permanent bodily state of "presenting" to the male.

A "breeder" to the slaveowner,[9] often depicted in jungle scenes in contemporary advertisements (Figure 2), the black woman carries

FIGURE 2

a triple burden of negative bodily associations. By virtue of her sex, she represents the temptations of the flesh and the source of man's moral downfall. By virtue of her race, she is instinctual animal, undeserving of privacy and undemanding of respect. She does not tease and then resist (as in the stereotype of the European temptress); she merely goes "into heat." Hispanic women are often similarly depicted as instinctual animals. But the legacy of slavery has added an additional element to effacements of black women's humanity. For in slavery her body is not only treated as an animal body but is *property*, to be "taken" and used at will. Such a body is denied even the dignity accorded a wild animal; its status approaches that of mere matter, thing-hood.

Through a cynical and cunning strategy, Clarence Thomas was able to neutralize the damage that could have been done to his case by unconscious racist images of the black man as oversexed animal; by bringing attention to these images and making an issue of them, he engineered a situation in which any white senator who did *not* treat him with the utmost delicacy and respect would seem a racist. Anita Hill, by contrast, bore the weight of the unexamined (at the hearings) construction of the black woman as mere body, whose moral and emotional sensibilities need not be treated with consideration. In the context of this legacy, the cool detachment with which the senators interrogated Hill about penises and pornography, while apologizing profusely to Thomas for the mere mention of such subjects, resonates with the historical effacement of black women's subjectivity.

ACTIVITY, PASSIVITY, AND GENDER

In "The Heavy Bear" the body is presented as haunting us with its passive materiality, its lack of agency, art, or even consciousness. Insofar as the "spirit's motive" is the guiding force, clarity and will dominate; the body, by contrast, simply *receives* and darkly, dumbly responds to impressions, emotions, passions. This duality of active spirit/passive body is also gendered, and it has been one of the most historically powerful of the dualities that inform Western ideologies of gender. First philosophically articulated by Aristotle (although embodied in many creation myths and associative schemes before him), it still informs contemporary images and ideology concerning reproduction. According to the Aristotelian version, the conception of a living being involves the vitalization of the purely material contribution of the female by the "effective and active" element, the male sperm:

> [T]here must needs be that which generates and that from which it generates; even if these be one, still they must be distinct in form and their essence must be different. . . . If, then, the male stands for the effective and active, and the female, considered as female, for the passive, it follows that what the female would contribute . . . would not be semen but material for the semen to work upon. This is just what we find to be the case, for the catamenia [menstrual materials] have in their nature an affinity to the primitive matter.[10]

So conceptually powerful (and perceptually determinative) was this view of things that when Leeuwenhoek in 1677 first examined sperm under the newly invented microscope, he saw tiny "animalcules" in it—the form of the future being, to be pressed out of the shapeless dough of the menstrual matter.

The dualism of male activity and female passivity is differently (but not incommensurably) represented by Hegel through an analogy with animals and plants:

> The difference between men and women is like that between animals and plants. Men correspond to animals, while women correspond to plants because their development is more placid and the principle that underlies it is the rather vague unity of feeling. . . . Women are educated—who knows how?—as it were by breathing in ideas, by living rather than by acquiring knowledge. The status of manhood, on the other hand, is attained only by the stress of thought and much technical exertion.[11]

Now, notice how these dualities—of male as active, striving, conscious subject and female as passive, vegetative, primitive matter—shape the following contemporary depiction, from Alan Guttmacher's drugstore guide to *Pregnancy, Birth, and Family Planning*:

> Some of the sperm swim straight up the one-inch, mucus-filled canal with almost purposeful success, while others bog down on the way, getting hopelessly stranded in tissue bays and coves. A small proportion of the total number ejaculated eventually reach the cavity of the uterus and begin their upward two-inch excursion through its length. Whether this progress results solely from the swimming efforts of the spermatozoa or whether they are aided by fluid currents

and muscular contractions of the uterus is still unknown. The un-daunted ones, those not stranded in this veritable everglade, reach the openings of the two fallopian tubes. . . . The one sperm that achieves its destiny has won against gigantic odds, several hundred million to one. . . . No one knows just what selective forces are responsible for the victory. Perhaps the winner had the strongest constitution; perhaps it was the swiftest swimmer of all the contes-tants entered in the race. . . . If ovulation occurred within several minutes to twenty-four hours before the sperm's journey ends, the ovum will be in the tube, awaiting fertilization; if ovulation took place more than twenty-four hours before insemination, the egg cell will already have begun to deteriorate and fragment, rendering it inca-pable of being fertilized by the time the spermatozoon reaches it. On the other hand, if ovulation has not yet occurred, but takes place within two or three days after intercourse, living spermatozoa will be cruising at the tubal site.[12]

So entrenched is our expectation that the male will be the "ef-fective and active" element and that the female must be the one to passively wait for him, that my students were shocked to discover that on most occasions when fertilization occurs it is actually the *egg* that travels to rendezvous with sperm that have been lolling around, for as much as three days, waiting for *her* to arrive. Gutt-macher, indeed, refuses to describe the sperm as "waiting" and depicts them instead as "cruising"—cruising down the strip, as it were, looking to pick up chicks. Such metaphors are continually reinforced by popular representations of conception such as the opening credits of *Look Who's Talking*, which depict the perilous race of "the undaunted ones" to the tune of "I Get Around" and per-sonify the one sperm "who achieves his destiny," having him provide a running oral commentary on his progress. The graphic simulates the consequences of an act of intercourse at ovulation (our imaginal paradigm, though by no means true of the majority of fertilizations); there at the end of the journey is the giant beach ball of an egg, languorously bobbing, awaiting the victor's arrival. Since the voice of the triumphant sperm is the same as that of Mikey, the baby who is conceived, Aristotle is confirmed: the male really *does* provide the form of the individual.

Clearly, then, mind/body dualism is no mere philosophical po-sition, to be defended or dispensed with by clever argument. Rather, it is a *practical* metaphysics that has been deployed and socially embodied in medicine, law, literary and artistic representations, the psychological construction of self, interpersonal relationships, popular culture, and advertisements—a metaphysics which will be deconstructed only through concrete transformation of the institutions and practices that sustain it. As a final illustration of how culturally sedimented (and often "innocently" and covertly reproduced) are the gendered dualities that I have discussed in this section, consider a Kmart advertisement for boy's and girl's bicycles. The ad describes three levels of bikes: one for toddlers (three-wheelers), one for pre-teeners, and one for teenagers. Each model has a boy's version and a girl's version, each with its own name. The toddler's models are named "Lion" and "Little Angel"; the pre-teeners, "Pursuit" and "St. Helen." But while the duality of male activity and female passivity is thus strikingly mapped onto pre-adolescence, once sexual maturity is reached other dualities emerge: the teenager's models are named "Granite Pass" and "White Heat"!

The gendered nature of mind/body dualism, and its wide-ranging institutional and cultural expression, is a recurring theme of many of the essays in this volume. In "Are Mothers Persons?" I explore how—despite an official rhetoric that insists on the embodied subjectivity of all persons—Western legal and medical practice concerning reproduction in fact divides the world into human subjects (fetus and father) and "mere" bodies (pregnant women). In "Hunger as Ideology" I consider how representations of men and women eating (for example, in contemporary advertisements) exhibit a dualistic pedagogy instructing women and men in very different attitudes toward the "heavy bear" and its hungers: women's appetites require containment and control, whereas male indulgence is legitimated and encouraged. In this essay, in "Anorexia Nervosa," and in "Reading the Slender Body," "the devouring woman" is seen to be as potent an image of dangerous female desire (particularly in contemporary culture) as the sexual temptress. I explore, as well, the social contexts that have encouraged the flourishing of this imagery.

In the latter two essays dualism is explored not only via gendered representations but as a more general contemporary construction of self that shapes male experience as well as female. Dualism, of course, was not invented in the twentieth century. But there are distinctive ways in which it is *embodied* in contemporary culture, giving the lie to the social mythology that ours is a body-loving, de-repressive era. We may be *obsessed* with our bodies, but we are hardly accepting of them. In "Anorexia Nervosa" I consider the way in which an agonistic experience of mind/body regulates the anorectic's sense of embodiment, as well as other obsessive body practices of contemporary culture. My aim, however, is not to portray these obsessions as bizarre or anomalous, but, rather, as the logical (if extreme) manifestations of anxieties and fantasies fostered by our culture. I develop this theme further in "Reading the Slender Body," where I decode the meanings of *fat* and *thin* in our culture to expose the moral significances attached to them, revealing the slender, fit body as a symbol of "virile" mastery over bodily desires that are continually experienced as threatening to overtake the self. This construction of self is then located within consumer culture and its contradictory requirement that we embody both the spiritual discipline of the work ethic and the capacity for continual, mindless consumption of goods.

Today, one often hears intellectuals urging that we "go beyond" dualisms, calling for the deconstruction of the hierarchical oppositions (male/female, mind/body, active/passive) that structure dualism in the West, and scorning others for engaging in "dualistic thinking." But it is not so easy to "go beyond dualism" in this culture, as I argue in a variety of ways in this volume. In "'Material Girl'" and in "Feminism, Postmodernism, and Gender Skepticism" I consider postmodern culture, poststructuralist thought, and some aspects of contemporary feminism as embodying fantasies of transcendence of the materiality and historicity of the body, its situatedness in space and time, and its gender.

ANGLO-AMERICAN FEMINISM, "WOMEN'S LIBERATION," AND THE POLITICS OF THE BODY

Considering the pervasiveness of associations such as those discussed in the preceding section, it is no surprise that feminist theorists turned to Western representations of the body with an analytic, deconstructive eye. From their efforts we have learned to read all the various texts of Western culture—literary works, philosophical works, artworks, medical texts, film, fashion, soap operas—less naively and more completely, educated and attuned to the historically pervasive presence of gender-, class-, and race-coded dualities, alert to their continued embeddedness in the most mundane, seemingly innocent representations. Since these dualities (although not these alone) mediate a good deal of our cultural reality, few representations—from high religious art to depictions of life at the cellular level—can claim innocence.[13]

Feminists first began to develop a critique of the "politics of the body," however, not in terms of the body as represented (in medical, religious, and philosophical discourse, artworks, and other cultural "texts"), but in terms of the material body as a site of political struggle. When I use the term *material*, I do not mean it in the Aristotelian sense of *brute* matter, nor do I mean it in the sense of "natural" or "unmediated" (for our bodies are necessarily cultural forms; whatever roles anatomy and biology play, they always interact with culture.) I mean what Marx and, later, Foucault had in mind in focusing on the "direct grip" (as opposed to representational influence) that culture has on our bodies, through the practices and bodily habits of everyday life. Through routine, habitual activity, our bodies learn what is "inner" and what is "outer," which gestures are forbidden and which required, how violable or inviolable are the boundaries of our bodies, how much space around the body may be claimed, and so on. These are often far more powerful lessons than those we learn consciously, through explicit instruction concerning the appropriate behavior for our gender, race, and social class.

The role of American feminism in developing a "political" understanding of body practice is rarely acknowledged. In describing the historical emergence of such an understanding, Don Hanlon Johnson leaps straight from Marx to Foucault, effacing the intellectual role played by the social movements of the sixties (both black power and women's liberation) in awakening consciousness of the body as "an instrument of power":

> Another major deconstruction [of the old notion of "the body"] is in the area of sociopolitical thought. Although Karl Marx initiated this movement in the middle of the 19th century, it did not gain momentum until the last 20 years due to the work of the late Michel Foucault. Marx argued that a person's economic class affected his or her experience and definition of "the body." . . . Foucault carried on these seminal arguments in his analysis of the body as the focal point for struggles over the shape of power. Population size, gender formation, the control of children and of those thought to be deviant

from the society's ethics are major concerns of political organization—and all concentrate on the definition and shaping of the body.
Moreover, the cultivation of the body is essential to the establishment
of one's social role.[14]

Not a few feminists, too, appear to accept this view of things. While
honoring French feminists Irigaray, Wittig, Cixous, and Kristeva for
their work on the body "as the site of the production of new modes
of subjectivity" and Beauvoir for the "understanding of the body as
a situation," Linda Zirelli credits Foucault with having "showed us
how the body has been historically disciplined"; to Anglo-American
feminism is simply attributed the "essentialist" view of the body as
an "archaic natural."[15]

Almost everyone who does the "new scholarship" on the body
claims Foucault as its founding father and guiding light. And certainly (as I will discuss later in this introduction) Foucault did articulate and delineate some of the central theoretical categories that
influenced that scholarship as it developed in the late 1980s and
early 1990s. "Docile bodies," "biopower," "micropractices"—these
are useful concepts, and Foucault's analyses, which employ them
in exploring historical changes in the organization and deployment
of power, are brilliant.[16] But neither Foucault nor any other poststructuralist thinker discovered or invented the idea, to refer again
to Johnson's account, that the "definition and shaping" of the body
is "the focal point for struggles over the shape of power." *That* was
discovered by feminism, and long before it entered into its marriage
with poststructuralist thought.

"There is no private domain of a person's life that is not political
and there is no political issue that is not ultimately personal. The old
barriers have fallen." Charlotte Bunch made this statement in 1968,
and although much has been written about "personal politics" in
the emergence of the second wave of feminism, not enough attention has been paid, I would argue, to its significance as an *intellectual*
paradigm, and in particular to the new understanding of the *body*
that "personal politics" ushered in. What, after all, is more personal
than the life of the body? And for women, associated with the body
and largely confined to a life centered *on* the body (both the beau-
tification of one's own body and the reproduction, care, and maintenance of the bodies of others), culture's grip on the body is a
constant, intimate fact of everyday life. As early as 1792, Mary

Wollstonecraft had provided a classic statement of this theme. As a privileged woman, she focuses on the social construction of femininity as delicacy and domesticity, and it is as clear an example of the production of a socially trained, "docile body" as Foucault ever articulated:

> To preserve personal beauty, woman's glory! the limbs and faculties are cramped with worse than Chinese bands, and the sedentary life which they are condemned to live, whilst boys frolic in the open air, weakens the muscles and relaxes the nerves. As for Rousseau's remarks, which have since been echoed by several writers, that they have naturally, that is since birth, independent of education, a fondness for dolls, dressing, and talking—they are so puerile as not to merit a serious refutation. That a girl, condemned to sit for hours together listening to the idle chat of weak nurses, or to attend to her mother's toilet, will endeavor to join the conversation, is, indeed, very natural; and that she will imitate her mother and aunts, and amuse herself by adorning her lifeless doll, as they do in dressing her, poor innocent babe! is undoubtedly a most natural consequence. . . . Nor can it be expected that a woman will resolutely endeavor to strengthen her constitution and abstain from enervating indulgences, if artificial notions of beauty, and false descriptions of sensibility, have been early entangled with her motives of action . . . Genteel women are, literally speaking, slaves to their bodies, and glory in their subjection, . . . women are everywhere in this deplorable state. . . . Taught from their infancy that beauty is woman's scepter, the mind shapes itself to the body, and, roaming round its gilt cage, only seeks to adorn its prison.[17]

A more activist generation urged escape from the prison, and, long before poststructuralist thought declared the body a political site, recognized that the most mundane, "trivial" aspects of women's bodily existence were in fact significant elements in the social construction of an oppressive feminine norm. In 1914, the first Feminist Mass Meeting in America—whose subject was "Breaking into the Human Race"—poignantly listed, among the various social and political rights demanded, "The right to ignore fashion."[18] Here, already, the material "micropractices" of everyday life— which would be extended by later feminists to include not only what one wears but who cooks and cleans (the classic "Politics of Housework" by Pat Mainardi),[19] and even, more recently, what one eats or does not eat—have been brought out of the realm of the purely personal and into the domain of the political. Here, for example, is a trenchant 1971 analysis, presented by way of a set of "conscious-ness-raising" exercises for men, of how female subjectivity is trained and subordinated by the everyday bodily requirements and vulnerabilities of "femininity":

> Sit down in a straight chair. Cross your legs at the ankles and keep your knees pressed together. Try to do this while you're having a conversation with someone, but pay attention at all times to keeping your knees pressed tightly together.
>
> Run a short distance, keeping your knees together. You'll find you have to take short, high steps if you run this way. Women have been taught it is unfeminine to run like a man with long, free strides. See how far you get running this way for 30 seconds.
>
> Walk down a city street. Pay a lot of attention to your clothing: make sure your pants are zipped, shirt tucked in, buttons done. Look straight ahead. Every time a man walks past you, avert your eyes and make your face expressionless. Most women learn to go through this act each time we leave our houses. It's a way to avoid at least some of the encounters we've all had with strange men who decided we looked available.[20]

Until I taught a course in the history of feminism several years ago, I had forgotten that the very first public act of second-wave feminist protest was the "No More Miss America" demonstration in August of 1968. The critique presented at that demonstration was far from the theoretically crude, essentializing program that caricatures of that era's feminism would suggest. Rather, the position paper handed out at the demonstration outlined a complex, nonreductionist analysis of the intersection of sexism, conformism, competition, ageism, racism, militarism, and consumer culture as they are constellated and crystallized in the pageant.[21] The "No More Miss America" demonstration was the event that earned "women's libbers" the reputation for being "bra-burners," an epithet many feminists have been trying to shed ever since. In fact, no bras *were* burned at the demonstration, although there was a huge "Freedom Trash Can" into which were thrown bras, along with girdles, curlers, false eyelashes, wigs, copies of the *Ladies' Home Journal*, *Cosmopolitan*, *Family Circle*, etc. The media, sensationalizing the event, and also no doubt influenced by the paradigm of draft-card burning as the act of political resistance par excellence, misreported or invented the burning of the bras. It stuck like crazy glue to the popular imagination; indeed, many of my students today still refer to feminists as "bra-burners." But whether or not bras were burned, the uneasy public with whom the image stuck surely got it right in recognizing the deep political meaning of women's refusal to "discipline" our breasts, culturally required to be so exclusively "for" the other—whether as instrument and symbol of nurturing love, or as erotic fetish.

And "whither the bra in the 90's?" Amy Collins, writing in 1991 for *Lear's* magazine, poses this question. She answers herself:

> Women are again playing up their bust lines with a little artifice. To give the breasts the solid, rounded shape that is currently desirable, La Perla is offering a Lycra bra with pre-formed, pressed-cotton cups. To provide a deeper cleavage, a number of lingerie companies are selling side-panel bras that gently nudge the breasts together. Perhaps exercising has made the idea of altering body contours acceptable once more. In any case, if anatomy is destiny, women are discovering new ways to reshape both.[22]

Indeed. In 1992, with the dangers of silicone implants on public trial, the media emphasis was on the irresponsibility of Dow, and the personal sufferings of women who became ill from their implants. To my mind, however, the most depressing aspect of the disclosures was the *cultural* spectacle: the large numbers of women who are having implants purely to enlarge or reshape their breasts and who consider any health risk worth the resulting boon to their self-esteem and "market value." These women take the risk, not because they have been passively taken in by media norms of the beautiful breast (almost always silicone-enhanced), but because they have correctly discerned that these norms shape the perceptions and desires of potential lovers and employers. They are neither dupes nor critics of sexist culture; rather, their overriding concern is their right to be desired, loved, and successful on its terms. Proposals to ban or even to regulate silicone breast implants are thus often viewed as totalitarian interference with self-determination, freedom, and choice. Many who argue in this way consider themselves feminists, and many feminist scholars today theorize explicitly *as* feminists "on their behalf." A recent article in the feminist philosophy journal *Hypatia*, for example, defends cosmetic surgery as being *"first and foremost* . . . about taking one's life into one's own hands."[23]

I examine this contemporary construction later in this volume. For now, I would only highlight how very different it is from the dominant feminist discourse on the body in the late sixties and seventies. *That* imagination of the female body was of a *socially* shaped and historically "colonized" territory, not a site of individual self-determination. As Andrea Dworkin described it:

> Standards of beauty describe in precise terms the relationship that an individual will have to her own body. They prescribe her motility, spontaneity, posture, gait, the uses to which she can put her body. *They define precisely the dimensions of her physical freedom.* And of course, the relationship between physical freedom and psychological development, intellectual possibility, and creative potential is an umbilical one.
>
> In our culture, not one part of a woman's body is left untouched, unaltered. No feature or extremity is spared the art, or pain, of improvement. . . . From head to toe, every feature of a woman's face, every section of her body, is subject to modification, alteration. This alteration is an ongoing, repetitive process. It is vital to the economy, the major substance of male-female differentiation, the most immediate physical and psychological reality of being a woman. From the age of 11 or 12 until she dies, a woman will spend a large part of her time, money, and energy on binding, plucking, painting and deodorizing herself. It is commonly and wrongly said that male transvestites through the use of makeup and costuming caricature the women they would become, but any real knowledge of the romantic ethos makes clear that these men have penetrated to the core experience of being a woman, a romanticized construct.[24]

Here, feminism inverted and converted the old metaphor of the Body Politic, found in Plato, Aristotle, Cicero, Seneca, Machiavelli, Hobbes, and many others, to a new metaphor: the politics of the body. In the old metaphor of the Body Politic, the state or society was imagined as a human body, with different organs and parts symbolizing different functions, needs, social constituents, forces, and so forth—the head or soul for the sovereign, the blood for the will of the people, or the nerves for the system of rewards and punishments. Now, feminism imagined the human body as *itself* a politically inscribed entity, its physiology and morphology shaped by histories and practices of containment and control— from foot-binding and corseting to rape and battering to compulsory heterosexuality, forced sterilization, unwanted pregnancy, and (in the case of the African American slave woman) explicit commodification:[25]

> [H]er head and her heart were separated from her back and her hands and divided from her womb and vagina. Her back and muscle were pressed into field labor where she was forced to work with men and work like men. Her hands were demanded to nurse and nurture the white man and his family as domestic servant whether she was technically enslaved or legally free. Her vagina, used for his sexual pleasure, was the gateway to the womb, which was his place of capital investment—the capital investment being the sex act and the resulting child the accumulated surplus, worth money on the slave market.[26]

One might rightly object that the body's literal bondage in slavery, described above by Barbara Omolade, is not to be compared to the metaphorical bondage of privileged nineteenth-century women to the corset, much less to the twentieth-century "tyranny of slenderness." No feminist writers considered them equivalent. But at the heart of the developing feminist model, for many writers, *was* the extension of the concept of enslavement to include the voluntary behaviors of privileged women. Problematic as this extension has come to seem, I think it is crucial to recognize that a staple of the prevailing sexist ideology against which the feminist model protested was the notion that in matters of beauty and femininity, it is women alone who are responsible for their sufferings from the whims and bodily tyrannies of fashion. According to that ideology, men's desires bear no responsibility, nor does the culture that subordinates women's desires to those of men, sexualizes and commodifies women's bodies, and offers them little other opportunity for social or personal power. Rather, it is in Woman's essential feminine nature to be (delightfully if incomprehensibly) drawn to such trivialities and to be willing to endure whatever physical inconvenience is entailed. In such matters, whether having her feet broken and shaped into four-inch "lotuses," or her waist straitlaced to fourteen inches, or her breasts surgically stuffed with plastic, she is her "own worst enemy." Set in cultural relief against this thesis, the feminist "anti-thesis"—the insistence that women are the *done to*, not the *doers*, here; that *men* and *their* desires bear the responsibility; and that female obedience to the dictates of fashion is better conceptualized as bondage than choice—was a crucial historical moment in the developing articulation of a new understanding of the sexual politics of the body.

BEYOND THE OPPRESSOR/OPPRESSED MODEL

The limitations of simple antithesis, however, ultimately disclosed themselves. Subsuming patriarchal institutions and practices under an oppressor/oppressed model which theorizes men as possessing and wielding power over women—who are viewed correspondingly as themselves utterly power*less*—proved inadequate to the social and historical complexities of the situations of men and women, and many different foci of criticism emerged in the 1980s and 1990s. A good many critics emphasized the necessity of constructing theory that would do better justice to racial, economic, and class differences among women. Others protested against what they viewed as a depiction of women as passive, without agency, a depiction that overlooks both women's collusions with patriarchal culture and their frequent efforts at resistance. Correlatively, the "old" feminist discourse has been charged with portraying men as the enemy and "essentializing" them as sexual brutes and cultural dominators. From more deconstructionist quarters, it has been criticized for its lack of textual sophistication—that is, its insensitivity to the multiplicity of meanings that can be read in every cultural act and practice. Within this type of critique, one may find arguments for the "creative" or "subversive" nature of practices and cultural forms, such as makeup, high heels, or cosmetic surgery, which the "old" feminist discourse would view as *simply* oppressive to women. In general, the "old" discourse is seen as having constructed an insufficiently textured, undiscerningly dualistic, overly pessimistic (if not paranoid) view of the politics of the body.

My own perspective on these criticisms will emerge in detail throughout this book. In this introduction, however, I want to provide some very general remarks, focusing in particular on the strengths and weaknesses of the old feminist discourse in the context of our increasingly image-dominated culture. I agree with the textual critique that the "old" discourse did not deal adequately with the multiplicity or contextuality of meaning. Rather, it laid down an initial lexicon, which others have elaborated and complicated. Susan Brownmiller's excellent book *Femininity*, for example, is extremely valuable in its examination of the body as a text saturated with gendered symbols and meanings.[27] The lexicon through which she interprets this text, however—for example, long hair, skirts, and high heels as symbolic of femininity—often cries out for further elaboration, both historical and contextual. With the exception of those eras in which certain styles were rigorously marked as masculine and forbidden to women (for example, trousers in the nineteenth century), the demonstration of "femininity" has involved the arrangement of items within a *system* that gives them their meaning. Context is everything, especially in our postmodern culture of pastiche and rearrangement. So, for example, a crew cut may be seen as "feminine" if the model's mouth is vividly colored and a lacy blouse is worn, but "masculine" when worn with no makeup, but with overalls and a confident body posture; men's jackets are hardly "masculine" when they overwhelm the body of an extremely petite sixteen-year-old, but they *do* carry connotations of maleness when they are tailored, accompanied by briefcase and a no-nonsense demeanor. Long hair on men has functioned as a symbol of resistance against establishment authority (as among hippies, rock stars, and bikers), and it also may function to *highlight* a man's "masculinity": long, straight ponytails are frequently worn by extremely muscular men. As to muscles themselves, are they invariably male, as Brownmiller says? Certainly they have been dominantly coded in this way, but (as I argue in "Reading the Slender Body"), they have also been race- and class-coded, and today they frequently symbolize qualities of character rather than class, race, or gender status.

Given the differences that race, class, gender, ethnicity, and so forth make to the determination of meaning, "reading" bodies becomes an extremely complex business. However, I do not agree with those who claim that images must always be read for "difference." Readers will indeed experience multiple responses to the same image or icon; a lesbian's "reading" of Madonna, for example, may be very different from that of a heterosexual "wanna be." But to focus *only* on multiple interpretations is to miss important effects of the everyday deployment of mass cultural representations of masculinity, femininity, beauty, and success.

First, the representations *homogenize*. In our culture, this means that they will smooth out all racial, ethnic, and sexual "differences" that disturb Anglo-Saxon, heterosexual expectations and identifications. Certainly, high-fashion images may contain touches of exotica: collagen-plumped lips or corn rows on white models, Barbra Streisand noses, "butch" styles of dress. Consumer capitalism depends on the continual production of novelty, of fresh images to stimulate desire, and it frequently drops into marginalized neighborhoods in order to find them. But such elements will either be explicitly *framed* as exotica or, within the overall system of meaning, they will not be permitted to overwhelm the representation and establish a truly alternative or "subversive" model of beauty or success. (White models may collagen their lips, but black models are usually light-skinned and Anglo-featured.) A definite (albeit not always fixed or determinate) system of boundaries sets limits on the validation of "difference."

Second, these homogenized images *normalize*—that is, they function as models against which the self continually measures, judges, "disciplines," and "corrects" itself. Cosmetic surgery is now a $1.75-billion-a-year industry in the United States, with almost 1.5 million people a year undergoing surgery of some kind, from face-lifts to calf implants. These operations have become more and more affordable to the middle class (the average cost of a nose job is $2,500), and almost all can be done on an outpatient basis—some during lunch hour. Lest it be imagined that most of these surgeries are to correct disfiguring accidents or birth defects, it should be noted that liposuction is the most frequently requested operation (average cost $1,500), with breast enlargement (average cost $2,000) a close second. Are diverse ethnic and racial styles of beauty asserting their "differences" through such surgery? Far from it. Does anyone in this culture have his or her nose reshaped to look more "African" or "Jewish"? Cher is typical here; her various surgeries have gradually replaced a strong, decidedly (if indeterminately) "ethnic" look with a much more symmetrical, delicate, Anglo-Saxon version of beauty. She also looks much younger at forty-six than she did at forty, as do most actresses of her generation, for whom face-lifts are virtually routine. These actresses, whose images surround us on television and in videos and films, are changing cultural expectations of what women "should" look like at forty-five and fifty. This is touted in the popular culture as a liberating development for older women; in the nineties, it is declared, fifty is still sexy. But in fact Cher, Jane Fonda, and others have not made the aging female body sexually more acceptable. They have established a new norm—achievable only through continual cosmetic surgery—in which the surface of the female body ceases to age physically as the body grows chronologically older.

Even within the context of homogenizing imagery, deciphering meaning is complicated. Female slenderness, for example, has a wide range of sometimes contradictory meanings in contemporary representations, the imagery of the slender body suggesting powerlessness and contraction of female social space in one context, autonomy and freedom in the next. It is impossible adequately to understand women's problems with food and body image unless these significations are unpacked, and this requires examining slenderness in multiple contexts. Although only one of the essays in this book claims to "read" the slender body, in fact all of the essays that discuss eating disorders do so. These are: "Hunger as Ideology," "Anorexia Nervosa," "The Body and the Reproduction of Femininity," "Reading the Slender Body," and "Whose Body Is This?"

To the extent that feminist discourse *has* employed a framework of oppressors and oppressed, villains and victims (and this, of course, is not equally true of all writers), it requires reconstruction if it is to be able adequately to theorize the pathways of modern power. In this reconstruction, the work of Michel Foucault has proved useful to much feminist thought, including my own work. Since several essays in this volume make use of Foucauldian categories and perspectives, it may be useful for me to provide an overview, in connection with the themes under discussion in this introduction. For Foucault, modern (as opposed to sovereign) power is non-authoritarian, non-conspiratorial, and indeed non-orchestrated; yet it nonetheless produces and normalizes bodies to serve prevailing relations of dominance and subordination. Understanding this new sort of power requires, according to Foucault, two conceptual changes. First, we must cease to imagine "power" as the *possession* of individuals or groups—as something people "have"— and instead see it as a dynamic or network of non-centralized forces. Second, we must recognize that these forces are *not* random or haphazard, but configure to assume particular historical forms, within which certain groups and ideologies *do* have dominance. Dominance here, however, is sustained not by decree or design "from above" (as sovereign power is exercised) but through multiple "processes, of different origin and scattered location," regulating the most intimate and minute elements of the construction of space, time, desire, embodiment.[28]

Here is one juncture where Foucauldian insights prove particularly useful to social and historical analysis of "femininity" and "masculinity." Where power works "from below," prevailing forms of selfhood and subjectivity (gender among them) are maintained, not chiefly through physical restraint and coercion (although social relations may certainly contain such elements), but through individual self-surveillance and self-correction to norms. Thus, as Foucault writes, "there is no need for arms, physical violence, material constraints. Just a gaze. An inspecting gaze, a gaze which each individual under its weight will end by interiorising to the point that he is his own overseer, each individual thus exercising this surveillance over, and against himself."[29]

Now, not all female submission is best understood in terms of such a model; women are frequently physically and emotionally terrorized and financially trapped in violent relationships and degrading jobs. But when it comes to the politics of appearance, such ideas are apt and illuminating.[30] In my own work, they have been extremely helpful both to my analysis of the contemporary disciplines of diet and exercise and to my understanding of eating disorders as arising out of and reproducing normative feminine practices of our culture, practices which train the female body in docility and obedience to cultural demands while at the same time being *experienced* in terms of power and control. Within a Foucauldian framework, power and pleasure do not cancel each other. Thus, the heady experience of feeling powerful or "in control," far from being a necessarily accurate reflection of one's social position, is always suspect as itself the product of power relations whose shape may be very different.

Foucault also emphasized, in later developments of his ideas, that power relations are never seamless but are always spawning new forms of culture and subjectivity, new opportunities for transformation. Where there is power, he came to see, there is also resistance.[31] Dominant forms and institutions are continually being penetrated and reconstructed by values, styles, and knowledges that have been developing and gathering strength, energy, and distinctiveness "at the margins." (This is why, I would argue, affirmative action should not be understood as only about redressing historical exclusions in the interests of justice to those groups excluded, but as essential to the diversification and reinvigoration of the dominant culture.) Such transformations do not occur in one fell swoop; they emerge only gradually, through local and often minute shifts in power. They may also be served, paradoxically, through conformity to prevailing norms. So, for example, the woman who goes into a rigorous weight-training program in order to achieve the currently stylish look may discover that her new muscles give her the self-confidence that enables her to assert herself more forcefully at work. Modern power-relations are thus unstable; resistance is perpetual and hegemony precarious.

Within a Foucauldian/feminist framework, it is indeed senseless to view men as the enemy: to do so would be to ignore, not only power differences in the racial, class, and sexual situations of men, but the fact that most men, equally with women, find themselves embedded and implicated in institutions and practices that they as individuals did not create and do not control—and that they frequently feel tyrannized by. (The best work being done out of the men's movement today explores this enmeshment;[32] unfortunately, it has frequently been eclipsed by best-selling and sensationalistic "reclamations" of masculinity.) Moreover, such a framework forces us to recognize the degree to which women collude in sustaining sexism and sexist stereotypes. For example, the continued popularity of the soap-opera villainess, mentioned earlier, is insured by the thousands of female viewers who delight both in the power and agency such characters manifest *and* in their inevitable neutralization (either through defeat or through personality conversion) by the forces of more conventional female behavior.

Many, if not most, women also are willing (often, enthusiastic) participants in cultural practices that objectify and sexualize us. Here, in its failure to admit female responsibility, I do think that much feminist analysis has been, and continues to be, inadequate—though understandably so, given the swiftness with which the acknowledgment that women *participate* in reproducing sexist culture gets converted to the ideas that we "are our own worst enemies," "do it to ourselves," "ask for it." In this climate of sedimented sexist ideology ready to become activated on the shallowest pretext, certain important discussions may become *verboten* because so strewn with dangerous mines threatening to go off. For example, I have always felt extremely torn, discussing *The Accused* in class, about how to deal with Jodie Foster's erotic dance in the bar. On the one hand, I think it is extremely important that we understand how beauty and sexuality can function as a medium of power and control for the otherwise powerless, and the scene provides an opportunity to discuss this. On the other hand, I *know* that as soon as we begin to discuss the dance in such terms, many students will immediately see this as corroborating that the woman was indeed a sexual temptress who led these men to rape. In the face of such crude but culturally powerful ideas, the relevant distinctions which I would then make stand a good chance of being utterly lost on my students.

FEMINISM AS SYSTEMIC CRITIQUE

The valuable reconceptualization of power suggested by Foucault should not be interpreted as entailing the view that all players are equal, or that positions of dominance and subordination are not sustained within networks of power. Men are not the enemy, but they often may have a higher stake in maintaining institutions within which they have historically occupied positions of dominance over women. That is why they have often *felt* like "the enemy" to women struggling to change those institutions. (Such a dual recognition seems essential, in particular, to theorizing the situation of men who have been historically subordinated on the basis of their race, class, or sexuality.) Moreover, the fact that cultural resistance is continual does not mean it is on an equal footing with forms that are culturally entrenched. It is simply absurd to suggest, as Dianne Johnson does in reviewing Naomi Wolf's *The Beauty Myth*, that the development of a "Happy to Be Me" Barbie-style doll of nonanorexic proportions signifies that feminist concerns over the cultural tyranny of slenderness are "out of date."[33] In "'Material Girl'" I strongly argue, against proponents of the absolute heterogeneity of culture, that in contemporary Western constructions of beauty there *are* dominant, strongly "normalizing" (racial and gendered) forms to contend with. To struggle effectively against the coerciveness of those forms it is first necessary to recognize that they *have* dominance, and not to efface such recognition through a facile and abstract celebration of "heterogeneity," "difference," "subversive reading," and so forth.

Recognizing that normalizing cultural forms exist does not entail, as some writers have argued, the view that women are "cultural dopes," blindly submitting to oppressive regimes of beauty.[34] Although many people *are* mystified (insisting, for example, that the current fitness craze is only about health or that plastic surgery to "correct" a "Jewish" or "black" nose is just an individual preference), often there will be a high degree of consciousness involved in the decision to diet or to have cosmetic surgery. People *know* the routes to success in this culture—they are advertised widely enough—and they are not "dopes" to pursue them. Often, given the racism, sexism, and narcissism of the culture, their personal happiness and economic security may depend on it.

In 1990 I lost twenty-five pounds through a national weight-loss program, a choice that some of my colleagues viewed as inconsistent and even hypocritical, given my work. But in my view, feminist cultural criticism is not a blueprint for the conduct of personal life (or political action, for that matter) and does not empower (or require) individuals to "rise above" their culture or to become martyrs to feminist ideals. It does not tell us what to *do* (although I continually get asked such questions when I speak at colleges)— whether to lose weight or not, wear makeup or not, lift weights or not. Its goal is edification and understanding, enhanced *consciousness* of the power, complexity, and *systemic* nature of culture, the interconnected webs of its functioning. It is up to the reader to decide how, when, and where (or whether) to put that understanding to further use, in the particular, complicated, and ever-changing context that is his or her life and no one else's.

The goal of consciousness-raising may seem, perhaps, to belong to another era. I believe, however, that in our present culture of mystification—a culture which continually pulls us away from systemic understanding and inclines us toward constructions that emphasize individual freedom, choice, power, ability—simply becoming *more conscious* is a tremendous achievement. (As Marx insisted, changes in consciousness *are* changes in life, and in a culture that counts on our remaining unconscious they are political as well.) Feminist cultural criticism cannot magically lift us into a transcendent realm of immunity to cultural images, but it ought to help guard against the feeling of comfortable oneness with culture and to foster a healthy skepticism about the pleasures and powers it offers. I know, for example, that although my weight loss has benefited me in a variety of ways, it has also diminished my efficacy as an alternative role model for my female students. I used to demonstrate the possibility of confidence, expressiveness, and success in a less than adequately normalized body. Today, my female students may be more likely to see me as confirmation that success comes only from playing by the cultural rules. This may affirm some of them, but what about those who cannot play by the rules? A small but possibly important source of self-validation and encouragement has been taken from them. Even though my choice to diet was a conscious and "rational" response to the system of cultural meanings that surround me (not the blind submission of a "cultural dope"), I should not deceive myself into thinking that my own feeling of enhanced personal comfort and power means that I am not servicing an oppressive system.

The "old" feminist discourse may have been insufficiently attentive to the multiplicity of meaning, the pleasures of shaping and decorating the body, or the role of female agency in reproducing patriarchal culture. What it did offer was a systemic critique capable of rousing women to collective action—something we do not have today. True, women are mobilizing around other issues—reproductive rights, for example. But on the sexualization and objectification of the female body contemporary feminism (with some notable exceptions)[35] is strikingly muted. Some forms of postmodern feminism (as I argue in " 'Material Girl' ") are worse than muted, they are distressingly at one with the culture in celebrating the creative agency of individuals and denying systemic pattern. It seems to me that feminist theory has taken a very strange turn indeed when plastic surgery can be described, as it has been by Kathy Davis, as *"first and foremost . . .* about taking one's life into one's own hands." I agree with Davis that as an *individual* choice that seeks to make life as livable and enjoyable as possible within certain cultural constraints and directives, of course such surgery can be experienced as liberating. But since when has the feminist critique of normalizing beauty practice ever been directed against individuals and their choices? Unlike Davis, I do not view cosmetic surgery as being first and foremost "about" self-determination *or* self-deception. Rather, my focus is on the complexly and densely institutionalized *system* of values and practices within which girls and women—and, increasingly, men and boys as well—come to believe that they are nothing (and are frequently treated as nothing) unless they are trim, tight, lineless, bulgeless, and sagless. In a cultural moment such as the present, within which a high level of physical attractiveness is continually presented as a prerequisite for romantic success and very often is demanded by employers as well, I believe that we desperately need the critical edge of systemic perspective.

My analysis of eating disorders—the core of the critique of normalizing practices presented in this book—is deeply informed by my experiences as a woman who has herself struggled with weight and body-image issues all her life. However, I do not recount that personal story in any of my pieces; I was trained as a philosopher, and that mode of writing does not come easily to me. Instead, I try to preserve the critical edge of the "old" feminist discourse, while incorporating a more postmodern appreciation of how subtle and multifaceted feminist discourse must be if it is to ring true to the complex experiences of contemporary women and men *and* provide systemic perspective on those experiences. Rather than attempt to "explain" eating disorders through one or another available model, I construct what Foucault has called a "polyhedron of intelligibility." I explore facets and intersections: cultural representations of female hunger and female eating, the role of consumer culture, long-standing philosophical and religious attitudes toward the body, similarities to other predominantly female disorders (agoraphobia, hysteria), connections with other contemporary body obsessions, continuities with "normal" female experience in our culture, and so forth. Each of these explorations is systemically located. I do not want the reader to lose sight of the fact that the escalation of eating disorders into a significant social phenomenon arises at the intersection of patriarchal culture and post-industrial capitalism.

My analysis is in this way "political." It is not, however, reductionist, and I hope it will help dispel the misperception, fostered by Joan Brumberg[36] and others, that the feminist cultural model reduces eating disorders to a simple pursuit of slenderness. Rather, such feminist/cultural analysis as Susie Orbach's *Hunger Strike* and Kim Chernin's *The Obsession* and *The Hungry Self* has always stressed the intersection of culture with family, economic, and historical developments and psychological constructions of gender.[37] Insofar as what Chernin first named the "tyranny of slenderness" has been seen as crucial to understanding eating disorders, that tyranny has rarely been viewed by feminists simply as a matter of arbitrary media images but has, rather, been seen as requiring cultural and historical analysis and interpretation. I deal more fully with the feminist paradigm, competing models, and ongoing resistance to the cultural perspective on eating disorders in the essay "Whose Body Is This?"

NATURE, CULTURE, AND THE BODY

Taken together, the feminist critiques of gendered representations and of the politics of the material body can also be seen as an extended argument against the notion that the body is a purely biological or natural form. In this way, American feminism has contributed significantly to what is arguably a major transformation in Western intellectual paradigms defining and representing the body. Within the traditional paradigms, despite significant historical variations certain features have been constant. First and foremost, the body is located (whether as wild beast or physiological clockwork) on the nature side of a nature/culture divide. As such, it is conceived as relatively historically unchanging in its most basic aspects, and unitary. That is, we speak of "the Body" as we speak of "Reason" or "Mind"—as though one model were equally and accurately descriptive of all human bodily experience, irrespective of sex, race, age, or any other personal attributes. That model is assumed to be a sort of neutral, generic core.

Over the past hundred and fifty years, under the influence of a variety of cultural forces, the body has been forced to vacate its long-term residence on the nature side of the nature/culture duality and encouraged to take up residence, along with everything else that is human, within culture. Karl Marx played a crucial role here, in reimagining the body as a historical and not merely a biological arena, an arena shaped by the social and economic organization of human life and, often, brutalized by it. Marx cut the first great slice into the unitary conception of "the Body" assumed by those who preceded him. It makes a difference, he insisted, *whose* body you are talking about—one that tills its own field, or one that works on an assembly line all day, or one that sits in an office managing the labor of others.

Gender and race, too, make a difference. The "generic" core is usually in reality a white or male body passing as the norm for all. For example, when the department of health lists "dairy products" as one of the four major food groups essential to health for all people, it excludes from its conception of the human norm those populations (African American, Mexican American, Asian Americans) among whom large numbers of individuals are lactose-intolerant. (Advising the inclusion of *calcium* in the diet would be less ethnocentric.) The definition of the "normal" human body temperature as 98.6 excludes most women during their fertile years for about two weeks every month (before ovulation, when progesterone levels should be low and body temperature below 98.6). Even the representation of groups who are themselves frequently rendered invisible in cultural constructions—as, for example, in assumptions of heterosexuality in discussions of sexuality, marriage, and parenthood—exhibit additional effacements of race and gender. Controversial findings on possible genetic factors in male homosexuality, for example, have continually been misrepresented in mass-media headlines as proposing a genetic basis for all homosexuality. A 1992 *Newsweek* cover story, for example, depicts two men holding hands; but the bold type asks the uninflected question, "Homosexuality: Born or Bred?"

The old metaphor of the Body Politic presented itself as a "generic" (that is, ostensibly human but covertly male) form. (It is interesting to note, however, that when the *natural* world was likened to a body—as it is in Plato's *Timaeus* and in many other ancient creation stories—it is gendered, and frequently female. It is only when a man-made rational form like the state is symbolized, a cultural invention imagined to bring order to the chaos of the "natural," that the fiction of genderlessness comes into play.) A good deal of feminist scholarship has focused on exposing such fictions and revealing their specificity (as white, male, historically located in various ways, and so forth). Others have focused on the cultural construction and historical experiences of the *female* body. The critique of cultural representations, discussed in the first section of this introduction, has also contributed to the feminist relocation of the body to the culture side of the nature/culture dualism. For one effect of this critique of the pervasive dualisms and metaphors that animate representations of the body is to call into question the assumption that we ever know or encounter the body—not only the bodies of others but our own bodies—directly or simply. Rather, it seems, the body that we experience and conceptualize is always *mediated* by constructs, associations, images of a cultural nature.

In various ways, all the essays in this volume exemplify a cultural approach to the body. My analysis of eating disorders, most explicitly, offers such a cultural perspective. The relevant essays span almost a decade of my thinking about anorexia, bulimia, and related issues and reflect different stages of information and understanding (both my own and the culture's). But although my analysis came to incorporate new elements over time (for example, my earliest essay, "Anorexia Nervosa," reflects my initial lack of knowledge about nineteenth-century anorexia), my understanding of eating disorders as complex crystallizations of culture has remained unaltered. Indeed, the more we learn about eating disorders and about women and their eating problems, both in the nineteenth century and today, the more the cultural model has been borne out, as I argue in "Whose Body Is This?"

In the case of eating disorders, the cultural evidence is by now so overwhelming, and by itself so overdetermines the phenomena, that the hunt for biological *explanations* (I do not deny that there are biological dynamics and effects involved) can only be understood as blind allegiance to the medical model. However, although I am convinced that anorexia and bulimia (as mass phenomena, not as the isolated cases that have been reported throughout history) have been culturally produced, I resist the general notion, quite dominant in the humanities and social sciences today, that the body is a tabula rasa, awaiting inscription by culture. When bodies are made into mere *products* of social discourse, they remain bodies in name only. Unless, as Richard Mohr argues, we are willing to grant that our corporeality is more than a "barren field," an "unchalked blackboard," "ineffective" apart from the social forces and discourses that script and shape it, then *those* forces are the "true body," and they—let's face it—look suspiciously more like "mind" than body, "emanating" (as Mohr describes it) "from the gas cloud-like social mind—or whatever it is that speaks social 'discourses'—as it brushes across the tabula rasa of the body."[38] In some areas biology may play a very great role in our destinies, and it always informs our lives to varying degrees. However, even in those areas where biology may play a more formidable role, its effect is never "pure," never untouched by history. We are creatures swaddled in culture from the moment we are designated one sex or the other, one race or another.

TRANSCENDENCE, "DIFFERENCE,"
AND CULTURAL TRANSFORMATION

Many feminists remain agnostic or ambivalent about the role of biology and sexual "difference"; justifiably fearful of ideas that seem to assert an unalterable, essential female nature, they are nonetheless concerned that too exclusive an emphasis on culture will obscure powerful, and potentially culturally transformative, aspects of women's experience. Is pregnancy merely a cultural construction, capable of being shaped into multitudinous social forms? Or does the unique configuration of embodiment presented in pregnancy—the having of an other within oneself, simultaneously both part of oneself and separate from oneself—constitute a distinctively female epistemological and ethical resource? Is PMS merely one more deployment in the ever-advancing medicalization of the body? Or is it also an opportunity (as Emily Martin argues) to access reserves of emotion, understanding, and creativity that normally remain dormant, repressed?[39]

One could reasonably answer that the female body is *both* construction *and* resource. It is important to recognize, however, that these ideas carry heavy ideological and personal freight. Women who suffer from blinding headaches, incapacitating back pain, and violent mood swings just before their periods may resent any suggestion that PMS is to the slightest degree culturally constructed. Women who have minimal or no symptoms but whose male partners and employers continually sneer or make jokes about women's behavior being dominated by their ovaries (ideas that hark back to nineteenth-century notions that women's physiology and psychology are ruled by their reproductive systems) may find themselves arguing that PMS is simply a cultural myth perpetuating male dominance in the public workplace. Moreover, the polarizing effects of the outbreak of phobias about "essentialism" have often found feminists lining up (or being lined up) on different sides of a divide. Joan Peters, in her witty account of the long, slow slide into menopause, sardonically describes this divide. On the one side are the "Transcenders"—for whom the female body, undetermined by nature or history, can be recreated anew by feminism. On the other side are the "Red Bloomers"—for whom the female body is a source of pleasure, knowledge, and power, to be revalued rather than remade. Of course, Peters intends these terms as caricatures.[40] But they are useful in highlighting, within the specific context of perspectives on the female body, the tension that Ann Snitow describes as being "as old as Western feminism": the tension between "needing to act as women and needing an identity not overdetermined by our gender."[41]

Clearly, both poles of this tension are necessary to feminist struggle and social change. If the efforts of "Red Bloomers" are needed for the deep transformation of culture, the arguments of "Transcenders" are needed to dismantle the barriers that prohibit entrance to domains reserved for men only. Now that I am a tenured professor, the "female" aspects of my identity, I hope, can operate transformatively, disturbing received notions of professorial and philosophical expertise and authority. When I was a graduate student, however, it was necessary to my professional survival that I demonstrate that I could argue "like the boys." Deciding how much one may "bloom" and how much one has to "transcend" in any given context is a tricky, subtle business (for movements as well as for individuals), and it is easy to lose track of who you are and what you wanted when you started, particularly if you were ambivalent to begin with. And what woman, growing up in a sexist culture, is *not* ambivalent about her "femaleness"?

Today, as I argue in several essays in this volume, the forces of "transcendence" seem to be in ascendance within postmodern feminism. In theorizing that ascendancy, I make use of much the same methodology I apply in my analysis of eating disorders. Rather than offer a causal explanation, I examine various elements as they intersect or crystallize in the phenomenon I am trying to understand. Some of these elements are *general* cultural attitudes; others have to do with *academic* cultures; still others have specifically to do with contemporary *feminism*. Throughout, my perspective on contemporary academic paradigms such as deconstructionism is to explore their *participation*, their embeddedness, in culture—as the expression, in an academic arena, of fantasies, anxieties, and fashions being played out in other, more "popular" or public contexts.

Although my language may not consistently reflect this, my overall analysis depends on a distinction between postmodern culture and poststructuralist thought. *Postmodern*, in the most general *cultural* sense, refers to the contemporary inclination toward the unstable, fluid, fragmented, indeterminate, ironic, and heterogeneous, for that which resists definition, closure, and fixity. Within this general categorization, many ideas that have developed out of poststructuralist thought—the emphasis on semiotic indeterminacy, the critique of unified conceptions of subjectivity, fascination with the instabilities of systems, and the tendency to focus on cultural resistance rather than dominant forms—are decidedly postmodern intellectual developments. But not all poststructuralist thought is postmodern. Foucault, as I read him, has both modern and postmodern moments. In his discussions of the discipline, normalization, and creation of "docile bodies," for instance, he is very much the descendant of Marx, whereas later revisions to his conception of power emphasize the ubiquity of resistance—a characteristically postmodern theme.

I view current postmodern tendencies thoroughly to "textualize" the body—exemplified in Judith Butler's analysis of drag as parody (see "Postmodern Subjects, Postmodern Bodies, Postmodern Resistance") and Susan McClary's reading of Madonna's music videos (see " 'Material Girl' ")—as giving a kind of free, creative rein to *meaning* at the expense of attention to the body's material locatedness in history, practice, culture. If the body is treated as pure text, subversive, destabilizing elements can be emphasized and freedom and self-determination celebrated; but one is left wondering, is there a *body* in this text? In " 'Material Girl' " I explore how a similar effacement of the body's materiality is played out *concretely* in our postmodern imagination of the body as malleable plastic, to be shaped to the meanings we choose.

Cultural expressions are all around us. Klan leader David Duke even had his eyes and nose reshaped to appear "kinder and gentler" to prospective voters. Contemporary movies are continually experimenting with the plasticity and deconstructive possibilities of the body: old bodies magically become young (*Sixteen Again*), young bodies become old (*Big*), death is transcended (*Cocoon*) or temporarily suspended (*Truly, Madly, Deeply*), reincarnation themes are played out (*Heaven Can Wait, Made in Heaven, Dead Again*). The extremely popular *Ghost* even plays with the notion that a well-disciplined and highly motivated (dead) spirit can push material objects (and living people) around without the aid of body. Talk shows evidence a special fascination with sex changes; one frequent guest is a person who has gone back and forth from man to woman to man several times. And, of course, there are the extravagant claims, made throughout the popular literature on "the new reproductive technologies," that *any* woman, regardless of age or medical problem, can become pregnant. In this literature, the difficult, painful, and disruptive regimes demanded by the new technology are continually effaced or trivialized: "You can still carry your own baby" even after menopause, assures Sherman Silber (currently the leading fertility expert/darling of the mass media); "*All that is needed* is an egg donor" (emphasis mine).[42]

My point here, I hope it is apparent, is *not* to criticize people who have plastic surgery, sex-change operations, or gamete intrafallopian transfers. It is to highlight a *discourse* that is gradually changing our conception and experience of our bodies, a discourse that encourages us to "imagine the possibilities" and close our eyes to limits and consequences. A postmodern intoxication with possibilities is expressed in some of the methodological and epistemological ideals of postmodern thought as well, as I argue in "Feminism, Postmodernism, and Gender Skepticism." Earlier in this introduction I spoke of the Cartesian fantasy of the philosopher's transcendence of the concrete locatedness of the body (and so of its perspectival limitations) in order to achieve the God's-eye view, the "view from nowhere." Today, I argue, a no less disembodied ideal is imagined by those who advocate "heterogeneity" and "indeterminacy" as principles for interpreting culture, history, and texts. This is not to deny that history and culture are indeed heterogeneous. Rather, I take issue with the fantasy of *capturing* that heterogeneity in our "readings" by continually seeking difference for its own sake, by being guided by the pure *possibilities* of interpretation rather than an embodied point of view. I call this the "view from everywhere" fantasy.

Thus, although I am strongly skeptical of certain tendencies in postmodern culture and poststructuralist thought, my perspective is by no means thoroughly negative. For one thing, as will be obvious to the reader, my own work makes liberal use of the insights of poststructuralist thought, particularly those of Foucault. More deeply, my approach to understanding cultural phenomena has been shaped by the experience of living in "postmodern times," and the unavoidable encounter with complexity, multiplicity, ambiguity that this has meant for me. In sorting out my own ambivalent relationship to postmodernity I have been greatly aided by bell hooks's *Yearning* and Jane Flax's *Thinking Fragments*, which I discuss in "Postmodern Subjects, Postmodern Bodies, Postmodern Resistance" and which model what I think of as an embodied postmodernism, incorporating the best of postmodern multiplicity with a constant acknowledgment of both the limitations of the self and the weight of collective history.

For neither Flax nor hooks does the fragmented nature of postmodern subjects and postmodern knowledge mean that we cannot or should not talk about "black identity" or "women's experiences" as historically constituted. In this, their approach is to be contrasted sharply to that of Jean Grimshaw and other writers for whom generalizations about gender, race, and class have become taboo, not only "politically" but *methodologically*. Although I recognize the validity of aspects of Grimshaw's critique, I have many concerns about the taboo on generalization, which I explore in connection with the Thomas/Hill hearings in "Feminism, Postmodernism, and Gender Skepticism." In that essay I also consider the related contemporary panic over "essentialism," suggesting, among other criticisms, that we look at that panic with a more psycho-cultural eye, as a possible expression of feminist anxiety over being identified with marginalized and devalued aspects of female identity. Such anxiety, however, cannot be adequately theorized only in terms of psychological ambivalence or inner conflict about our femaleness, our mothers, our bodies. Rather, it is also thoroughly continuous with the insistence on creative self-fashioning that is manifest throughout postmodern culture. And it must be located in the context of the *institutions* we practice in—institutions still dominated by masculinist, Eurocentric norms of "professional" behavior and accomplishment.

It is in this institutional context, I would argue, that we most need to "bloom" rather than "transcend." This does not mean alliance with determinist, essentializing ontologies. The most powerful revaluations of the female body have looked, not to nature or biology, but to the culturally inscribed and historically located body (or to historically developed *practices*) for imaginations of *alterity* rather than "the truth" about the female body. This is one of the elements that I read in the work of Luce Irigaray, Hélène Cixous, Adrienne Rich, Sarah Ruddick, ecofeminist Ynestra King, Alice Walker, Toni Morrison, Audre Lorde, and a good deal of lesbian-feminist and "cultural feminist" art and literature. Without imaginations (or embodiments) of alterity, from what vantage point can we seek transformation of culture? And how will we construct these imaginations and embodiments, if not through alliance with that which has been silenced, repressed, disdained? So, for example, feminist philosophers have frequently challenged dominant conceptions of rationality, morality, and politics through revaluations of those "female" qualities—spontaneity, practical knowledge, empathy—forbidden (or deemed irrelevant) to the "man of reason."

There are those who would claim that revaluing "female" resources only *inverts* the classic dualisms rather than challenging dualistic thinking itself. This position, which sounds incisive and which frequently has been pronounced authoritatively and received as gospel in contemporary poststructuralist feminist writing, in fact depends upon so abstract, disembodied, and ahistorical a conception of how cultural change occurs as to be worthy of inclusion in the most sterile philosophy text. The ongoing production, reproduction, and transformation of culture is not a conversation between talking heads, in which metaphysical positions are accepted or rejected wholesale. Rather, the metaphysics of a culture shifts piecemeal and through real, historical changes in relations of power, modes of subjectivity, the organization of life.

Dualism thus cannot be deconstructed in culture the way it can be on paper. To be concretely—that is, culturally—accomplished requires that we bring the "margins" to the "center," that we legitimate and nurture, in those institutions from which they have been excluded, marginalized ways of knowing, speaking, being. Because relocations of this sort are always concrete, historical events, enacted by real, historical people, they *cannot* challenge every insidious duality in one fell swoop, but neither can they reproduce exactly the same conditions as before, "in reverse." Rather, when we bring marginalized aspects of our identities (racial, gendered, ethnic, sexual) into the central arenas of culture they are themselves transformed, and *transforming*. Bell hooks (see "Postmodern Subjects, Postmodern Bodies, Postmodern Resistance" in this volume) provides the example of the African American philosopher Cornel West, who—by presenting a theoretical, academic talk in a passionate, dramatic sermon mode popular in black communities—concretely deconstructed, on that occasion and for that audience, the oppositions between intellect and passion, substance and style. Did he also deconstruct the gendered duality which has dominantly reserved the sermon mode for men? No. *That* challenge requires other occasions, other players.

If we do not struggle to force our work and workplaces to be informed by our histories of embodied experience, we participate in the cultural reproduction of dualism, both practically and representationally. The continuing masculinism of our public institutions (manifest not only in the styles of professionalism that they require but in their continued failure to accommodate and integrate the private—for instance, parenting—into the public sphere) has been exploited, clearly, in what Susan Faludi describes as the media-concocted fiction of a massive "flight" of unhappy women *from* those institutions and back to the home—the only place we can truly realize our feminine nature and completely fulfill our maternal responsibilities.[43] Most women, of course, could not afford to leave their job even if they wanted to. And whatever actual flight there has been, Faludi argues, is largely the result of panic caused by the media campaign rather than the other way around. But whatever the causality, the old dualities are clearly being culturally reinscribed. Glossy magazines and commercials are currently filled with images of domestic, reproductive bliss, of home as a cozy, plant-filled haven of babies, warmth, and light, skillfully managed and lovingly tended by women. The realm of the material, the care and reproduction of the body, we are reminded, is appropriately woman's. Only men, as Hegel said, are designed for the "stress" and "technical exertions" of the public domain.

PART ONE

DISCOURSES AND CONCEPTIONS
OF THE BODY

Whose Body Is This?

*Feminism, Medicine, and the Conceptualization
of Eating Disorders*

By the 1983 meetings of the New York Center for the Study of
Anorexia and Bulimia, palpable dissatisfaction was evident—
largely among female clinicians—over the absence of any theoretical focus on gender issues. In 1973, when Hilde Bruch published
her landmark work *Eating Disorders*, she made little use of the
concept of gender in her interpretation of anorexia. Kim Chernin,
in *The Obsession*, was the first to note that the vivid descriptions
Bruch provides of the anorectic's "battle" against the adult development of her body consistently lack one crucial element: recognition of the significance of the fact that this is a *female* body whose
development is being resisted.[1] Following Bruch, the etiological
models that dominated over the next decade emphasized developmental issues, family problems, and perceptual and/or cognitive
"dysfunction." In each, the understanding of the role played by the
construction of gender and other social factors was, at best, shallow
and unsystematic.

Developmental and family approaches conceptualized interactions between mother and child as occurring outside cultural time
and space; the father's role was simply ignored. Perceptual/cogni-
tive models theorized the role of "sociocultural factors" solely in
terms of "the pressure toward thinness," "indoctrination by the
thin ethic"; what passed for cultural analysis were statistical studies
demonstrating the dwindling proportions of *Playboy* centerfolds
and Miss America winners throughout the 1980s. And, in all of
this, transactions were imagined as occurring only between media
images and females, or females and other females (peer pressure to

conform; criticisms from the mother); the vulnerability of men and boys to popular imagery, the contribution of their desires and anxieties, the pressures thus brought to bear on girls and women, remained—as father/daughter incest was for Freud—a hidden and somehow unspeakable secret in the prevailing narratives.

In no place was the *meaning* of the ideal of slenderness explored, either in the context of the anorectic's experience or as a cultural formation that expresses ideals, anxieties, and social changes (some related to gender, some not) much deeper than the merely aesthetic. Rather, "the media," "Madison Avenue," and "the fashion industry" typically were collectively constructed as the sole enemy—a whimsical and capricious enemy, capable of indoctrinating and tyrannizing passive and impressionable young girls by means of whatever imagery it arbitrarily decided to promote that season. *Why* thinness should have become such a dominant cultural ideal in the twentieth century remained unaddressed; the interpretation of representations was viewed as outside the domain of clinical investigation.

The one clinical model for which gender *was* a key analytical category, the psychoanalytic, theorized the anorectic's resistance to developing a female body in the terms of traditional Freudianism, as expressing anxieties and fantasies of a purely psycho-sexual nature, such as fear of pregnancy or of attracting the sexual attention of men. Traditional Freudianism has been far more attuned than other models to the symbolic nature of the anorectic's symptoms, recognizing, for example, that the fear of fat on stomachs and breasts has gender associations that demand interpretation and is not merely indicative of compulsive slavery to the latest fashion trend. But Freudian theory nonetheless (and characteristically) has failed to situate the categories of its analysis in a sociocultural setting—to appreciate, for example, that fear of pregnancy may have more to do with fear of domestic entrapment than with suppressed Electra fantasies, or that anxieties about the dangers of sexual involvement might be a realistic response to the disclosure of the abusive and violent patterns that are all too common within domestic relationships. (Research has disclosed, too, that just as many of Freud's hysterics were very likely *actually* sexually abused, as he had originally hypothesized, so incidents of sexual abuse lie in the background of the so-called flight from sexuality of many anorectics, and in the histories of bulimics as well.)[2]

Thus, in 1983, gender either was absent or was theorized in essentialist terms by the leading authorities on eating disorders—a situation that organizers of the conference on anorexia and bulimia sought to rectify. To do so, they had to call on feminists who had been working at the margins of the official establishment: writing for audiences other than medical professionals, practicing therapy outside the framework of then-dominant models, and developing, over the preceding ten years, a very different approach to the understanding of eating disorders. The theme chosen for the 1983 conference was "Eating Disorders and the Psychology of Women," and Carol Gilligan and Susie Orbach were invited to be keynote speakers.

Gilligan's talk introduced the audience to Catherine Steiner-Adair's provocative study of high-school women, which revealed a striking association between problems with food and body image and emulation of the beautiful, independent, cool superwoman of media imagery.[3] Susie Orbach's talk was a moving argument, grounded in object-relations theory and situated in the sociocultural context of the construction of femininity, that the anorectic embodies, in an extreme and painfully debilitating way, a psychological struggle characteristic of the contemporary situation of women. That situation is one in which a constellation of social, economic, and psychological factors have combined to produce a generation of women who feel deeply flawed, ashamed of their needs, and not entitled to exist unless they transform themselves into worthy new selves (read: without need, without want, without *body*).[4] The mother-daughter relation is an important medium of this process. But it is not mothers who are to blame, stressed Orbach, for they too are children of their culture, deeply anxious over their own appetites and appearance and aware of the fact—communicated in a multitude of ways throughout our culture—that their daughters' ability to "catch a man" will depend largely on physical appearance, and that satisfaction in the role of wife and mother will hinge on learning to feed others rather than the self—metaphorically *and* literally.

For Orbach, anorexia represents one extreme on a continuum on which all women today find themselves, insofar as they are vulnerable, to one degree or another, to the requirements of the cultural construction of femininity. This notion provoked heated criticism from the (all-male) panel of commentators, two psychiatrists and one clinical psychologist. The political implications of Gilligan's talk had been missed by her respondents (and by Orbach's), all of whom chose to hear the paper solely as a lament for our culture's lack of esteem for the "female" values of connectedness, empathy, and other-directedness. Gilligan's talk was (mis)interpreted (as her work frequently is) as a simple celebration of traditional femininity rather than as a critique of the sexual division of labor that assigns "female" values to a separate domestic sphere while keeping the public, male space (and "masculinity") a bastion of autonomous selves.

Orbach's talk, unambiguous in its indictment of the normative construction of femininity in our culture, was much more troubling to the panelists. It elicited from them a passionate defense of "traditional women," with Orbach the feminist portrayed as unsisterly and unmotherly and the panelists cast as sympathetic protectors of those groups that Orbach had abused. So, for example, David Garner, co-author of *Anorexia Nervosa: A Multidimensional Perspective*, felt obliged to defend mothers against the "blame" Orbach had attributed to them and the "guilt" she had inflicted on them for "choosing traditional values" and being fulfilled by "nurturing." Steven Levenkron, author of *The Best Little Girl in the World*, came to the rescue of the anorectic herself—that "skinny kid in your office," as he called her, whose suffering Orbach had failed to appreciate adequately (in suggesting that her pain could be understood on a continuum with normative female suffering). Here, the feminist critique was charged with sacrificing the care of "helpless, chaotic, and floundering" children in the interests of a "rational" political agenda. The panelists thus represented themselves both as better feminists than Orbach (that is, more concerned with actual women's lives), better "women" (more empathic, more caring), and *at the same time* dazzlingly masculine Prince Charmings, rescuing women from the abstract and uncaring politics of feminism.

Even more provocative than Orbach's critique of the construction of femininity, however, was her questioning of the designation of eating disorders as "pathology." All the panelists, while remarking on how perfectly her interpretation tallied with and illuminated their own clinical experience, were uniform in criticizing her analysis for (as William Davis put it) its "[lack of] specific explanatory conceptions" and "indistinct and unconvincing" theorizing. How can it be that her analysis both explained and failed to explain? This apparent contradiction in the estimation of the panel can be accounted for only by the hidden stipulation that theory, no matter how well it illuminates a given phenomenon, is inadequate unless it also sets down general criteria to enable clear and precise distinguishing between "normal" and "pathological" members of a population. This, of course, is what Orbach's theory lacked—or, rather, contested. As such, it issued a profound challenge to one of the most basic and most thoroughly entrenched premises of the medical model.

PATHOLOGY, CULTURE, AND THE MEDICAL MODEL

In the clinical literature on eating disorders, the task of description, classification, and elaboration of "pathology" has driven virtually all research. In the leading journals, attempts to link eating disorders to one or another specific pathogenic situation (biological, psychological, familial) proliferate, along with studies purporting to demonstrate that eating disorders are members of some established category of disorder (depressive, affective, perceptual, hypothalamic . . .). Anorexia and bulimia are appearing in increasingly diverse populations of women, reducing the likelihood of describing a distinctive profile for each.[5] Yet the search for common pathologies still fuels much research.[6] As each proposed model is undermined by the actual diversity of the phenomena, ever more effort is put into precise classification of distinctive subtypes, and new "multidimensional" categories emerge (for instance, bulimia as a "biopsychosocial" illness)[7] that satisfy fantasies of precision and unification of phenomena that have become less and less amenable to scientific clarity and distinctness.

Where a unifying element *does* clearly exist—in the cultural context, and especially in the ideology and imagery that mediate the construction of gender—the etiological significance is described as merely contributory, facilitating, or a "modulating factor."[8] The prevailing understanding is that culture provokes, exacerbates, and gives distinctive form to an existing pathological condition. Such an understanding fails to come to grips with two striking facts about eating disorders. First, like hysteria in the nineteenth century, the incidence of eating disorders has always been disproportionately high among females: approximately 90 percent of sufferers are girls or women. Second, and again like hysteria, eating disorders are culturally and historically situated, in advanced industrial societies within roughly the past hundred years.[9] Individual cases have been documented, infrequently, throughout history, but it is not until the second half of the nineteenth century that something like a minor epidemic of anorexia nervosa is first described in medical accounts;[10] and that incidence pales beside the dramatic escalation of anorexia and bulimia in the 1980s and 1990s.[11]

These elements point to culture—working not only through ideology and images but through the organization of the family, the construction of personality, the training of perception—as not simply contributory but *productive* of eating disorders. A parallel exists in the formation of female hysteria. Thanks to the benefit of historical distance and the work of feminist scholars, almost all clinicians and theorists today agree that the ultimate sources of hysteria and neurasthenia as characteristic disorders of elite Victorian women are located in Victorian culture, and especially (although not exclusively) in ideology and upheavals related to gender. Most Victorian physicians, we should remember, lacked this perspective. It is only as hysteria has shed its symbolic, emotional, and professional freight, as it has become a historical phenomenon, that it has become possible to *see* it, in some ways, for the first time. Among the important elements now revealed is the clear continuum on which the normative and the disordered were located for Victorian women; it becomes possible to see the degree to which femininity itself required the holding of breath, the loss of air, the choking down of anger and desire, the relinquishing of voice, the denial of appetite, the constriction of body.

All this is visible in part because, from the perspective of the present, Victorian ideals of masculinity and femininity and the styles of behavior that regulated them seem *themselves* as dusty and distant as the disorders of the era. They are denaturalized for us, as our own constructions of gender cannot be, no matter how intellectually committed we may be to a social constructionist view. Too, contemporary medicine, protected by its myth of progress beyond the antiquated models and methods of the past, is able comfortably to acknowledge the thralldom of Victorian medicine to biologistic paradigms and its implication in a dualistic gender-politics that we pride ourselves on having transcended. Our contemporary medical models, gender identities, and other ideological beliefs are no longer enmeshed in a struggle to "conquer" hysteria and the mysterious, rebellious female world it once represented to mechanistic science and patriarchal culture. The cultural deconstruction of hysteria as a historically located intersection of Victorian gender-culture and Victorian medicine has thus become possible.

As was noted earlier, it was in the nineteenth century that self-starvation among elite women first surfaced with enough frequency to engage the general attention of the medical profession. But for the nineteenth century, "hysterical" symptoms such as paralysis and muteness expressed better than self-starvation did the contradictions faced by elite Victorian women, for whom the ideology of the compliant, refined, and thoroughly domestic lady was a coercive feminine ideal. Certainly, food refusal was an appropriate symptom in this cultural context, with its rigid prohibitions, both metaphorical and literal, against female appetite and desire, prohibitions that were locked in unstable and painful antithesis with a developing bourgeois culture of affluence and indulgence. But (for a variety of reasons discussed in essays throughout this volume) eating disorders have emerged as an overdetermined crystallization of cultural anxiety only in the second half of the twentieth century. The contemporary woman, who struggles to cope with social contradictions that first emerged in the Victorian era but who confronts those contradictions later in their historical development and as they intersect with specifically contemporary elements, is far more likely to develop an eating disorder than an hysterical paralysis.

It is one thing, apparently, to acknowledge the role played by culture in the production of a virtually extinct disorder, wrestled with by long-dead physicians who were working with now-discredited models.[12] It is another thing altogether for contemporary medicine similarly to interrogate the status of disorders it is still trying to subdue. Researchers do now acknowledge the preeminent role played by cultural ideology in the production of hysteria, but they still resist applying that historical lesson to the understanding of anorexia and bulimia. Although it is frequently acknowledged that cultural pressures may make women "especially vulnerable to eating disorders,"[13] that acknowledgment is usually quickly followed by the comment that not all individuals exposed to these pressures develop anorexia or bulimia. Hence, it is claimed, other "non-sociocultural" factors must be required in order for the disorder to be "produced" in a particular individual. These non-sociocultural factors (among those most frequently listed: "deficits" in autonomy, tendency to obesity, perfectionist personality traits and defective cognitive patterns, perceptual disturbances, biological factors, emotionally repressed familial interactions) are then weighted alongside sociocultural factors as *equally* determinative of the disorders. In this way we slide from the understanding that culture alone is not *sufficient* to "cause" anorexia or bulimia in an individual (which is true, and was true of hysteria as well) to mystification and effacement of culture's preeminent role in providing the necessary *ground* for the historical flourishing of the disorders. Eating disorders are indeed "multidimensional," as David Garner describes them. But that does not imply that all dimensions therefore play an *equal* role in the production of anorexia and bulimia.

Often, too, it is emphasized that "factors other than culture may be at work producing the high ratio of females to males." As the editors of the *Handbook of Eating Disorders* put it:

> What can explain the low prevalence of eating disorders in men? Certainly many men have the personality factors and family background of anorexic women. These men may also have role conflicts about profession and family, and they live in a culture that exerts no small pressure on males to be thin. . . . There could be complex physiological differences in the way males and females respond to chronic energy restriction. It is possible, for example, that males have a stronger counter-response to deprivation than do females, so that hunger, satiety, metabolism, or other factors exert stronger pressure for weight restoration. Males who are potentially anorexic may encounter stronger resistance to the self-imposed starvation, so fewer males progress from the early signs to the chronic condition.[14]

Similarly, in *New Hope for Binge Eaters* Harrison Pope and James Hudson suggest that bulimia may be biological ("Perhaps the hypothalamus, or some other part of the central nervous system concerned with eating behavior, is more easily affected in women than in men") or may be "the characteristic 'female' expression of [an] underlying disorder" which men express in different ways. These hypotheses are offered, equally valanced alongside sociocultural explanations, as part of a fascinating panoply of "possibilities," suggesting diverse "new areas of research."[15]

My point is not to deny that biological factors may play a contributory role in determining which individuals will prove most vulnerable to eating disorders. (It seems, however, virtually impossible to sort out cause and effect here; most proposed biological markers are just as likely to be the *result* of starvation as the cause.) But to suggest that biology may protect men from eating disorders is not to be open to possibilities; it is to close one's eyes to the obvious. Are the editors of the *Handbook* unaware of the statistics on dieting in this country? Do they not know that the overwhelming majority of those attending weight-loss clinics and purchasing diet products are women? Men *do* develop eating disorders, by the way, and, strikingly, those who do so are almost always models, wrestlers, dancers, and others whose profession demands a rigid regime of weight control. Looking to biology to explain the low prevalence of eating disorders among men is like looking to genetics to explain why nonsmokers do not get lung cancer as often as smokers. Certainly, genetic and other factors will play a role in determining an *individual's* level of vulnerability to the disease. But when tobacco companies try to deny that smoking is the preeminent source of lung cancer among smokers *as a group*, diverting attention by pointing to all the other factors that may have entered in particular cases, we are likely to see this as a willful obfuscation in the service of their professional interests.

I am *not* suggesting that, like the tobacco industry, eating-disorders researchers have a vested interest in keeping people addicted to their destructive behaviors. Nor do I mean to suggest that medical expertise has no place in the treatment of eating disorders. The conceptualization of eating disorders as pathology has produced some valuable research. But the medical model has a deep professional, economic, and philosophical stake in preserving the integrity of what it has demarcated as its domain, and the result has frequently been blindness to the obvious. This is not a conspiracy; rather, each discipline teaches aspiring professionals what to look at and what to ignore, as they choose their specialties and learn what lies outside the scope of their expertise, and as they come increasingly to converse "professionally" only with each other.

Arguments have been made, however, that are deeply threatening to the very presuppositions of the medical model and are therefore resisted more consciously and deliberately. What I will term the feminist/cultural perspective on eating disorders is such an argument, and in a later section of this essay I will discuss the resistance to it in more detail. Before I do that, however, I will first describe the broad contours of the feminist/cultural model, examine some specific contexts in which it has clearly issued a challenge to the medical model, and attempt to correct some common misconceptions about feminist/cultural criticism.

"BODY IMAGE DISTURBANCE" AND "BULIMIC THINKING"

The picture sketched in the last section is not seamless. The groundbreaking work of such investigators as Kim Chernin, Susie Orbach, and Marlene Boskind-White has helped to shape a very different paradigm which has been adopted by many eating-disorders professionals.

That feminist/cultural paradigm has: (1) cast into doubt the designation of anorexia and bulimia as psychopathology, emphasizing instead the learned, addictive dimension of the disorders; (2) reconstructed the role of culture and especially of gender as primary and productive rather than triggering or contributory; and (3) forced the reassignment, to social causes, of factors viewed in the standard medical model as pertaining to individual dysfunction. In connection with (3), many of the "non-sociocultural" factors that have been dominantly conceptualized as "distortions" and "delusions" specific to the "pathology" of anorexia and bulimia have been revealed to be prevalent among women in our culture. The ultimate consequence of this, for eating disorders, has been to call into question the clinical value of the normative/pathological duality itself.

The feminist perspective on eating disorders, despite significant differences among individual writers, has in general been distinguished by a prima facie commitment both to taking the perceptions of women seriously and to the necessity of systemic social analysis. These regulatory assumptions have predisposed feminists to explore the so-called perceptual disturbances and cognitive distortions of eating disorders as windows opening onto problems in the social world, rather than as the patient's "idiosyncratic" and "idiopathic . . . distortions of data from the outside world."[16] From the latter perspective, when a patient complains that her breasts are too large and insists that the only way to succeed in our culture is to be thin because, as one woman described it, "people . . . think that someone thin is automatically smarter and better,"[17] it is described as flawed reasoning, a misperception of reality that the therapist must work to correct. From a feminist/cultural perspective, this approach ignores the fact that for most people in our culture, slenderness is indeed equated with competence, self-control, and intelligence, and feminine curvaceousness (in particular, large breasts) with wide-eyed, giggly vapidity.[18]

Virtually every proposed hallmark of "underlying psychopathology" in eating disorders has been deconstructed to reveal a more widespread *cultural* disorder. A dramatic example is the case of BIDS, or Body Image Distortion Syndrome, first described by Hilde Bruch as "disturbance in size awareness,"[19] and for a long time seen as one of the hallmarks of anorexia nervosa, both in the popular imagination and in the diagnostic criteria. In both contexts BIDS has functioned to emphasize a discontinuity between anorexic and "normal" attitudes toward weight and body image. In the clinical literature, the initial theorizing of BIDS as a visuo-spatial problem, a perceptual defect, firmly placed anorexia within a medical, mechanistic model of illness (and a positivistic conception of perception, as well). A person who had this "defect" (sometimes conceived as the result of impaired brain-function; sometimes, as by Bruch, as part of a more general pattern of defective processing of body experiences due to inadequate infant development) was unable to see her body "realistically." In more popular renditions, the "bizarre" and mysterious nature of the symptom was emphasized; such descriptions were often accompanied by line drawings of the anorectic standing in front of a mirror that reflected back to her a grossly inflated and distorted image (Figure 3). As one not atypical 1984 article, from a magazine for nurses, described it:

> In a way, "anorexia" is a misnomer. Afflicted persons don't suffer from a loss of appetite. Instead, they have a *bizarre* preoccupation with eating—coupled with an obsessive desire to attain pencil-like thinness through restricted food intake and rigorous exercise. Even more *bizarre* is their distorted self-image; it's not unusual to hear a haggard, emaciated anorectic complain that she's still "too fat."[20]

In 1984, however, a study conducted by *Glamour* magazine and analyzed by Susan Wooley and Wayne Wooley revealed that 75

Anorexia and bulimia: eating habits that can kill

FIGURE 3

percent of the 33,000 women surveyed considered themselves "too fat," despite the fact that only one-quarter were deemed overweight by standard weight tables, and 30 percent were actually *under-weight*.[21] Similar studies followed, some specifically attempting to measure perception of body size, all with the same extraordinary results. A study by Kevin Thompson, for example, found that out of 100 women "free of eating-disorder symptoms" more than 95 percent overestimated their body size—on average one-fourth larger than they really were.[22] Such findings, of course, made the postulation of strictly perceptual defect problematic—unless it was supposed that most American women were suffering from perceptual malfunction.

The clinical response to these studies was to transfer the site of "distortion" from perceptual mechanism to affective/cognitive coloration: the contribution to perception of the mind's eye.[23] According to this model, it is not that women actually *see* themselves as fat; rather, they evaluate what they see by painfully self-critical standards. Lack of self-esteem now became the cause of women's body-image problems: "The better people feel about themselves," as Thompson concluded, "the less they tend to overestimate their size." But women, as study after study has shown, do *not* feel very good about their bodies.[24] Most women in our culture, then, are "disordered" when it comes to issues of self-worth, self-entitlement, self-nourishment, and comfort with their own bodies; eating disorders, far from being "bizarre" and anomalous, are utterly continuous with a dominant element of the experience of being female in this culture.

Attempts to reconceptualize BIDS as affective or cognitive rather than perceptual do not, of course, resolve the problem with the medical model; rather, they make it more apparent. For once such a symptom is reclassified as affective or cognitive the role of culture can no longer be easily effaced or mystified. Ultimately, that role is perceptual as well. Culture not only has taught women to be insecure bodies, constantly monitoring themselves for signs of imperfection, constantly engaged in physical "improvement"; it also is constantly teaching women (and, let us not forget, men as well) how to *see* bodies. As slenderness has consistently been visually glamorized, and as the ideal has grown thinner and thinner, bodies that a decade ago were considered slender have now come to seem fleshy. Consider, for example, the dramatic contrast between the "Maidenform woman" circa 1990 and circa 1960 (Figures 4 and 5). What was considered an ideal body in 1960 is currently defined as "full figure" (Figure 6), requiring special fashion accommodations! Moreover, as our bodily ideals have become firmer and more contained (we worship not merely slenderness but flablessness), *any* softness or bulge comes to be seen as unsightly—as disgusting, disorderly "fat," which must be "eliminated" or "busted," as popular exercise-equipment ads put it. Of course, the only bodies that do not transgress in this way are those that are tightly muscled or virtually skeletal. Short of meeting these standards, the slimmer the body, the more obtrusive will any lumps and bulges seem. Given this analysis, the anorectic does not "misperceive" her body; rather, she has learned all too well the dominant cultural standards of *how* to perceive.[25]

The case of BIDS is paradigmatic rather than exceptional. Consider, as another example, what have been termed the "disordered cognitions" or "distorted attitudes" proposed as distinctive to the psychopathology of anorexia and bulimia. These elements of "faulty thinking" or "flawed reasoning" standardly include: "magical thoughts" or "superstitious thinking" about the power of cer-

tain "forbidden" foods such as sweets to set off a binge, which perpetuate such "myths" as "If I have one cookie, I'll eat them all"; "selective abstraction" of thinness, as "the sole frame of reference for inferring self-worth" and "essential to her happiness and well-being" (I am special if I am thin), a belief which persists "in defiance of examples to the contrary"; "dichotomous reasoning" concerning food, eating, and weight ("If I'm not in complete control, I lose all control" or "If I gain one pound, I'll go on and gain a hundred pounds"); and "personalization" and "egocentric" interpretations of "impersonal events" ("I am embarrassed when other people see me eat").[26]

Each of these elements may indeed be characteristic of the sort of thinking that torments the lives of women with eating disorders. What I question here is the construction of such thinking as "faulty," "flawed," "distorted," "myths," the product of invalid logic, poor reasoning, or mythological thinking. These constructions portray the anorectic and bulimic as incorrectly processing "data"[27] from an external reality whose *actual* features are very different from her cognitions and perceptions. But in fact each of these "distorted attitudes" is a fairly accurate representation of

FIGURES 4 AND 5 (*OPPOSITE*);
FIGURE 6 (*LEFT*)

social attitudes toward slenderness or the biological realities involved in dieting.

For example, many of the "faulty beliefs" associated with eating disorders are *accurate* descriptions of psychological and physiological dynamics that we now know are endemic to dieting itself, particularly to the extremes reached by anorectics and bulimics. It is now well known, for example, that the body has a powerful system of automatic compensations that respond to food deprivation as though to starvation, by setting off cravings, binge behavior, and obsessional thoughts about food.[28] It has been shown, moreover, that people are better able to stay on diets if they are permitted no solid food at all rather than limited amounts of food;[29] the bulimic is thus not so unreasonable in thinking that total control over food is required in order for *any* control to be maintained. But of course total control is ultimately unsustainable; most people on very low-calorie diets eventually gain back all the weight they lose.[30] The general point here is that "the diet" is itself a precarious, unstable, self-defeating state for a body to be in—a reality that the "disordered cognitions" of bulimics and anorectics are confronting all too clearly and painfully.

To turn to the bulimic's "flawed reasoning" concerning the importance of slenderness in our culture: the absurdity of categorizing the belief that "I am special if I am thin" and women's embarrassment over being seen eating as "distorted" attitudes ought to be apparent. What reality do they distort? Our culture is one in which Oprah Winfrey, a dazzling role model for female success, has said that the most "significant achievement of her life" was losing sixty-seven pounds on a liquid diet. (She gained it all back within a year.) It is a culture in which commercial after commercial depicts female eating as a furtive activity, properly engaged in behind closed doors, and even under those circumstances requiring restriction and restraint (see "Hunger as Ideology" in this volume). It is a culture in which my "non–eating disordered" female students write in their journals of being embarrassed to go to the ice cream counter for fear of being laughed at by the boys in the cafeteria; a culture in which Sylvester Stallone has said that he likes his women "anorexic" (his then girlfriend, Cornelia Guest, immediately lost twenty-four pounds);[31] a culture in which personal ads consistently list "slim," "lean," or "trim" as *required* of prospective dates. The anorectic thus appears, not as the victim of a unique and "bizarre" pathology, but as the bearer of very distressing tidings about our culture.

THE CULTURAL ARGUMENT:
MYTHS AND MISCONCEPTIONS

In this section I will attempt to answer some frequently raised concerns about and criticisms of feminist/cultural approaches to eating disorders. I hope thereby to clarify what is being claimed by the cultural argument.

At the 1983 meetings of the New York Center for the Study of Anorexia and Bulimia, Steven Levenkron charged feminism with sacrificing the care of "helpless, chaotic, and floundering" children in the interests of a "rational" political agenda. Is he right? Does maintaining a continuity between eating disorders and "normal" female behavior entail a denial of the fact that anorexia and bulimia are extreme and debilitating disorders? I think not. The feminist perspective has never questioned the reality of the anorectic's disorder or the severity of her suffering. Rather, what is at stake is the conception of the pathological as the indicator of a special "profile" (psychological or biological) that distinguishes the eating-disordered woman from the women who "escape" disorder. Feminist analysts see no firm boundary on one side of which a state of psychological comfort and stability may be said to exist. They see, rather, only varying degrees of disorder, some more "functional" than others, but all undermining women's full potential.

At one end of this continuum we find anorexia and bulimia, extremes which set into play physiological and psychological dynamics that lead the sufferer into addictive patterns and medical and emotional problems outside the "norms" of behavior and experience. But it is not only anorectics and bulimics whose lives are led into "disorder." This is a culture in which rigorous dieting and exercise are being engaged in by more and younger girls all the time—girls as young as seven or eight, according to some studies.[32] These little girls live in constant fear—a fear reinforced by the attitudes of the boys in their classes—of gaining a pound and thus ceasing to be "attractive." They jog daily, count their calories obsessively, and risk serious vitamin deficiencies and delayed reproductive maturation. We may be producing a generation of young, privileged women with severely impaired menstrual, nutritional, and intellectual functioning.

But how can a cultural analysis account for the fact that only *some* girls and women develop full-blown eating disorders, despite the fact that we are all subject to the same sociocultural pressures? Don't we require the postulation of a distinctive underlying pathology (familial or psychological) to explain why some individuals are more vulnerable than others? The first of these questions is frequently presented by medical professionals as though it dealt a decisive blow to the cultural argument, and it is extraordinary how often it is indeed accepted as a devastating critique. It is based, however, on an important and common misunderstanding (or misrepresentation) of the feminist position as involving the positing of an *identical* cultural situation for all *women* rather than the description of ideological and institutional parameters governing the construction of *gender* in our culture. The difference is crucial, yet even such a sophisticated thinker as Joan Brumberg misses it completely. "Current cultural models," Brumberg argues, "fail to explain why so many individuals *do not* develop the disease, even though they have been exposed to the same cultural environment."[33] But of course we are *not* all exposed to "the same cultural environment." What we *are* all exposed to, rather, are homogenizing and normalizing images and ideologies concerning "femininity" and female beauty. Those images and ideology press for conformity to dominant cultural norms. But people's identities are not formed *only* through interaction with such images, powerful as they are. The unique configurations (of ethnicity, social class, sexual orientation, religion, genetics, education, family, age, and so forth) that make up each person's life will determine how each *actual* woman is affected by our culture.

The search for distinctive patterns, profiles, and abnormalities underlying anorexia nervosa and bulimia is thus not, as many researchers claim, *conceptually* demanded; a myriad of heterogeneous factors, "family resemblances" rather than essential features, unpredictable combinations of elements, may be at work in determining who turns out to be most susceptible. It may be, too, that patterns and profiles could once be assembled but are now breaking apart under the pressure of an increasingly coercive mass culture with its compelling, fabricated images of beauty and success.

For example, from its nineteenth-century emergence as a cultural phenomenon, anorexia has been a class-biased disorder, appearing predominantly among the daughters of families of relative affluence.[34] The reasons for this are several. Slenderness and rejection of food have, of course, very different meanings in conditions of deprivation and scarcity than in those of plenty. Demonstrating an ability to "rise above" the need to eat imparts moral or aesthetic superiority only where others are prone to overindulgence. Where people are barely managing to put nutritious food on the table, the fleshless, "dematerialized" body suggests death, not superior detachment, self-control, or resistance to parental expectations. Moreover, the possibility of success in attaining dominant ideals (for example, that of the glamorous superwoman so many anorectics emulate)[35] depends on certain material preconditions which economically struggling women lack; hence, they may be "protected" (so to speak) against eating disorders by their despair of ever embodying the images of feminine success that surround them. However, studies suggest that eating disorders have for some time been on the rise among *all* socioeconomic groups;[36] within a culture which is continually drawing us into an invented world of attainable power, actual material restrictions on our lives may not limit the imagination as decisively as they once did.

To give another example of the tension between "difference" and homogenizing culture: it has been argued that certain ethnic and racial conceptions of female beauty, often associated with different cultural attitudes toward female power and sexuality, may provide resistance to normalizing images and ideologies. This has been offered as an explanation, for example, as to why eating disorders have been less common among blacks than whites.[37] Without disputing the significance of such arguments, we should be cautious about assuming too *much* "difference" here. The equation of slenderness and success in this culture continually undermines the preservation of alternative ideals of beauty. A legacy of reverence for the zaftig body has not protected Jewish women from eating disorders; the possibility of greater upward mobility is now having a similar effect on young African American women, as the numerous diet and exercise features appearing in *Essence* magazine make clear. To imagine that African American women are immune to the standards of slenderness that reign today is, moreover, to come very close to the racist notion that the art and glamour—the culture—of femininity belong to the white woman alone. The black woman, by contrast, is woman in her earthy, "natural," state, uncorseted by civilization. "Fat is a black woman's issue, too," insisted the author of a 1990 *Essence* article, bitterly criticizing the high-school guidance counselor who had told her she did not have to worry about managing her weight because "black women aren't seen as sex objects but as women. So really, you're lucky because you can go beyond the stereotypes of woman as sex object. . . . Also, fat [women] are more acceptable in the black community." Apparently, as the author notes, the guidance counselor had herself not "gone beyond" stereotypes of the maternal, desexualized Mammy as the prototype of black womanhood. Saddled with these projected racial notions, the young woman, who had struggled with compulsive eating and yo-yo dieting for years, was left alone to deal with an eating disorder that she wasn't "supposed" to have.[38]

RESPONSES TO THE FEMINIST CHALLENGE:
CHANGE AND RESISTANCE

The feminist/cultural contribution to the study of eating disorders has, as was said earlier, altered the clinical terrain. Clinicians have become much more aware of how widespread are women's problems with food, eating, and body image and of how stressful and fragmenting are the contradictory role-demands placed on contemporary women. Family interactions are no longer imagined, as they once were, as consisting solely of relations between the patient and an over-controlling, overly dependent mother. Studies are beginning to explore the role played by the teasing and criticism of fathers and boyfriends,[39] as well as the disturbing incidence of sexual abuse in the backgrounds of eating-disordered women.[40] Some clinicians previously hostile to feminism are even beginning to talk about the hyper-valuation of masculinist values in our culture.[41]

But the deepest implications of the feminist challenge to the concept of pathology are continually resisted. For example, rather than acknowledge how normative the obsession with body weight is in our culture, Michael Strober, editor of the *Journal of Eating Disorders*, suggests that "the intensifying preoccupation with body shape and dieting so common in nonclinical adolescent populations" may be "indicative of a symptomatically milder or partial expression of the illness."[42] The difference, I would suggest, is not merely semantic. Rather, Strober is so intent on retaining the notions of "illness" and "disease" that he is willing to "medicalize" the majority of adolescent women into the bargain.

Or consider the work of Joan Brumberg. Unlike dominant clinical models, Brumberg's work offers itself as a cultural analysis and is especially notable for its fine, historical account of the medicalization of anorexia nervosa in the nineteenth century, which reconstructed the bizarre behavior of "fasting girls" from miraculous occurrence to pathological condition. "Disease," Brumberg concludes, "is a cultural artifact, defined and redefined over time."[43]

But despite the historical detachment Brumberg brings to her discussion of the transformation of the anorectic from sainthood to patienthood, she is full of sanctimonious outrage at what she sees as the attempts of contemporary feminists to "demedicalize" anorexia. Constructing a straw-woman distortion of feminist arguments that anorexia is a voiceless, unconscious, self-destructive scream of protest, Brumberg charges feminists with "venerating" and "romanticizing" anorectics as "heroic freedom fighters" who "freely choose" a hunger strike as a form of intentional political action.[44] Feminists, she goes on, argue that "merely by speaking up about sexism and subordination, women with eating disorders can cure themselves and society." Against these fabricated and inaccurate claims Brumberg positions herself, much as the panel of commentators positioned themselves at the 1983 conference on anorexia and bulimia. The anorectic, she insists, is a "helpless and desperate" individual whose voice is not that of "social protest" but expresses only "frustration and fear." Instead of "dignifying" her disorder, we should acknowledge the "infantile," self-preoccupied, deluded nature of anorectic behavior (at one point Brumberg compares the pursuit of thinness to "a paranoid schizophrenic's attempts to elude imagined enemies") and recognize that eating disorders will only be "cured" through treatment of the "biomedical component of this destructive illness."[45]

All of Brumberg's criticisms might be summed up by the headline of a letter that was published several years ago in *Newsday*, in angry response to a column by Karen DeCrow and Robert Seidenberg (who had articulated a version of the "social protest" thesis). The headline read: "Anorexia Nervosa Is a Disease, Not a Protest."[46] The opposition (*either* "disease" *or* "protest") presupposes a model within which to recognize the debilitating, self-consuming nature of a disorder is therefore to situate it outside the realm of the political. Within this model, helplessness and desperation, frustration and fear define and exhaust the reality of the disordered body; it is deemed incompatible that the subject be both "helpless and desperate" *and* locked in a struggle that has some meaning, trying to find honor on the ruinous terms of her culture and therefore communicating an excruciating message about the gender politics that regulate our lives. Of course, to acknowledge that a deep and embodied *understanding* of what culture demands might be the *source* of the anorectic's (or hysteric's) suffering is to suppose that the patient might have as much to teach the "experts" as the other way around.

Instead of this recognition, we find medical reassertions of expertise. New demarcations of "true" illness and disease are staked out, and as each anomaly has emerged to challenge the dominant paradigms, more rigorous criteria and stiffer definitions are demanded to distinguish between anorexia and "anorexic-like behaviors," "true anorectics" and "me, too, anorectics," "bulimic thinking" and normal female "weight-preoccupation," "true bulimics" and those women who do not binge and purge frequently enough to threaten their lives, or "vocational bulimics" (for example, ballet dancers) who exhibit the same behaviors but lack the accompanying "pathology."[47]

It is not that some of these distinctions cannot be made. Distinctions can *always* be made. And because distinctions can always be made, it is crucial that we always ask not merely whether a distinction holds at some level of analysis or description but what purposes it serves and what elements it obscures. What is obscured by the medicalization of eating disorders, whether "full-blown" anorexia and bulimia or "ordinary" weight-preoccupation, is an adequate understanding of the ubiquitous and thoroughly *routine* grip that culture has had and continues to have on the female body, how *commonplace* experiences of depreciation, shame, and self-hatred are, and why this situation has gotten worse, not better, in the culture of the eighties.[48] In this historical era, when the parameters defining women's "place" have indeed been challenged, it is disturbing that we are spending so much of our time and energy obsessed, depressed, and engaging in attempts at anxious transformation (most frequently, reduction) of our bodies. It is hard to escape the recognition, as is suggested throughout the essays in this volume, that a political battle is being waged over the energies and resources of the female body, a battle in which at least some feminist agendas for women's empowerment are being defeated (or, at a minimum, assaulted by backlash).

BEYOND THE MEDICAL MODEL

Since the seventeenth century, science has "owned" the study of the body and its disorders. This proprietorship has required that the body's meanings be utterly transparent and accessible to the qualified specialist (aided by the appropriate methodology and technology) and utterly opaque to the patient herself. It has required, too, the exorcising of all pre-modern notions that the body might obey a spiritual, emotional, or associational rather than a purely mechanical logic. In the context of such requirements, hysteria and anorexia have challenged modern science, not only with their seeming insistence on the power of the body to behave irrationally and inexplicably (Weir Mitchell once called hysteria "Mysteria"; anorexia was an "enigma" to Hilde Bruch),[49] but also because of the spectacle each presents of the *patient* (however unconsciously or self-destructively) creating and bestowing meaning on her own body, in a form that is opaque and baffling to the Cartesian mind of the scientist. Ultimately, Freud enabled psychoanalysis to rationalize and make clear the meanings of hysteria and to bring the hysterical body under the proprietorship of the scientist/analyst. Today the same sort of struggle is being waged over the body of the eating-disordered woman.

In the medical model, the body of the subject is the passive tablet on which disorder is inscribed. Deciphering that inscription is usually seen as a matter of determining the "cause" of the disorder; sometimes (as with psychoanalysis) *interpretation* of symptoms will be involved. But always the process requires a trained—that is to say, highly specialized—professional whose expertise alone can unlock the secrets of the disordered body. For the feminist analyst, by contrast, the disordered body, like all bodies, is engaged in a process of making meaning, of "labor on the body." From this perspective, anorexia (for example) is never *merely* regressive, never *merely* a fall into illness and chaos. Nor is it facilitated simply by bedazzlement by cultural images, "indoctrination" by what happens, arbitrarily, to be in fashion at this time. Rather, the "relentless pursuit of excessive thinness"[50] is an attempt to embody certain values, to create a body that will speak for the self in a meaningful and powerful way.

The tools of this labor are supplied: the vocabulary and the syntax of the body, like those of all languages, are culturally given. The anorectic cannot simply decide to make slenderness mean whatever she wishes it to. This is not to say, however, that the meaning of slenderness is univocal or fixed or clear. On the contrary, the fact that slenderness is so compelling in the contemporary context (and not only to anorectics, of course) suggests that in our culture slenderness is, rather, *overdetermined*, freighted with multiple significances. As such, it is capable of being used as a vehicle for the expression of a range of (sometimes contradictory) anxieties, aspirations, dilemmas. Within such a framework, interpreting anorexia requires, not technical or professional expertise, but awareness of the many layers of cultural signification that are crystallized in the disorder.

Among such significations, which I explore in detail in other essays in this volume, are: (1) the promise of transcendence of domestic femininity and admission to the privileged public world, a world in which admiration is granted not to softness but to will, autonomy, and rigor; (2) the symbolic and practical control of female hunger (read: desire), continually constructed as a problem in patriarchal cultures (particularly in times when gender relations have become unsettled) and internalized in women's shame over their own needs and appetites; (3) the symbolic recircumscription of woman's limited "place" in the world; and (4) the tantalizing (and mystifying) ideal of a perfectly managed and regulated self, within a consumer culture which has made the actual management of hunger and desire intensely problematic. In this last context, food refusal, weight loss, commitment to exercise, and ability to tolerate bodily pain and exhaustion have become cultural metaphors for self-determination, will, and moral fortitude.

The decoding of slenderness to reveal deep associations with autonomy, will, discipline, conquest of desire, enhanced spirituality, purity, and transcendence of the female body suggests that the continuities proposed by Rudolph Bell between contemporary anorexia and the self-starvation of medieval saints are not so farfetched as such critics as Brumberg have claimed.[51] Brumberg argues that attempts to find common psychological or political features in the anorexia of medieval saints and that of contemporary women founder on the fact that anorexia mirabilia was centered on a quest for spiritual perfection, "while the modern anorectic strives for perfection in terms of society's ideal of physical rather than spiritual beauty."[52] But Brumberg here operates on the assumption—an assumption challenged by the essays in this volume—that there *is* such a thing as purely "physical" beauty.

Granted, the medieval saint was utterly uninterested in attaining a slender appearance. But it does not follow that the contemporary obsession with slenderness is without deep "spiritual" dimensions, and that these cannot share important—that is, illuminating—affinities with the ascetic ambitions of medieval saints. Here, one anorectic explicitly makes the connection: "My soul seemed to grow as my body waned," she recalls. "I felt like one of those early Christian saints who starved themselves in the desert sun."[53] This is not to say that the meaning of self-starvation for the fasting nuns of the Middle Ages can be simply equated with its meaning for adolescent anorectics of today. But in the context of enduring historical traditions that have dominantly coded appetite, lack of will, temptation, and, indeed, the body itself as female, surely we would expect that women's projects to transcend hunger and desire would reveal some continuous elements.

The shallow and unanalyzed conception of slenderness as merely "an external body configuration *rather than* an internal spiritual state,"[54] an ideal without psychological or moral depth, still predominates in the literature on anorexia and bulimia. Why? One explanation is that so long as eating disorders remain situated within a medical model, those who are entrusted with the conceptualization of anorexia and bulimia will be medical professionals who have little experience in or inclination toward cultural interpretation and criticism. But more important is the fact that to begin to incorporate such interpretation and criticism within the medical model would be to transform that model itself. Susceptibility to *images* can still be conceptualized in terms of a passive subject and a mechanical process. To acknowledge, however, that meaning is continually being produced at all levels—by the culture, by the subject, by the clinician as well—and that in a fundamental sense there *is* no body that exists neutrally, outside this process of making meaning, no body that passively awaits the objective deciphering of trained experts, is to question the presuppositions on which much of modern science is built and around which our highly specialized, professionalized, and compartmentalized culture revolves. Or, to put this another way: it is to suggest that the study of the disordered body is as much the proper province of cultural critics in every field and of nonspecialists, ordinary but critically questioning citizens, as it is of the "experts." This audacious challenge is the legacy of the feminist reconceptualization of eating disorders.

Are Mothers Persons?

*Reproductive Rights and the Politics
of Subject-ivity*

Many people, both in academic and nonacademic circles, have come to regard feminist arguments concerning the biases and exclusions of Western culture either as outmoded by progressive changes in gender relations, or as paranoid delusions, fueled by a mania for "political correctness" rather than truth. These notions persist despite increasingly strong cultural evidence to the contrary. As the Clarence Thomas/Anita Hill hearings demonstrated, images of the woman as lying temptress still triumph in this culture over women's rights to an equal hearing under the law. Women still earn significantly less than men for equal work. And the feminist ideal of an egalitarian domestic division of labor so far appears no match for an ideology that insists women must continue to bear the major responsibility for cooking, cleaning, and child-care even when they are also working full-time in jobs and professions formerly reserved for men.

Some of the most resilient inequalities in our legal and social treatment of women lie in the domain of reproductive control. But despite the highly publicized and turbulent nature of the battles that have been fought in this domain, the most glaring inequalities have yet to receive the exposure and emphasis they deserve. This omission results at least in part, I would argue, from the fact that, although abortion rights are a prominent issue, both pro-choice and pro-life arguments are locked into rhetoric and strategies that fail to situate the struggle within the broader context of reproductive control. In this essay I will attempt to locate the struggle over abortion rights within that context.

The first three sections of the essay will be largely devoted to exposing and interpreting some remarkable, pernicious contradictions in legal and medical practices concerning the protection of the "subject" and to examining some of the cultural ideology, metaphors, and images that animate those contradictions. Although law and medicine claim to have a unified and coherent tradition concerning individual rights, in fact two different traditions have been established, one for embodied subjects, and the other for those who come to be treated as mere bodies despite an official rhetoric that vehemently forswears such treatment of human beings. I will also explore the expression of this practical metaphysics—this deeply sedimented, cultural duality—in more everyday arenas, and as it has crystallized in movements for fetal and father's rights. In the last section of the essay I will briefly consider some implications my analysis holds for feminist discourse on reproduction.

My examinations of the legal double standard concerning the bodily integrity of pregnant and nonpregnant bodies, the construction of women as fetal incubators, the bestowal of "super-subject" status to the fetus, and the emergence of a father's-rights ideology will reveal, I believe, that feminist anger and frustration are far from paranoid or anachronistic. I hope they will demonstrate, as well, that the current terms of the abortion debate—as a contest between fetal claims to personhood and women's right to choose—are limited and misleading. In the context of my analysis in this essay, the current battle over reproductive control emerges as an assault on the personhood of *women*.

EMBODIED SUBJECTS AND DE-SUBJECTIFIED BODIES

Our legal tradition officially places a high—some might say inordinately high—value on bodily integrity. As the United States Supreme Court acknowledged over one hundred years ago:

> No right is held more sacred, or is more carefully guarded, by the common law, than the right of every individual to the possession and control of his own person, free from all restraint or interference of others, unless by a clear and unquestionable authority of law. As well said by Judge Cooley, "The right to one's person may be said to be a right of complete immunity: to be let alone."[1]

Bodily integrity and the "right to one's person" are philosophically knit together by the Cartesian conception of the human body as the "home" of the person—the "ghost in the machine," as Gilbert Ryle has called it[2]—the self-conscious, willing, desiring, dreaming, creating "inner" self, the "I." The historical influence of this construction on Western modernity, especially on legal conceptions of bodily integrity, privacy, and personhood, has been sweeping and profound. Yet, as we will see, the "ghost in the machine" is not always the legislating metaphor in concrete social practice; sometimes entirely mechanistic conceptions of the body dominate, conceptions from which all concern for the inner self have vanished. In practice, our legal tradition divides the human world as Descartes divided all of reality: into conscious subjects and mere bodies (*res extensa*). And in the social expression of that duality, some groups have clearly been accorded subject-status and its protections, while others have regularly been denied those protections, becoming for all medical and legal purposes pure *res extensa*, bodies stripped of their animating, dignifying, and humanizing "subject-ivity."

First let us examine the tradition regarding embodied subjects. This is one in which bodily integrity is privileged so highly that judges have consistently refused to force individuals to submit without consent to medical treatment even though the life of another hangs in the balance. So, for example, in the case of *McFall v. Shimp* (1979), Shimp's bodily integrity was legally protected to the extent that he was permitted to refuse a procedure (a bone-marrow extraction and donation) that could have prevented his cousin's otherwise certain death from aplastic anemia. (McFall did indeed die two weeks after the decision was handed down.) Other similar suits have been equally unsuccessful, including highly publicized ones such as that pressed by a Seattle woman to have the father of her leukemic child donate his marrow, and that of an Illinois father who sued the mother of his son's twin half-siblings to have tests done to see if their marrow matched his son's.[3] Many of us—and I include myself—may find Shimp's action and similar refusals morally repugnant. They are, however, thoroughly sanctioned by law, which insists on *informed consent* for any medical procedure, and which permits us to be Bad Samaritans in the interests of preserving *principles* that are viewed as constituting (in the words of the *McFall* decision) "the very essence . . . of our society."[4]

The doctrine of informed consent is, in a very real sense, a protection of the *subjectivity* of the person involved—that is, it is an acknowledgment that the body can never be regarded merely as a site of quantifiable processes that can be assessed objectively, but must be treated as invested with personal meaning, history, and value that are ultimately determinable only by the subject who lives "within" it. According to the doctrine of informed consent, even when it is "for the good" of the patient, no one else—neither relative nor expert—may determine for the embodied subject what medical risks are worth taking, what procedures are minimally or excessively invasive, what pain is minor. When that meaning-bestowing function is in danger of being taken away from the subject, the prevailing ideology (and the accompanying legal response) conceptualizes the situation as a violent invasion of the personal space of the body. For example, physicians performing unconsented-to treatment are legally guilty of battery.[5] Or consider the impassioned justification for his decision given by the judge who ruled on *McFall v. Shimp*:

> For a society which respects the rights of *one* individual, to sink its teeth into the jugular vein or neck of one of its members and suck from it sustenance for *another* member, is revolting to our hard-wrought concepts of jurisprudence. Forcible extraction of living body tissue causes revulsion to the judicial mind. Such would raise the specter of the swastika and the Inquisition, reminiscent of the horrors this portends.[6]

The key metaphor of this description, vampirism, not only evokes the pulsing, flowing, *vital* nature of the human body but suggests that to invade it is tantamount to parasitism, a stealing of the inner essence of the person. The body here, clearly, is no mere physical entity but a self embodied, or (to put it the other way around) a body suffused with subjectivity. The system which would countenance its invasion is likened to Nazi Germany and the Inquisition, or (as in *Rochin v. California* [1952]), to medieval torture:

> Illegally breaking into the privacy of the petitioner, the struggle to open his mouth and remove what was there, the forcible extraction of his stomach contents—this course of proceeding by agents of government to obtain evidence is bound to offend even hardened sensibilities. They are methods too close to the rack and the screw to permit of constitutional differentiation.[7]

Rochin, a suspected drug dealer, had merely been made to regurgitate two capsules he had swallowed. Moreover, the invasion of

Rochin's privacy falls within a clearly recognized category of possible exception to the protection of bodily integrity: invasion of a minimal nature may be permitted when it is required to promote the state's interest in the prosecution of criminals.[8] So, for example, blood-alcohol tests may be required of drivers suspected of intoxication.[9] But even for suspected criminals, the law has emphatically drawn the line at major surgery. In *Winston v. Lee* (1985), law-enforcement authorities needed a bullet, lodged in the defendant's chest, as evidence against him. Both the circuit court and the Supreme Court ruled against the state, the Supreme Court arguing that "surgery without the patient's consent, performed under a general anesthetic to search for evidence of a crime, involves a virtually total divestment of the patient's ordinary control over surgical probing beneath his skin." Both the circuit court and the Supreme Court, interestingly, were especially emphatic concerning the degrading and "demeaning" nature of "drugging" this citizen "into a state of unconsciousness" against his will.[10]

In contrast to all this privileging of the hallowed ground of "the subject's" body[11] is the casual and morally imperious approach medicine and law have taken to nonconsensual medical interference in the reproductive lives of women—particularly when they are of non-European descent, poor, or non-English-speaking. In this arena we see racism, classism, and sexism interlock virulently, whether we are looking at the history of involuntary sterilization in this country, the statistics on court-ordered obstetrical intervention, or the Supreme Court's *Rust v. Sullivan* decision, which forbids doctors in federally funded clinics to discuss or offer information about abortion or to indicate where such information might be available, even when a woman has no other access to medical advice.[12]

The history of involuntary sterilization, overwhelmingly aimed at the "mentally defective" ("feeble-minded," "retarded," "mentally ill") and one of the most blatant examples of medical and legal disregard for the personhood of certain groups in this country, has been strongly shaped by the politics of race, class, and gender. From 1900 to 1960, 60,000 persons in the United States were sterilized without their consent, many never even informed of the nature of the operation.[13] Initially fueled by nineteenth-century versions of evolutionary theory (almost invariably racist) and the eugenics-inspired vision of a society purged of "defective genes," the history of involuntary sterilization of the "mentally defective" in this country has in practice largely affected those groups considered genetically suspect and racially inferior: those convicted of crimes, the poor, African Americans, Native Americans, Spanish Americans, and Puerto Ricans.[14]

Less often noted is the overwhelming gender-bias that began to develop in the 1930s and 1940s, as the Depression shifted the concerns of those officials empowered to sterilize from the prevention of genetic defect to the prevention of parenthood in those individuals deemed unable to *care* adequately for their children. Philip Reilly, in *The Surgical Solution*, notes the change in ideology and the increasingly glaring disparity between the numbers of men and of women sterilized.[15] He fails, however, to see the connection between the two. Today, virtually all sterilization abuse (as well as proposals for less drastic bodily invasions, such as the use of Norplant) is directed against women on welfare, and is rationalized by the "inability to care" model. Often, as in the case of *Rust*, the reproductive rights of poor women are threatened without outright legal deprivation of those rights. In *Walker v. Pierce*, for example, the defendant admitted that his practice was to require consent for postpartum sterilization of his Medicaid patients who came to him pregnant with a third child. If consent was not given, he would refuse to treat the patient, and on occasion he threatened to try to have their state assistance terminated. He did not insist on these conditions for patients *not* on Medicaid, no matter how many children they had.[16]

Turning to court-ordered obstetrical interventions—and these include forced cesarean sections, detention of women against their will, and intrauterine transfusions—the statistics make clear that in this culture the pregnant, poor woman (especially if she is of non-European descent) comes as close as a human being can get to being regarded, medically and legally, as "mere body," her wishes, desires, dreams, religious scruples of little consequence and easily ignored in (the doctor's or judge's estimation of) the interests of fetal well-being. In 1987, the *New England Journal of Medicine* reported that of twenty-one cases in which court orders for obstetrical intervention were sought, 86 percent were obtained. Eighty-one percent of the women involved were black, Asian, or Hispanic.[17]

In one of the most extreme and revealing of the forced-cesarean cases, George Washington University Hospital won a court order requiring that a cesarean section be performed on a terminally ill patient, Angela Carder, before her fetus was viable, and against the wishes of the woman, her husband, and the doctors on staff. Both the woman and her baby died shortly after the operation. The District of Columbia Court of Appeals, in affirming the order against a requested stay, ruled that the woman's right to avoid bodily intrusion could justifiably be put aside, as she had "at best two days left of sedated life."[18] Here, clearly, a still living human subject had become, for all legal purposes, dead matter, a mere fetal container. A woman whom *no court in the country would force to undergo a blood transfusion for a dying relative* had come to be legally regarded, when pregnant, as a mere life-support system for a fetus.

It is important to emphasize here that the legal analogues to cases such as these are *not* interventions such as those involved, for example, when a Jehovah's Witness is ordered to permit a dependent child to receive a blood transfusion, but precisely cases such as *McFall v. Shimp*, in which the *body* of the person subject to the court order is required for the intervention. This is why the protection of bodily integrity is an issue in cases of this latter sort, but not in cases solely involving the overriding of parental wishes, where the body of the parent is not itself involved. With the correct moral analogues in mind, it is clear that even granting full personhood to the fetus does not mute the force and depth of the legal and moral inconsistency here. On the one hand, we have Shimp's refusal to submit to a procedure that could have saved his cousin's life, a refusal which was upheld by law on the grounds that to do otherwise would be a gross invasion of the privileged territory of the subject's own body. On the other hand, we have numerous cases in which judges not only have ordered pregnant women to submit to highly invasive procedures[19] but have conceptualized these interventions as the protection of the fetus's rights against the inappropriate and selfish maternal evaluations of the physical, emotional, and religious acceptability of those procedures.

Consider the language of court orders for medical treatment of pregnant women. These orders, in striking contrast to the rhetoric of violent subjugation, the metaphors of the rack and the screw, the analogies with fascist regimes employed in the rulings on *McFall v.*

Shimp and *Rochin v. California*, often dismiss the proposed intervention as minor, inconsequential, of significance only to an individual whose desires for personal freedom and "convenience" are
excessive. So, the judge in *Taft v. Taft* (1982), in issuing an order for
cervical surgery against the will of the woman (the order had been
sought by her husband), referred to the procedure as "the operation
of a *few sutures* . . . to hold the pregnancy."[20] This is clearly to
sidestep utterly, in the case of the pregnant woman, the doctrine of
informed consent, which requires that the individual affected be the
final judge of the degree of invasiveness and risk that is acceptable.
Without that requirement, informed consent has no meaning at all.

Even, however, if we are likely to agree that cerclage is a minimally invasive procedure,[21] let us not forget the judicial horror
expressed at even less intrusive procedures carried out on the bodies of suspected criminals (such as the forced regurgitation that was
the issue in *Rochin*). The discomfort, risk, and invasiveness of cesareans are another matter. The court record has made it abundantly
clear (cf. *Winston*) that major surgery without consent is an extreme
and demeaning violation of bodily integrity and control; it is also
risky, no matter how "routine" the procedure. If marrow transfusions and even blood tests have not been required, surely a refusal
to undergo the "massive intrusion"[22] of a major surgical procedure
such as a cesarean section should be honored. Yet when Ayesha
Madyun refused a cesarean on religious grounds the judge ruled
that for him *not* to issue a court order forcing her to have the
operation would be to "indulge" Madyun's "desires" at the expense
of the safety of her fetus.[23]

As a number of analysts have pointed out, there are no legal
justifications for the discrepancies between the treatment accorded
pregnant women and that given to nonpregnant persons.[24] Rather,
to explain such contradictions we must leave the realm of rationality
and enter the realm of gender ideology (and, in many cases, of racial
prejudice as well). These decisions, clearly, are mediated by normative conceptions of the pregnant woman's appropriate role and
function. Note the judge's choice, in the *Madyun* case, of the term
desires (over, for example, the more legally conventional *wishes*). The
idea of female "desire" is potent and threatening in our culture,
with its sexual overtones and suggestions of personal gratification
and capricious self-interest—particularly when paired with the no-

tion of indulgence, as in this judge's ruling. Madyun's objections, we should remember, were religious (as are most maternal refusals of obstetrical intervention).[25] For the judge, however, religious scruples are on a par with the flightiest of personal whims when they come into conflict with the supreme role the pregnant woman should be playing: that of incubator to her fetus. In fulfilling that function, the pregnant woman is *supposed* to efface her own subjectivity, if need be. When she refuses to do so, that subjectivity comes to be construed as excessive, wicked. (The cultural archetype of the cold, selfish mother—the evil goddesses, queens, and stepmothers of myth and fairy tale—clearly lurks in the imaginations of many of the judges issuing court orders for obstetrical intervention.)

Thus, ontologically speaking, the pregnant woman has been seen by our legal system as the mirror-image of the abstract subject whose bodily integrity the law is so determined to protect. For the latter, subjectivity is the essence of personhood, not to be sacrificed even in the interests of the preservation of the life of another individual. Personal valuation, choice, and consciousness itself (remember the *Winston* court's horror at unconsented-to anesthesia) are the given values, against which any claims to state interest or public good must be rigorously argued and are rarely granted. The essence of the pregnant woman, by contrast, is her biological, purely mechanical role in preserving the life of another. In her case, *this* is the given value, against which her claims to subjectivity must be rigorously evaluated, and they will usually be found wanting insofar as they conflict with her life-support function. In the face of such a conflict, her valuations, choices, consciousness are expendable.[26]

Intersecting with this gender ideology, in cases such as *Madyun*, is our historical tradition of effacement of the personhood of people of color, racist beliefs about their "irresponsibility," and disdain for religious and cultural diversity. These elements can come into play at both ends of the spectrum of reproductive abuse—coerced sterilization, and coerced cesareans. In coerced-sterilization cases the mediating racist image is often that of the promiscuous breeder, populating the world irresponsibly, like an unspayed animal. One of the witnesses in *Walker v. Pierce* said that Pierce lectured her: "And, he said, 'Listen here young lady . . . this is my tax money paying for something like this. . . . I am tired of people going around here having babies and my tax money paying for it.'"[27] In forced-cesarean cases like *Madyun*, the mediating racist image may be that of the ignorant, uncivilized primitive whose atavistic religious beliefs are in conflict with the enlightened attitudes of modern science.

FETAL SUPER-SUBJECTS AND MATERNAL INCUBATORS

> As a one-time cocaine abuser, Debbie abused her son in the womb. Now, thanks to support from Alliance, she's learned how to be the responsible parent little Ricky needs.
>
> *From the 1991* United Way *brochure*

Clearly, there has been one legal tradition for those who occupy the cultural location of the subject and another for those who are marked as "other." Some acknowledgment of the injustice of forced cesareans was finally made when the District of Columbia Court of Appeals, in a widely publicized decision, set aside the original ruling on Angela Carder's case and even raised the question of whether "there could ever be a situation extraordinary or compelling enough to justify a massive intrusion into a person's body, such as a cesarean section, against that person's will." (It is not to depreciate the court's ruling to note that Angela Carder was a white woman.) The appeal had been filed by the American Medical Association and thirty-nine other organizations, whose consciousness had been significantly raised by the efforts of Lynn Paltrow of the American Civil Liberties Union, George Annas of the Boston University School of Medicine, and several others who brought the Carder case and others to national attention.[28] In 1987, 47 percent of the obstetricians surveyed by the *New England Journal of Medicine* had approved of forced cesareans and had agreed that the precedent set by the courts in cases requiring emergency cesarean sections for the sake of the fetus should be extended to include other procedures such as intrauterine transfusion.[29] Since the Angela Carder case, these attitudes may be changing. Yet there are extremely vocal and powerful advocates of pervasive obstetrical intervention,[30] and pregnant women continue to be treated as fetal incubators in other ways as well. The past few years have seen increasing numbers of cases in which brain-dead pregnant women have been kept alive for as long as seven or eight weeks, until the fetus is mature enough to deliver by cesarean section,[31] and the Catholic church has declared life-sustaining treatment to be mandatory for a pregnant patient "if continued treatment may benefit her unborn child."[32]

Indeed, I believe the ideology of woman-as-fetal-incubator is stronger than ever and is making ever greater encroachments into pregnant women's lives. The difference is that today it is most likely to emerge in the context of issues concerning the "life-styles" of pregnant women. In 1986, Lawrence Nelson and his colleagues warned that "compelling pregnant women to undergo medical treatment sets an unsavory precedent for further invasions of a woman's privacy and bodily integrity." As though imagining the horrifying terrain of a future dystopia (such as that depicted in Margaret Atwood's *The Handmaid's Tale*), they list such potential intrusions:

> [These] could include court orders prohibiting pregnant women from using alcohol, cigarettes, or other possibly harmful substances, forbidding them from continuing to work because of the presence of fetal toxins in the workplace, forcing them to take drugs or accept intrauterine blood transfusions, requiring pregnant anorexic teenagers to be force-fed, forcing women to undergo prenatal screening and diagnostic procedures such as amniocentesis, sonography, or fetoscopy, or mandating that women submit to *in utero* or extra-uterine surgery for the fetus. . . . The prospect of courts literally managing the lives of pregnant women and extensively intruding into their daily activities is frightening and antithetical to the fundamental role that freedom of action plays in our society.[33]

Just five years later, this landscape no longer seems so futuristic. Although the Supreme Court has banned employers from adopting "fetal protection" policies that would bar women of childbearing age from hazardous jobs, this decision seems almost anomalous in the contemporary zeitgeist, within which the protection of fetal rights has burgeoned into a national obsession. Prosecutions and preventive detentions of pregnant women for fetal endangerment, once a rarity, are becoming more and more common. Since the Pamela Rae Stewart case of 1985, in which Stewart was charged with criminal neglect of her child for failing to follow medical advice during pregnancy, such cases have multiplied. In 1989, a Florida judge sentenced twenty-three-year-old Jennifer Johnson to fifteen years' probation on her conviction of delivering illegal drugs via the umbilical cord to her two babies. A Massachusetts woman who miscarried after an automobile accident in which she was intoxicated was prosecuted for vehicular homicide of her fetus. A Connecticut woman was charged with endangering her fetus by swallowing cocaine as police moved to arrest her. A Washington judge sent Brenda Vaughan to jail for nearly four months to protect her fetus, because a drug test, taken after she was arrested for forging a check, revealed cocaine use.[34] In 1990, a Wyoming woman was charged by the police with the crime of drinking while pregnant and was prosecuted for felony child abuse. In South Carolina, a dozen women have been arrested after the hospitals they went to for maternity care tested them for cocaine use and turned them in to the police for fetal abuse.[35]

In some ways even more disturbing than these legal actions are changes in the everyday attitudes of people. In March 1991, two waiters were fired from their jobs when they tried to persuade a nine-months-pregnant customer not to order a rum daiquiri because drinking alcohol could harm her fetus.[36] Soon after, they appeared on the "Oprah Winfrey" show, where many members of the audience indicated their strong support for the waiters' action. As might be expected, the customer's action was construed as reckless and "selfish," even though it is highly unlikely that one drink at her advanced stage of pregnancy could affect the fetus's health. Audience members were insistent, as was columnist Cal Thomas, that pregnant women who engage in *any* activities that have even the *slightest* risk are behaving "selfishly" and that others are only acting responsibly in pointing this out to them. In Thomas's condemnation of the customer, all distinctions—between levels of harm, between fetuses and children, between prohibitions that affect the deployment of the mother's own body and those that do not—are effaced:

> What if the woman had come in a month from now with her newborn child and ordered two drinks, one for her and one to put in the baby's bottle, because the child had been crying and the mother thought this was a good way to get it to sleep? Would the waiter have been justified in refusing service to the baby because it is underage? Of course. Then what's the difference between wanting to protect a child that is newly born and one that is about to be born?[37]

Once again the specter of the evil mother looms large. The biting injustice is that pregnant women are in general probably the Best Samaritans of our culture. The overwhelming majority will suffer considerable personal inconvenience, pain, risk, and curtailment of their freedom to do what their doctors advise is in the best interests of their fetuses. As one obstetrical surgeon put it, most of the women he sees "would cut off their heads to save their babies."[38] In the specific case of the customer who ordered the daiquiri, by her own account she had been extremely careful throughout her pregnancy and thought hard before ordering the drink:

> I was a week overdue . . . and I thought it would be safe to have just this one drink, which I ordered with dinner. . . . I've always made it a point to read everything I could find about alcohol in pregnancy. I felt guilty enough as it was for ordering the drink. . . . They tried to make me feel like a child abuser.[39]

Most poignant about this quote is the woman's internal sense of transgression, which I interpret as an indication, not of her recognition of the *actual* threat of one drink to her fetus's health, but of the extraordinary levels of vigilance now expected of and taken upon themselves by pregnant women. Yet at the same time as supererogatory levels of care are demanded of the pregnant woman, neither the father nor the state nor private industry is held responsible for any of the harms they may be inflicting on developing fetuses, nor are they required to contribute to their care. Fathers' drug habits, smoking, alcoholism, reckless driving, and psychological and physical treatment of pregnant wives are part of the fetus's "environment," too—sometimes indirectly, through their effect on the mother's well-being, but sometimes directly as well (through the effects of secondhand smoke and crack dust in the air, physical abuse, and alcohol's deleterious effect on the quality of sperm, to give a few examples). But fathers are nonetheless off the hook, as is the health system that makes it so difficult for poor women to obtain adequate prenatal care and for addicted mothers to get help.[40] As Katha Pollitt points out:

> Judges order pregnant addicts to jail, but they don't order drug treatment programs to accept them, or Medicaid, which pays for heroin treatment, to cover crack addiction—let alone order landlords not to evict them, or obstetricians to take uninsured women as pa-

tients, or the federal government to fund fully the Women, Infants, and Children supplemental feeding program, which reaches only two-thirds of those who are eligible. The policies that have underwritten maternal and infant health in most of the industrialized west since World War II—a national health service, paid maternity leave, direct payments to mothers, government-funded day care, home health visitors for new mothers, welfare payments that reflect the cost of living—are still regarded in the United States by even the most liberal as hopeless causes, and by everyone else as budget-breaking giveaways to the undeserving, pie-in-the-sky items from a mad socialist's wish list.[41]

While public service announcements on television target the smoking and alcohol habits of pregnant women as though they were the sole causes of low birth-weight and infant disability, a task force commissioned by the government concluded that "if we just delivered routine clinical care and social services to pregnant women, we could prevent one-quarter to one-third of infant mortality." As things now stand, one out of every three pregnant women gets insufficient prenatal care (a situation that is not helped, of course, if drug-addicted mothers avoid seeking medical help, for fear they will be turned in to the police). Among other improvements, the task force recommends a public information campaign and a "nurturing approach" to pregnant women's needs, with home visits by nurses, social workers, and other counselors. The Bush White House, however, acted on none of this, withholding most of the report from Congress in the interests of preserving "the confidentiality of the deliberative process" in the Executive branch.[42]

Only the pregnant woman, apparently, has the "duty of care."[43] Indeed, according to the construction examined in the first section of this essay, this is her essential function. That it is framed, moreover, in entirely mechanistic terms—as fleshy incubator—is revealed by the exclusive attention given to her physiological state. The facts that a drink now and then might relax and soothe her, and that continual vigilance over the "environment" she is providing (if not the threat of public scrutiny and condemnation itself) may make her perpetually tense and worried, and that such factors may also affect the well-being of the fetus are not considered. Rather, a crudely mechanistic portrayal of her bodily connection with the fetus prevails. One daiquiri taken by the mother is imagined as equivalent to serving the fetus a cocktail. This image is so distasteful that it is then easy to leap to the further equation: one drink = fetal alcohol syndrome.

Sometimes the womb is described not as incubator but as prison. "The viable unborn child is literally captive within the mother's body," argued the dissenting judge in the appeal of the Carder case. Anti-choice spokesperson Barnard Nathanson describes the fetus as "bricked in, as it were, behind . . . an impenetrable wall of flesh, muscle, bone and blood."[44] Perhaps such images can be dismissed as those of an ideologue. Michael Harrison's description, then, will serve as an example of the increasing *subjectification* of fetal being. For, strikingly, as the personhood of the pregnant woman has been drained from her and her function as fetal incubator activated, the subjectivity of the *fetus* has been elevated:

> The fetus could not be taken seriously as long as he remained a medical recluse in an opaque womb; and it was not until the last half of this century that the prying eye of the ultrasonogram rendered the once opaque womb transparent, stripping the veil of mystery from the dark inner sanctum, and letting the light of scientific observation fall on the shy and secretive fetus. . . . The sonographic voyeur, spying on the unwary fetus, finds him or her a surprisingly active little creature, and not at all the passive parasite we had imagined. . . . The fetus has come a long way—from biblical "seed" and mystical "homunculus" to an individual with medical problems that can be diagnosed and treated, that is, a patient. Although he cannot make an appointment and seldom complains, this patient will at all times need a physician.[45]

The gender ideology that permeates this quotation is various and obvious, and need not be belabored here. Here, I need only highlight the duality Harrison constructs between the "opaque," impenetrable womb, a territory itself bereft of the light of consciousness, a cave, a place merely to sleep, and the psychologically complex, fully personified fetus, at once "shy and secretive" and vitally "active." (And, of course, unlike his mother, he "seldom complains"—an ideal "patient"!) Ruth Hubbard notes, as well, the remarkable arrogance of the assumption that before developments in ultrasound, "we" had imagined the fetus to be a "passive parasite." Who is this "we"? she asks. "Surely not," she points out, "women who have been awakened by the painful kicks of a fetus!"[46] Those women, of course, have been rendered metaphorically unconscious by Harrison; only their inert, shrouded wombs remain.

Of course, the increasingly routine use of ultrasound *has* made the fetus seem more of a person, both to the doctor and to the mother.[47] Because of such changes in the perception of the fetus's status, combined with the advancing technologies that enable the doctor to treat the fetus directly, as an autonomous patient, doctors have come to feel confused, angry, and, perhaps, morally outraged when mothers refuse a recommended treatment. I can understand their discomfort and frustration. But the disturbing fact remains that increased empathy for the fetus has often gone hand in hand with decreased respect for the autonomy of the mother.[48] And, in general, the New Reproductive Technology has been a confusingly mixed bag as far as the subjectivity of women is concerned. On the one hand, women now have a booming technology seemingly focused on fulfilling *their* desires: to conceive, to prevent miscarriage, to deliver a healthy baby at term. On the other hand, proponents and practitioners continually encourage women to treat their bodies as passive instruments of those goals, ready and willing, "if they want a child badly enough," to endure however complicated and invasive a regime of diagnostic testing, daily monitoring, injections, and operative procedures may be required. Thus, one element of women's subjectivity is indeed nurtured, while all other elements (investment in career, other emotional needs, importance of other personal relationships, etc.) are minimized, marginalized, and (when they refuse to be repressed) made an occasion for guilt and self-questioning.

One of the most disturbing examples is presented by Dr. Stefan Semchyshyn. Semchyshyn argues for an extremely aggressive approach to the prevention of miscarriage, dismissing the (generally accepted) belief that many early miscarriages are the inevitable result of genetic defect and ought not to be rigorously prevented. He reassures readers that genetic testing (amniocentesis and ultrasound) will pick up those defects at the beginning of the second trimester, when the women can still elect to have an abortion.[49] Semchyshyn is, I presume, aware of the physical pain and (well-documented) psychological trauma involved in a second-trimester abortion; yet, apparently, these factors are too trivial for him to mention even as possible considerations.[50] In our present cultural context, the New Reproductive Technologies *do* cater to women's desires (that is, to the desires of women who can afford them), but only when they are the *right* desires, desires that will subordinate all else (even in the face of technological success rates which continue to be very discouraging) to the project of producing a child.

Gradually over the last century, and steeply accelerating over the decade of the 1980s, the legal status of the fetus has been greatly enhanced as well.[51] For over half a century, the *Dietrich* rule (1884), which established that damages (for instance, accidental death or injury) incurred on a fetus were not separately recoverable, because the fetus was "a part of the mother," prevailed.[52] Then, in 1946, in what has been described as "the most spectacular abrupt reversal of a well settled rule in the whole history of the law of torts,"[53] a federal district court in *Bonbrest v. Kotz* held that there may be recovery for injury to a viable fetus subsequently born alive.[54] Nelson points out that even this change, however, did not recognize the fetus as a person with full legal rights; the point of the ruling was to allow damaged *born* persons in need of special medical treatment, schooling, and so forth to be compensated for injuries wrongly suffered when they were not yet legal persons.

The same intent, on Nelson's analysis, is behind the New Jersey Supreme Court's unfortunately worded statement, in *Smith v. Brennan* (1960) that "a child has a legal right to begin life with a sound mind and body." *Smith,* recognizing a child's cause of action for negligently inflicted prenatal injury, explicitly denies that this entails recognition of fetal personhood. The point is simply to establish the legitimacy of the *live-born* child's injury claim.[55] Yet the phrase taken by itself (out of context of the decision) *is* problematic, not only suggesting an unprecedented scope of rights, but ambiguous concerning to whom they belong. Over the past thirty years this ambiguity has been frequently exploited at the expense of the intent of the ruling, as advocates of obstetrical intervention have freely invoked the *fetus's* right to "begin life with a sound mind and body" as justification for their suits. The slippage here, from a live-born child's right to bring action against injuries suffered when in the fetal state to the right of the *fetus* to force its mother to accept treatment against her will, is profound and pernicious.

But let us, for the sake of argument, lay aside the issue of misapplication of tort law. Let us grant a fetus's right to be born healthy and sound and to be provided with a safe, healthy environment to promote this end. If we grant this, we are obliged to recognize also that this gives the fetus rights that *no one else* in this society has. Here we are once again confronted with the strange set of affairs entailed by fetal-rights arguments, that a two-year-old child has far fewer rights than a six-month-old fetus![56]

My point here is *not* to deny protection or dignity to the fetus or to suggest that it is no more than tissue or an appendage to the mother. In fact, I will later argue very strongly against such perspectives. Rather, my object is to bring attention to the ontological construction that is entailed (but never openly acknowledged) by the fetal-rights position, a position that is increasingly becoming conventional wisdom in many quarters of our culture. Very simply put, that construction is one in which pregnant women are not subjects at all (neither under the law nor in the zeitgeist) while fetuses are *super*-subjects. It is as though the subjectivity of the pregnant body were siphoned from it and emptied into fetal life.

FATHER'S RIGHTS

This offspring was begot without a Mother.

Montesquieu, epigraph to
The Spirit of the Law

O why did God,
Creator wise, that peopl'd highest Heav'n
With Spirits Masculine, create at last
This noveltie on Earth, this fair defect
Of Nature, and not fill the World at once
With Men as Angels without Feminine,
Or find some other way to generate
Mankind?

Milton, Paradise Lost,
Book X, *lines 888–895*

Alongside attempts to define the pregnant woman's status as that of mere incubator, we have seen a corresponding emergence of a more and more vocal movement for father's rights. James Bopp, a highly visible advocate of this movement and general counsel of the National Right to Life Committee, has marketed a "Father's Rights Litigation Kit," a how-to guide for bringing suit against wives and girlfriends.[57] And although such cases have thus far invariably been defeated in higher courts, in November of 1989 the Pennsylvania State Senate passed legislation that has gone further than any other in addressing father's rights, requiring that women notify their husbands of abortion plans and holding physicians who perform an abortion without a form showing that the husband has been notified liable for civil damages to the husband and punitive damages of $5,000.[58]

One reason why the movement for father's rights has grown so rapidly is the culturally powerful rhetoric of "equality" with which the movement has trumpeted its cause. "It's a balancing of rights," says James Bopp.[59] But it is a mystification to conceptualize father's-rights cases in this way, as though equitable distribution is the goal, like the allocation of a child's time in a custody case. For the basis for these cases is always a concrete occasion when the mother's and the father's goals are mutually exclusive. In that context, equal treatment *cannot* be achieved. Rather, one must prevail over the other in the dispute. Any father seeking his "rights" in such a case is claiming that his desires should not merely *equal* but *supersede* those of the mother. That is, what is being sought in father's-rights cases is not equality for fathers but the *privileging* of paternal interests.

The imagination of the father as not merely half-partner in the creation of life but the true parent of the child is a construction that has deep roots in Western culture. In *The Furies*, which dramatizes the triumph of rational, impartial Apollonic justice over matriarchal "blood" justice, Aeschylus has Apollo argue, pointing to the motherless Pallas Athene, who sprang fully formed from the head of Zeus, that the "true parent" is "he who mounts":

> The mother is no parent of that which is called
> her child, but only nurse of the new-planted seed
> that grows. The parent is he who mounts. A stranger she
> preserves a stranger's seed, if no god interfere.
> I will show you proof of what I have explained. There can
> be a father without any mother. There she stands,
> the living witness, daughter of Olympian Zeus,
> she who was never fostered in the dark of the womb
> yet such a child as no goddess could bring to birth.[60]

James Hillman has argued that the Genesis story, which reverses the actualities of birth, making the "male . . . the precondition of the female and the ground of its possibility rather than vice versa," is another version of the "male as true parent" fantasy.[61] And certainly the dominant seventeenth-century account of reproduction, which spruces up the Aristotelian theory of generation with modern, mechanistic dress, is another.

From Aristotle to contemporary representations of the romance of the sperm and the egg,[62] the male contribution has been portrayed as the "effective and active" element in reproduction,[63] the female as passive, unformed matter, waiting to be individuated and vivified by the valiant sperm who wins her. But the mechanistic theory of preformation and embodiment went still further, representing the female body not even as providing the *material* stuff out of which the human being is formed (Aristotle's view), but merely as a *container* for the housing and incubation of already formed human beings, originally placed in Adam's semen by God, and parceled out, over the ages, to all his male descendants.[64] In 1577 the Dutch microscopist Antonie van Leeuwenhoek received what was for him decisive confirmation of this theory, when he discovered tiny tadpole-like creatures—"animalcules"—in the semen of male animals. He declared that this discovery empirically established Aristotle's intuition "that it is exclusively the male semen that forms the fetus, and that all that the woman may contribute only serves to receive the semen and feed it."[65] The imagination of woman as fetal incubator, in disturbing ascendance today, and of male as true parent (clearly attempting a comeback) has, then, deep historical roots.

In 1976 the Supreme Court clearly and resoundingly rejected the father's-rights argument, ruling in *Planned Parenthood of Central Missouri v. Danforth* that a spouse has no right that competes with, balances, or limits the woman's right to choose abortion. The court recognized both "the deep and proper concern and interest that a devoted and protective husband has in his wife's pregnancy and in the growth and development of the fetus" *and* the fact that an implication of the *Danforth* ruling (as of *Roe*) was that there would be cases when the mother might act unilaterally, without the approval of her husband. But the court insisted that since "only one of the two marriage partners can prevail" and since "it is the woman who physically bears the child and who is the more directly and immediately affected by the pregnancy . . . the balance weighs in her favor."[66]

The seemingly incontrovertible fact that only the mother experiences pregnant *embodiment* (obscured by the current fashion of speaking of *couples* as pregnant) is a powerful impediment to the father's-rights position, as those who have brought suit against their wives have obviously recognized, judging from the rhetoric and strategy of their arguments. Listen, for example, to Erin Conn, one of James Bopp's clients, as he describes his case on a "Nightline" show of July, 1988:

> My rights—I'm the—father of the child. My wife and I were joined in matrimony, and there's a bond there which makes me the father of the children that come out of our family. God—you know, the way the system's set up, the woman carries the child. And if I could carry the child, I would. But that's not the way the system's set up. But the thing is, that after that child is born, half of that child—part of that child is me. And I'm part of that child. And I feel like by her having the right to abort that child is her having the right to destroy a part of me without me having any say-so. And—she—you know, she wants control of her body. But what about me? Am I not allowed to have control of my body? That baby is a part of my body also.[67]

For Erin Conn, the biological reality of pregnancy is described as "the way the system's set up." This mechanistic imagery, I would suggest, although instinctively rather than methodically chosen by Conn, is not accidental. Conn has inchoately recognized that he must divest pregnancy of all emotional, spiritual, religious significance, of all evocation of hardship or burden, of all connection with the *experience* of the pregnant woman. He must turn the fact that women bear children into merely one instance of the impersonal, arbitrary functioning of an impersonal, arbitrary "system." In this imagination of things, there are no female subjects, only "carriers" (as Conn puts it) of fetuses, and the only true loci of subjective experience are the men who (it is implied) have been so cruelly and unfairly excluded (by the "system") from serving as "carriers." It's been "set up" that way; what's a poor fellow to do?

It is easy, of course, for Conn to say that if he *could* carry the child, he would—for he can't. But details like this pale alongside Conn's impassioned description of himself as so intertwined and interconnected with the fetus that not only is *he* "part of that child"—which is true—but *the child* is a "part of [Conn's] body" as well—which is not true. The slippage from father-as-part-of-the-child to child-as-part-of-the-father allows Conn actually to evoke the image—emotional, if not visual—of himself as pregnant, and from there to appropriate and emotionally manipulate the rhetoric of the pro-choice movement (and indeed of his own wife's case): "She wants control of her body. But what about me? Am I not allowed to have control of my body?" Such exploitation of ideas that feminists have introduced to the culture is a typical strategy of father's-rights arguments. In a September, 1989, hearing, one litigant went so far as to claim—shamelessly equating his situation with that of a woman whose body has been invaded against her will—that he would feel "raped of his reproductive rights" if he lost the case.[68]

Such rhetoric attempts to strangle feminism with its own rope ("reproductive rights") and to win sympathy for the man as brutalized "rape" victim. More deeply, it attempts to create an image of the man as *woman* (that is, as women have been imagined in our culture). As "woman" he can lay claim to sensitivity, nurturing instinct, tenderness, and caring—the construction of subjectivity that has been assigned to us, and in many people's minds the justification for privileging maternal over paternal claims. To win father's-rights cases, that justification must be undercut; thus, the men who have brought these cases to court have rarely been ashamed to cry, to speak of their helplessness, to "feminize" themselves. "I just felt helpless," said Gary Bell, describing his feelings after his girlfriend had an abortion. "I cried for hours. I hurt so bad inside."[69]

The strategy is to underscore that men have tender feelings too, especially tender feelings of a parental nature. That they *do* have such feelings (and many others discouraged from full expression by dominant Western constructions of masculinity) is indisputably true. My point, once again—as in my argument concerning fetal rights—is not to dehumanize men or challenge their claims to enhanced subjectivity, but to point out the corresponding price that *women's* subjectivity has been required to pay. In the father's-rights cases, every assertion of male feeling has been accompanied by a corresponding denial of *female* sensibility; every attempt to prove that men can be nurturers, too, has involved an attempted discreditation of the *woman's* nurturing capabilities—for instance, picturing her as lacking the qualities of caring, selflessness, and so forth that are required of a "true parent." While the men describe themselves as tender flowers, easily bruised and damaged, the women are portrayed as cold, ruthless destroyers of fetal life, running rough-shod over paternal sensibilities.

In one of the most striking of these cases, an Indiana man sought an injunction prohibiting his girlfriend's abortion, arguing that her reasons for wanting an abortion were that "she wishes to look nice in a bathing suit this summer . . . not to be pregnant in the sum-mertime . . . and not to share the petitioner with the baby." The judge granted the man's petition (without hearing from the woman), ruling that since the woman was not in school, was un-employed, and was living with her mother, "the continuance of her pregnancy would not interfere with either her employment or ed-ucation." Moreover, he went on, "The appearance and demeanor of the respondent . . . indicated that she is a very pleasant young lady, slender in stature, healthy, and well able to carry a baby to delivery without an undue burden."[70] Are we in a courtroom, or at an auction for prize heifers?

RECLAIMING REPRODUCTIVE SUBJECTIVITY

The future of *Roe v. Wade* is now the central cultural arena for the battle over reproductive control. In this essay, however, I have emphasized the necessity of locating the struggle for abortion rights in a broader context. What gets obscured when abortion rights are considered in abstraction from issues involving forced medical treat-ment, legal and social interference in the management of preg-nancy, and so forth, is the fact that it is not only women's repro-ductive rights that are currently being challenged but women's status as *subjects*, within a system in which—for better or worse—the protection of "the subject" remains a central value. What also may get obscured are the interlocking and mutually supporting effacements of subjectivity that are involved when the woman is perceived as a racial or economic "other" as well. So long as the debate over reproductive control is conceptualized solely in the dominant terms of the abortion debate—that is, as a conflict be-tween the fetus's right to life and the woman's right to choose—we are fooled into thinking that it is only the fetus whose ethical and legal status is at issue. The pregnant woman (whose ethical and legal status as a person is not constructed as a question in the abortion debate, and which most people wrongly assume is fully protected legally) is seen as fighting, not for her *personhood*, but "only" for her right to control her reproductive destiny.

The nature of pregnancy is such, however, that to deprive the woman of control over her reproductive life—whether by means of involuntary or coerced sterilization, court-ordered cesarean, or forbidden abortion—is necessarily also to mount an assault on her personal integrity and autonomy (the essence of personhood in our culture) and to treat her merely as pregnant *res extensa*, material incubator of fetal subjectivity. Unfortunately, feminists have in the past sometimes colluded in such constructions, arguing that reproduction and pregnancy are "functions" that are disengagable from the being of the subject and—like all alienated labor—amenable to being sold or rented to another. Over time, the severe limitations of this model, crystallized for many feminists by the "Baby M"/Mary Beth Whitehead surrogacy case, have become clear. It is crucial, I believe, that we now shift our discourse and strategies away from an abstract rhetoric of choice to one focused on (1) exposing the contradictions in our legal tradition regarding bodily integrity and insisting that women's equal protection under the law requires that they be resolved,[71] and (2) challenging the fetal-container conception, by reclaiming (from the right wing, which now holds a monopoly on such ideas) the view of pregnancy and abortion as *experientially* profound events. Only on the basis of such a reclamation can we assert women's moral authority, not only by virtue of our distinctive embodiment but also by virtue of our social histories, to adjudicate the complex ethical dilemmas that arise out of our reproductivity.

The foregoing contains several notions that may give contemporary feminists pause, and that require some further explanation. First, there is the problematic notion of women's "experience," and the concomitant danger of essentializing the experiences of some groups of women while effacing the histories and experiences of others. Although I acknowledge that danger, I believe that invoking women's embodied experience need not be equivalent to an alliance with "essentialism," so long as we remain mindful of the historical, racial, and cultural diversity of that experience—for example, so long as we recognize the different social histories within which the freedom and economic conditions that permit women to *have* children have been as tenuous as the right *not* to have them. At the same time, consciousness of our diversity ought not to be permitted to dilute recognition that, *as women*, we *all* have an "authority of experience" that men lack, and that gives us "a privileged critical location from which to speak" concerning reproduction.[72] Women's varied historical experiences of reproduction and birth—such as those described by Emily Martin[73] and Angela Davis,[74] and including the experiences of the infertile and the voluntarily childless—provide such locations of authority for us. So, too, do more philosophical, reconstructive accounts, such as Iris Young's study of "pregnant embodiment."[75]

Feminists may be made queasy, too, by the idea of emphasizing the experiential significance of pregnancy and birth, out of a fear of the conceptual proximity of such notions to constructions of mothering as the one true destiny for women. I believe, however, that we stand a better chance of successfully contesting such ideology if we engage in the construction of a public, feminist discourse on pregnancy and birth rather than leaving it in the hands of the "pro-lifers." It now seems to me, for example, that feminists should never have permitted debate over the status of the fetus to have achieved center stage in the public imagination, but ought, rather, to have attempted to preempt that debate with a strong *feminist* perspective acknowledging and articulating the ethical and emotional value of the fetus.[76] (I suspect that we would have developed such a perspective if African American women, with their historical experience of having not only their bodies but their children appropriated from them, had played a more central role in framing the rhetoric and arguments of earlier feminist politics.) Granting value, even personhood, to the fetus does not make social control of women's reproduction any less problematic, as I have argued in this essay. Attempts to *devalue* fetal life, on the other hand, have fed powerfully into the right-wing imagination of a possible world in which women would be callously and casually scraping fetuses out of their bodies like leftovers off a plate. This image—so cruelly unrepresentative of most women's experiences—must be challenged, must be shown to be a projection of "evil mother" archetypes, reflective of deep cultural *anxieties* about women's autonomy rather than the *realities* of its exercise.

And, finally, there is the currently problematic status of concepts such as authority and the subject, concepts which have played a crucial role in Western modernity but are now in various philosophical and literary quarters being declared decentered, dying, or dead. This is not the place to detail those arguments. But it is easy, I believe, to call for the wholesale deconstruction of concepts such as subjectivity, authority, and identity only so long as we remain on the plane of high theory, where they function as abstractions. Once we begin to examine the role played by such concepts as they are institutionally and socially embodied in contexts such as law and medicine, in which the philosophical blueprint is transformed into real social architecture, a different agenda may suggest itself. This is what I have argued in this essay with regard to the politics and rhetoric of subjectivity as they are played out in the arena of the current legal and social battle over reproductive control.

Within this battle, we cannot afford, whether in the interests of theoretical avant-gardism or political correctness, to abandon conceptions such as subjectivity, authority, embodied consciousness, and personal integrity. But this does not mean that we will be reproducing them in precisely the form in which we have inherited them. We need to remember that when poststructuralist writers declare that the "author" or "man" (or "metaphysics" or "philosophy") is dead, they refer to conceptions that were historically developed by European men, under conditions of their cultural dominance. Under those conditions, subjectivity took a very particular form by virtue of the experiences excluded from it. Iris Young's study of pregnant embodiment, for example, suggests that pregnancy makes uniquely available (although it does not guarantee) a very different experience of the relationship between mind and body, inner and outer, self and other than that presumed by Descartes, Hobbes, Locke, and other architects of the modernist subject. The conception of autonomy assumed by that model, for example, is challenged by an embodiment that literally houses "otherness" within the self.

Young's argument makes us aware of the fact that invoking the authority of marginalized subjects may ultimately result in a reconstruction of subjectivity itself. This is not to say that the (historical) subjectivities of subordinate groups have developed fully *outside* of or unaffected by dominant constructions of the subject. (It is not as though, for example, women have not sought autonomy or cherished possibilities for individuation and self-development.) But our relation to these values has been different: more ambivalent, less purely identified; one could even say, less oppressed.[77] Historically excluded from participation in the making of philosophy, law, and politics, we have nonetheless created culture in our own assigned "spheres," and these cultures now provide a valuable resource for us as we begin to make philosophy, law, and politics in the public arena.

Hunger as Ideology

In a television commercial, two little French girls are shown dressing up in the feathery finery of their mother's clothes. They are exquisite little girls, flawless and innocent, and the scene emphasizes both their youth and the natural sense of style often associated with French women. (The ad is done in French, with subtitles.) One of the girls, spying a picture of the other girl's mother, exclaims breathlessly, "Your mother, she is so slim, so beautiful! Does she eat?" The daughter, giggling, replies: "Silly, just not so much," and displays her mother's helper, a bottle of FibreThin. "Aren't you jealous?" the friend asks. Dimpling, shy yet self-possessed, deeply knowing, the daughter answers, "Not if I know her secrets."

Admittedly, women are continually bombarded with advertisements and commercials for weight-loss products and programs, but this commercial makes many of us particularly angry. On the most obvious level, the commercial affronts with its suggestion that young girls begin early in learning to control their weight, and with its romantic mystification of diet pills as part of the obscure, eternal arsenal of feminine arts to be passed from generation to generation. This romanticization, as often is the case in American commercials, trades on our continuing infatuation with (what we imagine to be) the civility, tradition, and savoir-faire of "Europe" (seen as the stylish antithesis to our own American clumsiness, aggressiveness, crudeness). The little girls are fresh and demure, in a way that is undefinably but absolutely recognizably "European"—as defined, that is, within the visual vocabulary of popular American culture. And FibreThin, in this commercial, is nothing so crass and "medical" and pragmatic (read: American) as a diet pill, but a mysterious, prized (and, it is implied, age-old) "secret," known only to those with both history and taste.

But we expect such hype from contemporary advertisements. Far more unnerving is the psychological acuity of the ad's focus, not on the size and shape of bodies, but on a certain *subjectivity*, represented by the absent but central figure of the mother, the woman who eats, only "not so much." We never see her picture; we are left to imagine her ideal beauty and slenderness. But what she looks like is not important, in any case; what is important is the fact that she has achieved what we might call a "cool" (that is, casual) relation to food. She is not starving herself (an obsession, indicating the continuing power of food), but neither is she desperately and shamefully binging in some private corner. Eating has become, for her, no big deal. In its evocation of the lovely French mother who doesn't eat much, the commercial's metaphor of European "difference" reveals itself as a means of representing that enviable and truly foreign "other": the woman for whom food is merely ordinary, who can take it or leave it.

Another version, this time embodied by a sleek, fashionable African American woman, playfully promotes Virginia Slims Menthol (Figure 7). This ad, which appeared in *Essence* magazine, is one of a series specifically targeted at the African American female consumer. In contrast to the Virginia Slims series concurrently appearing in *Cosmo* and *People*, a series which continues to associate the product with historically expanded opportunities for women ("You've come a long way, baby" remains the motif and slogan), Virginia Slims pitches to the *Essence* reader by mocking solemnity and self-importance *after* the realization of those opportunities: "Why climb the ladder if you're not going to enjoy the view?" "Big girls don't cry. They go shopping." And, in the variant depicted in Figure 7: "Decisions are easy. When I get to a fork in the road, I eat."

Arguably, the general subtext meant to be evoked by these ads is the failure of the dominant, white culture (those who *don't* "enjoy the view") to relax and take pleasure in success. The upwardly mobile black consumer, it is suggested, will do it with more panache, with more cool—and of course with a cool, Virginia Slims Menthol in hand. In this particular ad, the speaker scorns obsessiveness, not only over professional or interpersonal decision-making, but over food as well. Implicitly contrasting herself to those who worry and fret, she presents herself as utterly "easy" in her relationship with food. Unlike the FibreThin mother, she eats any-

FIGURE 7

time she wants. But *like* the FibreThin mother (and this is the key similarity for my purposes), she has achieved a state beyond craving. Undominated by unsatisfied, internal need, she eats not only freely but without deep desire and without apparent consequence. It's "easy," she says. Presumably, without those forks in the road she might forget about food entirely.

The Virginia Slims woman is a fantasy figure, her cool attitude toward food as remote from the lives of most contemporary African American women as from any others. True, if we survey cultural attitudes toward women's appetites and body size, we find great variety—a variety shaped by ethnic, national, historical, class, and other factors. My eighty-year-old father, the child of immigrants, asks at the end of every meal if I "got enough to eat"; he considers me skinny unless I am plump by my own standards. His attitude reflects not only memories of economic struggle and a heritage of Jewish-Russian preference for zaftig women, but the lingering, well into this century, of a once more general Anglo-Saxon cultural appreciation for the buxom woman. In the mid-nineteenth century, hotels and bars were adorned with Bouguereau-inspired paintings of voluptuous female nudes; Lillian Russell, the most photographed woman in America in 1890, was known and admired for her hearty appetite, ample body (over two hundred pounds at the height of her popularity), and "challenging, fleshly arresting" beauty.[1] Even as such fleshly challenges became less widely appreciated in the twentieth century, men of Greek, Italian, Eastern European, and African descent, influenced by their own distinctive cultural heritages, were still likely to find female voluptuousness appealing. And even in the late 1960s and early 1970s, as Twiggy and Jean Shrimpton began to set a new norm for ultra-slenderness, lesbian cultures in the United States continued to be accepting—even celebrating—of fleshy, space-claiming female bodies.

Even more examples could be produced, of course, if we cast our glance more widely over the globe and back through history. Many cultures, clearly, have revered expansiveness in women's bodies and appetites. Some still do. But in the 1980s and 1990s an increasingly universal equation of slenderness with beauty and success has rendered the competing claims of cultural diversity ever feebler. Men who were teenagers from the mid-seventies on, whatever their ethnic roots or economic class, are likely to view long, slim legs, a flat stomach, and a firm rear end as essentials of female beauty.

Unmuscled heft is no longer as acceptable as it once was in lesbian communities. Even Miss Soviet Union has become lean and tight, and the robust, earthy actresses who used to star in Russian films have been replaced by slender, Westernized types.

Arguably, a case could once be made for a contrast between (middle-class, heterosexual) white women's obsessive relations with food and a more accepting attitude toward women's appetites within African American communities. But in the nineties, features on diet, exercise, and body-image problems have grown increasingly prominent in magazines aimed at African American readers, reflecting the cultural reality that for most women today—whatever their racial or ethnic identity, and increasingly across class and sexual-orientation differences as well—free and easy relations with food are at best a relic of the past. (More frequently in *Essence* than in *Cosmo*, there may be a focus on health problems associated with overweight among African Americans, in addition to the glamorization of slenderness.) Almost all of us who can afford to be eating well are dieting—and hungry—almost all of the time.

It is thus Dexatrim, not Virginia Slims, that constructs the more realistic representation of women's subjective relations with food. In Dexatrim's commercial that shows a woman, her appetite-suppressant worn off, hurtling across the room, drawn like a living magnet to the breathing, menacing refrigerator, hunger is represented as an insistent, powerful force with a life of its own. This construction reflects the physiological reality of dieting, a state the body is unable to distinguish from starvation.[2] And it reflects its psychological reality as well; for dieters, who live in a state of constant denial, food is a perpetually beckoning presence, its power growing ever greater as the sanctions against gratification become more stringent. A slender body may be attainable through hard work, but a "cool" relation to food, the true "secret" of the beautiful "other" in the FibreThin commercial, is a tantalizing reminder of what lies beyond the reach of the inadequate and hungry self. (Of course, as the ads suggest, a psychocultural transformation remains possible, through FibreThin and Virginia Slims.)

PSYCHING OUT THE FEMALE CONSUMER

Sometimes, when I am analyzing and interpreting advertisements and commercials in class, students accuse me of a kind of paranoia about the significance of these representations as carriers and re-producers of culture. After all, they insist, these are just images, not "real life"; any fool knows that advertisers manipulate reality in the service of selling their products. I agree that on some level we "know" this. However, were it a meaningful or *usable* knowledge, it is unlikely that we would be witnessing the current spread of diet and exercise mania across racial and ethnic groups, or the explosion of technologies aimed at bodily "correction" and "enhancement."

Jean Baudrillard offers a more accurate description of our cultural estimation of the relation and relative importance of image and "reality." In *Simulations*, he recalls the Borges fable in which the cartographers of a mighty empire draw up a map so detailed that it ends up exactly covering the territory of the empire, a map which then frays and disintegrates as a symbol of the coming decline of the empire it perfectly represents. Today, Baudrillard suggests, the fable might be inverted: it is no longer the territory that provides the model for the map, but the map that defines the territory; and it is the *territory* "whose shreds are slowly rotting across the map." Thinking further, however, he declares even the inverted fable to be "useless." For what it still assumes is precisely that which is being lost today—namely, the distinction between the territory and its map, between reality and appearance. Today, all that we experience as meaningful are appearances.[3]

Thus, we all "know" that Cher and virtually every other female star over the age of twenty-five is the plastic product of numerous cosmetic surgeries on face and body. But, in the era of the "hyperreal" (as Baudrillard calls it), such "knowledge" is as faded and frayed as the old map in the Borges tale, unable to cast a shadow of doubt over the dazzling, compelling, authoritative images themselves. Like the knowledge of our own mortality when we are young and healthy, the knowledge that Cher's physical appearance is fabricated is an empty abstraction; it simply does not compute. It is the created image that has the hold on our most vibrant, immediate sense of what *is*, of what matters, of what we must pursue for ourselves.

In *constructing* the images, of course, continual use is made of knowledge (or at least what is imagined to be knowledge) of consumers' lives. Indeed, a careful reading of contemporary advertisements reveals continual and astute manipulation of problems that psychology and the popular media have targeted as characteristic dilemmas of the "contemporary woman," who is beset by conflicting role demands and pressures on her time. "Control"—a word that rarely used to appear in commercial contexts—has become a common trope in advertisements for products as disparate as mascara ("Perfect Pen Eyeliner. Puts *you* in control. And isn't that nice for a change?") and cat-box deodorant ("Control. I strive for it. My cat achieves it"). *"Soft felt tip gives you absolute control of your line"* (Figure 8). It is virtually impossible to glance casually at this ad without reading "line" as "life"—which is, of course, the subliminal coding such ads intend. "Mastery" also frequently figures in ads for cosmetics and hair products: "Master your curls with new Adaptable Perm." The rhetoric of these ads is interestingly contrasted to the rhetoric of mastery and control directed at male consumers. Here, the message is almost always one of mastery and control over *others* rather than the self: "Now it's easier than ever to achieve a position of power in Manhattan" (an ad for a Manhattan health club), or "Don't just serve. Rule" (an ad for Speedo tennis shoes).

Advertisers are aware, too, of more specific *ways* in which women's lives are out of control, including our well-documented food disorders; they frequently incorporate the theme of food obsession into their pitch. The Sugar Free Jell-O Pudding campaign exemplifies a typical commercial strategy for exploiting women's eating problems while obscuring their dark realities. (The advertisers themselves would put this differently, of course.) In the "tip of my tongue" ad (Figure 9), the obsessive mental state of the compulsive eater is depicted fairly accurately, guaranteeing recognition from people with that problem: "If I'm not eating dessert, I'm talking about it. If I'm not talking about it, I'm eating it. And I'm always thinking about it . . . It's just always on my mind."

These thoughts, however, belong to a slender, confident, and—most important—decidedly not depressed individual, whose upbeat, open, and accepting attitude toward her constant hunger is far from that of most women who eat compulsively. "The inside of a binge," Geneen Roth writes, "is deep and dark. At the core . . . is deprivation, scarcity, a feeling that you can never get enough."[4] A student described her hunger as "a black hole that I had to fill up." In the Sugar Free Jell-O ad, by contrast, the mental state depicted is most like that of a growing teenage boy; to be continually hungry

FIGURE 8

FIGURE 9

is represented as a normal, if somewhat humorous and occasionally annoying, state with no disastrous physical or emotional consequences.

The use of a male figure is one strategy, in contemporary ads, for representing compulsive eating as "natural" and even lovable. Men are *supposed* to have hearty, even voracious, appetites. It is a mark of the manly to eat spontaneously and expansively, and manliness is a frequent commercial code for amply portioned products: "Manwich," "Hungry Man Dinners," "Manhandlers." Even when men advertise diet products (as they more frequently do, now that physical perfection is increasingly being demanded of men as well as women), they brag about their appetites, as in the Tommy Lasorda commercials for Slim-Fast, which feature three burly football players (their masculinity beyond reproach) declaring that if Slim-Fast can satisfy *their* appetites, it can satisfy anyone's. The displacement of the female by a male figure (displacement when the targeted consumer is in fact a woman) thus dispels thoughts of addiction, danger, unhappiness, and replaces them with a construction of compulsive eating (or thinking about food) as benign indulgence of a "natural" inclination. Consider the ad shown in Figure 10, depicting a male figure diving with abandon into the "tempered-to-full-flavor-consistency" joys of Häagen-Dazs deep chocolate.

Emotional heights, intensity, love, and thrills: it is women who habitually seek such experiences from food and who are most likely to be overwhelmed by their relationship to food, to find it dangerous and frightening (especially rich, fattening, soothing food like ice cream). The marketers of Häagen-Dazs know this; they are aware of the well-publicized prevalence of compulsive eating and binge behaviors among women. Indeed, this ad exploits, with artful precision, exactly the sorts of associations that are likely to resonate with a person for whom eating is invested with deep emotional meaning. Why, then, a male diver? In part, as I have been arguing, the displacement is necessary to insure that the grim actualities of women's eating problems remain obscured; the point, after all, is to sell ice cream, not to remind people of how dangerous food actually *is* for women. Too, the advertisers may reckon that women might enjoy seeing a man depicted in swooning surrender to ice cream,

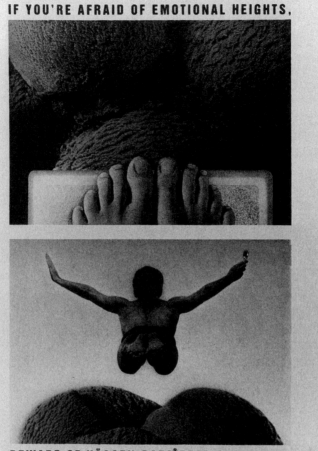

IF YOU'RE AFRAID OF EMOTIONAL HEIGHTS,

BEWARE OF HÄAGEN-DAZS®DEEP CHOCOLATE.

If intensity scares you, great pleasure upsets you or love makes you flee, please don't try our new Deep Chocolate Ice Creams. The shock of real Callebaut Belgian chocolate might be a tad overwhelming. And even if you can handle the thrill of Deep Chocolate alone, beware of Deep Chocolate Peanut Butter and Deep Chocolate Fudge. Or Belgian Chocolate Chocolate, found exclusively in our Shoppes. Häagen-Dazs Deep Chocolate. Surrender or stay away.

Available at participating Häagen-Dazs Ice Cream Shoppes and your favorite grocery.

© 1989 The Häagen-Dazs Company, Inc.

Häagen-Dazs

DEEP CHOCOLATE
THE FINEST ICE CREAM IN THE WORLD™

FIGURE 10

as a metaphor for the emotional surrender that so many women crave from their husbands and lovers.

I would argue, however, that more than a purely profit-maximizing, ideologically neutral, Madison Avenue mentality is at work in these ads. They must also be considered as gender ideology—that is, as specifically (consciously or unconsciously) servicing the cultural reproduction of gender difference and gender inequality, quite independent of (although at times coinciding with) marketing concerns. As gender ideology, the ads I have been discussing are not distinctively contemporary but continue a well-worn representational tradition, arguably inaugurated in the Victorian era, in which the depiction of women eating, particularly in sensuous surrender to rich, exciting food, is taboo.[5]

In exploring this dimension, we might begin by attempting to imagine an advertisement depicting a young, attractive woman indulging as freely, as salaciously as the man in the Post cereal ad shown in Figure 11. Such an image would violate deeply sedimented expectations, would be experienced by many as disgusting and transgressive. When women are positively depicted as sensuously voracious about food (almost never in commercials, and only very rarely in movies and novels), their hunger for food is employed solely as a metaphor for their sexual appetite. In the eating scenes in *Tom Jones* and *Flashdance*, for example, the heroines' unrestrained delight in eating operates as sexual foreplay, a way of prefiguring the abandon that will shortly be expressed in bed. Women are permitted to lust for food itself only when they are pregnant or when it is clear they have been near starvation—as, for example, in *McCabe and Mrs. Miller*, in the scene in which Mrs. Miller, played by Julie Christie, wolfs down half a dozen eggs and a bowl of beef stew before the amazed eyes of McCabe. Significantly, the scene serves to establish Mrs. Miller's "manliness"; a woman who eats like this is to be taken seriously, is not to be trifled with, the movie suggests.

The metaphorical situation is virtually inverted in the representation of male eaters. Although voracious eating may occasionally code male sexual appetite (as in *Tom Jones*), we frequently also find

FIGURE 11

sexual appetite operating as a metaphor for eating pleasure. In commercials that feature male eaters, the men are shown in a state of wild, sensual transport over heavily frosted, rich, gooey desserts. Their total lack of control is portrayed as appropriate, even adorable; the language of the background jingle is unashamedly aroused, sexual and desiring:

> I'm thinking about you the whole day through [crooned to a Pillsbury cake]. I've got a passion for you.
>
> You're my one and only, my creamy deluxe [Betty Crocker frosting].
>
> You butter me up, I can't resist, you leave me breathless [Betty Crocker frosting].
>
> Your brownies give me fever. Your cake gives me chills [assorted Betty Crocker mixes].

I'm a fool for your chocolate. I'm wild, crazy, out of control [assorted Betty Crocker mixes].

I've got it bad, and I should know, 'cause I crave it from my head right down to my potato [for Pillsbury Potatoes Au Gratin].

Can't help myself. It's Duncan Hines [assorted cake mixes] and nobody else.

In these commercials food is constructed as a sexual object of desire, and eating is legitimated as much more than a purely nutritive activity. Rather, food is *supposed* to supply sensual delight and succor—not as metaphorically standing for something else, but as an erotic experience in itself. Women are permitted such gratification from food only in measured doses. In another ad from the Diet Jell-O series, eating is metaphorically sexualized: "I'm a girl who just can't say no. I insist on dessert," admits the innocently dressed but flirtatiously posed model (Figure 12). But at the same time that eating is mildly sexualized in this ad, it is also contained. She is permitted to "feel good about saying 'Yes'"—but ever so demurely, and to a harmless low-calorie product. Transgression beyond such limits is floridly sexualized, as an act of "cheating" (Figure 13). Women may be encouraged (like the man on the Häagen-Dazs high board) to "dive in"—not, however, into a dangerous pool of Häagen-Dazs Deep Chocolate, but for a "refreshing dip" into Weight Watchers linguini (Figure 14). Targeted at the working woman ("Just what you need to revive yourself from the workday routine"), this ad also exploits the aquatic metaphor to conjure up images of female independence and liberation ("Isn't it just like us to make waves?").

All of this may seem peculiarly contemporary, revolving as it does around the mass marketing of diet products. But in fact the same metaphorical universe, as well as the same practical prohibitions against female indulgence (for, of course, these ads are not only selling products but teaching appropriate behavior) were characteristic of Victorian gender ideology. Victorians did not have *Cosmo* and television, of course. But they did have conduct manuals, which warned elite women of the dangers of indulgent and overstimulating eating and advised how to consume in a feminine way (as little as possible and with the utmost precaution against unseemly show of desire). *Godey's Lady's Book* warned that it was vulgar for women to load their plates; young girls were admonished

FIGURE 12

You'll think
you're cheating
But you know you're not...
It's Wonder® Light bread.
Should you tell?
Should you tell your
friend that each full-size slice
of great tasting Wonder
Light is only 40 calories?
You can't just let her
suffer through carrot sticks
and rice cakes... Can you?

WONDER LIGHT   WONDER LIGHT

The lighter slice of America.

FIGURE 13

to "be frugal and plain in your tastes."[6] Detailed lexicons offered comparisons of the erotic and cooling effects of various foods, often with specific prescriptions for each sex.[7] Sexual metaphors permeate descriptions of potential transgression:

> Every luxurious table is a scene of temptation, which it requires fixed principles and an enlightened mind to withstand. . . . Nothing can be more seducing to the appetite than this arrangement of the viands which compose a feast; as the stomach is filled, and the natural desire for food subsides, the palate is tickled by more delicate and relishing dishes until it is betrayed into excess.[8]

Today, the same metaphors of temptation and fall appear frequently in advertisements for diet products (see Figure 15). And in the Victorian era, as today, the forbiddenness of rich food often resulted in private binge behavior, described in *The Bazaar Book of Decorum* (1870) as the "secret luncheon," at which "many of the most abstemious at the open dinner are the most voracious . . . swallowing cream tarts by the dozen, and caramels and chocolate drops by the pound's weight."[9]

The emergence of such rigid and highly moralized restrictions on female appetite and eating are, arguably, part of what Bram Dijkstra

FIGURE 14

Dive in.

Just what you need to revive yourself from the workday routine. A refreshing dip into our new Seafood Linguini. Generous chunks of seafood with whole shrimp, together with tender cuts of broccoli florets, carrots and zucchini. All in a light garlic sauce, and served amid a sea of linguini.

Weight Watchers Seafood Linguini. Something deliciously different to add to your schedule.

Isn't it just like us to make waves?

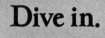

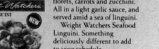

© 1987, Weight Watchers Intl., Inc., owner of trademark.

This is living!

FIGURE 15

has interpreted as a nineteenth-century "cultural ideological counter-offensive" against the "new woman" and her challenge to prevailing gender arrangements and their constraints on women.[10] Mythological, artistic, polemical, and scientific discourses from many cultures and eras certainly suggest the symbolic potency of female hunger as a cultural metaphor for unleashed female power and desire, from the blood-craving Kali (who in one representation is shown eating her own entrails) to the *Malleus Malificarum* ("For the sake of fulfilling the mouth of the womb, [witches] consort even with the devil") to Hall and Oates's contemporary rock lyrics: "Oh, oh, here she comes, watch out boys, she'll chew you up."[11]

In *Tom Jones* and *Flashdance*, the trope of female hunger as female sexuality is embodied in attractive female characters; more frequently, however, female hunger as sexuality is represented by Western culture in misogynist images permeated with terror and loathing rather than affection or admiration. In the figure of the man-eater the metaphor of the devouring woman reveals its deep psychological underpinnings. Eating is not really a metaphor for the sexual act; rather, the sexual act, when initiated and desired by a woman, is imagined as itself an act of eating, of incorporation and destruction of the object of desire. Thus, women's sexual appetites must be curtailed and controlled, because they threaten to deplete and consume the body and soul of the male. Such imagery, as Dijkstra has demonstrated, flourishes in the West in the art of the late nineteenth century. Arguably, the same cultural backlash (if not in the same form) operates today—for example, in the ascendancy of popular films that punish female sexuality and independence by rape and dismemberment (as in numerous slasher films), loss of family and children (*The Good Mother*), madness and death (*Fatal Attraction, Presumed Innocent*), and public humiliation and disgrace (*Dangerous Liaisons*).

Of course, Victorian prohibitions against women eating were not *only* about the ideology of gender. Or, perhaps better put, the ideology of gender contained other dimensions as well. The construction of "femininity" had not only a significant moral and sexual aspect (femininity as sexual passivity, timidity, purity, innocence) but a class dimension. In the reigning body symbolism of the day, a frail frame and lack of appetite signified not only spiritual transcendence of the desires of the flesh but *social* transcendence of the laboring, striving "economic" body. Then, as today, to be aristocratically cool and unconcerned with the mere facts of material survival was highly fashionable. The hungering bourgeois wished to appear, like the aristocrat, above the material desires that in fact ruled his life. The closest he could come was to possess a wife whose ethereal body became a sort of fashion statement of *his* aristocratic tastes. If he could not be or marry an aristocrat, he could have a wife who looked like one, a wife whose non-robust beauty and delicate appetite signified her lack of participation in the taxing "public sphere."[12]

MEN EAT AND WOMEN PREPARE

The metaphorical dualities at work here, whatever their class meanings, presuppose an idealized (and rarely actualized) gendered division of labor in which men strive, compete, and exert themselves in the public sphere while women are cocooned in the domestic arena (which is romanticized and mystified as a place of peace and leisure, and hence connotes transcendence of the laboring, bourgeois body). In the necessity to make such a division of labor appear natural we find another powerful ideological underpinning (perhaps the most important in the context of industrialized society) for the cultural containment of female appetite: the notion that women are most gratified by feeding and nourishing *others*, not themselves. As a literal activity, of course, women fed others long before the "home" came to be identified as women's special place; Caroline Bynum argues that there is reason to believe that food preparation was already a stereotypically female activity in the European Middle Ages.[13] But it was in the industrial era, with its idealization of the domestic arena as a place of nurture and comfort for men and children, that feeding others acquired the extended emotional meaning it has today.

In "An Ode to Mothers" columnist Bud Poloquin defines *Moms* as "those folks who, upon seeing there are only four pieces of pie for five people, promptly announce they never did care for the stuff."[14] Denial of self and the feeding of others are hopelessly enmeshed in this construction of the ideal mother, as they are in the nineteenth-century version of the ideal wife as "she who stands . . . famished before her husband, while he devours, stretched at ease, the produce of her exertions; waits his tardy permission without a word or a look of impatience, and feeds, with the humblest gratitude, and the shortest intermission of labor, on the scraps and offals which he disdains."[15] None of this self-sacrifice, however, is felt as such by the "paragon of womanhood" (as Charles Butler calls her), for it is here, in the care and feeding of others, that woman experiences the one form of desire that is appropriately hers: as Elias Canetti so succinctly puts it, "Her passion is to give food."[16]

Over a decade ago, John Berger trenchantly encapsulated the standard formula he saw as regulating the representation of gender difference, both throughout the history of art and in contemporary advertising: "Men act, and women appear."[17] Today, that opposition no longer seems to hold quite as rigidly as it once did (women are indeed objectified more than ever, but, in this image-dominated culture, men increasingly are too). But if this duality no longer strictly applies, the resilience of others is all the more instructive. Let me replace Berger's formulation with another, apparently more enduring one: "Men eat and women prepare." At least in the sphere of popular representations, this division of labor is as prescriptive in 1991 as in 1891. Despite the increasing participation of women of all ages and classes in the "public" sphere, her "private" role of nurturer remains ideologically intact.

To be sure, we have inherited some of these representations from a former era—for example, the plump, generous Mammys and Grandmas who symbolically have prepared so many products: Aunt Jemima, Mrs. Smith, Mrs. Paul, Grandma Brown. But our cultural penchant for nostalgia does not get us off the hook here. At the start of the 1990s (and this seems to be even more striking now than five years ago), popular representations almost never depict a man *preparing* food as an everyday activity, routinely performed in the unpaid service of others. Occasionally, men *are* shown serving food—in the role of butler or waiter. They may be depicted roasting various items around a campfire, barbecuing meat, preparing a salad for a special company dinner, or making *instant* coffee (usually in a getaway cabin or vacation boat). But all of these are nonroutine, and their exceptional nature is frequently underscored in the ad. In one commercial, a man fixes instant coffee to serve to his wife in bed on her birthday. "How tough can it be?" he asks. "She makes breakfast every morning." In another ad, a man is shown preparing pancakes for his son's breakfast (Figure 16). "My pancakes deserve the rich maple flavor of Log Cabin Syrup," reads the bold type, suggesting ("my pancakes") male proprietorship and ease in the kitchen. The visual image of the father lovingly serving the son undoubtedly destabilizes cultural stereotypes (racial as well as gendered). But in the smaller print below the image we are told that this is a "special moment" with his son. Immediately the destabilizing image reconfigures into a familiar one: like Dad's secret recipe for barbecue sauce, this father's pancakes make their appearance only on special occasions. Or perhaps it is the very fact that Dad is doing the cooking that *makes* this a significant, intimate occasion for sharing. (Imagine a woman instead of a man in the ad; would "special moment" not then seem odd?)

Continually, in representations that depict men preparing food, there will be a conspicuously absent wife or mother (for instance, in the hospital having a baby) who, it is implied, is *normally* re-

FIGURE 16

sponsible for the daily labor of food preparation and service. Even when men or boys are used to advertise convenience foods, the product has usually been left for them with expert instructions added by Mom. In the Jell-O Heritage ad (Figure 17), this absent maternal figure (whether mother or grandmother is not clear) appears in the small insert to the upper right of the larger image, which depicts a young man away at college, well supplied with Jell-O pudding snacks. Significantly (although somewhat absurdly), she is associated with the provision of a "strong foundation" by virtue of the fact that *she* prepares instant pudding from a mix rather than merely opening up an already prepared pudding snack. Jell-O, of course, could not present nostalgic images of Grandma preparing *real* "scratch" pudding, since it does not want to evoke longing for a time when women did not depend on its products. But in terms of the oppositions exploited in this ad, instant pudding works just as well; compared to flipping the lid off a pudding snack, preparing instant pudding *is* a laborious task. It thus belongs to women's world. Men are almost *never* shown lavishing time on cooking. *Real* coffee is always prepared by women, as are all the cakes and casseroles that require more than a moment to put together. When men *are* shown cooking an elaborate meal, it is always *with* one or two other yuppie men, converting the activity from an act of everyday service into a festive, "Big Chill" occasion. But even these representations are rare. In all the many dinner parties that Hope and Michael hosted on "Thirtysomething," no man has ever appeared in the kitchen except to sneak a bit of the meal being prepared by Hope, Nancy, and Melissa.

FOOD AND LOVE

At the beginning of the 1992 U.S. presidential campaign, Hillary Clinton, badgered by reporters' endless questions concerning her pursuit of a professional career, shot back defensively and sarcastically: "Well, I suppose I could have stayed home and baked cookies and had teas . . ." Media audiences never got to hear the end of her remark (or the questioning that preceded it); the "cookies and teas" sound-bite became *the* gender-transgression of the campaign, replayed over and over, and presented by opponents as evidence of Hillary's rabid feminism and disdain for traditional maternal

FIGURE 17

values. Rightly protesting this interpretation, Hillary Clinton tried to prove her true womanhood by producing her favorite recipe for oatmeal chocolate chip cookies. Barbara Bush, apparently feeling that a gauntlet had been thrown down, responded in kind with a richer, less fibre-conscious recipe of her own. Newspapers across the country asked readers to prepare both and vote on which First Lady had the better cookie.

   That the cookie itself should have become the symbol and center of the national debate about Hillary Clinton's adequacy as wife and mother is not surprising. Food is equated with maternal and wifely love throughout our culture. In nearly all commercials that feature men eating—such as the cake commercials whose sexualized rhetoric was quoted earlier—there is a woman in the background (either visible or implied) who has *prepared* the food. (The "Betty Crocker, You Sweet Talker" series has two women: the possessor of the clearly feminine hands offering the cakes, and Betty Crocker herself, to whom all the passionate croonings—"I'm a fool for your chocolate. I'm wild, crazy, out of control"—are addressed.) Most significantly, *always*, the woman in the background speaks the language of love and care through the offering of food: "Nothin' says lovin' like something from the oven"; "Give me that great taste of love"; "Nothing says 'Cookie, I love you' like Nestle's Toll House Cookies Do." In these commercials, male eating is inextricably tied to female offerings of love. This is not represented, however, as female self-abnegation. Rather, it is suggested that women receive *their* gratification through nourishing others, either in the old-fashioned way (taste and emotional pleasure) or in the health-conscious mode:

> *Her voice, heard off:* He's like a little boy—normally serious, *then* he eats English muffins with butter [shot of man's face transported with childlike delight] and *I* get to enjoy watching him. A little butter brings a lot of joy.
>
> *He:* What are you doing?
> *She:* I'm listening to your heart.
> *He:* What does it say?
> *She:* It says that it's glad that you've started jogging, and that you're eating healthier. It's happy that I'm giving us new Promise margarine. Eating foods low in cholesterol is good for you and your heart.
> *He:* Know what else is good for me?
> *She:* What?
> *He:* You.
> *She beams, snuggling deeper into man's chest.*

My analysis, I want to emphasize, is not meant to disparage caring for the physical and emotional well-being of others, "maternal" work that has been scandalously socially undervalued even as it has been idealized and sanctified. Nor am I counterposing to the argument of these ads the construction that women are simply oppressed by such roles. This would be untrue to the personal experiences of many women, including myself. I remember the pride and pleasure that radiated from my mother, who was anxious and unhappy in most other areas of her life, when her famous stuffed cabbage was devoured enthusiastically and in voluminous quantities by my father, my sisters, and me. As a little girl, I loved watching her roll each piece, enclosing just the right amount of filling, skillfully avoiding tearing the tender cabbage leaves as she folded them around the meat. I never felt so safe and secure as at those moments. She was visibly pleased when I asked her to teach me exactly how to make the dish and thrilled when I even went so far as to write the quantities and instructions down as she tried to formulate them into an official recipe (until then, it had been passed through demonstration from mother to daughter, and my mother considered that in writing it down I was conferring a higher status on it). Those periods in my life when I have found myself too busy writing, teaching, and traveling to find the time and energy to prepare special meals for people that I love have been periods when a deep aspect of my self has felt deprived, depressed.

Nor would I want my critique to be interpreted as effacing the collective, historical experiences of those groups, forced into servitude for the families of others, who have been systematically deprived of the freedom *to* care for their own families. Bell hooks points out, for example, that black women's creation of "home-place," of fragile and hard-won "spaces of care and nurturance" for the healing of deep wounds made by racism, sexism, and poverty, was less a matter of obedience to a tyrannical gender-norm than the construction of a "site of cultural resistance."[18] With this in mind, it is clear that the Jell-O Heritage ad discussed earlier is more complex than my interpretation has thus far allowed. Part of an extensive General Foods series aimed at the African American consumer and promoting America's historically black colleges, the ad's association of the maternal figure with "strong foundations" runs far deeper than a nostalgic evocation of Mom's traditional cooking. In this ad, the maternal figure is linked with a black "heritage," with the preservation and communication of culture.

However, at the same time that hooks urges that contemporary black culture should honor the black woman's history of service to her family and her community, she also cautions against the ideological construction of such service as woman's natural role. (Despite the pleasure I take in cooking, in relationships where it has been expected of me I have resented it deeply.) It is this construction that is reinforced in the representations I have been examining, through their failure to depict males as "naturally" fulfilling that role, and—more perniciously—through their failure to depict females as appropriate *recipients* of such care. Only occasionally are little girls represented as being *fed*; more often, they (but never little boys) are shown learning how to feed others (Figure 18). In this

FIGURE 18

way, caring is representationally "reproduced" as a quintessentially and exclusively female activity. It is significant and disquieting that the General Foods series does not include any ads that portray female students discovering their black heritage (or learning how to rely on convenience foods!) at college. It is possible that the ad series is very deliberate here, exploiting contemporary notions that the "crisis in black manhood" is the fault of black women and identifying its products with an imagined world in which opportunities for black men go hand in hand with "natural," prefeminist gender relations. Black men will find their way to college, it is suggested, so long as women remain in the background, encouraging and supporting rather than competing and undermining.

The ubiquitous configuration of woman-food-man, with food expressing the woman's love for the man and at the same time satisfying woman's desire to bestow love, establishes male hunger as thoroughly socially integrated into the network of heterosexual family and love relations. Men can eat *and* be loved; indeed, a central mode by which they receive love is through food from women. For women, by contrast (who are almost never shown being fed by others), eating—in the form of private, *self*-feeding—is represented as a *substitute* for human love. Weight Watchers transparently offers itself as such in its "Who says you can't live on love?" ad (Figure 19). In other ads, it offers its low-cal spaghetti sauce as "A Friend." Diet Coke, emphasizing the sexual, insists that "sometimes the best relationships are purely fizzical." Miracle Whip Light offers itself as "a light that turns you on."

Notice that in these ads there is no partner, visible or implied, offering the food and thus operating as the true bestower of "love." In many ads—virtually a genre, in fact—the absence of the partner is explicitly thematized, a central aspect of the narrative of the ad. One commercial features a woman in bed, on the phone, refusing date after date in favor of an evening alone with her ice-cream bon bons: "Your Highness? Not tonight!" "The inauguration? Another year!" In another, a woman admits to spending a lot of time alone with her "latest obsession," a chocolate drink, because it gives her "the same feeling as being in love" and "satisfies her innermost cravings anytime [she] wants." She pleads with us, the viewers, not to tell Michael, her boyfriend.

These commercials hit a painful nerve for women. The bon bon commercial may seem merely silly, but the chocolate drink ad begins to evoke, darkly and disturbingly, the psychological and material realities of women's food problems. The talk of "obsession" and "innermost cravings," the furtiveness, the secrecy, the use of food to satisfy emotional needs, all suggest central elements of binge behavior. Frusen Glädjé supplies another piece and gives an important lie to the other, more upbeat commercials (Figure 20): "He never called. So, Ben and I went out for a walk to pick up a pint of Frusen Glädjé. Ben's better looking anyway." Frusen Glädjé: "It feels so good." Here, as in the Häagan-Dazs ad discussed earlier, the sensuousness of the ice-cream experience is emphasized; unlike the Häagan-Dazs ad, however, Frusen Glädjé offers solace from emotional depths rather than the thrill of emotional heights. This is, indeed, the prevailing gender reality. For women, the emotional comfort of self-feeding is rarely turned to in a state of pleasure and independence, but in despair, emptiness, loneliness, and desperation. Food is, as one woman put it, "the only thing that will take care of *me*."[19]

FIGURE 19

FIGURE 20

FOOD AS TRANSGRESSION

An extremely interesting fact about male bulimics: they rarely binge alone. They tend to binge at mealtime and in public places, whereas women almost always eat minimally at meals and gorge later, in private.[20] Even in our disorders (or perhaps especially in our disorders) we follow the gender rules. In the commercials I have been discussing, female eating is virtually always represented as private, secretive, illicit. The woman has stolen away from the world of husband, family, friends to a secret corner where she and the food can be alone. A "Do Not Disturb" sign hangs on the door to the room where the women sits munching on her "purple passion," New York Deli Potato Chips. A husband returns home to discover that in his absence his wife, sitting on the floor, has eaten all the Frusen Glädjé; her voice is mildly defiant, although soft—"I ate all the Frusen Glädjé"—but her face is sheepish and her glance averted. Men sing openly of their wild cravings for Betty Crocker cakes; women's cravings are a dirty, shameful secret, to be indulged in only when no one is looking.

More often than not, however, women are not even permitted, even in private, indulgences so extravagant in scope as the full satisfaction of their hungers. Most commonly, women are used to advertise, *not* ice cream and potato chips (foods whose intake is very difficult to contain and control), but individually wrapped pieces of tiny, bite-size candies: Andes candies, Hershey's kisses, Mon Cheri bon bons. Instead of the mounds of cake and oozing frosting typical of commercials featuring male eaters, women are confined to a "tiny scoop" of flavor, a "tiny piece" of chocolate. As in the Weight Watchers linguini advertisement ("Dive in"), the rhetoric of indulgence is invoked, only to be contained by the product itself: "Indulge a little," urges Andes Candies. "Satisfy your urge to splurge in five delicious bite-size ways." The littleness of the candy and the amount of taste that is packed within its tiny boundaries are frequently emphasized: "Each bite-size piece packs a wallop of milk chocolate crunch." Instead of the emphasis on undifferentiated feelings of sensuous delight that we see in commercials showing men, the pitch aimed at women stresses the exquisite pleasure to be had from a sensually focused and limited experience. The message to women is explicit: "Indulge a *little*." (And only out of sight; even these minuscule bon bons are eaten privately, in isolation, behind closed doors.)

If one genre of commercials hints at the dark secrets of binge behavior—the refusal of female desire to remain circumscribed and repressed; the frustrations of "feeding" others and never being fed yourself—the "bite-size" candy genre represents female hunger as successfully contained within the bounds of appropriate feminine behavior. It is significant, surely, that in all these commercials the woman is found "indulging" only after a day spent serving others. In these commercials, it is permissible for women to feed the self (if such dainty nibbling merits this description) only after first feeding others:

> For my angel, I sewed for days. Now I deserve a little praise. I thank me very much with Andes Candies.

> Chances are you spent the day doing things for others. Don't you deserve something for yourself? Try a Mon Cheri. [The woman is in the bathtub; in the background, dimly heard are the voices of the day gone by: "Honey, did you pick up my dry cleaning?" "Mrs. Jones, will you type this letter?" "Mommy, we want to go to the park!" She sinks down into the tub, unwrapping the candy, in exquisite anticipation.]

These commercials, no less than the Victorian conduct manuals, offer a virtual blueprint for disordered relations to food and hunger. The representation of unrestrained appetite as inappropriate for women, the depiction of female eating as a private, transgressive act, make restriction and denial of hunger central features of the construction of femininity and set up the compensatory binge as a virtual inevitability. Such restrictions on appetite, moreover, are not merely about food intake. Rather, the social control of female hunger operates as a practical "discipline" (to use Foucault's term) that trains female bodies in the knowledge of their limits and possibilities. Denying oneself food becomes the central micro-practice in the education of feminine self-restraint and containment of impulse.

Victorian women were told that it was vulgar to load their plates; in 1990, women students of mine complain of the tortures of the cafeteria—the embarrassment of eating ice cream in front of the male students, the pressure to take just a salad or, better yet, refuse food altogether. Later at night, when they are alone, they confront the deprived and empty feeling left in the wake of such a regimen. As in the commercials, the self-reward and solace is food. The problem, however, after a day of restraint is the requirement for any further containment of the now ravenous self. Unlike the women in the Andes candy commercials, few women who have spent the day submerging their desires, either for the sake of their families or to project the appropriately attractive lack of appetite to a cafeteria full of adolescent boys, really feel rewarded by a bite-size piece of candy, no matter how much chocolate "wallop" it packs. In private, shamefully and furtively, we binge.

When, in my classes, we discuss contemporary representations, I encourage my students to bring in examples that appear to violate traditional gender-dualities and the ideological messages contained in them. Frequently, my students view our examination of these "subversive" representations as an investigation and determination of whether or not "progress" has been made. My students want very much to believe that progress is being made, and so do I. But "progress" is not an adequate description of the cultural status of the counter-examples they bring me. Rather, they almost always display a complicated and bewitching tangle of new possibilities and old patterns of representation. They reflect the instabilities that trouble the continued reproduction of the old dualities and ideologies, but they do not show clearly just where we are going.

A television commercial for Hormel microwaveable Kid's Kitchen Meals, for example, opens with two young girls trying to fix a bicycle. A little boy, watching them, offers to help, claiming that "I can fix anything. My dad lets me fix his car. My mom lets me fix dinner." When the girls are skeptical ("Yeah? Well, prove it!"), he fixes a Hormel's Kid's Kitchen Meal for them. Utterly impressed with his culinary skill and on the basis of this ready to trust his mechanical aptitude, they ask, "You know how to fix a bike?" "What? Yeah, I do!" he eagerly replies. Now, is this ad "progressive" or "regressive"? The little girls cannot fix their own bike, a highly traditional, "feminine" limitation. Yet they do not behave in helpless or co-quettish ways in the commercial. Far from it. They speak in rough voices and challenging words to the boy, who is physically smaller (and, it appears, younger) than they; "Give me a break!" they mutter scornfully when he claims he can "fix anything." Despite their mechanical inability, they do not act deferential, and in a curious way this neutralizes the gendered meanings of the activities depicted. Not being able to fix a bike is something that could happen to anyone, they seem to believe. And so we may begin to see it this way too.

Then, too, there is the unusual representation of the male cooking for and serving the females. True, it only required a touch of the

FIGURE 21

microwave panel. But this is, after all, only a little boy. One message this commercial may be delivering is that males can engage in traditionally "feminine" activities without threat to their manhood. Cooking for a woman does not mean that she won't respect you in the morning. She will still recognize your authority to fix her bike (indeed, she may become further convinced of it precisely by your mastery of "her" domain). The expansion of possibilities for boys thus extracts from girls the price of continued ineptitude in certain areas (or at least the show of it) and dependence on males. Yet, in an era in which most working women find themselves with two full-time jobs—their second shift beginning at five o'clock, when they return from work to meet their husband's expectations of dinner, a clean and comfortable home, a sympathetic ear—the message that cooking and serving others is not "sissy," though it may be problematic and nonprogressive in many ways, is perhaps the single most *practically* beneficial (to women) message we can convey to little boys.

In its provision of ambiguous and destabilizing imagery, the in-

Enter the State of Häagen-Dazs

Häagen-Dazs

VANILLA FUDGE

FIGURE 22

flux of women into the professional arena has had a significant effect on the representation of gender. Seeking to appeal to a population that wishes to be regarded (at least while on the job) as equal in power and ability to the men with whom they work, advertisers have tried to establish gender symmetry in those representations that depict or evoke the lives of professional couples. Minute Rice thus has two versions of its "I wonder what 'Minute' is cookin' up for dinner tonight?" commercial. In one, father and children come home from work and school to find mother "cookin' up" an elaborate chicken stir-fry to serve over Minute Rice. In the other, a working woman returns to find her male partner "cookin' up" the dinner. The configuration is indeed destabilizing, if only because it makes us aware of how very rare it is to see. But, significantly, there are no children in this commercial, as there are in the more traditional version; the absence of children codes the fact that this is a yuppie couple, the group to which this version is designed to appeal.

And now Häagen-Dazs, the original yuppie ice cream, has designed an ad series for this market (Figures 21 and 22). These ads perfectly illustrate the unstable location of contemporary gender advertisements: they attempt to satisfy representational conventions that still have a deep psychic grip on Western culture, while at the same time registering every new rhythm of the social heartbeat. "Enter the State of Häagen-Dazs"—a clear invocation of the public world rather than the domestic domain. The man and woman are dressed virtually identically (making small allowances for gender-tailoring) in equally no-nonsense, dark business suits, styled for power. Their hair-styles are equivalent, brushed back from the face, clipped short but not punky. They have similar expressions: slightly playful, caught in the act but certainly not feeling guilty. They appear to be indulging in their ice-cream break in the middle of a workday; this sets up both the fetching representational incongruity of the ad and its realism. Ice cream has always been represented as relaxation food, to be *indulged* in; it belongs to a different universe than the work ethic, performance principle, or spirit of competition. To eat it in a business suit is like having "quickie" sex in the office, irregular and naughty. Yet everyone knows that people *do* eat ice cream on their breaks and during their lunch hours. The ad thus appears both realistic and *representationally* odd; we realize that we are seeing images we have not seen before *except* in real life. And, of course, in real life, women *do* eat Häagen-Dazs, as much as, if not more than, men.

And yet, intruding into this world of gender equality and eating realism that is designed to appeal to the sensibilities of "progressive" young men and women is the inescapable disparity in how much and how the man and woman are eating. He: an entire pint of vanilla fudge, with sufficient abandon to topple the carton, and greedy enough to suck the spoon. She: a restrained Eve-bite (already taken; no licks or sucks in process here), out of a single brittle bar (aestheticized as "artfully" nutty, in contrast to his bold, unaccessorized "Vanilla Fudge." Whether unconsciously reproduced or deliberately crafted to appeal to the psychic contradictions and ambivalence of its intended audience, the disparity comes from the recesses of our most sedimented, unquestioned notions about gender.

PART TWO

THE SLENDER BODY AND OTHER CULTURAL FORMS

In 1983, preparing to teach an interdisciplinary course in "Gender, Culture, and Experience," I felt the need for a topic that would enable me to bring feminist theory alive for a generation of students that seemed increasingly suspicious of feminism. My sister, Binnie Klein, who is a therapist, suggested that I have my class read Kim Chernin's *The Obsession: Reflections on the Tyranny of Slenderness*. I did, and I found my Reagan-era students suddenly sounding like the women in the consciousness-raising sessions that had first made me aware of the fact that my problems as a woman were not mine alone. While delighted to have happened on a topic that was so intensely meaningful to them, I was also disturbed by what I was reading in their journals and hearing in the privacy of my office. I had identified deeply with the general themes of Chernin's book. But my own disordered relations with food had never reached the point of anorexia or bulimia, and I was not prepared for the discovery that large numbers of my students were starving, binging, purging, and filled with self-hatred and desperation. I began to read everything I could find on eating disorders. I found that while the words and diaries of patients were enormously illuminating, most of the clinical theory was not very helpful. The absence of cultural perspective—particularly relating to the situation of women—was striking.

As a philosopher, I was also intrigued by the classically dualistic language my students often used to describe their feelings, and I decided to incorporate a section on contemporary attitudes toward the body in my metaphysics course. There, I discovered that although it was predominantly my female students who experienced their lives as a perpetual battle with their bodies, quite a few of my male students expressed similar ideas when writing about running. I found myself fascinated by what seemed to me to be the cultural emergence of a set of attitudes about the body which, while not new as *ideas*, were finding a special kind of embodiment in contemporary culture, and I began to see all sorts of evidence for this cultural hypothesis. So began a project that has since occupied a good deal of my attention and that has, I believe, progressively been validated.

In 1983, the body practices and attitudes that I viewed as supporting my tentative intuitions were a mere ripple on the cultural scene compared to the place I have watched them assume since then.

"Anorexia Nervosa: Psychopathology as the Crystallization of Culture," first published in 1985, was the result of my initial exploration of the various cultural axes to which my students' experiences guided me in my "Gender, Culture, and Experience" and metaphysics courses. "The Body and the Reproduction of Femininity" and "Reading the Slender Body," both first published in 1989, are in a sense an extension of that earlier piece, in that they explore the dynamics of further axes on which eating disorders are located: the historically female psychological disorders, changes in historical attitudes toward what constitutes "fat" and "thin," and the structural tensions of consumer society. These axes are not, however, meant make up an exhaustive list. Ultimately, these essays do not so much explain eating disorders as *follow* them through a series of cultural interconnections and intersections.

Since the "Anorexia Nervosa" essay first appeared, in 1985, there has, of course, been an explosion of written material, media attention, and clinical study devoted to eating disorders. I have not attempted to incorporate new studies or statistics into these previously published pieces, although much of the new information strongly bears out my observations and interpretations. Nor have I tried to bring my original formulations into line with developments in my thinking. I have chosen instead to let the evolution of my ideas—and in some cases the evolution of the phenomena themselves—manifest themselves through the essays. Some sections of the original essays have been deleted to avoid redundancy, a few formulations clarified, a number of new illustrations added, and endnotes revised when accuracy demanded it. Otherwise, the essays in this section of the book appear substantially as they did in their original versions.

Anorexia Nervosa

Psychopathology as the
Crystallization of Culture

Historians long ago began to write the history of the body. They have studied the body in the field of historical demography or pathology; they have considered it as the seat of needs and appetites, as the locus of physiological processes and metabolisms, as a target for the attacks of germs or viruses; they have shown to what extent historical processes were involved in what might seem to be the purely biological "events" such as the circulation of bacilli, or the extension of the lifespan. But the body is also directly involved in a political field; power relations have an immediate hold upon it; they invest it, mark it, train it, torture it, force it to carry out tasks, to perform ceremonies, to emit signs.

> *Michel Foucault*, Discipline and Punish

I believe in being the best I can be,
I believe in watching every calorie . . .

> *Crystal Light television commercial*

EATING DISORDERS, CULTURE, AND THE BODY

Psychopathology, as Jules Henry has said, "is the final outcome of all that is wrong with a culture."[1] In no case is this more strikingly true than in that of anorexia nervosa and bulimia, barely known a century ago, yet reaching epidemic proportions today. Far from being the result of a superficial fashion phenomenon, these disorders, I will argue, reflect and call our attention to some of the central ills of our culture—from our historical heritage of disdain for the body, to our modern fear of loss of control over our future, to the disquieting meaning of contemporary beauty ideals in an era of greater female presence and power than ever before.

Changes in the incidence of anorexia[2] have been dramatic.[3] In 1945, when Ludwig Binswanger chronicled the now famous case of Ellen West, he was able to say that "from a psychiatric point of view we are dealing here with something new, with a new symptom."[4] In 1973, Hilde Bruch, one of the pioneers in understanding and treating eating disorders, could still say that anorexia was "rare indeed."[5] Today, in 1984, it is estimated that as many as one in every 200–250 women between the ages of thirteen and twenty-two suffer from anorexia, and that anywhere from 12 to 33 percent of college women control their weight through vomiting, diuretics, and laxatives.[6] The New York Center for the Study of Anorexia and Bulimia reports that in the first five months of 1984 it received 252 requests for treatment, as compared to the 30 requests received in all of 1980.[7] Even correcting for increased social awareness of eating disorders and a greater willingness of sufferers to report their illnesses, these statistics are startling and provocative. So, too, is the fact that 90 percent of all anorectics are women, and that of the 5,000 people each year who have part of their intestines removed as an aid in losing weight 80 percent are women.[8]

Anorexia nervosa is clearly, as Paul Garfinkel and David Garner have called it, a "multidimensional disorder," with familial, perceptual, cognitive, and, possibly, biological factors interacting in varying combinations in different individuals to produce a "final common pathway."[9] In the early 1980s, with growing evidence, not only of an overall increase in frequency of the disease, but of its higher incidence in certain populations, attention has begun to turn, too, to cultural factors as significant in the pathogenesis of eating disorders.[10] Until very recently, however, the most that could be expected in the way of cultural or social analysis, with very few exceptions, was the (unavoidable) recognition that anorexia is related to the increasing emphasis that fashion has placed on slenderness over the past fifteen years.[11] This, unfortunately, is only to replace one mystery with another, more profound than the first.

What we need to ask is *why* our culture is so obsessed with keeping our bodies slim, tight, and young that when 500 people were asked what they feared most in the world, 190 replied, "Getting fat."[12] In an age when our children regularly have nightmares of nuclear holocaust, that as adults we should give *this* answer—that we most fear "getting fat"—is far more bizarre than the anorectic's misperceptions of her body image, or the bulimic's compulsive vomiting. The nightmares of nuclear holocaust and our desperate fixation on our bodies as arenas of control—perhaps one of the few available arenas of control we have left in the twentieth century—are not unconnected, of course. The connection, if explored, could be significant, demystifying, instructive.

So, too, we need to explore the fact that it is women who are most oppressed by what Kim Chernin calls "the tyranny of slenderness," and that this particular oppression is a post-1960s, post-feminist phenomenon. In the fifties, by contrast, with middle-class women once again out of the factories and safely immured in the home, the dominant ideal of female beauty was exemplified by Marilyn Monroe—hardly your androgynous, athletic, adolescent body type. At the peak of her popularity, Monroe was often described as "femininity incarnate," "femaleness embodied"; last term, a student of mine described her as "a cow." Is this merely a change in what size hips, breasts, and waist are considered attractive, or has the very idea of incarnate femaleness come to have a different meaning, different associations, the capacity to stir up different fantasies and images, for the culture of the eighties? These are the sorts of questions that need to be addressed if we are to achieve a deep understanding of the current epidemic of eating disorders.

The central point of intellectual orientation for this essay is expressed in its subtitle. I take the psychopathologies that develop within a culture, far from being anomalies or aberrations, to be characteristic expressions of that culture; to be, indeed, the crystallization of much that is wrong with it. For that reason they are important to examine, as keys to cultural self-diagnosis and self-scrutiny. "Every age," says Christopher Lasch, "develops its own peculiar forms of pathology, which express in exaggerated form its underlying character structure."[13] The only aspect of this formulation with which I would disagree, with respect to anorexia, is the idea of the expression of an underlying, unitary cultural character structure. Anorexia appears less as the extreme expression of a character structure than as a remarkably overdetermined *symptom* of some of the multifaceted and heterogeneous distresses of our age. Just as anorexia functions in a variety of ways in the psychic economy of the anorexic individual, so a variety of cultural currents or streams converge in anorexia, find their perfect, precise expression in it.

I will call those streams or currents "axes of continuity": *axes* because they meet or converge in the anorexic syndrome; *continuity* because when we locate anorexia on these axes, its family resemblances and connections with other phenomena emerge. Some of these axes represent anorexia's *synchronicity* with other contemporary cultural practices and forms—bodybuilding and jogging, for example. Other axes bring to light *historical* connections: for instance, between anorexia and earlier examples of extreme manipulation of the female body, such as tight corseting, or between anorexia and long-standing traditions and ideologies in Western culture, such as our Greco-Christian traditions of dualism. The three axes that I will discuss in this essay (although they by no means exhaust the possibilities for cultural understanding of anorexia) are the *dualist axis*, the *control axis*, and the *gender/power axis*.[14]

Throughout my discussion, it will be assumed that the body, far from being some fundamentally stable, acultural constant to which we must *contrast* all culturally relative and institutional forms, is constantly "in the grip," as Foucault puts it, of cultural practices. Not that this is a matter of cultural *repression* of the instinctual or natural body. Rather, there is no "natural" body. Cultural practices, far from exerting their power *against* spontaneous needs, "basic" pleasures or instincts, or "fundamental" structures of body experience, are already and always inscribed, as Foucault has emphasized, "on our bodies and their materiality, their forces, energies, sensations, and pleasures."[15] Our bodies, no less than anything else that is human, are constituted by culture.

Often, but not always, cultural practices have their effect on the body as experienced (the "lived body," as the phenomenologists put it) rather than the physical body. For example, Foucault points to the medicalization of sexuality in the nineteenth century, which recast sex from being a family matter into a private, dark, bodily secret that was appropriately investigated by such specialists as doctors, psychiatrists, and school educators. The constant probing and interrogation, Foucault argues, ferreted out, eroticized and solidified all sorts of sexual types and perversions, which people then experienced (although they had not done so originally) as defining their bodily possibilities and pleasures. The practice of the medical confessional, in other words, in its constant foraging for sexual secrets and hidden stories, actually *created* new sexual secrets—and eroticized the acts of interrogation and confession, too.[16] Here, social practice changed people's *experience* of their bodies and their possibilities. Similarly, as we shall see, the practice of dieting—of saying no to hunger—contributes to the anorectic's increasing sense of hunger as a dangerous eruption from some alien part of the self, and to a growing intoxication with controlling that eruption.

The *physical* body can, however, also be an instrument and medium of power. Foucault's classic example in *Discipline and Punish* is public torture during the Ancien Régime, through which, as Dreyfus and Rabinow put it, "the sovereign's power was literally and publicly inscribed on the criminal's body in a manner as controlled, scenic and well-attended as possible."[17] Similarly, the nineteenth-century corset caused its wearer actual physical incapacitation, but it also served as an emblem of the power of culture to impose its designs on the female body.

Indeed, female bodies have historically been significantly more vulnerable than male bodies to extremes in both forms of cultural manipulation of the body. Perhaps this has something to do with the fact that women, besides *having* bodies, are also *associated* with the body, which has always been considered woman's "sphere" in family life, in mythology, in scientific, philosophical, and religious ideology. When we later consider some aspects of the history of medicine and fashion, we will see that the social manipulation of the female body emerged as an absolutely central strategy in the maintenance of power relations between the sexes over the past hundred years. This historical understanding must deeply affect our understanding of anorexia and of our contemporary preoccupation with slenderness.

This is *not* to say that I take what I am doing here to be the unearthing of a long-standing male conspiracy against women or the fixing of blame on any particular participants in the play of social forces. In this I once again follow Foucault, who reminds us that although a perfectly clear logic, with perfectly decipherable aims and objectives, may characterize historical power relations, it is nonetheless "often the case that no one was there to have invented" these aims and strategies, either through choice of individuals or through the rational game plan of some presiding "headquarters."[18] We are not talking, then, of plots, designs, or overarching strategies. This does not mean that individuals do not *consciously* pursue goals that in fact advance their own position. But it does deny that in doing so they are consciously directing the overall movement of power relations or engineering their shape. They may not even know what that shape is. Nor does the fact that power relations involve domination by particular groups—say, of prisoners by guards, females by males, amateurs by experts—entail that the dominators are in anything like full control of the situation or that the dominated do not sometimes advance and extend the situation themselves.[19] Nowhere, as we shall see, is this collaboration in oppression more clear than in the case of anorexia.

THE DUALIST AXIS

I will begin with the most general and attenuated axis of continuity, the one that begins with Plato, winds its way to its most lurid expression in Augustine, and finally becomes metaphysically solidified and scientized by Descartes. I am referring, of course, to our dualistic heritage: the view that human existence is bifurcated into two realms or substances: the bodily or material, on the one hand; the mental or spiritual, on the other. Despite some fascinating historical variations which I will not go into here, the basic imagery of dualism has remained fairly constant. Let me briefly describe its central features; they will turn out, as we will see, to comprise the basic body imagery of the anorectic.

First, the body is experienced as *alien*, as the not-self, the not-me. It is "fastened and glued" to me, "nailed" and "riveted" to me, as Plato describes it in the *Phaedo*.[20] For Descartes, the body is the brute material envelope for the inner and essential self, the thinking thing; it is ontologically distinct from that inner self, is as mechanical in its operations as a machine, is, indeed, comparable to animal existence.

Second, the body is experienced as *confinement and limitation*: a "prison," a "swamp," a "cage," a "fog"—all images that occur in Plato, Descartes, and Augustine—from which the soul, will, or mind struggles to escape. "The enemy ["the madness of lust"] held my will in his power and from it he made a chain and shackled me," says Augustine.[21] In the work of all three philosophers, images of the soul being "dragged" by the body are prominent. The body is "heavy, ponderous," as Plato describes it; it exerts a downward pull.[22]

Third, the body is *the enemy*, as Augustine explicitly describes it time and again, and as Plato and Descartes strongly suggest in their diatribes against the body as the source of obscurity and confusion in our thinking. "A source of countless distractions by reason of the mere requirement of food," says Plato; "liable also to diseases which overtake and impede us in the pursuit of truth; it fills us full of loves, and lusts, and fears, and fancies of all kinds, and endless foolery, and in very truth, as men say, takes away from us the power of thinking at all. Whence come wars, and fightings, and factions? Whence but from the body and the lusts of the body."[23]

And, finally, whether as an impediment to reason or as the home of the "slimy desires of the flesh" (as Augustine calls them), the body is the locus of *all that threatens our attempts at control*. It overtakes, it overwhelms, it erupts and disrupts. This situation, for the dualist, becomes an incitement to battle the unruly forces of the body, to show it who is boss. For, as Plato says, "Nature orders the soul to rule and govern and the body to obey and serve."[24]

All three—Plato, Augustine, and, most explicitly, Descartes—provide instructions, rules, or models of how to gain control over the body, with the ultimate aim—for this is what their regimen finally boils down to—of learning to live without it.[25] By that is meant: to achieve intellectual independence from the lure of the body's illusions, to become impervious to its distractions, and, most important, to kill off its desires and hungers. Once control has become the central issue for the soul, these are the only possible terms of victory, as Alan Watts makes clear:

> Willed control brings about a sense of duality in the organism, of consciousness in conflict with appetite. . . . But this mode of control is a peculiar example of the proverb that nothing fails like success. For the more consciousness is individualized by the success of the will, the more everything outside the individual seems to be a threat—including . . . the uncontrolled spontaneity of one's own body. . . . Every success in control therefore demands a further success, so that the process cannot stop short of omnipotence.[26]

Dualism here appears as the offspring, the by-product, of the identification of the self with control, an identification that Watts sees as lying at the center of Christianity's ethic of anti-sexuality. The attempt to subdue the spontaneities of the body in the interests of control only succeeds in constituting them as more alien and more powerful, and thus more needful of control. The only way to win this no-win game is to go beyond control, to kill off the body's spontaneities entirely—that is, to cease to *experience* our hungers and desires.

This is what many anorectics describe as their ultimate goal. "[I want] to reach the point," as one put it, "when I don't need to eat at all."[27] Kim Chernin recalls her surprise when, after fasting, her hunger returned: "I realized [then] that my secret goal in dieting must have been the intention to kill off my appetite completely."[28]

It is not usually noted, in the popular literature on the subject, that anorexic women are as obsessed with *hunger* as they are with being slim. Far from losing her appetite, the typical anorectic is haunted by it—in much the same way that Augustine describes being haunted by sexual desire—and is in constant dread of being overwhelmed by it. Many describe the dread of hunger, "of not having control, of giving in to biological urge," to "the craving, never satisfied thing,"[29] as the "original fear" (as one puts it),[30] or, as Ellen West describes it, "the real obsession." "I don't think the dread of becoming fat is the real . . . neurosis," she writes, "but the constant desire for food. . . . [H]unger, or the dread of hunger, pursues me all morning. . . . Even when I am full, I am afraid of the coming hour in which hunger will start again." Dread of becoming fat, she interprets, rather than being originary, served as a "brake" to her horror of her own unregulatable, runaway desire for food.[31] Bruch reports that her patients are often terrified at the prospect of taking just one bite of food, lest they never be able to stop.[32] (Bulimic anorectics, who binge on enormous quantities of food—sometimes consuming up to 15,000 calories a day[33]—indeed *cannot* stop.)

These women experience hunger as an alien invader, marching to the tune of its own seemingly arbitrary whims, disconnected from any normal self-regulating mechanisms. Indeed, it could not possibly be so connected, for it is experienced as coming from an area *outside* the self. One patient of Bruch's says she ate breakfast because "my stomach wanted it," expressing here the same sense of alienation from her hunger (and her physical self) as Augustine's when he speaks of his "captor," "the law of sin that was in my member."[34]

Bruch notes that this "basic delusion," as she calls it, "of not owning the body and its sensations" is a typical symptom of all eating disorders. "These patients act," she says, "as if for them the regulation of food intake was outside [the self]."[35] This experience of bodily sensations as foreign is, strikingly, not limited to the experience of hunger. Patients with eating disorders have similar problems in identifying cold, heat, emotions, and anxiety as originating in the self.[36]

While the body is experienced as alien and outside, the soul or will is described as being trapped or confined in this alien "jail," as one woman describes it.[37] "I feel caught in my body," "I'm a prisoner in my body":[38] the theme is repeated again and again. A typical fantasy, evocative of Plato, imagines total liberation from the bodily prison: "I wish I could get out of my body entirely and fly!"[39] "Please dear God, help me. . . . I want to get out of my body, I want to get out!"[40] Ellen West, astute as always, sees a central meaning of her self-starvation in this "ideal of being too thin, of being *without a body*."[41]

Anorexia is not a philosophical attitude; it is a debilitating affliction. Yet, quite often a highly conscious and articulate scheme of images and associations—virtually a metaphysics—is presented by these women. The scheme is strikingly Augustinian, with evocations of Plato. This does not indicate, of course, that anorectics are followers of Plato or Augustine, but that the anorectic's metaphysics makes explicit various elements, historically grounded in Plato and Augustine, that run deep in our culture.[42] As Augustine often speaks of the "two wills" within him, "one the servant of the flesh, the other of the spirit," who "between them tore my soul apart," so the anorectic describes a "spiritual struggle," a "contest between good and evil," often conceived explicitly as a battle between mind or will and appetite or body.[43] "I feel myself, quite passively," says West, "the stage on which two hostile forces are mangling each other."[44] Sometimes there is a more aggressive alliance with mind against body: "When I fail to exercise as often as I prefer, I become guilty that I have let my body 'win' another day from my mind. I can't wait 'til this semester is over. . . . My body is going to pay the price for the lack of work it is currently getting. I can't wait!"[45]

In this battle, thinness represents a triumph of the will over the body, and the thin body (that is to say, the nonbody) is associated with "absolute purity, hyperintellectuality and transcendence of the flesh. My soul seemed to grow as my body waned; I felt like one of those early Christian saints who starved themselves in the desert sun. I felt invulnerable, clean and hard as the bones etched into my silhouette."[46] Fat (that is to say, becoming *all* body) is associated with the taint of matter and flesh, "wantonness,"[47] mental stupor and mental decay.[48] One woman describes how after eating sugar she felt "polluted, disgusting, sticky through the arms, as if some-thing bad had gotten inside."[49] Very often, sexuality is brought into this scheme of associations, and hunger and sexuality are psychi-cally connected. Cherry Boone O'Neill describes a late-night binge, eating scraps of leftovers from the dog's dish:

> I started slowly, relishing the flavor and texture of each marvelous bite. Soon I was ripping the meager remains from the bones, stuffing the meat into my mouth as fast as I could detach it.
>   [Her boyfriend surprises her, with a look of "total disgust" on his face.]
>   I had been caught red-handed . . . in an animalistic orgy on the floor, in the dark, alone. Here was the horrid truth for Dan to see. I felt so evil, tainted, pagan. . . . In Dan's mind that day, I had been whoring after food.[50]

A hundred pages earlier, she had described her first romantic in-volvement in much the same terms: "I felt secretive, deceptive, and . . . tainted by the ongoing relationship" (which never went beyond kisses).[51] Sexuality, similarly, is "an abominable business" to Aimee Liu; for her, staying reed-thin is seen as a way of avoiding sexuality, by becoming "androgynous," as she puts it.[52] In the same way, Sarah, a patient of Levenkron's, connects her dread of gaining weight with "not wanting to be a 'temptation' to men."[53] In Liu's case, and in Sarah's, the desire to appear unattractive to men is connected to anxiety and guilt over earlier sexual abuse. Whether or not such episodes are common to many cases of anorexia,[54] "the avoidance of any sexual encounter, a shrinking from all bodily contact," is, according to Bruch, characteristic of anorectics.[55]

THE CONTROL AXIS

Having examined the axis of continuity from Plato to anorexia, we should feel cautioned against the impulse to regard anorexia as expressing entirely modern attitudes and fears. Disdain for the body, the conception of it as an alien force and impediment to the soul, is very old in our Greco-Christian traditions (although it has usually been expressed most forcefully by male philosophers and theologians rather than adolescent women!).

But although dualism is as old as Plato, in many ways contemporary culture appears *more* obsessed than previous eras with the control of the unruly body. Looking now at contemporary American life, a second axis of continuity emerges on which to locate anorexia. I call it the *control axis*.

The young anorectic, typically, experiences her life as well as her hungers as being out of control. She is a perfectionist and can never carry out the tasks she sets herself in a way that meets her own rigorous standards. She is torn by conflicting and contradictory expectations and demands, wanting to shine in all areas of student life, confused about where to place most of her energies, what to focus on, as she develops into an adult. Characteristically, her parents expect a great deal of her in the way of individual achievement (as well as physical appearance), yet have made most of the important decisions for her.[56] Usually, the anorexic syndrome emerges, not as a conscious decision to get as thin as possible, but as the result of her having begun a diet fairly casually, often at the suggestion of a parent, having succeeded splendidly in taking off five or ten pounds, and then having gotten hooked on the intoxicating feeling of accomplishment and control.

Recalling her anorexic days, Aimee Liu recreates her feelings:

> The sense of accomplishment exhilarates me, spurs me to continue on and on. It provides a sense of purpose and shapes my life with distractions from insecurity. . . . I shall become an expert [at losing weight]. . . . The constant downward trend [of the scale] somehow comforts me, gives me visible proof that I can exert control.[57]

The diet, she realizes, "is the one sector of my life over which I and I alone wield total control."[58]

The frustrations of starvation, the rigors of the constant physical activity in which anorectics engage, the pain of the numerous physical complications of anorexia: these do not trouble the anorectic. Indeed, her ability to ignore them is further proof to her of her mastery of her body. "This was something I could control," says one of Bruch's patients. "I still don't know what I look like or what size I am, but I know my body can take anything."[59] "Energy, discipline, my own power will keep me going," says Liu. "Psychic fuel, I need nothing and no one else, and I will prove it. . . . Dropping to the floor, I roll. My tailbone crunches on the hard floor. . . . I feel no pain. I will be master of my own body, if nothing else, I vow."[60] And, finally, from one of Bruch's patients: "*You make of your own body your very own kingdom where you are the tyrant, the absolute dictator.*"[61]

Surely we must recognize in this last honest and explicit statement a central modus operandi for the control of contemporary bourgeois anxiety. Consider compulsive jogging and marathon-running, often despite shin splints and other painful injuries, with intense agitation over missing a day or not meeting a goal for a particular run. Consider the increasing popularity of triathlon events such as the Iron Man, whose central purpose appears to be to allow people to find out how far they can push their bodies— through long-distance swimming, cycling, and running—before they collapse. Consider lawyer Mike Frankfurt, who runs ten miles every morning: "*To run with pain is the essence of life.*"[62] Or consider the following excerpts from student journals:

> The best times I like to run are under the most unbearable conditions. I love to run in the hottest, most humid and steepest terrain I can find. . . . For me running and the pain associated with it aren't enough to make me stop. I am always trying to overcome it and the biggest failure I can make is to stop running because of pain. Once I ran five of a ten-mile run with a severe leg cramp but wouldn't stop—it would have meant failure.[63]

> When I run I am free. . . . The pleasure is closing off my body—as if the incessant pounding of my legs is so total that the pain ceases to exist. There is no grace, no beauty in the running—there is the jarring reality of sneaker and pavement. Bright pain that shivers and splinters sending its white hot arrows into my stomach, my lung, but it cannot pierce my mind. I am on automatic pilot—there is no remembrance of pain, there is freedom—I am losing myself, peeling out of this heavy flesh. . . . Power surges through me.[64]

None of this is to dispute that the contemporary concern with fitness has nonpathological, nondualist dimensions as well. Particularly for women, who have historically suffered from the ubiquity of rape and abuse, from the culturally instilled conviction of our own helplessness, and from lack of access to facilities and programs for rigorous physical training, the cultivation of strength, agility, and confidence clearly has a positive dimension. Nor are the objective benefits of daily exercise and concern for nutrition in question here. My focus, rather, is on a subjective stance, become increasingly prominent, which, although preoccupied with the body and deriving narcissistic enjoyment from its appearance, takes little pleasure in the *experience* of embodiment. Rather, the fundamental identification is with mind (or will), ideals of spiritual perfection, fantasies of absolute control.

Not everyone, of course, for whom physical training is a part of daily routine exhibits such a stance. Here, an examination of the language of female body-builders is illustrative. Body-building is particularly interesting because on the surface it appears to have the opposite structure to anorexia: the body-builder is, after all, building the body *up*, not whittling it down. Body-building develops strength. We imagine the body-builder as someone who is proud, confident, and perhaps most of all, conscious of and accepting of her physicality. This is, indeed, how some female body-builders experience themselves:

> I feel . . . tranquil and stronger [says Lydia Cheng]. Working out creates a high everywhere in my body. I feel the heat. I feel the muscles rise, I see them blow out, flushed with lots of blood. . . . My whole body is sweating and there's few things I love more than working up a good sweat. That's when I really feel like a woman.[65]

Yet a sense of joy in the body as active and alive is *not* the most prominent theme among the women interviewed by Trix Rosen. Many of them, rather, talk about their bodies in ways that resonate disquietingly with typical anorexic themes.

There is the same emphasis on will, purity, and perfection: "I've learned to be a stronger person with a more powerful will . . . pure concentration, energy and spirit." "I want to be as physically perfect as possible." "Body-building suits the perfectionist in me." "My goal is to have muscular perfection."[66] Compulsive exercisers—whom Dinitia Smith, in an article for *New York* magazine calls "The New Puritans"—speak in similar terms: Kathy Krauch, a New York art director who bikes twelve miles a day and swims two and a half, says she is engaged in "a quest for perfection." Mike Frankfurt, in describing his motivation for marathon running, speaks of "the purity about it." These people, Smith emphasizes, care little about their health: "They pursue self-denial as an end in itself, out of an almost mystical belief in the purity it confers."[67]

Many body-builders, like many anorectics, unnervingly conceptualize the body as alien, not-self:

> I'm constantly amazed by my muscles. The first thing I do when I wake up in the morning is look down at my "abs" and flex my legs to see if the "cuts" are there. . . . My legs have always been my most stubborn part, and I want them to develop so badly. Every day I can see things happening to them. . . . I don't flaunt my muscles as much as I thought I would. I feel differently about them; they are my product and I protect them by wearing sweaters to keep them warm.[68]

Most strikingly, body-builders put the same emphasis on *control*: on feeling their life to be fundamentally out of control, and on the feeling of accomplishment derived from total mastery of the body. That sense of mastery, like the anorectic's, appears to derive from two sources. First, there is the reassurance that one can overcome all physical obstacles, push oneself to any extremes in pursuit of one's goals (which, as we have seen, is a characteristic motivation of compulsive runners, as well). Second, and most dramatic (it is spoken of time and again by female body-builders), is the thrill of being in total charge of the shape of one's body. "Create a masterpiece," says *Fit* magazine. "Sculpt your body contours into a work of art." As for the anorectic—who literally cannot *see* her body as other than her inner reality dictates and who is relentlessly driven by an ideal image of ascetic slenderness—so for the body-builder a purely mental conception comes to have dominance over her life: "You visualize what you want to look like . . . and then create the form." "The challenge presents itself: to rearrange things." "It's up to you to do the chiseling; you become the master sculptress." "What a fantasy, for your body to be changing! . . . I keep a picture in my mind as I work out of what I want to look like and what's happened to me already."[69] Dictation to nature of one's own chosen design for the body is the central goal for the body-builder, as it is for the anorectic.

The sense of security derived from the attainment of this goal appears, first of all, as the pleasure of control and independence.

"Nowadays," says Michael Sacks, associate professor of psychiatry at Cornell Medical College, "people no longer feel they can control events outside themselves—how well they do in their jobs or in their personal relationships, for example—but they can control the food they eat and how far they can run. Abstinence, tests of endurance, are ways of proving their self-sufficiency."[70] In a culture, moreover, in which our continued survival is often at the mercy of "specialists," machines, and sophisticated technology, the body acquires a special sort of vulnerability and dependency. We may live longer, but the circumstances surrounding illness and death may often be perceived as more alien, inscrutable, and arbitrary than ever before.

Our contemporary body-fetishism expresses more than a fantasy of self-mastery in an increasingly unmanageable culture, however. It also reflects our alliance *with* culture against all reminders of the inevitable decay and death of the body. "Everybody wants to live forever" is the refrain from the theme song of *Pumping Iron*. The most youth-worshipping of popular television shows, "Fame," opens with a song that begins, "I want to live forever." And it is striking that although the anorectic may come very close to death (and 15 percent do indeed die), the dominant experience throughout the illness is of *invulnerability*.

The dream of immortality is, of course, nothing new. But what is unique to modernity is that the defeat of death has become a scientific fantasy rather than a philosophical or religious mythology. We no longer dream of eternal union with the gods; instead, we build devices that can keep us alive indefinitely, and we work on keeping our bodies as smooth and muscular and elastic at forty as they were at eighteen. We even entertain dreams of halting the aging process completely: "Old age," according to Durk Pearson and Sandy Shaw, authors of the popular *Life Extension*, "is an unpleasant and unattractive affliction."[71] The mega-vitamin regime they prescribe is able, they claim, to prevent and even to reverse the mechanisms of aging.

Finally, it may be that in cultures characterized by gross excesses in consumption, the "will to conquer and subdue the body" (as Chernin calls it) expresses an aesthetic or moral rebellion.[72] Anorectics initially came from affluent families, and the current craze for long-distance running and fasting is largely a phenomenon of young, upwardly mobile professionals (Dinitia Smith calls it "Deprivation Chic").[73] To those who are starving *against* their wills, of course, starvation cannot function as an expression of the power of the will. At the same time, we should caution against viewing anorexia as a trendy illness of the elite and privileged. Rather, its most outstanding feature is powerlessness.

THE GENDER/POWER AXIS

Ninety percent of all anorectics are women. We do not, of course, need to know that particular statistic to realize that the contemporary "tyranny of slenderness" is far from gender-neutral. Women are more obsessed with their bodies than men, less satisfied with them,[74] and permitted less latitude with them by themselves, by men, and by the culture. In a 1984 *Glamour* magazine poll of 33,000 women, 75 percent said they thought they were "too fat." Yet by Metropolitan Life Insurance Tables, themselves notoriously affected by cultural standards, only 25 percent of these women were heavier than their optimal weight, and a full 30 percent were *below* that weight.[75] The anorectic's distorted image of her body—her inability to see it as anything but too fat—although more extreme, is not radically discontinuous, then, from fairly common female misperceptions.

Consider, too, actors like Nick Nolte and William Hurt, who are permitted a certain amount of softening, of thickening about the waist, while still retaining romantic-lead status. Individual style, wit, the projection of intelligence, experience, and effectiveness still go a long way for men, even in our fitness-obsessed culture. But no female can achieve the status of romantic or sexual ideal without the appropriate *body*. That body, if we use television commercials as a gauge, has gotten steadily leaner since the mid 1970s.[76] What used to be acknowledged as an extreme required only of high fashion models is now the dominant image that beckons to high-school and college women. Over and over, extremely slender women students complain of hating their thighs or their stomachs (the anorectic's most dreaded danger spot); often, they express concern and anger over frequent teasing by their boyfriends. Janey, a former student, is 5′10″ and weighs 132 pounds. Yet her boyfriend Bill, also a student of mine, calls her "Fatso" and "Big Butt" and insists she should be 110 pounds because (as he explains in his journal for my class) "that's what Brooke Shields weighs." He calls this "constructive criticism" and seems to experience extreme anxiety over the possibility of her gaining any weight: "I can tell it bothers her yet I still continue to badger her about it. I guess that I think that if I continue to remind her things will change faster."[77] This sort of relationship, in which the woman's weight has become a focal issue, is not at all atypical, as I have discovered from student journals and papers.

Hilda Bruch reports that many anorectics talk of having a "ghost" inside them or surrounding them, "a dictator who dominates me," as one woman describes it; "a little man who objects when I eat" is the description given by another.[78] The little ghost, the dictator, the "other self" (as he is often described) is always male, reports Bruch. The anorectic's *other* self—the self of the uncontrollable appetites, the impurities and taints, the flabby will and tendency to mental torpor—is the body, as we have seen. But it is also (and here the anorectic's associations are surely in the mainstream of Western culture) the *female* self. These two selves are perceived as at constant war. But it is clear that it is the male side—with its associated values of greater spirituality, higher intellectuality, strength of will—that is being expressed and developed in the anorexic syndrome.[79]

What is the meaning of these gender associations in the anorectic? I propose that there are two levels of meaning. One has to do with fear and disdain for traditional female roles and social limitations. The other has to do, more profoundly, with a deep fear of "the Female," with all its more nightmarish archetypal associations of voracious hungers and sexual insatiability.

Adolescent anorectics express a characteristic fear of growing up to be mature, sexually developed, and potentially reproductive women. "I have a deep fear," says one, "of having a womanly body, round and fully developed. I want to be tight and muscular and thin."[80] Cherry Boone O'Neill speaks explicitly of her fear of womanhood.[81] If only she could stay thin, says yet another, "I would never have to deal with having a woman's body; like Peter Pan I could stay a child forever."[82] The choice of Peter Pan is telling here—what she means is, stay a *boy* forever. And indeed, as Bruch reports, many anorectics, when children, dreamt and fantasized about growing up to be boys.[83] Some are quite conscious of playing out this fantasy through their anorexia; Adrienne, one of Levenkron's patients, was extremely proud of the growth of facial and body hair that often accompanies anorexia, and especially proud of her "skinny, hairy arms."[84] Many patients report, too, that their father had wanted a boy, were disappointed to get "less than" that, or had emotionally rebuffed their daughter when she began to develop sexually.[85]

In a characteristic scenario, anorexia develops just at the outset of puberty. Normal body changes are experienced by the anorectic, not surprisingly, as the takeover of the body by disgusting, womanish fat. "I grab my breasts," says Aimee Liu, "pinching them until they hurt. If only I could eliminate them, cut them off if need be, to become as flat-chested as a child again."[86] The anorectic is exultant when her periods stop (as they do in *all* cases of anorexia[87] and as they do in many female runners as well). Disgust with menstruation is typical: "I saw a picture at a feminist art gallery," says another woman. "There was a woman with long red yarn coming out of her, like she was menstruating. . . . I got that *feeling*—in that part of my body that I have trouble with . . . my stomach, my thighs, my pelvis. That revolted feeling."[88]

Some authors interpret these symptoms as a species of unconscious feminist protest, involving anger at the limitations of the traditional female role, rejection of values associated with it, and fierce rebellion against allowing their futures to develop in the same direction as their mothers' lives.[89] In her portrait of the typical anorexic family configuration, Bruch describes nearly all of the mothers as submissive to their husbands but very controlling of their children.[90] Practically all had had promising careers which they had given up to care for their husbands and families full-time, a task they take very seriously, although often expressing frustration and dissatisfaction.

Certainly, many anorectics appear to experience anxiety about falling into the life-style they associate with their mothers. It is a prominent theme in Aimee Liu's *Solitaire*. Another woman describes her feeling that "[I am] full of my mother . . . she is in me even if she isn't there" in nearly the same breath as she complains of her continuous fear of being "not human . . . of ceasing to exist."[91] And Ellen West, nearly a century earlier, had quite explicitly equated becoming fat with the inevitable (for an elite woman of her time) confinements of domestic life and the domestic stupor she associates with it:

Dread is driving me mad . . . the consciousness that ultimately I will lose everything; all courage, all rebelliousness, all drive for doing; that it—my little world—will make me flabby, flabby and fainthearted and beggarly.[92]

Several of my students with eating disorders reported that their anorexia had developed after their families had dissuaded them from choosing or forbidden them to embark on a traditionally male career.

Here anorexia finds a true sister-phenomenon in the epidemic of female invalidism and "hysteria" that swept through the middle and upper-middle classes in the second half of the nineteenth century.[93] It was a time that, in many ways, was very like our own, especially in the conflicting demands women were confronting: the opening up of new possibilities versus the continuing grip of the old expectations. On the one hand, the old preindustrial order, with the father at the head of a self-contained family production unit, had given way to the dictatorship of the market, opening up new, nondomestic opportunities for working women. On the other hand, it turned many of the most valued "female" skills—textile and garment manufacture, food processing—out of the home and over to the factory system.[94] In the new machine economy, the lives of middle-class women were far emptier than they had been before.

It was an era, too, that had been witnessing the first major feminist wave. In 1840, the World Anti-Slavery Conference had been held, at which the first feminists spoke loudly and long on the connections between the abolition of slavery and women's rights. The year 1848 saw the Seneca Falls Convention. In 1869, John Stuart Mill published his landmark work "On the Subjection of Women." And in 1889 the Pankhursts formed the Women's Franchise League. But it was an era, too (and not unrelatedly, as I shall argue later), when the prevailing ideal of femininity was the delicate, affluent lady, unequipped for anything but the most sheltered domestic life, totally dependent on her prosperous husband, providing a peaceful and comfortable haven for him each day after his return from his labors in the public sphere.[95] In a now famous letter, Freud, criticizing John Stuart Mill, writes:

It really is a still-born thought to send women into the struggle for existence exactly as men. If, for instance, I imagine my gentle sweet girl as a competitor it would only end in my telling her, as I did seventeen months ago, that I am fond of her and that I implore her to withdraw from the strife into the calm uncompetitive activity of my home.[96]

This is exactly what male doctors *did* do when women began falling ill, complaining of acute depression, severe headaches, weakness, nervousness, and self-doubt.[97] Among these women were such noted feminists and social activists as Charlotte Perkins Gilman, Jane Addams, Elizabeth Cady Stanton, Margaret Sanger, British activist Josephine Butler, and German suffragist Hedwig Dohm. "I was weary myself and sick of asking what I am and what I ought to be," recalls Gilman,[98] who later went on to write a fictional account of her mental breakdown in the chilling novella *The Yellow Wallpaper*. Her doctor, the famous female specialist S. Weir Mitchell, instructed her, as Gilman recalls, to "live as domestic a life as possible. Have your child with you all the time. . . . Lie down an hour every day after each meal. Have but two hours intellectual life a day. And never touch pen, brush or pencil as long as you live."[99]

Freud, who favorably reviewed Mitchell's 1887 book and who advised that psychotherapy for hysterical patients be combined with Mitchell's rest cure ("to avoid new psychical impressions"),[100] was as blind as Mitchell to the contribution that isolation, boredom, and intellectual frustration made to the etiology of hysteria. Nearly all of the subjects in *Studies in Hysteria* (as well as the later *Dora*) are acknowledged by Freud to be unusually intelligent, creative, energetic, independent, and, often, highly educated. (Berthe Pappenheim—"Anna O."—as we know, went on after recovery to become an active feminist and social reformer.) Freud even comments, criticizing Janet's notion that hysterics were "psychically insufficient," on the characteristic coexistence of hysteria with "gifts of the richest and most original kind."[101] Yet Freud never makes the connection (which Breuer had begun to develop)[102] between the monotonous domestic lives these women were expected to lead after they completed their schooling, and the emergence of compulsive daydreaming, hallucinations, dissociations, and hysterical conversions.

Charlotte Perkins Gilman does make that connection. In *The Yellow Wallpaper* she describes how a prescribed regime of isolation and enforced domesticity eventuates, in her fictional heroine, in the development of a full-blown hysterical symptom, madness, and collapse. The symptom, the hallucination that there is a woman trapped in the wallpaper of her bedroom, struggling to get out, is at once a perfectly articulated expression of protest and a completely debilitating idée fixe that allows the woman character no distance on her situation, no freedom of thought, no chance of making any progress in leading the kind of active, creative life her body and soul crave.

So too for the anorectic. It is indeed essential to recognize in this illness the dimension of protest against the limitations of the ideal of female domesticity (the "feminine mystique," as Betty Friedan called it) that reigned in America throughout the 1950s and early 1960s—the era when most of their mothers were starting homes and families. This was, we should recall, the era following World War II, an era during which women were fired en masse from the jobs they had held during the war and shamelessly propagandized back into the full-time job of wife and mother. It was an era, too, when the "fuller figure," as Jane Russell now calls it, came into fashion once more, a period of "mammary madness" (or "resurgent Victorianism," as Lois Banner calls it), which glamorized the voluptuous, large-breasted woman.[103] This remained the prevailing fashion tyranny until the late 1960s and early 1970s.

But we must recognize that the anorectic's protest, like that of the classical hysterical symptom, is written on the bodies of anorexic women, not embraced as a conscious politics—nor, indeed, does it reflect any social or political understanding at all. Moreover, the symptoms themselves function to preclude the emergence of such an understanding. The idée fixe—staying thin—becomes at its farthest extreme so powerful as to render any other ideas or life-projects meaningless. Liu describes it as "all encompassing."[104] West writes: "I felt all inner development was ceasing, that all becoming and growing were being choked, because a single idea was filling my entire soul."[105]

Paradoxically—and often tragically—these pathologies of female protest (and we must include agoraphobia here, as well as hysteria and anorexia) actually function as if in collusion with the cultural conditions that produced them.[106] The same is true for more moderate expressions of the contemporary female obsession with slenderness. Women may feel themselves deeply attracted by the aura of freedom and independence suggested by the boyish body ideal of today. Yet, each hour, each minute spent in anxious pursuit of that ideal (for it does not come naturally to most mature women) is in fact time and energy taken from inner development and social achievement. As a feminist protest, the obsession with slenderness is hopelessly counterproductive.

It is important to recognize, too, that the anorectic is terrified and repelled, not only by the traditional female domestic role—which she associates with mental lassitude and weakness—but by a certain archetypal image of the female: as hungering, voracious, all-needing, and all-wanting. It is this image that shapes and permeates her experience of her own hunger for food as insatiable and out of control, that makes her feel that if she takes just one bite, she will not be able to stop.

Let us explore this image. Let us break the tie with food and look at the metaphor: hungering . . . voracious . . . extravagantly and excessively needful . . . without restraint . . . always wanting . . . always wanting too much affection, reassurance, emotional and sexual contact, and attention. This is how many women frequently experience themselves, and, indeed, how many men experience women. "Please, God, keep me from telephoning him," prays the heroine in Dorothy Parker's classic "A Telephone Call,"[107] experiencing her need for reassurance and contact as being as out of control and degrading as the anorectic does her desire for food. The male counterpart to this is found in Paul Morel in Lawrence's *Sons and Lovers*: "Can you never like things without clutching them as if you wanted to pull the heart out of them?" he accuses Miriam as she fondles a flower. "Why don't you have a bit more restraint, or reserve, or something. . . . You're always begging things to love you, as if you were a beggar for love. Even the flowers, you have to fawn on them."[108] How much psychic authenticity do these images carry in 1980s America? One woman in my class provided a stunning insight into the connection between her perception of herself and the anxiety of the compulsive dieter. "You know," she said, "the anorectic is always convinced she is taking up too much space, eating too much, wanting food too much. I've never felt that way, but I've often felt that I was *too much*—too much emotion, too much need, too loud and demanding, too much *there*, if you know what I mean."[109]

The most extreme cultural expressions of the fear of woman as "too much"—which almost always revolve around her sexuality—are strikingly full of eating and hungering metaphors. "Of woman's unnatural, *insatiable* lust, what country, what village doth not complain?" queries Burton in *The Anatomy of Melancholy*.[110] "You are the true hiennas," says Walter Charleton, "that allure us with the fairness of your skins, and when folly hath brought us within your reach, you leap upon us and *devour* us."[111]

The mythology/ideology of the devouring, insatiable female (which, as we have seen, is the image of her female self the anorectic has internalized) tends historically to wax and wane. But not without rhyme or reason. In periods of gross environmental and social crisis, such as characterized the period of the witch-hunts in the fifteenth and sixteenth centuries, it appears to flourish.[112] "All witchcraft comes from carnal lust, which is in women *insatiable*," say Kramer and Sprenger, authors of the official witch-hunters handbook, *Malleus Malificarum*. For the sake of fulfilling the "*mouth* of the womb . . . [women] consort even with the devil."[113]

Anxiety over women's uncontrollable hungers appears to peak, as well, during periods when women are becoming independent and are asserting themselves politically and socially. The second half of the nineteenth century, concurrent with the first feminist wave discussed earlier, saw a virtual flood of artistic and literary images of the dark, dangerous, and evil female: "sharp-teethed, devouring" Sphinxes, Salomes, and Delilahs, "biting, tearing, murderous women." "No century," claims Peter Gay, "depicted woman as vampire, as castrator, as killer, so consistently, so programmatically, and so nakedly as the nineteenth."[114] No century, either, was so obsessed with sexuality—particularly female sexuality—and its medical control. Treatment for excessive "sexual excitement" and masturbation in women included placing leeches on the womb,[115] clitoridectomy, and removal of the ovaries (also recommended for "troublesomeness, eating like a ploughman, erotic tendencies, persecution mania, and simple 'cussedness'").[116] The importance of female masturbation in the etiology of the "actual neurosis" was a topic in which the young Freud and his friend and colleague Wilhelm Fliess were especially interested. Fliess believed that the secret to controlling such "sexual abuse" lay in the treatment of nasal "genital spots"; in an operation that was sanctioned by Freud, he attempted to "correct" the "bad sexual habits" of Freud's patient Emma Eckstein by removal of the turbinate bone of her nose.[117]

It was in the second half of the nineteenth century, too, despite a flurry of efforts by feminists and health reformers,[118] that the stylized "S-curve," which required a tighter corset than ever before, came into fashion.[119] "While the suffragettes were forcefully propelling all women toward legal and political emancipation," says Amaury deRiencourt, "fashion and custom imprisoned her physically as she had never been before."[120] Described by Thorstein Veblen as a "mutilation, undergone for the purpose of lowering the subject's vitality and rendering her permanently and obviously unfit for work," the corset indeed did just that.[121] In it a woman could barely sit or stoop, was unable to move her feet more than six inches at a time, and had difficulty in keeping herself from regular fainting fits. (In 1904, a researcher reported that "monkeys laced up in these corsets moped, became excessively irritable and within weeks sickened and died"!)[122] The connection was often drawn in popular magazines between enduring the tight corset and the exercise of self-restraint and control. The corset is "an ever present monitor," says one 1878 advertisement, "of a well-disciplined mind and well-regulated feelings."[123] Today, of course, we diet to achieve such control.

It is important to emphasize that, despite the practice of bizarre and grotesque methods of gross physical manipulation and external control (clitoridectomy, Chinese foot-binding, the removal of bones of the rib cage in order to fit into the tight corsets), such control plays a relatively minor role in the maintenance of gender/power relations. For every historical image of the dangerous, aggressive woman there is a corresponding fantasy—an ideal femininity, from which all threatening elements have been purged—that women have mutilated themselves *internally* to attain. In the Victorian era, at the same time that operations were being performed to control female sexuality, William Acton, Richard von Krafft-Ebing, and others were proclaiming the official scientific doctrine that women are naturally passive and "not very much troubled with sexual feelings of any kind."[124] Corresponding to this male medical fantasy was the popular artistic and moral theme of woman as ministering angel; sweet, gentle, domestic, without intensity or personal ambition of any sort.[125] Peter Gay suggests, correctly, that these ideals must be understood as a reaction-formation to the era's "pervasive sense of manhood in danger," and he argues that few women actually fit the "insipid goody" (as Kate Millett calls it) image.[126] What Gay forgets, however, is that most women *tried* to fit—working classes as well as middle were affected by the "tenacious and all-pervasive" ideal of the perfect lady.[127]

On the gender/power axis the female body appears, then, as the unknowing medium of the historical ebbs and flows of the fear of woman as "too much." That, as we have seen, is how the anorectic experiences her female, bodily self: as voracious, wanton, needful of forceful control by her male will. Living in the tide of cultural backlash against the second major feminist wave, she is not alone in constructing these images. Christopher Lasch, in *The Culture of Narcissism*, speaks of what he describes as "the apparently aggressive overtures of sexually liberated women" which "convey to many males the same message—that women are *voracious, insatiable*," and call up "early fantasies of a possessive, suffocating, *devouring* and castrating mother."[128]

Our contemporary beauty ideals, by contrast, seemed purged, as Kim Chernin puts it, "of the power to conjure up memories of the past, of all that could remind us of a woman's mysterious power."[129] The ideal, rather, is an "image of a woman in which she is not yet a woman": Darryl Hannah as the lanky, newborn mermaid in *Splash*; Lori Singer (appearing virtually anorexic) as the reckless, hyperkinetic heroine of *Footloose*; the Charley Girl; "Cheryl Tiegs in shorts, Margaux Hemingway with her hair wet; Brooke Shields naked on an island;"[130] the dozens of teenage women who appear in Coke commercials, in jeans commercials, in chewing gum commercials.

The images suggest amused detachment, casual playfulness, flirtatiousness without demand, and lightness of touch. A refusal to take sex, death, or politics too deadly seriously. A delightfully unconscious relationship to her body. The twentieth century has seen this sort of feminine ideal before, of course. When, in the 1920s, young women began to flatten their breasts, suck in their stomachs, bob their hair, and show off long colt-like legs, they believed they were pursuing a new freedom and daring that demanded a carefree, boyish style. If the traditional female hourglass suggested anything, it was confinement and immobility. Yet the flapper's freedom, as Mary McCarthy's and Dorothy Parker's short stories brilliantly reveal, was largely an illusion—as any obsessively cultivated sexual style must inevitably be. Although today's images may suggest androgynous independence, we need only consider who is on the receiving end of the imagery in order to confront the pitiful paradox involved.

Watching the commercials are thousands of anxiety-ridden women and adolescents (some of whom may well be the very ones appearing in the commercials) with anything *but* an unconscious relation to their bodies. They are involved in an absolutely contradictory state of affairs, a totally no-win game: caring desperately, passionately, obsessively about attaining an ideal of coolness, effortless confidence, and casual freedom. Watching the commercials is a little girl, perhaps ten years old, whom I saw in Central Park, gazing raptly at her father, bursting with pride: "Daddy, guess what? I lost two pounds!" And watching the commercials is the anorectic, who associates her relentless pursuit of thinness with power and control, but who in fact destroys her health and imprisons her imagination. She is surely the most startling and stark illustration of how cavalier power relations are with respect to the motivations and goals of individuals, yet how deeply they are etched on our bodies, and how well our bodies serve them.

The Body and the
Reproduction of Femininity

The body—what we eat, how we dress, the daily rituals through which we attend to the body—is a medium of culture. The body, as anthropologist Mary Douglas has argued, is a powerful symbolic form, a surface on which the central rules, hierarchies, and even metaphysical commitments of a culture are inscribed and thus reinforced through the concrete language of the body.[1] The body may also operate as a metaphor for culture. From quarters as diverse as Plato and Hobbes to French feminist Luce Irigaray, an imagination of body morphology has provided a blueprint for diagnosis and/or vision of social and political life.

The body is not only a *text* of culture. It is also, as anthropologist Pierre Bourdieu and philosopher Michel Foucault (among others) have argued, a *practical*, direct locus of social control. Banally, through table manners and toilet habits, through seemingly trivial routines, rules, and practices, culture is *"made* body," as Bourdieu puts it—converted into automatic, habitual activity. As such it is put "beyond the grasp of consciousness . . . [untouchable] by voluntary, deliberate transformations."[2] Our conscious politics, social commitments, strivings for change may be undermined and betrayed by the life of our bodies—not the craving, instinctual body imagined by Plato, Augustine, and Freud, but what Foucault calls the "docile body," regulated by the norms of cultural life.[3]

Throughout his later "genealogical" works (*Discipline and Punish*, *The History of Sexuality*), Foucault constantly reminds us of the primacy of practice over belief. Not chiefly through ideology, but through the organization and regulation of the time, space, and movements of our daily lives, our bodies are trained, shaped, and impressed with the stamp of prevailing historical forms of selfhood, desire, masculinity, femininity. Such an emphasis casts a dark and disquieting shadow across the contemporary scene. For women, as study after study shows, are spending more time on the management and discipline of our bodies than we have in a long, long time. In a decade marked by a reopening of the public arena to women, the intensification of such regimens appears diversionary and subverting. Through the pursuit of an ever-changing, homogenizing, elusive ideal of femininity—a pursuit without a terminus, requiring that women constantly attend to minute and often whimsical changes in fashion—female bodies become docile bodies—bodies whose forces and energies are habituated to external regulation, subjection, transformation, "improvement." Through the exacting and normalizing disciplines of diet, makeup, and dress—central organizing principles of time and space in the day of many women—we are rendered less socially oriented and more centripetally focused on self-modification. Through these disciplines, we continue to memorize on our bodies the feel and conviction of lack, of insufficiency, of never being good enough. At the farthest extremes, the practices of femininity may lead us to utter demoralization, debilitation, and death.

Viewed historically, the discipline and normalization of the female body—perhaps the only gender oppression that exercises itself, although to different degrees and in different forms, across age, race, class, and sexual orientation—has to be acknowledged as an amazingly durable and flexible strategy of social control. In our own era, it is difficult to avoid the recognition that the contemporary preoccupation with appearance, which still affects women far more powerfully than men, even in our narcissistic and visually oriented culture, may function as a backlash phenomenon, reasserting existing gender configurations against any attempts to shift or transform power relations.[4] Surely we are in the throes of this backlash today. In newspapers and magazines we daily encounter stories that promote traditional gender relations and prey on anxieties about change: stories about latch-key children, abuse in day-care centers, the "new woman's" troubles with men, her lack of marriageability, and so on. A dominant visual theme in teenage magazines involves women hiding in the shadows of men, seeking solace in their arms, willingly contracting the space they occupy.

The last, of course, also describes our contemporary aesthetic ideal for women, an ideal whose obsessive pursuit has become the central torment of many women's lives. In such an era we desperately need an effective political discourse about the female body, a discourse adequate to an analysis of the insidious, and often paradoxical, pathways of modern social control.

Developing such a discourse requires reconstructing the feminist paradigm of the late 1960s and early 1970s, with its political categories of oppressors and oppressed, villains and victims. Here I believe that a feminist appropriation of some of Foucault's later concepts can prove useful. Following Foucault, we must first abandon the idea of power as something possessed by one group and leveled against another; we must instead think of the network of practices, institutions, and technologies that sustain positions of dominance and subordination in a particular domain.

Second, we need an analytics adequate to describe a power whose central mechanisms are not repressive, but *constitutive*: "a power bent on generating forces, making them grow, and ordering them, rather than one dedicated to impeding them, making them submit, or destroying them." Particularly in the realm of femininity, where so much depends on the seemingly willing acceptance of various norms and practices, we need an analysis of power "from below," as Foucault puts it; for example, of the mechanisms that shape and proliferate—rather than repress—desire, generate and focus our energies, construct our conceptions of normalcy and deviance.[5]

And, third, we need a discourse that will enable us to account for the subversion of potential rebellion, a discourse that, while insisting on the necessity of objective analysis of power relations, social hierarchy, political backlash, and so forth, will nonetheless allow us to confront the mechanisms by which the subject at times becomes enmeshed in collusion with forces that sustain her own oppression.

This essay will not attempt to produce a general theory along these lines. Rather, my focus will be the analysis of one particular arena where the interplay of these dynamics is striking and perhaps exemplary. It is a limited and unusual arena, that of a group of gender-related and historically localized disorders: hysteria, agoraphobia, and anorexia nervosa.[6] I recognize that these disorders have also historically been class- and race-biased, largely (although not exclusively) occurring among white middle- and upper-middle-class women. Nonetheless, anorexia, hysteria, and agoraphobia may provide a paradigm of one way in which potential resistance is not merely undercut but *utilized* in the maintenance and repro-duction of existing power relations.[7]

The central mechanism I will describe involves a transformation (or, if you wish, duality) of meaning, through which conditions that are objectively (and, on one level, experientially) constraining, enslaving, and even murderous, come to be experienced as liber-ating, transforming, and life-giving. I offer this analysis, although limited to a specific domain, as an example of how various con-temporary critical discourses may be joined to yield an understand-ing of the subtle and often unwitting role played by our bodies in the symbolization and reproduction of gender.

THE BODY AS A TEXT OF FEMININITY

The continuum between female disorder and "normal" feminine practice is sharply revealed through a close reading of those dis-orders to which women have been particularly vulnerable. These, of course, have varied historically: neurasthenia and hysteria in the second half of the nineteenth century; agoraphobia and, most dra-matically, anorexia nervosa and bulimia in the second half of the twentieth century. This is not to say that anorectics did not exist in the nineteenth century—many cases were described, usually in the context of diagnoses of hysteria[8]—or that women no longer suffer from classical hysterical symptoms in the twentieth century. But the taking up of eating disorders on a mass scale is as unique to the culture of the 1980s as the epidemic of hysteria was to the Victorian era.[9]

The symptomatology of these disorders reveals itself as textuality. Loss of mobility, loss of voice, inability to leave the home, feeding others while starving oneself, taking up space, and whittling down the space one's body takes up—all have symbolic meaning, all have *political* meaning under the varying rules governing the historical construction of gender. Working within this framework, we see that whether we look at hysteria, agoraphobia, or anorexia, we find the body of the sufferer deeply inscribed with an ideological construc-tion of femininity emblematic of the period in question. The construction, of course, is always homogenizing and normalizing, erasing racial, class, and other differences and insisting that all women aspire to a coercive, standardized ideal. Strikingly, in these disorders the construction of femininity is written in disturbingly concrete, hyperbolic terms: exaggerated, extremely literal, at times virtually caricatured presentations of the ruling feminine mystique. The bodies of disordered women in this way offer themselves as an aggressively graphic text for the interpreter—a text that insists, actually demands, that it be read as a cultural statement, a statement about gender.

Both nineteenth-century male physicians and twentieth-century feminist critics have seen, in the symptoms of neurasthenia and hysteria (syndromes that became increasingly less differentiated as the century wore on), an exaggeration of stereotypically feminine traits. The nineteenth-century "lady" was idealized in terms of delicacy and dreaminess, sexual passivity, and a charmingly labile and capricious emotionality.[10] Such notions were formalized and scientized in the work of male theorists from Acton and Krafft-Ebing to Freud, who described "normal," mature femininity in such terms.[11] In this context, the dissociations, the drifting and fogging of perception, the nervous tremors and faints, the anesthesias, and the extreme mutability of symptomatology associated with nineteenth-century female disorders can be seen to be concretizations of the feminine mystique of the period, produced according to rules that governed the prevailing construction of femininity. Doctors described what came to be known as the hysterical personality as "impressionable, suggestible, and narcissistic; highly labile, their moods changing suddenly, dramatically, and seemingly for inconsequential reasons . . . egocentric in the extreme . . . essentially asexual and not uncommonly frigid"[12]—all characteristics normative of femininity in this era. As Elaine Showalter points out, the term *hysterical* itself became almost interchangeable with the term *feminine* in the literature of the period.[13]

The hysteric's embodiment of the feminine mystique of her era, however, seems subtle and ineffable compared to the ingenious literalism of agoraphobia and anorexia. In the context of our culture this literalism makes sense. With the advent of movies and television, the rules for femininity have come to be culturally transmitted more and more through standardized visual images. As a result, femininity itself has come to be largely a matter of constructing, in the manner described by Erving Goffman, the appropriate surface presentation of the self.[14] We are no longer given verbal descriptions or exemplars of what a lady is or of what femininity consists. Rather, we learn the rules directly through bodily discourse: through images that tell us what clothes, body shape, facial expression, movements, and behavior are required.

In agoraphobia and, even more dramatically, in anorexia, the disorder presents itself as a virtual, though tragic, parody of twentieth-century constructions of femininity. The 1950s and early 1960s, when agoraphobia first began to escalate among women, was a period of reassertion of domesticity and dependency as the feminine ideal. *Career woman* became a dirty word, much more so than it had been during the war, when the economy depended on women's willingness to do "men's work." The reigning ideology of femininity, so well described by Betty Friedan and perfectly captured in the movies and television shows of the era, was childlike, nonassertive, helpless without a man, "content in a world of bedroom and kitchen, sex, babies and home."[15] The housebound agoraphobic lives this construction of femininity literally. "You want me in this home? You'll have me in this home—with a vengeance!" The point, upon which many therapists have commented, does not need belaboring. Agoraphobia, as I. G. Fodor has put it, seems "the logical—albeit extreme—extension of the cultural sex-role stereotype for women" in this era.[16]

The emaciated body of the anorectic, of course, immediately presents itself as a caricature of the contemporary ideal of hyperslenderness for women, an ideal that, despite the game resistance of racial and ethnic difference, has become the norm for women today. But slenderness is only the tip of the iceberg, for slenderness itself requires interpretation. "C'est le sens qui fait vendre," said Barthes, speaking of clothing styles—it is meaning that makes the sale.[17] So, too, it is meaning that makes the body admirable. To the degree that anorexia may be said to be "about" slenderness, it is about slenderness as a citadel of contemporary and historical meaning, not as an empty fashion ideal. As such, the interpretation of slenderness yields multiple readings, some related to gender, some not. For the purposes of this essay I will offer an abbreviated, gender-focused reading. But I must stress that this reading illuminates only partially, and that many other currents not discussed here—economic, psychosocial, and historical, as well as ethnic and class dimensions—figure prominently.[18]

We begin with the painfully literal inscription, on the anorectic's body, of the rules governing the construction of contemporary femininity. That construction is a double bind that legislates contradictory ideals and directives. On the one hand, our culture still widely advertises domestic conceptions of femininity, the ideological moorings for a rigorously dualistic sexual division of labor that casts woman as chief emotional and physical nurturer. The rules for this construction of femininity (and I speak here in a language both symbolic and literal) require that women learn to feed others, not the self, and to construe any desires for self-nurturance and self-feeding as greedy and excessive.[19] Thus, women must develop a totally other-oriented emotional economy. In this economy, the control of female appetite for food is merely the most concrete expression of the general rule governing the construction of femininity: that female hunger—for public power, for independence, for sexual gratification—be contained, and the public space that women be allowed to take up be circumscribed, limited. Figure 23, which appeared in a women's magazine fashion spread, dramatically illustrates the degree to which slenderness, set off against the resurgent muscularity and bulk of the current male body-ideal, carries connotations of fragility and lack of power in the face of a decisive male occupation of social space. On the body of the anorexic woman such rules are grimly and deeply etched.

On the other hand, even as young women today continue to be taught traditionally "feminine" virtues, to the degree that the professional arena is open to them they must also learn to embody the "masculine" language and values of that arena—self-control, determination, cool, emotional discipline, mastery, and so on. Female bodies now speak symbolically of this necessity in their slender spare shape and the currently fashionable men's-wear look. (A contemporary clothing line's clever mirror-image logo, shown in Figure 24, offers women's fashions for the "New Man," with the model posed to suggest phallic confidence combined with female allure.) Our bodies, too, as we trudge to the gym every day and fiercely resist both our hungers and our desire to soothe ourselves, are becoming more and more practiced at the "male" virtues of

FIGURE 23

control and self-mastery. Figure 25 illustrates this contemporary equation of physical discipline with becoming the "captain" of one's soul. The anorectic pursues these virtues with single-minded, unswerving dedication. "Energy, discipline, my own power will keep me going," says ex-anorectic Aimee Liu, recreating her anorexic days. "I need nothing and no one else. . . . I will be master of my own body, if nothing else, I vow."[20]

The ideal of slenderness, then, and the diet and exercise regimens that have become inseparable from it offer the illusion of meeting, through the body, the contradictory demands of the contemporary ideology of femininity. Popular images reflect this dual demand. In a single issue of *Complete Woman* magazine, two articles appear, one on "Feminine Intuition," the other asking, "Are You

FIGURE 24

the New Macho Woman?" In *Vision Quest*, the young male hero falls in love with the heroine, as he says, because "she has all the best things I like in girls and all the best things I like in guys," that is, she's tough and cool, but warm and alluring. In the enormously popular *Aliens*, the heroine's personality has been deliberately constructed, with near–comic book explicitness, to embody traditional nurturant femininity alongside breathtaking macho prowess and control; Sigourney Weaver, the actress who portrays her, has called the character "Rambolina."

In the pursuit of slenderness and the denial of appetite the traditional construction of femininity intersects with the new requirement for women to embody the "masculine" values of the public arena. The anorectic, as I have argued, embodies this intersection,

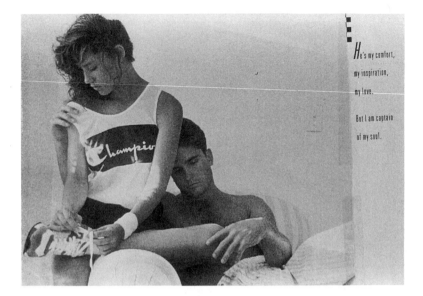

He's my comfort,
my inspiration,
my love.
But I am captain
of my soul.

FIGURE 25

this double bind, in a particularly painful and graphic way.[21] I mean *double bind* quite literally here. "Masculinity" and "femininity," at least since the nineteenth century and arguably before, have been constructed through a process of mutual exclusion. One cannot simply add the historically feminine virtues to the historically mas- culine ones to yield a New Woman, a New Man, a new ethics, or a new culture. Even on the screen or on television, embodied in created characters like the *Aliens* heroine, the result is a parody. Unfortunately, in this image-bedazzled culture, we find it increasingly difficult to discriminate between parodies and possibilities for the self. Explored as a possibility for the self, the "androgynous" ideal ultimately exposes its internal contradiction and becomes a war that tears the subject in two—a war explicitly thematized, by many anorectics, as a battle between male and female sides of the self.[22]

PROTEST AND RETREAT IN THE SAME GESTURE

In hysteria, agoraphobia, and anorexia, then, the woman's body may be viewed as a surface on which conventional constructions of femininity are exposed starkly to view, through their inscription in extreme or hyperliteral form. They are written, of course, in languages of horrible suffering. It is as though these bodies are speaking to us of the pathology and violence that lurks just around the corner, waiting at the horizon of "normal" femininity. It is no wonder that a steady motif in the feminist literature on female disorder is that of pathology as embodied *protest*—unconscious, inchoate, and counterproductive protest without an effective language, voice, or politics, but protest nonetheless.

American and French feminists alike have heard the hysteric speaking a language of protest, even or perhaps especially when she was mute. Dianne Hunter interprets Anna O.'s aphasia, which manifested itself in an inability to speak her native German, as a rebellion against the linguistic and cultural rules of the father and a return to the "mother-tongue": the semiotic babble of infancy, the language of the body. For Hunter, and for a number of other feminists working with Lacanian categories, the return to the semiotic level is both regressive and, as Hunter puts it, an "expressive" communication "addressed to patriarchal thought," "a self-repudiating form of feminine discourse in which the body signifies what social conditions make it impossible to state linguistically."[23] "The hysterics are accusing; they are pointing," writes Catherine Clément in *The Newly Born Woman*; they make a "mockery of culture."[24] In the same volume, Hélène Cixous speaks of "those wonderful hysterics, who subjected Freud to so many voluptuous moments too shameful to mention, bombarding his mosaic statute / law of Moses with their carnal, passionate body-words, haunting him with their inaudible thundering denunciations." For Cixous, Dora, who so frustrated Freud, is "the core example of the protesting force in women."[25]

The literature of protest includes functional as well as symbolic approaches. Robert Seidenberg and Karen DeCrow, for example, describe agoraphobia as a "strike" against "the renunciations usually demanded of women" and the expectations of housewifely functions such as shopping, driving the children to school, accompanying their husband to social events.[26] Carroll Smith-Rosenberg presents a similar analysis of hysteria, arguing that by preventing the woman from functioning in the wifely role of caretaker of others, of "ministering angel" to husband and children, hysteria "became one way in which conventional women could express—in most cases unconsciously—dissatisfaction with one or several aspects of their lives."[27] A number of feminist writers, among whom Susie Orbach is the most articulate and forceful, have interpreted anorexia as a species of unconscious feminist protest. The anorectic is engaged in a "hunger strike," as Orbach calls it, stressing that this is a political discourse, in which the action of food refusal and dramatic transformation of body size "expresses with [the] body what [the anorectic] is unable to tell us with words"—her indictment of a culture that disdains and suppresses female hunger, makes women ashamed of their appetites and needs, and demands that women constantly work on the transformation of their body.[28]

The anorectic, of course, is unaware that she is making a political statement. She may, indeed, be hostile to feminism and any other critical perspectives that she views as disputing her own autonomy and control or questioning the cultural ideals around which her life is organized. Through embodied rather than deliberate demonstration she exposes and indicts those ideals, precisely by pursuing them to the point at which their destructive potential is revealed for all to see.

The same gesture that expresses protest, moreover, can also signal retreat; this, indeed, may be part of the symptom's attraction. Kim Chernin, for example, argues that the debilitating anorexic fixation, by halting or mitigating personal development, assuages this generation's guilt and separation anxiety over the prospect of surpassing our mothers, of living less circumscribed, freer lives.[29] Agoraphobia, too, which often develops shortly after marriage, clearly functions in many cases as a way to cement dependency and attachment in the face of unacceptable stirrings of dissatisfaction and restlessness.

Although we may talk meaningfully of protest, then, I want to emphasize the counterproductive, tragically self-defeating (indeed, self-deconstructing) nature of that protest. Functionally, the symptoms of these disorders isolate, weaken, and undermine the sufferers; at the same time they turn the life of the body into an all-absorbing fetish, beside which all other objects of attention pale into unreality. On the symbolic level, too, the protest collapses into its opposite and proclaims the utter capitulation of the subject to the contracted female world. The muteness of hysterics and their return to the level of pure, primary bodily expressivity have been interpreted, as we have seen, as rejecting the symbolic order of the patriarchy and recovering a lost world of semiotic, maternal value. But *at the same time*, of course, muteness is the condition of the silent, uncomplaining woman—an ideal of patriarchal culture. Protesting the stifling of the female voice through one's own voicelessness— that is, employing the language of femininity to protest the conditions of the female world—will always involve ambiguities of this sort. Perhaps this is why symptoms crystallized from the language of femininity are so perfectly suited to express the dilemmas of middle-class and upper-middle-class women living in periods poised on the edge of gender change, women who have the social and material resources to carry the traditional construction of femininity to symbolic excess but who also confront the anxieties of new possibilities. The late nineteenth century, the post–World War II period, and the late twentieth century are all periods in which gender becomes an issue to be discussed and in which discourse proliferates about "the Woman Question," "the New Woman," "What Women Want," "What Femininity Is."

COLLUSION, RESISTANCE, AND THE BODY

The pathologies of female protest function, paradoxically, as if in collusion with the cultural conditions that produce them, reproducing rather than transforming precisely that which is being protested. In this connection, the fact that hysteria and anorexia have peaked during historical periods of cultural backlash against attempts at reorganization and redefinition of male and female roles is significant. Female pathology reveals itself here as an extremely interesting social formation through which one source of potential for resistance and rebellion is pressed into the service of maintaining the established order.

In our attempt to explain this formation, objective accounts of power relations fail us. For whatever the objective social conditions are that create a pathology, the symptoms themselves must still be produced (however unconsciously or inadvertently) by the subject. That is, the individual must invest the body with meanings of various sorts. Only by examining this productive process on the part of the subject can we, as Mark Poster has put it, "illuminate the mechanisms of domination in the processes through which meaning is produced in everyday life"; that is, only then can we see how the desires and dreams of the subject become implicated in the matrix of power relations.[30]

Here, examining the context in which the anorexic syndrome is produced may be illuminating. Anorexia will erupt, typically, in the course of what begins as a fairly moderate diet regime, undertaken because someone, often the father, has made a casual critical remark. Anorexia *begins in*, emerges out of, what is, in our time, conventional feminine practice. In the course of that practice, for any number of individual reasons, the practice is pushed a little beyond the parameters of moderate dieting. The young woman discovers what it feels like to crave and want and need and yet, through the exercise of her own will, to triumph over that need. In the process, a new realm of meanings is discovered, a range of values and possibilities that Western culture has traditionally coded as "male" and rarely made available to women: an ethic and aesthetic of self-mastery and self-transcendence, expertise, and power over others through the example of superior will and control. The experience is intoxicating, habit-forming.

At school the anorectic discovers that her steadily shrinking body is admired, not so much as an aesthetic or sexual object, but for the strength of will and self-control it projects. At home she discovers, in the inevitable battles her parents fight to get her to eat, that her actions have enormous power over the lives of those around her. As her body begins to lose its traditional feminine curves, its breasts and hips and rounded stomach, begins to feel and look more like a spare, lanky male body, she begins to feel untouchable, out of reach of hurt, "invulnerable, clean and hard as the bones etched into my silhouette," as one student described it in her journal. She despises, in particular, all those parts of her body that continue to mark her as female. "If only I could eliminate [my breasts]," says Liu, "cut them off if need be."[31] For her, as for many anorectics, the breasts represent a bovine, unconscious, vulnerable side of the self. Liu's body symbolism is thoroughly continuous with dominant cultural associations. Brett Silverstein's studies on the "Possible Causes of the Thin Standard of Bodily Attractiveness for Women"[32] testify empirically to what is obvious from every comedy routine involving a dramatically shapely woman: namely, our cultural association of curvaceousness with incompetence. The anorectic is also quite aware, of course, of the social and sexual vulnerability involved in having a female body; many, in fact, were sexually abused as children.

Through her anorexia, by contrast, she has unexpectedly discovered an entry into the privileged male world, a way to become what is valued in our culture, a way to become safe, to rise above it all—for her, they are the same thing. She has discovered this, paradoxically, by pursuing conventional feminine behavior—in this case, the discipline of perfecting the body as an object—to excess. At this point of excess, the conventionally feminine deconstructs, we might say, into its opposite and opens onto those values our culture has coded as male. No wonder the anorexia is experienced as liberating and that she will fight family, friends, and therapists in an effort to hold onto it—fight them to the death, if need be. The anorectic's experience of power is, of course, deeply and dangerously illusory. To reshape one's body into a male body is *not* to put on male power and privilege. To *feel* autonomous and free while harnessing body and soul to an obsessive body-practice is to serve, not transform, a social order that limits female possibilities. And, of course, for the female to become male is only for her to locate herself on the other side of a disfiguring opposition. The new "power look" of female body-building, which encourages women to develop the same hulklike, triangular shape that has been the norm for male body-builders, is no less determined by a hierarchical, dualistic construction of gender than was the conventionally "feminine" norm that tyrannized female body-builders such as Bev Francis for years.

Although the specific cultural practices and meanings are different, similar mechanisms, I suspect, are at work in hysteria and agoraphobia. In these cases too, the language of femininity, when pushed to excess—when shouted and asserted, when disruptive and demanding—deconstructs into its opposite and makes available to the woman an illusory experience of power previously forbidden to her by virtue of her gender. In the case of nineteenth-century femininity, the forbidden experience may have been the bursting of fetters—particularly moral and emotional fetters. John Conolly, the asylum reformer, recommended institutionalization for women who "want that restraint over the passions without which the female character is lost."[33] Hysterics often infuriated male doctors by their lack of precisely this quality. S. Weir Mitchell described these patients as "the despair of physicians," whose "despotic selfishness wrecks the constitution of nurses and devoted relatives, and in unconscious or half-conscious self-indulgence destroys the comfort of everyone around them."[34] It must have given the Victorian patient some illicit pleasure to be viewed as capable of such disruption of the staid nineteenth-century household. A similar form of power, I believe, is part of the experience of agoraphobia.

This does not mean that the primary reality of these disorders is not one of pain and entrapment. Anorexia, too, clearly contains a dimension of physical addiction to the biochemical effects of starvation. But whatever the physiology involved, the ways in which the subject understands and thematizes her experience cannot be reduced to a mechanical process. The anorectic's ability to live with minimal food intake allows her to feel powerful and worthy of admiration in a "world," as Susie Orbach describes it, "from which at the most profound level [she] feels excluded" and unvalued.[35] The literature on both anorexia and hysteria is strewn with battles of will between the sufferer and those trying to "cure" her; the latter, as Orbach points out, very rarely understand that the psychic values she is fighting for are often more important to the woman than life itself.

TEXTUALITY, PRAXIS, AND THE BODY

The "solutions" offered by anorexia, hysteria, and agoraphobia, I have suggested, develop out of the practice of femininity itself, the pursuit of which is still presented as the chief route to acceptance and success for women in our culture. Too aggressively pursued, that practice leads to its own undoing, in one sense. For if femininity is, as Susan Brownmiller has said, at its core a "tradition of imposed limitations,"[36] then an unwillingness to limit oneself, even in the pursuit of femininity, breaks the rules. But, of course, in another sense the rules remain fully in place. The sufferer becomes wedded to an obsessive practice, unable to make any effective change in her life. She remains, as Toril Moi has put it, "gagged and chained to [the] feminine role," a reproducer of the docile body of femininity.[37]

This tension between the psychological meaning of a disorder, which may enact fantasies of rebellion and embody a language of protest, and the practical life of the disordered body, which may utterly defeat rebellion and subvert protest, may be obscured by too exclusive a focus on the symbolic dimension and insufficient attention to praxis. As we have seen in the case of some Lacanian feminist readings of hysteria, the result of this can be a one-sided interpretation that romanticizes the hysteric's symbolic subversion of the phallocentric order while confined to her bed. This is not to say that confinement in bed has a transparent, univocal meaning—in powerlessness, debilitation, dependency, and so forth. The "practical" body is no brute biological or material entity. It, too, is a culturally mediated form; its activities are subject to interpretation and description. The shift to the practical dimension is not a turn to biology or nature, but to another "register," as Foucault puts it, of the cultural body, the register of the "useful body" rather than the "intelligible body."[38] The distinction can prove useful, I believe, to feminist discourse.

The intelligible body includes our scientific, philosophic, and aesthetic representations of the body—our cultural *conceptions* of the body, norms of beauty, models of health, and so forth. But the same representations may also be seen as forming a set of *practical* rules and regulations through which the living body is "trained, shaped, obeys, responds," becoming, in short, a socially adapted and "useful body."[39] Consider this particularly clear and appropriate example: the nineteenth-century hourglass figure, emphasizing breasts and hips against a wasp waist, was an intelligible *symbolic* form, representing a domestic, sexualized ideal of femininity. The sharp cultural contrast between the female and the male form, made possible by the use of corsets and bustles, reflected, in symbolic terms, the dualistic division of social and economic life into clearly defined male and female spheres. At the same time, to achieve the specified look, a particular feminine *praxis* was required—straitlacing, minimal eating, reduced mobility—rendering the female body unfit to perform activities outside its designated sphere. This, in Foucauldian terms, would be the "useful body" corresponding to the aesthetic norm.

The intelligible body and the useful body are two arenas of the same discourse; they often mirror and support each other, as in the above illustration. Another example can be found in the seventeenth-century philosophic conception of the body as a machine, mirroring an increasingly more automated productive machinery of labor. But the two bodies may also contradict and mock each other. A range of contemporary representations and images, as noted earlier, have coded the transcendence of female appetite and its public display in the slenderness ideal in terms of power, will, mastery, the possibilities of success in the professional arena. These associations are carried visually by the slender superwomen of prime-time television and popular movies and promoted explicitly in advertisements and articles appearing routinely in women's fashion magazines, diet books, and weight-training publications. Yet the thousands of slender girls and women who strive to embody these images and who in that service suffer from eating disorders, exercise compulsions, and continual self-scrutiny and self-castigation are anything *but* the "masters" of their lives.

Exposure and productive cultural analysis of such contradictory and mystifying relations between image and practice are possible only if the analysis includes attention to and interpretation of the "useful" or, as I prefer to call it, the practical body. Such attention, although often in inchoate and theoretically unsophisticated form, was central to the beginnings of the contemporary feminist movement. In the late 1960s and early 1970s the objectification of the female body was a serious political issue. All the cultural paraphernalia of femininity, of learning to please visually and sexually through the practices of the body—media imagery, beauty pageants, high heels, girdles, makeup, simulated orgasm—were seen as crucial in maintaining gender domination.

Disquietingly, for the feminists of the present decade, such focus on the politics of feminine praxis, although still maintained in the work of individual feminists, is no longer a centerpiece of feminist cultural critique.[40] On the popular front, we find *Ms.* magazine presenting issues on fitness and "style," the rhetoric reconstructed for the 1980s to pitch "self-expression" and "power." Although feminist theory surely has the tools, it has not provided a critical discourse to dismantle and demystify this rhetoric. The work of French feminists has provided a powerful framework for understanding the inscription of phallocentric, dualistic culture on gendered bodies, but it has offered very little in the way of concrete analyses of the female body as a locus of practical cultural control. Among feminist theorists in this country, the study of cultural representations of the female body has flourished, and it has often been brilliantly illuminating and instrumental to a feminist rereading of culture.[41] But the study of cultural representations alone, divorced from consideration of their relation to the practical lives of bodies, can obscure and mislead.

Here, Helena Mitchie's significantly titled *The Flesh Made Word* offers a striking example. Examining nineteenth-century representations of women, appetite, and eating, Mitchie draws fascinating and astute metaphorical connections between female eating and female sexuality. Female hunger, she argues, and I agree, "figures unspeakable desires for sexuality and power."[42] The Victorian novel's "representational taboo" against depicting women eating (an activity, apparently, that only "happens offstage," as Mitchie puts it) thus functions as a "code" for the suppression of female sexuality, as does the general cultural requirement, exhibited in etiquette and sex manuals of the day, that the well-bred woman eat little and delicately. The same coding is drawn on, Mitchie argues, in contemporary feminist "inversions" of Victorian values, inversions that celebrate female sexuality and power through images exulting in female eating and female hunger, depicting it explicitly, lushly, and joyfully.

Despite the fact that Mitchie's analysis centers on issues concerning women's hunger, food, and eating practices, she makes no mention of the grave eating disorders that surfaced in the late nineteenth century and that are ravaging the lives of young women today. The practical arena of women dieting, fasting, straitlacing, and so forth is, to a certain extent, implicit in her examination of Victorian gender ideology. But when Mitchie turns, at the end of her study, to consider contemporary feminist literature celebrating female eating and female hunger, the absence of even a passing glance at how women are *actually* managing their hungers today leaves her analysis adrift, lacking any concrete social moorings. Mitchie's sole focus is on the inevitable failure of feminist literature to escape "phallic representational codes."[43] But the feminist celebration of the female body did not merely deconstruct on the written page or canvas. Largely located in the feminist counterculture of the 1970s, it has been culturally displaced by a very different contemporary reality. Its celebration of female flesh now presents itself in jarring dissonance with the fact that women, feminists included, are starving themselves to death in our culture.

This is not to deny the benefits of diet, exercise, and other forms of body management. Rather, I view our bodies as a site of struggle, where we must *work* to keep our daily practices in the service of resistance to gender domination, not in the service of docility and gender normalization. This work requires, I believe, a determinedly skeptical attitude toward the routes of seeming liberation and pleasure offered by our culture. It also demands an awareness of the often contradictory relations between image and practice, between rhetoric and reality. Popular representations, as we have seen, may forcefully employ the rhetoric and symbolism of empowerment, personal freedom, "having it all." Yet female bodies, pursuing these ideals, may find themselves as distracted, depressed, and physically ill as female bodies in the nineteenth century were made when pursuing a feminine ideal of dependency, domesticity, and delicacy. The recognition and analysis of such contradictions, and of all the other collusions, subversions, and enticements through which culture enjoins the aid of our bodies in the reproduction of gender, require that we restore a concern for female praxis to its formerly central place in feminist politics.

Reading the Slender Body

In the late Victorian era, arguably for the first time in the West, those who could afford to eat well began systematically to deny themselves food in pursuit of an aesthetic ideal.[1] Certainly, other cultures had dieted. Aristocratic Greek culture made a science of the regulation of food intake, as a road to self-mastery and the practice of moderation in all things.[2] Fasting, aimed at spiritual purification and domination of the flesh, was an important part of the repertoire of Christian practice in the Middle Ages.[3] These forms of diet can clearly be viewed as instruments for the development of a "self"—whether an "inner" self, for the Christians, or a public self, for the Greeks—constructed as an arena in which the deepest possibilities for human excellence may be realized. Rituals of fasting and asceticism were therefore reserved for the select few, aristocratic or priestly, who were deemed capable of achieving such excellence of spirit. In the late nineteenth century, by contrast, the practices of body management begin to be middle-class preoccupations, and concern with diet becomes attached to the pursuit of an idealized physical weight or shape; it becomes a project in service of body rather than soul. Fat, not appetite or desire, became the declared enemy, and people began to measure their dietary achievements by the numbers on the scale rather than by the level of their mastery of impulse and excess. The bourgeois "tyranny of slenderness" (as Kim Chernin has called it)[4] had begun its ascendancy (particularly over women), and with it the development of numerous technologies—diet, exercise, and, later on, chemicals and surgery—aimed at a purely physical transformation.

Today, we have become acutely aware of the massive and multifaceted nature of such technologies and the industries built around them. To the degree that a popular critical consciousness exists, however, it has been focused largely (and not surprisingly) on what has been viewed as pathological or extreme—on the unfortunate minority who become "obsessed" or go "too far." Television talk shows feature tales of disasters caused by stomach stapling, gastric bubbles, gastrointestinal bypass operations, liquid diets, compulsive exercising. Magazines warn of the dangers of fat-reduction surgery and liposuction. Books and articles about bulimia and anorexia nervosa proliferate. The portrayal of eating disorders by the popular media is often lurid; audiences gasp at pictures of skeletal bodies or at item-by-item descriptions of the mounds of food eaten during an average binge. Such presentations create a "side show" relationship between the ("normal") audience and those on view ("the freaks"). To the degree that the audience may nonetheless recognize themselves in the behavior or reported experiences of those on stage, they confront themselves as "pathological" or outside the norm.

Of course, many of these behaviors *are* outside the norm, if only because of the financial resources they require. But preoccupation with fat, diet, and slenderness are not abnormal.[5] Indeed, such preoccupation may function as one of the most powerful normalizing mechanisms of our century, insuring the production of self-monitoring and self-disciplining "docile bodies" sensitive to any departure from social norms and habituated to self-improvement and self-transformation in the service of those norms. Seen in this light, the focus on "pathology," disorder, accident, unexpected disaster, and bizarre behavior obscures the normalizing function of the technologies of diet and body management. For women, who are subject to such controls more profoundly and, historically, more ubiquitously than men, the focus on "pathology" (unless embedded in a political analysis) diverts recognition from a central means of the reproduction of gender.

In this essay I examine the normalizing role of diet and exercise by analyzing popular representations through which their cultural meaning is crystallized, metaphorically encoded, and transmitted. More specifically, I pursue here Mary Douglas's insight that images of the "microcosm"—the physical body—may symbolically reproduce central vulnerabilities and anxieties of the "macrocosm"—the social body.[6] I will explore this insight by reading, as the text or surface on which culture is symbolically written, some dominant meanings that are connected, in our time, to the imagery of slenderness.[7]

The first step in my argument is a decoding of the contemporary slenderness ideal so as to reveal the psychic anxieties and moral valuations contained within it—valuations concerning correct and incorrect management of impulse and desire. In the process I describe a key contrast between two different symbolic functions of body shape and size: (1) the designation of social position, such as class status or gender role; and (2) the outer indication of the spiritual, moral, or emotional state of the individual. Next, aided by the significant work of Robert Crawford, I turn to the social body of consumer culture in order to demonstrate how the "correct" management of desire in that culture, requiring as it does a contradictory double-bind construction of personality, inevitably produces an unstable bulimic personality-type as its norm, along with the contrasting extremes of obesity and self-starvation.[8] These symbolize, I will argue, the contradictions of the social body—contradictions that make self-management a continual and virtually impossible task in our culture. Finally, I introduce gender into this symbolic framework, showing how additional resonances (concerning the cultural management of female desire, on the one hand, and female flight from a purely reproductive destiny, on the other) have overdetermined slenderness as the current ideal for women.

CONTEMPORARY ANXIETY AND THE ENEMY FLAB

In the magazine show "20/20," several ten-year-old boys were shown some photos of fashion models. The models were pencil-thin. Yet the pose was such that a small bulge of hip was forced, through the action of the body, into protuberance—as is natural, unavoidable on any but the most skeletal or the most tautly developed bodies. We bend over, we sit down, and the flesh coalesces in spots. These young boys, pointing to the hips, disgustedly pronounced the models to be "fat." Watching the show, I was appalled at the boys' reaction. Yet I could not deny that I had also been surprised at my own current perceptions while re-viewing female bodies in movies from the 1970s; what once appeared slender and fit now seemed loose and flabby. *Weight* was not the key element

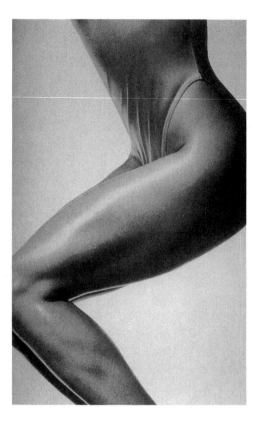

FIGURE 26

in these changed perceptions—my standards had not come to favor *thinner* bodies—rather, I had come to expect a tighter, smoother, more contained body profile (see Figure 26, which dramatically captures the essence of this ideal).

The self-criticisms of the anorectic, too, are usually focused on particular soft, protuberant areas of the body (most often the stomach) rather than on the body as a whole. Karen, in Ira Sacker and Marc Zimmer's *Dying to Be Thin*, tries to dispel what she sees as the myth that the anorectic misperceives her whole body as fat:

> I hope I'm expressing myself properly here, because this is important. You have to understand. I don't see my whole body as fat. When I look in the mirror I don't really see a fat person there. I see certain things about me that are really thin. Like my arms and legs. But I can

tell the minute I eat certain things that my stomach blows up like a pig's. I know it gets distended. And it's disgusting. That's what I keep to myself—hug to myself.[9]

Or Barbara, from Dalma Heyn's article on "Body Vision":

Sometimes my body looks so bloated, I don't want to get dressed. I like the way it looks for exactly two days each month: usually, the eighth and ninth days after my period. Every other day, my breasts, my stomach—they're just awful lumps, bumps, bulges. My body can turn on me at any moment; it is an out-of-control mass of flesh.[10]

Much has been made of such descriptions, from both psychoanalytic and feminist perspectives. But for now I wish to pursue these images of unwanted bulges and erupting stomachs in another direction than that of gender symbolism. I want to consider them as a metaphor for anxiety about internal processes out of control—uncontained desire, unrestrained hunger, uncontrolled impulse. Images of bodily eruption frequently function symbolically in this way in contemporary horror movies and werewolf films (*The Howling*, *A Teen-Age Werewolf in London*) and in David Cronenberg's remake of *The Fly*. The original *Fly* imagined a mechanical joining of fly parts and person parts, a variation on the standard "half-man, half-beast" image. In Cronenberg's *Fly*, as in the werewolf genre, a new, alien, libidinous, and uncontrollable self literally bursts through the seams of the victims' old flesh. (A related, frequently copied image occurs in *Alien*, where a parasite erupts from the chest of the human host.) In advertisements, the construction of the body as an alien attacker, threatening to erupt in an unsightly display of bulging flesh, is a ubiquitous cultural image.

Until the 1980s, excess weight was the target of most ads for diet products; today, one is much more likely to find the enemy constructed as bulge, fat, or flab. "Now," a typical ad runs, "get rid of those embarrassing bumps, bulges, large stomach, flabby breasts and buttocks. Feel younger, and help prevent cellulite buildup. . . . Have a nice shape with no tummy." To achieve such results (often envisioned as the absolute eradication of body, as in "no tummy") a violent assault on the enemy is usually required; bulges must be "attacked" and "destroyed," fat "burned," and stomachs (or, more disgustedly, "guts") must be "busted" and "eliminated" (Figure 27). The increasing popularity of liposuction, a far from

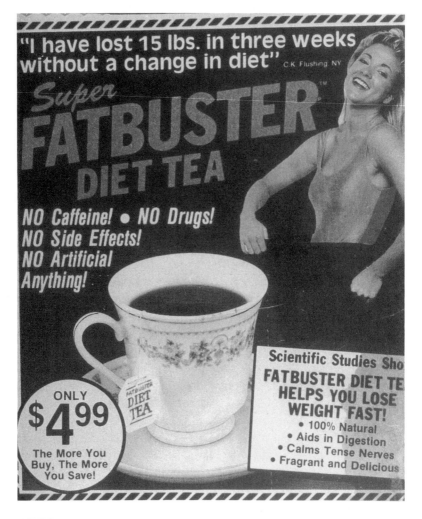

FIGURE 27

totally safe technique developed specifically to suck out the unwanted bulges of people of normal weight (it is not recommended
for the obese), suggests how far our disgust with bodily bulges has
gone. The ideal here is of a body that is absolutely tight, contained,
"bolted down," firm: in other words, a body that is protected
against eruption from within, whose internal processes are under
control. Areas that are soft, loose, or "wiggly" are unacceptable,

even on extremely thin bodies. Cellulite management, like liposuction, has nothing to do with weight loss, and everything to do with the quest for firm bodily margins.

This perspective helps illuminate an important continuity of meaning in our culture between compulsive dieting and body-building, and it reveals why it has been so easy for contemporary images of female attractiveness to oscillate between a spare, "minimalist" look and a solid, muscular, athletic look. The coexistence of these seemingly disparate images does not indicate that a postmodern universe of empty, endlessly differentiating images now reigns. Rather, the two ideals, though superficially very different, are united in battle against a common enemy: the soft, the loose; unsolid, excess flesh. It is perfectly permissible in our culture (even for women) to have substantial weight and bulk—so long as it is tightly managed. Simply to be slim is not enough—the flesh must not "wiggle" (Figure 28). Here we arrive at one source of insight into why it is that the image of ideal slenderness has grown thinner and thinner throughout the 1980s and early 1990s, and why women with extremely slender bodies often still see themselves as fat. Unless one takes to muscle-building, to achieve a flab-free, excess-free body one must trim very near the bone.

SLENDERNESS AND THE INNER STATE OF THE SELF

The moral—and, as we shall see, economic—coding of the fat/slender body in terms of its capacity for self-containment and the control of impulse and desire represents the culmination of a developing historical change in the social symbolism of body weight and size. Until the late nineteenth century, the central discriminations marked were those of class, race, and gender; the body indicated social identity and "place." So, for example, the bulging stomachs of successful mid-nineteenth-century businessmen and politicians were a symbol of bourgeois success, an outward manifestation of their accumulated wealth.[11] By contrast, the gracefully slender body announced aristocratic status; disdainful of the bourgeois need to display wealth and power ostentatiously, it commanded social space invisibly rather than aggressively, seemingly above the commerce in appetite or the need to eat. Subsequently, this ideal began to be appropriated by the status-seeking middle

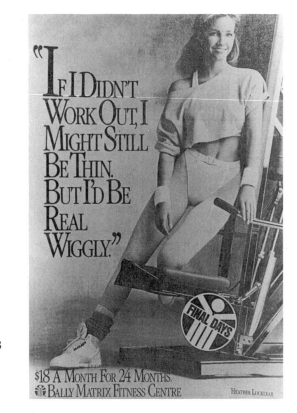

FIGURE 28

class, as slender wives became the showpieces of their husbands' success.[12]

Corpulence went out of middle-class vogue at the end of the century (even William Howard Taft, who had weighed over three hundred pounds while in office, went on a reducing diet). Social power had come to be less dependent on the sheer accumulation of material wealth and more connected to the ability to control and manage the labor and resources of others. At the same time, excess body weight came to be seen as reflecting moral or personal inadequacy, or lack of will.[13] These associations are possible only in a culture of overabundance—that is, in a society in which those who control the production of "culture" have more than enough to eat. The moral requirement to diet depends on the material preconditions that make the *choice* to diet an option and the possibility of personal "excess" a reality. Although slenderness continues to re-

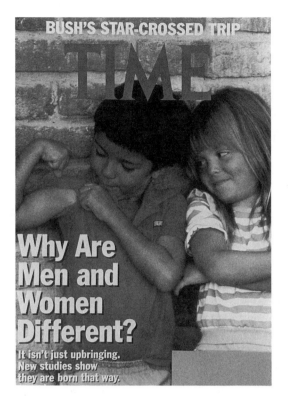

FIGURE 29

tain some of its traditional class associations ("a woman can never be too rich or too thin"), the importance of this equation has eroded considerably since the 1970s. Increasingly, the size and shape of the body have come to operate as a market of personal, internal order (or disorder)—as a symbol for the emotional, moral, or spiritual state of the individual.

Consider one particularly clear example, that of changes in the meaning of the muscled body. Muscularity has had a variety of cultural meanings that have prevented the well-developed body from playing a major role in middle-class conceptions of attractiveness. Of course, muscles have chiefly symbolized and continue to symbolize masculine power as physical strength, frequently operating as a means of coding the "naturalness" of sexual difference, as a *Time* cover and a Secret ad illustrate (Figures 29 and 30). But at the same time (and as the Secret ad illustrates), they have been

FIGURE 30

associated with manual labor and proletarian status, and they have often been suffused with racial meaning as well (as in numerous film representations of sweating, glistening bodies belonging to black slaves and prizefighters). Under the racial and class biases of our culture, muscles thus have been associated with the insensitive, unintelligent, and animalistic (recall the well-developed Marlon Brando as the emotionally primitive, physically abusive Stanley Kowalski in *A Streetcar Named Desire*). Moreover, as the body itself is dominantly imagined within the West as belonging to the "nature" side of a nature/culture duality, the *more* body one has had, the more uncultured and uncivilized one has been expected to be.

Today, however, the well-muscled body has become a cultural icon; "working out" is a glamorized and sexualized yuppie activity. No longer signifying inferior status (except when developed to extremes, at which point the old association of muscles with brute, unconscious materiality surfaces once more), the firm, developed body has become a symbol of correct *attitude*; it means that one "cares" about oneself and how one appears to others, suggesting willpower, energy, control over infantile impulse, the ability to "shape your life" (Figure 31). "You exercise, you diet," says Heather Locklear, promoting Bally Matrix Fitness Centre on television, "and you can do anything you want." Muscles express sexuality, but controlled, managed sexuality that is not about to erupt in unwanted and embarrassing display.[14]

To the degree that the question of class still operates in all this, it relates to the category of social mobility (or lack of it) rather than class *location*. So, for example, when associations of fat and lower-class status exist, they are usually mediated by moral qualities—fat being perceived as indicative of laziness, lack of discipline, unwillingness to conform, and absence of all those "managerial" abilities that, according to the dominant ideology, confer upward mobility (Figure 32). Correspondingly, in popular teen movies such as *Flashdance* and *Vision Quest*, the ability of the (working-class) heroine and hero to pare, prune, tighten, and master the body operates as a clear symbol of successful upward aspiration, of the penetrability of class boundaries to those who have "the right stuff." These movies (as one title makes explicit) are contemporary "quest myths"; like their prototype, *Rocky*, they follow the struggle of an individual to attain a personal grail, against all odds and through numerous trials. But

FIGURE 31

You don't just shape your body.
You shape your life.

**JOIN NOW AND PAY NOTHING
FOR 30 DAYS. ASK ABOUT OUR
PAY AS YOU GO PROGRAM.**

This year, keep your New Year's resolution to get in shape. Join Bally's now through January 31 and you'll pay nothing for 30 days. This offer applies to any renewable membership using our credit card automatic payment plan. Your membership gives you access to an unmatched selection of the most advanced exercise equipment. Including Lifecycles, Stairmasters® and Gravitrons® Plus aerobics and our exclusive 30-Minute Workout® Join Bally's today.

Bally's.
HEALTH CLUB
An Equal Opportunity Club

unlike the film quests of a previous era (which sent Mr. Smith to Washington and Mr. Deeds to town to battle the respective social evils of corrupt government and big business), *Flashdance* and *Vision Quest* render the hero's and heroine's commitment, will and spiritual integrity through the metaphors of weight loss, exercise, and tolerance of and ability to conquer physical pain and exhaustion. (In *Vision Quest*, for example, the audience is encouraged to admire the young wrestler's perseverance when he ignores the fainting spells and nosebleeds caused by his rigorous training and dieting.)

Not surprisingly, young people with eating disorders often thematize their own experience in similar terms, as in the following excerpt from an interview with a young woman runner:

> Well, I had the willpower, I could train for competition, and I could turn down food any time. I remember feeling like I was on a constant high. And the pain? Sure, there was pain. It was incredible. Between

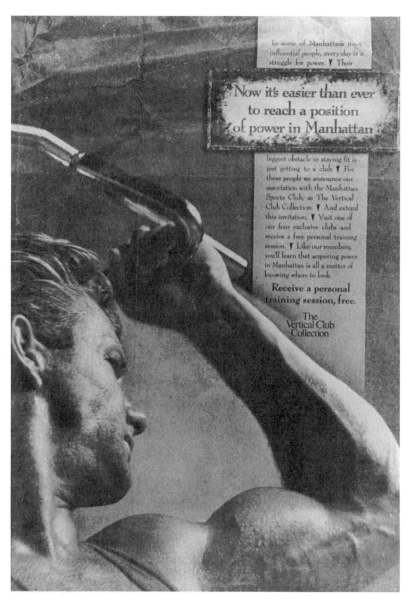

FIGURE 32

the hunger and the muscle pain from the constant workouts? I can't tell you how much I hurt.

You may think I was crazy to put myself through constant, intense pain. But you have to remember, I was fighting a battle. And when you get hurt in a battle, you're proud of it. Sure, you may scream inside, but if you're brave and really good, then you take it quietly, because you know it's the price you pay for winning. And I needed to win. I really felt that if I didn't win, I would die . . . all these enemy troops were coming at me, and I had to outsmart them. If I could discipline myself enough—if I could keep myself lean and strong— then I could win. The pain was just a natural thing I had to deal with.[15]

As in *Vision Quest*, the external context is training for an athletic event. But here, too, that goal becomes subordinated to an internal one. The real battle, ultimately, is with the self. At this point, the limitations of the brief history presented in the opening paragraph of this essay are revealed. In that paragraph, the contemporary preoccupation with diet is contrasted to historical projects of body management that were suffused with moral meaning. In this section, however, I have suggested that examination of even the most shallow representations (teen movies) discloses a moral ideology— one, in fact, seemingly close to the aristocratic Greek ideal described by Foucault in *The Use of Pleasure*. The central element of that ideal, as Foucault describes it, is "an agonistic relation with the self"— aimed, not at the extirpation of desire and hunger in the interests of "purity" (as in the Christian strain of dualism), but at a "virile" mastery of desire through constant "spiritual combat."[16]

For the Greeks, however, the "virile" mastery of desire took place in a culture that valorized moderation. The culture of contemporary body-management, struggling to manage desire in a system dedicated to the proliferation of desirable commodities, is very different. In cultural fantasies such as *Vision Quest* and *Flashdance*, self-mastery is presented as an attainable and stable state; but, as I argue in the next section of this essay, the reality of the contemporary agonism of the self is another matter entirely.

SLENDERNESS AND THE SOCIAL BODY

Mary Douglas, looking on the body as a system of "natural symbols" that reproduce social categories and concerns, has argued that anxiety about the maintenance of rigid bodily boundaries (manifested, for example, in rituals and prohibitions concerning excreta, saliva, and the strict delineation of "inside" and "outside") is most evident and intense in societies whose external boundaries are under attack.[17] Let me hypothesize, similarly, that preoccupation with the "internal" management of the body (that is, management of its desires) is produced by instabilities in what could be called the macro-regulation of desire within the system of the social body.

In advanced consumer capitalism, as Robert Crawford has elegantly argued, an unstable, agonistic construction of personality is produced by the contradictory structure of economic life.[18] On the one hand, as producers of goods and services we must sublimate, delay, repress desires for immediate gratification; we must cultivate the work ethic. On the other hand, as consumers we must display a boundless capacity to capitulate to desire and indulge in impulse; we must hunger for constant and immediate satisfaction. The regulation of desire thus becomes an ongoing problem, as we find ourselves continually besieged by temptation, while socially condemned for overindulgence. (Of course, those who cannot afford to indulge their desires as consumers, teased and frustrated by the culture, face a much harsher dilemma.)

Food and diet are central arenas for the expression of these contradictions. On television and in popular magazines, with a flip of the page or barely a pause between commercials, images of luscious foods and the rhetoric of craving and desire are replaced by advertisements for grapefruit diets, low-calorie recipes, and exercise equipment. Even more disquieting than these manifest oppositions, however, are the constant attempts by advertisers to mystify them, suggesting that the contradiction doesn't really exist, that one can "have it all." Diets and exercise programs are accordingly presented with the imagery of instant gratification ("From Fat to Fabulous in 21 Days," "Size 22 to Size 10 in No Time Flat," "Six Minutes to an Olympic-Class Stomach") and effortlessness ("3,000 Sit-Ups Without Moving an Inch . . . 10 Miles of Jogging Lying Flat on Your Back" [Figure 33], "85 Pounds Without Dieting," and even, shamelessly, "Exercise Without Exercise"). In reality, however, the opposition is not so easily reconciled. Rather, it presents a classic double bind, in which the self is torn in two mutually incompatible directions. The contradiction is not an abstract one but stems from

FIGURE 33

the specific historical construction of a "consuming passion" from which all inclinations toward balance, moderation, rationality, and foresight have been excluded.

Conditioned to lose control at the mere sight of desirable products, we can master our desires only by creating rigid defenses against them. The slender body codes the tantalizing ideal of a well-managed self in which all is kept in order despite the contradictions of consumer culture. Thus, whether or not the struggle is played out in terms of food and diet, many of us may find our lives vacillating between a daytime rigidly ruled by the "performance principle" and nights and weekends that capitulate to unconscious "letting go" (food, shopping, liquor, television, and other addictive drugs). In this way, the central contradiction of the system inscribes itself on our bodies, and bulimia emerges as a characteristic modern personality construction. For bulimia precisely and explicitly expresses the extreme development of the hunger for unrestrained consumption (exhibited in the bulimic's uncontrollable food binges) existing in unstable tension alongside the requirement that we sober up, "clean up our act," get back in firm control on Monday morning (the necessity for purge—exhibited in the bulimic's vomiting, compulsive exercising, and laxative purges).

The same structural contradiction is inscribed in what has been termed (incorrectly) the "paradox" that we have an "epidemic" of anorexia nervosa in this country "despite the fact that we have an overweight majority."[19] Far from paradoxical, the coexistence of anorexia and obesity reveals the instability of the contemporary personality construction, the difficulty of finding homeostasis between the producer and the consumer sides of the self. Bulimia embodies the unstable double bind of consumer capitalism, while anorexia and obesity embody an attempted resolution of that double bind. Anorexia could thus be seen as an extreme development of the capacity for self-denial and repression of desire (the work ethic in absolute control); obesity, as an extreme capacity to capitulate to desire (consumerism in control). Both are rooted in the same consumer-culture construction of desire as overwhelming and overtaking the self. Given that construction, we can only respond either with total submission or rigid defense.

Neither anorexia nor obesity is accepted by the culture as an appropriate response. The absolute conquest of hunger and desire (even in symbolic form) can never be tolerated by a consumer system—even if the Christian dualism of our culture also predisposes us to be dazzled by the anorectic's ability seemingly to transcend the flesh. Anorectics are proud of this ability, but, as the disorder progresses, they usually feel the need to hide their skeletal bodies from those around them. If cultural attitudes toward the anorectic are ambivalent, however, reactions to the obese are not. As Marcia Millman documents in *Such a Pretty Face*, the obese elicit blinding rage and disgust in our culture and are often viewed in terms that suggest an infant sucking hungrily, unconsciously at its mother's breast: greedy, self-absorbed, lazy, without self-control or willpower.[20] People avoid sitting next to the obese (even when the space they take up is not intrusive); comics feel no need to restrain their cruelty; socially, they are considered unacceptable at public functions (one man wrote to "Dear Abby," saying that he was planning to replace his brother and sister-in-law as honor attendants at his wedding, because "they are both quite overweight"). Significantly, the part of the obese anatomy most often targeted for vicious attack, and most despised by the obese themselves, is the stomach, symbol of consumption (in the case of the obese, unrestrained consumption taking over the organism; one of Marcia Millman's interviewees recalls how the husband of a friend called hers "an awful, cancerous-looking growth").[21]

SLENDERNESS, SELF-MANAGEMENT,
AND NORMALIZATION

Self-management in consumer culture, I have been arguing, becomes more elusive as it becomes more pressing. The attainment of an acceptable body is extremely difficult for those who do not come by it "naturally" (whether aided by genetics, metabolism, or high activity-level) and as the ideal becomes firmer and tauter it begins to exclude more and more people. Constant watchfulness over appetite and strenuous work on the body itself are required to conform to this ideal, while the most popular means of "correction"—dieting—often insures its own failure, as the experience of deprivation leads to compensatory binging, with its attendant feelings of defeat, worthlessness, and loss of hope. Between the media images of self-containment and self-mastery and the reality of constant, everyday stress and anxiety about one's appearance lies the chasm that produces bodies habituated to self-monitoring and self-normalization.

Ultimately, the body (besides being evaluated for its success or failure at getting itself in order) is seen as demonstrating correct or incorrect attitudes toward the demands of normalization itself. The obese and anorectic are therefore disturbing partly because they embody resistance to cultural norms. Bulimics, by contrast, typically strive for the conventionally attractive body shape dictated by their more "normative" pattern of managing desire. In the case of the obese, in particular, what is perceived as their defiant rebellion against normalization appears to be a source of the hostility they inspire. The anorectic at least pays homage to dominant cultural values, outdoing them in their own terms:

> I wanted people to look at me and see something special. I wanted to look in the face of a stranger and see admiration, so that I would know that I accomplished something that was just about impossible for most people, especially in our society. . . . From what I've seen, more people fail at losing weight than at any other single goal. I found out how to do what everyone else couldn't: I could lose as much or as little weight as I wanted. And that meant I was better than everyone else.[22]

The anorectic thus strives to stand above the crowd by excelling at its own rules; in so doing, however, she exposes the hidden penalties. But the obese—particularly those who claim to be happy although overweight—are perceived as not playing by the rules at all. If the rest of us are struggling to be acceptable and "normal," we cannot allow them to get away with it; they must be put in their place, be humiliated and defeated.

A number of talk shows have made this abundantly clear. On one, much of the audience reaction was given over to disbelief and to the attempt to prove to one obese woman that she was *not* happy: "I can't believe you don't want to be slim and beautiful, I just can't believe it." "I heard you talk a lot about how you feel good about yourself and you like yourself, but I really think you're kidding yourself." "It's hard for me to believe that Mary Jane is really happy . . . you don't fit into chairs, it's hard to get through the doorway. My God, on the subway, forget it." When Mary Jane persisted in her assertion that she was happy, she was warned, in a viciously self-righteous tone, that it would not last: "Mary Jane, to be the way you are today, you had better start going on a diet soon, because if you don't you're going to get bigger and bigger and bigger. It's true."[23] On another show, in an effort to subdue an increasingly hostile and offensive audience one of the doctor-guests kept trying to reassure them that the "fat and happy" target of their attacks did not *really* mean that she didn't *want* to lose weight; rather, she was simply tired of trying and failing. This construction allows people to give their sympathy to the obese, assuming as it does the obese person's acknowledgment that to be "normal" is the most desired goal, elusive only because of personal inadequacy. Those who are willing to present themselves as pitiable, in pain, and conscious of their own unattractiveness—often demonstrated, on these shows, by self-admissions about intimate physical difficulties, orgies of self-hate, or descriptions of gross consumption of food, win the sympathy and concern of the audience.

SLENDERNESS AND GENDER

It has been amply documented that women in our culture are more tyrannized by the contemporary slenderness ideal than men are, as they typically have been by beauty ideals in general. It is far more important to men than to women that their partner be slim.[24] Women are much more prone than men to perceive themselves as too fat.[25] And, as is by now well known, girls and women are more likely to engage in crash dieting, laxative abuse, and compulsive exercising and are far more vulnerable to eating disorders than males. But eating disorders are not only "about" slenderness, any more than (as I have been arguing) slenderness is only—or even chiefly—about being physically thin. My aim in this section, there-fore, is not to "explain" facts about which so much has now been written from historical, psychological, and sociological points of view. Rather, I want to remain with the image of the slender body, confronting it now both as a gendered body (the slender body as female body—the usual form in which the image is displayed) (Figure 34) and as a body whose gender meaning is never neutral. This layer of gender-coded signification, suffusing other meanings,

FIGURE 34

overdetermines slenderness as a contemporary ideal of specifically *female* attractiveness.

The exploration of contemporary slenderness as a metaphor for the correct management of desire must take into account the fact that throughout dominant Western religious and philosophical traditions, the capacity for self-management is decisively coded as male. By contrast, all those bodily spontaneities—hunger, sexuality, the emotions—seen as needful of containment and control have been culturally constructed and coded as female.[26] The management of specifically female desire, therefore, is in phallocentric cultures a doubly freighted problem. Women's desires are by their very nature excessive, irrational, threatening to erupt and challenge the patriarchal order.

Some writers have argued that female hunger (as a code for female desire) is especially problematized during periods of disruption and change in established gender-relations and in the position of women. In such periods (of which our own is arguably one), nightmare images of what Bram Dijkstra has called "the consuming woman" theme proliferate in art and literature (images representing female desire unleashed), while dominant constructions of the female body become more sylphlike—unlike the body of a fully developed woman, more like that of an adolescent or boy (images that might be called female desire unborn). Dijkstra argues such a case concerning the late nineteenth century, pointing to the devouring sphinxes and bloodsucking vampires of *fin-de-siècle* art, and the accompanying vogue for elongated, "sublimely emaciated" female bodies.[27] A commentator of the time vividly describes the emergence of a new body-style, not very unlike our own:

> Women can change the cut of their clothes at will, but how can they change the cut of their anatomies? And yet, they have done just this thing. Their shoulders have become narrow and slightly sloping, their throats more slender, their hips smaller and their arms and legs elongated to an extent that suggest that bed, upon which the robber, Procrustes, used to stretch his victims.[28]

The fact that our own era has witnessed a comparable shift (from the hourglass figure of the fifties to the androgynous, increasingly elongated, slender look that has developed over the past decade) cries out for interpretation. This shift, however, needs to be interpreted not only from the standpoint of male anxiety over women's desires (Dijkstra's analysis, while crucial, is only half the story) but also from the standpoint of the women who embrace the "new look." For them it may have a very different meaning; it may symbolize, not so much the containment of female desire, as its liberation from a domestic, reproductive destiny. The fact that the slender female body can carry both these seemingly contradictory

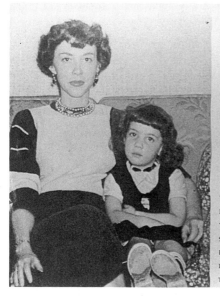

FIGURE 35

meanings is one reason, I would suggest, for its compelling attraction in periods of gender change.[29]

To elaborate this argument in more detail: earlier, I presented some quotations from interviews with eating-disordered women in which they describe their revulsion to breasts, stomachs, and all other bodily bulges. At that point I subjected these quotations to a gender-neutral reading. While not rescinding that interpretation, I want to overlay it now with another reading, which I present in "Anorexia Nervosa: Psychopathology as the Crystallization of Culture." There, I suggest that the characteristic anorexic revulsion toward hips, stomach, and breasts (often accompanied by disgust at menstruation and relief at amenorrhoea) might be viewed as expressing rebellion against maternal, domestic femininity—a femininity that represents both the suffocating control the anorectic experiences her own mother as having had over her, *and* the mother's actual lack of position and authority outside the domestic arena. (A Nike ad [Figure 35] embodies both these elements, as the "strength" of the mother is depicted in the containing arm that encircles her small daughter, while young women reading the ad are reassured that they can exercise *their* strength in other, non-maternal ways.) Here we encounter another reason for anxiety over soft, protuberant body-parts. They evoke helpless infancy and symbolize maternal femininity as it has been constructed over the past hundred years in the West. That femininity, as Dorothy Dinnerstein has argued, is perceived as both frighteningly powerful and, as the child comes increasingly to recognize the hierarchical nature of the sexual division of labor, utterly powerless.[30]

The most literal symbolic form of maternal femininity is represented by the nineteenth-century hourglass figure, emphasizing breasts and hips—the markers of reproductive femaleness—against a fragile wasp waist.[31] It is not until the post–World War II period, with its relocation of middle-class women from factory to home and its coercive bourgeois dualism of the happy homemaker-mother and the responsible, provider-father, that such clear bodily demarcation of "male" and "female" spheres surfaces again. The era of the cinch belt, the pushup bra, and Marilyn Monroe could be viewed, for the body, as an era of "resurgent Victorianism."[32] It was also the last coercively normalizing body-ideal to reign before boyish slenderness began its ascendancy in the mid-1960s.

From this perspective, one might speculate that the boys who reacted with disgust or anxiety to fleshy female parts were reacting to evocations of maternal power, newly threatening in an age when women are making their way into arenas traditionally reserved for men: law, business, higher education, politics, and so forth.[33] The buxom Sophia Loren was a sex goddess in an era when women were encouraged to define their deepest desires in terms of service to home, husband, and family. Today, it is required of female desire, loose in the male world, to be normalized according to the professional (and male) standards of that world; female bodies, accordingly, must be stripped of all psychic resonances with maternal power. From the standpoint of male anxiety, the lean body of the career businesswoman today may symbolize such a neutralization. With her body and her dress she declares symbolic allegiance to the professional, white, male world along with her lack of intention to subvert that arena with alternative "female values." At the same time, insofar as she is clearly "dressing up," *playing* male (almost always with a "softening" fashion touch to establish traditional feminine decorativeness, and continually cautioned against the dire

Is your face paying the price of success?

FIGURE 36

consequences of allotting success higher priority than her looks), she represents no serious competition (symbolically, that is) to the real men of the workplace (Figures 36 and 37).

For many women, however, disidentification with the maternal body, far from symbolizing reduced power, may symbolize (as it did in the 1890s and 1920s) freedom from a reproductive destiny and a construction of femininity seen as constraining and suffocating. Correspondingly, taking on the accoutrements of the white, male world may be experienced as empowerment by women themselves, and as their chance to embody qualities—detachment, self-containment, self-mastery, control—that are highly valued in our culture. The slender body, as I have argued earlier, symbolizes such qualities. "It was about power," says Kim Morgan, speaking in the documentary *The Waist Land* of the obsession with slenderness that led to her anorexia, "that was the big thing . . . something I could throw in people's faces, and they would look at me and I'd only weigh this much, but I was strong and in control, and

clothes minded

Crystal-and-drop earrings

How to Make a Guy's Look Girlish

Add the right accents to handsome haberdashery and you can give it a frankly feminine air. Here are a few softening touches worth trying.

● **SCARVES** Drape a lacy scarf around your shoulders, tie a chiffon scarf in a floppy bow at your throat or let a lace-trimmed hanky peak out of your jacket or shirt pocket.

Lace-trimmed pocket square

● **TIES** Knot a softly woven or paisley print tie and wear it the way no man would—with a strand or two of pearls.

● **JEWELRY** Gems are the definitive differentiating pieces. Try: long link chains with fake jewels, rhinestone pendants, pretty pins and elegant drop earrings.

Colorful fau gemstone pins

● **BAGS** Carry a clutch in soft brightly colored leather—it has a businesslike shape with a casual flair.

● **SHOES** Go for mannish wing tip oxfords or Loafers with feminine details— pointed toes, under-slung heels, two-tone styling, leather bows or tassels—and wear them with bright or patterned tights or delicate crocheted socks. ●

Red reptilian-leather clutch

Pointy-toed wing tip oxfords

Anne Klein II notch lapel shirt, V-neck sweater, blazer and pants. Amy Sinaiko crystal-and-pearl drop earrings. Yves St. Laurent faux-gemstone pins. Levire pointy-toed wing tip oxfords. Hair by Lee Emmack; makeup by Roxanna Floyd.

#9

FIGURE 37

Aerobics are terrific for the cardio-vascular system. And even for burning calories.

But when it comes to firming your body, there's no substitute for a progressive resistance system.

Like the Bodybar 2000. The world's finest home gym. Designed by the people who have been making institutional fitness equipment for nearly 40 years.

The Bodybar 2000 offers over 32 firming exercises. The kind you'd do at a health spa.

Only, now you can do them in the privacy of your own home. With no time wasted waiting for a machine to be free. Or time wasted driving to and from the spa.

Look for the Bodybar 2000 at better sporting goods stores everywhere. Or call **1-800-62-MARCY**, Ext. 47 for information.

Because if you have a problem with firmness, Marcy can help you iron it out.

⊘ MARCY
WHEN YOU FINALLY GET SERIOUS.

THE JOY OF COOKING.

FIGURE 38

hey *you're* sloppy."[34] The taking on of "male" power as self-mastery is another locus where, for all their surface dissimilarities, the shedding of weight and the development of muscles intersect. Appropriately, the new "Joy of Cooking" takes place in the gym, in one advertisement that shamelessly exploits the associations of female body-building with liberation from a traditional, domestic destiny (Figure 38).

In the intersection of these gender issues and more general cultural dilemmas concerning the management of desire, we see how the tightly managed body—whether demonstrated through sleek, minimalist lines or firmly developed muscles—has been overdetermined as a contemporary ideal of specifically female attractiveness. The axis of consumption/production is gender-overlaid, as I have argued, by the hierarchical dualism that constructs a dangerous, appetitive, bodily "female principle" in opposition to a masterful "male" will. We would thus expect that when the regulation of desire becomes especially problematic (as it is in advanced consumer cultures), women and their bodies will pay the greatest symbolic and material toll. When such a situation is compounded by anxiety about *women's* desires in periods when traditional forms of gender organization are being challenged, this toll is multiplied. It would be wrong to suppose, however, that it is exacted through the simple *repression* of female hunger. Rather, here as elsewhere, power works also "from below," as women associate slenderness with self-management, by way of the experience of newfound freedom (from a domestic destiny) and empowerment in the public arena. In this connection we might note the difference between contemporary ideals of slenderness, coded in terms of self-mastery and expressed through traditionally "male" body symbolism, and mid-Victorian ideals of female slenderness, which symbolically emphasized reproductive femininity corseted under tight "external" constraints. But whether externally bound or internally managed, no body can escape either the imprint of culture or its gendered meanings.

PART THREE

POSTMODERN BODIES

Feminism, Postmodernism, and
Gender Skepticism

In 1987, I heard a feminist historian claim that there were absolutely no common areas of experience between the wife of a plantation owner in the pre–Civil War South and the female slaves her husband owned. Gender, she argued, is so thoroughly fragmented by race, class, historical particularity, and individual difference as to be useless as an analytical category. The "bonds of womanhood," she insisted, are a feminist fantasy, born out of the ethnocentrism of white, middle-class academics.

• • •

A central point of a book by a feminist philosopher is the refutation of all feminist attempts to articulate a sense in which the history of philosophy reveals distinctively "male" perspectives on reality. All such attempts, the author argues, "do violence" to the history of philosophy and "injustice" to the "extremely variegated nature" of male experience. Indeed, any attempt to "cut" reality and perspective along gender lines is methodologically flawed and essentializing.[1]

• • •

For some feminist literary theorists, gender has become a discursive formation, inherently unstable and continually self-deconstructing. The meaning of gender is constantly deferred, endlessly multiple. We must "get beyond the number two," as one writer has described it, and move toward a "dizzying accumulation of narratives."[2] (A new journal is entitled *Genders*.) Not to do so is to perpetuate a hierarchical, binary construction of reality.

• • •

In the November, 1987, issue of *Ms.* magazine, an article appeared on the art of Georgia O'Keeffe. It included the text of a letter from O'Keeffe to Mabel Luhan:

> I thought you could write something about me that the men
> can't—What I want written—I do not know—I have no def-
> inite idea of what it should be—but a woman who has lived
> many things and who sees lines and colors as an expression
> of living—might say something that a man can't—I feel there
> is something unexplored about women that only a woman
> can explore—Men have done all they can do about it. Does
> that mean anything to you—or doesn't it?

The article itself, written by a staff reporter, begins: "Georgia
O'Keeffe. The woman of our century who made it clear once
and for all that painting has no gender."

CONTEMPORARY FEMINISM AND GENDER SKEPTICISM

In the 1970s, the feminist imagination was fueled by the insight that
the template of gender could disclose aspects of culture and history
previously concealed. The male-normative view of the world, feminists argued, had obscured its own biases through its fictions of
unity (History, Reason, Culture, Tradition . . .). Each of those unities was shown to have a repressed shadow, an *"other"* whose
material history, values, and perspective had yet to be written.

Today, many feminists are critical of what they now see as the
oversimplifications and overgeneralizations of this period in feminism. Challenges have arisen—sometimes emotionally charged—
targeted at classics of feminist theory and their gendered readings
of culture and history. Where once the prime objects of academic
feminist critique were the phallocentric narratives of our male-dom-
inated disciplines, now feminist criticism has turned to its own
narratives, finding them reductionist, totalizing, inadequately nu-
anced, valorizing of gender difference, unconsciously racist, and
elitist. Feminism may be developing a new direction, a new skepticism about the use of gender as an analytical category.

Such skepticism is by no means universal; contemporary feminism remains a diverse and pluralist enterprise. Nor does gender
skepticism take a single characteristic form. Rather, it has emerged
(as my opening montage suggests) across disciplines and theoretical
affiliations, speaking in different voices and crystallized around
different concerns. Naming and criticizing such a phenomenon is

a slippery, perilous business. Yet, it is my contention that we are seeing an important cultural formation here, the analysis of which must become a pressing concern for feminists.

Like all cultural formations, feminist gender-skepticism is complexly constructed out of diverse elements—intellectual, psychological, institutional, and sociological. Arising not from monolithic design but from an interplay of factors and forces, it is best understood not as a discrete, definable position which can be adopted or rejected but as an emerging coherency which is being fed by a variety of currents, sometimes overlapping, sometimes quite distinct. In this essay, I critically examine four such currents and the (sometimes unintentional) routes by which they empty into the waters of gender skepticism.

The first current is the result of an academic marriage that has brought well-founded feminist concerns over the ethnocentrism and unconscious racial biases of gender theory into a theoretical alliance with (a highly programmatic appropriation of) the more historicist, politically oriented wing of poststructuralist thought (e.g., Foucault, Lyotard). This union, I argue, has contributed to the development of a new feminist methodologism that lays claims to an authoritative critical framework, legislating "correct" and "incorrect" approaches to theorizing identity, history, and culture. This methodologism, which eschews generalizations about gender a priori on theoretical grounds, is in danger of discrediting and disabling certain kinds of feminist cultural critique; it also often implicitly (and mistakenly) supposes that the adoption of a "correct" theoretical approach makes it possible to *avoid* ethnocentrism.

The second current that I discuss in this chapter is the result of certain feminist appropriations of deconstructionism. Here, a postmodern recognition of interpretive multiplicity, of the indeterminacy and heterogeneity of cultural meaning and meaning-production, is viewed as calling for new narrative approaches, aimed at the adequate representation of textual "difference." From this perspective, the template of gender is criticized for its fixed, binary structuring of reality and is replaced by a narrative ideal of ceaseless textual play. But this ideal, I argue, although it arises out of a critique of modernist epistemological pretensions to represent reality adequately by achieving what Thomas Nagel has called the "view from nowhere," remains animated by its own fantasies of attaining an epistemological perspective free of the locatedness and limitations of embodied existence—a fantasy that I call a "dream of everywhere."

Through these critical concerns, I hope to encourage caution among those who are ready to celebrate wholeheartedly the emergence of postmodern feminism. The programmatic appropriation of poststructuralist insight, I argue, is, in shifting the focus of crucial feminist concerns about the representation of cultural diversity from practical contexts to questions of adequate theory, highly problematic for feminism. Not only are we thus diverted from attending to the professional and institutional mechanisms through which the politics of exclusion operate most powerfully in intellectual communities, but we also deprive ourselves of still vital analytical tools for critique of those communities and the hierarchical, dualistic power structures that sustain them.[3]

If this is so, then what mechanisms have drawn feminists into participation with such a development? The last two currents I examine provide foci for examining such issues, through an exploration of the institutions of knowledge and power that still dominate our masculinist public arena and that now threaten, I argue, to harness and tame the visionary and critical energy of feminism as a movement of cultural resistance and transformation.

FROM THE "VIEW FROM NOWHERE" TO FEMINIST METHODOLOGISM

Let me begin with a story, told from my perspective as a feminist philosopher, about the emergence of gender analytics and the difficulties into which it later fell.[4]

In 1979, Richard Rorty's *Philosophy and the Mirror of Nature* burst onto the philosophical scene in the United States. Its author, established and respected in the very traditions he now set out to deconstruct, was uniquely situated to legitimate a simple yet subversive argument. That argument, earlier elaborated in different ways by Marx, Nietzsche, and Dewey, and being developed on the Continent in the work of Derrida and Foucault, held that ideas are the creation of social beings rather than the (more or less adequate) representations or "mirrorings" of nature.

Rorty's presentation of this argument was philosophically elegant, powerful, and influential. But it was not Rorty, rebellious member of the club (or, indeed, *any* professional intellectual voice), who was ultimately responsible for uncovering the pretensions and illusions of the ideals of epistemological objectivity, universal foundations of reason, and neutral judgment. That uncovering first occurred, not in the course of philosophical conversation, but in political practice. Its agents were the liberation movements of the sixties and seventies, emerging not only to assert the legitimacy of marginalized cultures and suppressed perspectives but also to expose the biases of the official accounts. Now those accounts could no longer claim to descend from the heavens of pure rationality or to reflect the inevitable and progressive logic of intellectual or scientific discovery. They had to be seen, rather, as the products of historically situated individuals with very particular class, race, and gender interests. The imperial categories that had provided justification for those accounts—Reason, Truth, Human Nature, History, Tradition—were now displaced by the (historical, social) questions: *Whose* truth? *Whose* nature? *Whose* version of reason? *Whose* history? *Whose* tradition?

Feminism, appropriately enough, initiated the cultural work of exposing and articulating the gendered nature of history, culture, and society. It was a cultural moment of revelation and relief. The category of the "human"—a standard against which all difference translates to lack, insufficiency—was brought down to earth, given a pair of pants, and reminded that it was not the only player in town. Our students still experience this moment of critical and empowering insight when, for example, they learn from Gilligan and others that the language of "rights" is, not the ethical discourse of God or Nature, but the ideological superstructure of a particular construction of masculinity.[5]

Gender theorists Dinnerstein, Chodorow, Gilligan,[6] and many others uncovered patterns that resonate experientially and illuminate culturally. They cleared a space, described a new territory, that radically altered the male-normative terms of discussion about reality and experience; they forced recognition of the difference gender makes. Academic disciplines were challenged, sometimes in their most basic self-conceptions and categories—as in philosophy, which has made an icon of the ideal of an abstract, universal reason unaffected by the race, class, gender, or history of the reasoner (Nagel's "view from nowhere").[7] There *is* no view from nowhere, feminists insisted; indeed, the "view from nowhere" may itself be a male construction on the possibilities for knowledge.

The unity of the "gendered human," however, often proved to be as much a fiction as the unity of abstract, universal "man." In responding to the cultural imperative to describe the difference gender makes, gender theorists (along with those who attempt to speak for a "black experience" uninflected by gender or class) often glossed over other dimensions of social identity and location, dimensions which, when considered, cast doubt on the proposed gender (or racial) generalizations. Chodorow, for example, has frequently been criticized for implicitly elevating one pattern of difference between men and women, characteristic at most of a particular historical period and form of family organization, to the status of an essential "gender reality." Since the patterns described in gender analysis have often been based on the experiences of white, middle-class men and women, such accounts are guilty, feminists have frequently pointed out, of perpetuating the same sort of unconscious privilegings and exclusions characteristic of the male-normative theories they criticize.

As was the case when the first challenges were presented to the imperial unities of the phallocentric worldview, the agents of critical insight into the biases of gender theory were those excluded: women of color, lesbians, and others who found their history and culture ignored in the prevailing discussions of gender. What I wish to emphasize here is that these challenges, arising out of concrete experiences of exclusion, neither were grounded in a conception of adequate theory nor demanded a theoretical response. Rather, as new narratives began to be produced, telling the story of the diversity of woman's experiences, the chief intellectual imperative was to *listen*, to become aware of one's biases, prejudices, and ignorance, to begin to stretch the emotional and intellectual borders of what Minnie Bruce Pratt calls "the narrow circle of the self."[8] A new personal attitude was called for, a greater humility and greater attentiveness to what one did not know and could only learn from others with a different experience and perspective. The corresponding institutional imperative, for academics, was to stretch the established, culturally narrow borders of required curriculum, course reading lists, lecture series, research designs, student and faculty recruitment, and so forth.

We also *should* have learned that although it is imperative to struggle continually against racism and ethnocentrism in all its forms, it is impossible to be "politically correct." For the dynamics of inclusion and exclusion (as history had just taught us) are played out on multiple and shifting fronts, and all ideas (no matter how liberating in some contexts or for some purposes) are condemned to be haunted by a voice from the margins, either already speaking or presently muted but awaiting the conditions for speech, that awakens us to what has been excluded, effaced, damaged.[9] However, nothing in the early feminist critique of gender theory, it should be noted, declared the theoretical impossibility of discovering common ground among diverse groups of people or insisted that the abstraction of gender coherencies across cultural difference is *bound* to lapse into a pernicious universalization. It is only as feminism has become drawn into what Barbara Christian has called the "race for theory,"[10] that problems of racism, ethnocentrism, and historicism have become wedded to general methodological concerns about the legitimacy of gender generalization and abstraction.

Frequently (although not exclusively),[11] the categories of postmodern thinkers have been incorporated in statements of these concerns. Nancy Fraser and Linda Nicholson, for example, urge feminists to adopt a "postmodern-feminist theory" of identity, in which general claims about "male" and "female" reality are eschewed in favor of "complexly constructed conceptions . . . treating gender as one relevant strand among others, attending also to class, race, ethnicity, age, and sexual orientation."[12] Conceptions of gender (and, presumably, of race, class, sexual orientation, and so forth) that are not constructed in this way are totalizing; that is, they create a false unity out of heterogeneous elements, relegating the submerged elements to marginality. Much past feminist theory, Fraser and Nicholson argue, is guilty of this practice. Like the "grand narratives of legitimation" (of the white, male, Western intellectual tradition) criticized by Lyotard and others, the narratives of gender analysis harbor, either fully (as in Chodorow) or in "trace" form (as in Gilligan), "an overly grandiose and totalizing conception of theory."[13] Donna Haraway, too, describes gender theory in the same terms used by postmodernists to criticize phallocentric culture: as appropriation, totalization, incorporation, suppression.[14]

These proposals for more adequate approaches to identity begin from the invaluable insight that gender forms only one axis of a complex, heterogeneous construction, constantly interpenetrating, in historically specific ways, with multiple other axes of identity. I want to question, however, the conversion of this insight into *the* authoritative insight, and thence into a privileged critical framework, a "neutral matrix" (to borrow Rorty's term) that legislates the appropriate terms of all intellectual efforts and is conceived as capable of determining who is going astray and who is on the right track. This is a result that Fraser and Nicholson would also deplore, given their obvious commitment to feminist pluralism; their ideal is that of a "tapestry composed of threads of many different hues."[15] I share this ideal, but I question whether it is best served through a new postmodern-feminist theoretical agenda.

Certainly, feminist scholarship will benefit from more local, historically specific study and from theoretical projects that analyze the relations of diverse axes of identity. Too often, however (for instance, in grant, program, and conference guidelines and descriptions), this focus has translated to the coercive, mechanical requirement that *all* enlightened feminist projects attend to "the intersection of race, class, and gender." What happened to ethnicity? Age? Sexual orientation? In any case, just how many axes can one include and still preserve analytical focus or argument? Even more troubling is the (often implicit, sometimes explicit) dogma that the only "correct" perspective on race, class, and gender is the affirmation of difference; this dogma reveals itself in criticisms that attack gender generalizations as *in principle* essentialist or totalizing. Surely such charges should require concrete examples of *actual* differences that are being submerged by any particular totality in question.

We also need to guard against the "view from nowhere" supposition that if we only employ the right method we can avoid ethnocentrism, totalizing constructions, and false universalizations. No matter how local and circumscribed the object or how attentive the scholar is to the axes that constitute social identity, some of those axes will be ignored and others selected. This is an inescapable fact of human embodiment, as Nietzsche was the first to point out: "The eye . . . in which the active and interpreting forces, through which alone seeing becomes seeing *something*, are supposed to be lacking [is] an absurdity and a nonsense. There is *only* a perspectival seeing, *only* a perspectival knowing."[16] This selectivity, moreover, is never innocent. We always "see" from points of view that are invested with our social, political, and personal interests, inescapably -centric in one way or another, even in the desire to do justice to heterogeneity.

Nor does attentiveness to difference assure the adequate representation of difference. Certainly, we often err on the side of exclusion and thus submerge large areas of human history and experience. But attending *too* vigilantly to difference can just as problematically construct an "other" who is an exotic alien, a breed apart. As Foucault has reminded us, "everything is dangerous"— and every new context demands that we reassess the "main danger." This requires a "hyper- and pessimistic activism," not an alliance with one, true theory.[17] No theory, that is to say—not even one that measures its adequacy in terms of justice to heterogeneity, locality, complexity—can place itself beyond danger.

Indeed, it is possible, as we all know, to advance the most vociferously anti-totalizing theories, and yet to do so in the context of an intellectual discourse and professional practice (governing hiring, tenure, promotion, publications) whose very language requires membership to understand, and that remains fundamentally closed to difference (regarding it as "politically incorrect," "theoretically unsophisticated," "unrigorous"). We deceive ourselves if we believe that poststructuralist theory is attending to the "problem of difference" so long as so many concrete others are excluded from the conversation. Moreover, in the context of a practice that *is* attentive to issues of exclusion and committed to developing the conditions under which many voices can speak and be heard, clear, accessible, stimulating general hypotheses (eschewed by postmodern feminists) can be dialogically invaluable. Such ideas reconfigure the realities we take for granted; they allow us to examine our lives freshly; they bring history and culture to new life and invite our critical scrutiny. Showing a bold hand, they can encourage difference to reveal itself well.

In terms of such practical criteria, feminist gender theory deserves a somewhat different historical evaluation than is currently being written.[18] Certainly it is undeniable that such theory, as Fraser and Nicholson persuasively argue, has overly universalized.

(Chodorow's work, for example, requires careful historical circumscription and contextualization; it then becomes enormously edifying for certain purposes.) Such overgeneralization, as I suggested earlier, reflects the historical logic conditioning the emergence of contemporary feminist thought and is not *merely* symptomatic of the ethnocentrism of white, middle-class feminists. We all—and postmodernists especially—stand on the shoulders of this work (and on the shoulders of those who spoke, often equally univocally, for black experience and culture). Could we now speak of the differences that inflect gender and race (and that may confound and fragment gender and racial generalizations) if each had not first been shown to make a difference?

While in theory all totalizing narratives may be equal, in the context of Western history and of the actual relations of power characteristic of that history, key differences distinguish the universalizations of gender theory from the meta-narratives arising out of the propertied, white, male, Western intellectual tradition. That tradition, we should remember, reigned for thousands of years and was able to produce powerful works of philosophy, literature, art, and religion before its hegemony began, under great protest, to be dismantled. Located at the very center of power, at the intersection of three separate axes of privilege—race, class, and gender—that tradition had little stake in the recognition of difference (other than to construct it as inferior or threatening "other"). This is not to say that this tradition is univocal. Indeed, elsewhere I have argued that it has produced many "recessive" and subversive strains of philosophizing.[19] Rather, my point is that it produced no practice of self-interrogation and critique of its racial, class, and gender biases—because they were largely invisible to it.

Feminist theory—even the work of white, upper-class, heterosexual women—is not located at the *center* of cultural power. The axes whose intersections form the cultural locations of feminist authors give some of us positions of privilege, certainly; but *all* women, *as* women, also occupy subordinate positions, positions in which they feel ignored or denigrated. Contemporary feminism, emerging out of that recognition, has from the beginning exhibited an interest in restoring to legitimacy that which has been marginalized and disdained, an interest, I would suggest, that has affected its intellectual practice significantly. As an outsider discourse, that is, as a movement born out of the experience of marginality, contemporary feminism has been unusually highly attuned to issues of exclusion and invisibility. This does not mean, of course, that the work of feminists has not suffered deeply from class, racial, and other biases. But I find Donna Haraway's charge that "white feminists . . . were forced kicking and screaming to notice" those biases to be remarkable.[20] It is a strange (perhaps a postmodern) conception of intellectual and political responsiveness that views white feminism, now critically scrutinizing (and often utterly discrediting) its conceptions of female reality and morality and its gendered readings of culture, *barely more than a decade after they began to be produced*, as "resistant" to recognizing its own fictions of unity.

Assessing where we are now, it seems to me that feminism stands less in danger of the totalizing tendencies of feminists than of an increasingly paralyzing anxiety over falling (from what grace?) into ethnocentrism or "essentialism." (The often-present implication that such a fall indicates deeply conservative and racist tendencies, of course, intensifies such anxiety.) Do we want to delegitimate a priori the exploration of experiential continuity and structural common ground among women? Journals and conferences are now coming to be dominated by endless debates about method, reflections on how feminist scholarship should proceed and where it has gone astray. We need to consider the degree to which this serves, not the empowerment of diverse cultural voices and styles, but the academic hegemony (particularly in philosophy and literary studies) of detached, metatheoretical discourse.[21] If we wish to empower diverse voices, we would do better, I believe, to shift strategy from the methodological dictum that we forswear talk of "male" and "female" realities (which, as I will argue later, can still be edifying and useful) to the messier, more slippery, practical struggle to create institutions and communities that will not permit *some* groups of people to make determinations about reality for *all*.

THE "VIEW FROM NOWHERE"
AND THE DREAM OF EVERYWHERE

In theory, deconstructionist postmodernism stands against the ideal of disembodied knowledge and declares that ideal to be a mystification and an impossibility. There is no Archimedean viewpoint; rather, history and culture are texts, admitting an endless proliferation of readings, each of which is itself unstable. I have no dispute with this epistemological critique, or with the metaphor of the world as text, as a means of undermining various claims to authoritative, transcendent insight into the nature of reality. The question remains, however, how the human knower is to negotiate this infinitely perspectival, destabilized world. Deconstructionism answers with, as an alternative ideal, a constant vigilant suspicion of all determinate readings of culture and a partner aesthetic of ceaseless textual play. Here is where deconstruction may slip into its own fantasy of escape from human locatedness—by supposing that the critic can become wholly protean, adopting endlessly shifting, seemingly inexhaustible vantage points, none of which is "owned" by either the critic or the author of a text under examination.

Deconstructionism has profoundly affected certain feminist approaches to gender as a grid for the reading of culture. Such readings, these feminists argue, only reproduce the dualistic logic which has held the Western imagination in its grip. Instead, contemporary feminism should attempt, as Susan Suleiman describes it, "to get beyond, not only the number one—the number that determines unity of body or of self—but also to get beyond the number two, which determines difference, antagonism and exchange."[22] "One is too few," as Donna Haraway writes, "but two are too many."[23] The "number one" clearly represents for Suleiman the fictions of unity, stability, and identity characteristic of the phallocentric worldview. The "number two" represents the grid of gender, which feminists have used to expose the hierarchical, oppositional structure of that worldview. "Beyond the number two" is, not some other number, but "endless complication" and a "dizzying accumulation of narratives." Suleiman here refers to Derrida's often quoted interview with Christie McDonald, in which he speaks of "a 'dream' of the innumerable, . . . a desire to escape the combinatory . . . to invent incalculable choreographies."[24]

Such images from Derrida have been used in a variety of ways by feminists. Drucilla Cornell and Adam Thurschwell interpret Derrida as offering a utopian vision of human life no longer organized by gender duality and hierarchy.[25] But Suleiman interprets him as offering an *epistemological* or narrative ideal. As such, key contrasts with traditional (most particularly, Cartesian) images of knowing are immediately evident. Metaphors of dance and movement have replaced the ontologically fixing stare of the motionless spectator. The lust for finality has been banished. The dream is of "incalculable choreographies," not the clear and distinct "mirrorings" of nature, seen from the heights of "nowhere." But, I would argue, the philosopher's fantasy of transcendence has not yet been abandoned. The historical specifics of the modernist, Cartesian version have simply been replaced by a new, postmodern configuration of detachment, a new imagination of disembodiment: a dream of being *everywhere*.

My point can best be seen through examination of the role of the body—that is, of the metaphor of the body—in these (seemingly contrasting) epistemologies of "nowhere" and "everywhere." For Cartesian epistemology, the body—conceptualized as the site of epistemological limitation, as that which fixes the knower in time and space and therefore situates and relativizes perception and thought—requires transcendence if one is to achieve the view from nowhere, the God's-eye view. Once one has achieved that view (has become *object*-ive), one can see nature as it really is, undistorted by human perspective. For postmodern Suleiman, by contrast, there is no escape from human perspective, from the process of human making and remaking of the world. The body, accordingly, is reconceived. No longer an obstacle to knowledge (for knowledge in the Cartesian sense is an impossibility, and the body is incapable of being transcended in pursuit of it), the body is seen instead as the vehicle of the human making and remaking of the world, constantly shifting location, capable of revealing endlessly new points of view.

Beneath the imagery of a moving (but still unified) body is the deeper postmodern imagery of a body whose very unity has been shattered by the choreography of multiplicity. For the "creative movement" (as Suleiman describes it) of human interpretation, of course, "invents" (and reinvents) the body itself.[26] Donna Haraway imaginatively and evocatively describes this fragmented postmodern body through the image of the cyborg, which becomes a metaphor for the "disassembled and reassembled, postmodern collective and personal self [which] feminists must code." The cyborg is not only culturally "polyvocal"; she (?) "speaks in tongues."[27] Looked at with the aid of the imagery of archetypal typology rather

than science fiction, the postmodern body is the body of the mythological Trickster, the shape-shifter: "of indeterminate sex and
changeable gender . . . who continually alters her/his body, creates
and recreates a personality . . . [and] floats across time" from period to period, place to place.[28]

The appeal of such archetypes is undeniable. Set against the
masculinist hubris of the Cartesian ideal of the magisterial, universal knower whose privileged epistemological position reveals reality
as it is, the postmodern ideal of narrative "heteroglossia" (as Haraway calls it) appears to celebrate a "feminine" ability to enter into
the perspectives of others, to accept fluidity as a feature of reality.
At a time when the rigid demarcations of the clear and distinct
Cartesian universe are crumbling, and the notion of the unified
subject is no longer tenable, the Trickster and the cyborg invite us
to "take pleasure" in (as Haraway puts it) the "confusion of boundaries," in the fragmentation and fraying of the edges of the self that
have already taken place.[29]

However, the spirit of epistemological *jouissance* suggested by the
images of cyborg, Trickster, the metaphors of dance, and so forth
obscures the located, limited, inescapably partial, and *always* personally invested nature of human "story making." This is not
merely a theoretical point. Deconstructionist readings that enact
this protean fantasy are continually "slip-slidin' away"; through
paradox, inversion, self-subversion, facile and intricate textual
dance, they often present themselves (maddeningly, to one who
wants to enter into critical dialogue with them) as having it any way
they want. They refuse to assume a shape for which they must take
responsibility.

Recognition of this responsibility, however, forces one to take a
more humble approach to the project of embracing heterogeneity.
That project, taken as anything other than an ideal of social *process*,
is self-deconstructing. Any attempt to do justice to heterogeneity,
entertained as an epistemological (or narrative) goal, devours its
own tail. For the appreciation of difference requires the acknowledgment of some point beyond which the dancer cannot go. If she
were able to go everywhere, there would *be* no difference, nothing
that eludes. Denial of the unity and stability of identity is one thing.
The epistemological fantasy of *becoming* multiplicity—the dream of
limitless multiple embodiments, allowing one to dance from place

to place and self to self—is another. What sort of body is it that is free to change its shape and location at will, that can become anyone and travel anywhere? If the body is a metaphor for our locatedness in space and time and thus for the finitude of human perception and knowledge, then the postmodern body is no body at all.

The deconstructionist erasure of the body is not effected, as it is in the Cartesian version, by a trip to "nowhere," but by a resistance to the recognition that one is always *somewhere*, and limited. Here, it becomes clear that to overcome Cartesian hubris it is not sufficient to replace metaphors of spectatorship with metaphors of dance; it is necessary to relinquish all fantasies of epistemological conquest, not only those that are soberly fixed on necessity and unity but also those that are intoxicated with possibility and plurality. Despite its explicit rejection of conceptions of knowledge that view the mind as a "mirror of nature," deconstructionism reveals a longing for adequate representations—unlike Cartesian conceptions, but no less ambitious—of a relentlessly heterogeneous reality.[30]

THE RETREAT FROM FEMALE OTHERNESS

The preceding discussion of the body as epistemological metaphor for locatedness has focused on deconstructionism's *theoretical* deconstruction of locatedness. In the next two sections of this essay, I want to shift gears and pursue the issue of locatedness—or, rather, the denial of locatedness—in more concrete directions.

It is striking to me that there is often a curious selectivity at work in contemporary feminist criticisms of gender-based theories of identity. The analytics of race and class—the two other giants of modernist social critique—do not seem to be undergoing quite the same deconstruction. Women of color often construct "white feminists" as a unity, without attention to the class, ethnic, and religious differences that situate and divide us, and white feminists tend to accept this (as I believe they should) as enabling crucial sorts of criticisms to be made. It is usually acknowledged, too, that the experience of being a person of color in a racist culture creates some similarities of position across class and gender. At the very least, the various notions of identity that have come out of race consciousness are regarded as what Nietzsche would call "life enhancing fictions."[31] Donna Haraway, for example, applauds the homogenizing unity "women of color" as "a cyborg identity, a potent subjectivity synthesized from fusions of outsider identities."[32]

I have heard feminists insist, too, that race and class each have a material base that gender lacks. When the suggestion is made that perhaps such a material base exists, for gender, in women's reproductive role, the wedges of cultural diversity and multiple interpretation suddenly appear. Women have perceived childbearing, as Jean Grimshaw points out, both as "the source of their greatest joy and as the root of their worst suffering."[33] She concludes that the differences in various social constructions of reproduction, the vast disparities in women's experiences of childbirth, and so forth preclude the possibility that the practices of reproduction can meaningfully be interrogated as a source of insight into the difference gender makes. I find this conclusion remarkable. Women's reproductive experiences, of course, differ widely, but surely not as widely as they do from those of men, *none* of whom (up to now—technology may alter this) has had even the possibility of carrying a child under any circumstances.[34] Why, it must be asked, are we so ready to deconstruct what have historically been the most ubiquitous elements of the gender axis, while we remain so willing to defer to the authority and integrity of race and class axes as fundamentally grounding?

In attempting to answer this question, I no longer focus on postmodern theory, for the current of gender skepticism I am exploring here is not particularly characteristic of postmodern feminism. Rather, it flows through all theoretical schools of feminist thought, revealing itself in different ways. In place of my previous focus on postmodernism, I organize my discussion around a heuristic distinction between two historical moments of feminist thought, representing two different perspectives on "female otherness."

A previous generation of feminist thought (whose projects, of course, many feminists continue today) set out to connect the work that women have historically done (typically regarded as belonging to the material, practical arena, and thus of no epistemological or intellectual significance) with distinctive ways of experiencing and knowing the world. As such, the imagination of female alterity was a "life-enhancing fiction," providing access to coherent visions of utopian change and cultural transformation. Within this moment, too, a developing focus on the role of mothering in the construction of infant gender-identity (and thus of culture) was central to the ongoing feminist deconstruction of the phallocentric worldview. (Within that worldview it is the father/theologian/philosopher who is the sole source of morality, logic, language.)

The feminist recovery of female otherness from the margins of culture had both a materialist wing (Ruddick, Hartsock, Rich, and others) and a psychoanalytic wing (Dinnerstein, Chodorow, Kristeva, Cixous, Irigaray), the latter attempting to reconstruct developmental theory with the pre-oedipal mother rather than the phallic father at its center. I think it is instructive to note the difference between the way feminists once described this work and how it is often described now. In a 1982 *Diacritics* review of Dinnerstein, Rich, and Chodorow, Coppélia Kahn describes what these authors have in common:

> To begin with, they all regard gender less as a biological fact than as a social product, an institution learned through and perpetuated by culture. And they see this gender system not as a mutually beneficial and equitable division of roles, but as a perniciously symbiotic polarity which denies full humanity to both sexes while meshing—and helping to create—their neuroses. Second, they describe the father-absent, mother-involved nuclear family as creating the gender identities which perpetuate patriarchy and the denigration of women. . . . They question the assumption that the sexual division of labor, gender personality, and heterosexuality rest on a biological and instinctual base. . . . They present, in effect, a collective vision of how maternal power in the nursery defines gender so as to foster patriarchal power in the public world.[35]

In a 1987 talk, Jean Grimshaw describes these same texts as depicting motherhood "as a state of regression" in which the relation between mother and child is "idealized" in its symbiotic nondifferentiation.[36] Chodorow's ethnocentrism or lack of historical specificity was not the issue here; what was, as Grimshaw saw it, was Chodorow's portrayal of a suffocating reality as a cozy, blissful state and an implicit criticism of women who do not experience maternity in this way. Similarly, Toril Moi, in a talk devoted to reviving Freud's view of reason *against* the revisions of feminist object-relations theory, describes the theory as involving "an idealization of pre-Oedipal mother-child relations," a "biologistic" view of development, and a "romanticization of the maternal."[37] Are Grimshaw and Moi discussing the same works as Kahn?

Of course the answer is *no*. For the context has changed, and these texts are now being read by their critics from the perspective of a different concrete situation than that which existed when Kahn produced her reading of Chodorow, Dinnerstein, and Rich. My point is not that Kahn's reading was the "correct" one; there is no timeless text against which to measure historical interpretations. Rather, I wish to encourage confrontation with the present context. It is the present context that has supplied the specter of "biologism," "romanticization," and "idealization." The dangers that we are responding to are not in the texts, but in our social reality and in ourselves.

In speaking of social reality, I am not *only* referring to the danger of feminist notions of male and female realities or perspectives entering into a conservative zeitgeist where they will function as an ideological mooring for the reassertion of the traditional gender roles, although in this time of great backlash against changes in gender-power relations, that danger is certainly real enough. What I am primarily interested in here, however, are the changing meanings of female "otherness" for women, as we attempt to survive, in historically unprecedented numbers, within our still largely masculinist public institutions.

Changes in the professional situation of academic feminists during the 1980s may be exemplary here. A decade ago, the exploration and revaluation of that which has been culturally constructed as female set the agenda for academic feminists of many disciplines, at a time when feminism was just entering the (white, male) academy. We were outsiders, of suspect politics (most of us had been "political" feminists before or during our professional training) and inappropriate sex (a *woman* philosopher?). At that time, few of us were of other than European descent. But nonetheless to be a feminist academic was to be constantly aware of one's "otherness"; that one was a woman was brought home to one daily. The feminist imagination was fueled precisely by what it was never allowed to forget: the analysis of the historical construction of male power and female "otherness" became our theoretical task.

Today, women have been "accepted." That is, it has been acknowledged (seemingly) that women can indeed "think like men," and those women who are able to adopt the prevailing standards of professional "balance," critical detachment, rigor, and the appropriate insider mentality have been rewarded for their efforts. Those who are unable or unwilling to do so (along with those men who are similarly unable or unwilling) continue to be denied acceptance, publication, tenure, promotions. At this juncture, women may discover that they have a new investment in combating notions that gender locates and limits.

In such a world any celebration of "female" ways of knowing or thinking may be felt by some to be dangerous professionally and perhaps a personal regression as well. For, within the masculinist institutions we have entered, relational, holistic, and nurturant attitudes continue to be marked as flabby, feminine, and soft. In this institutional context, as we are permitted "integration" into the professional sphere, the category of female "otherness," which has spoken to many feminists of the possibility of institutional and cultural change, of radical transformation of the values, metaphysical assumptions, and social practices of our culture, may become something from which we wish to dissociate ourselves. We need instead to establish our leanness, our critical incisiveness, our proficiency at clear and distinct dissection.

I was startled, at a conference in 1987, by the raw hostility of a number of responses to a talk on "female virtue"; I have often been dismayed at the anger that (white, middle-class) feminists have exhibited toward the work of Gilligan and Chodorow. This sort of visceral reaction to theorists of gender difference (unlike the critiques discussed in the first section in this chapter) is not elicited by their ethnocentrism or ahistoricism; it is specifically directed against what is perceived as their romanticization of female values such as empathy and nurturing. Such a harsh critical stance is protection, perhaps, against being tarred by the brush of female "otherness," of being contaminated by things "female." Of course, to romanticize *anything* is the last thing that any rigorous scholar would do. Here, disdain for female "sentimentality" intersects with both the modern fashion for the cool and the cult of professionalism in our culture.

THE PLACE OF DUALITY IN A PLURAL UNIVERSE

Generalizations about gender can of course obscure and exclude. I would suggest, however, that such determinations cannot be made by methodological fiat but must be decided by context. The same is true of the representation of heterogeneity and complexity. There are dangers in too wholesale a commitment to either dual *or* multiple grids. Only the particular context can determine when general categories of analysis—race, class, gender—are perniciously homogenizing and when they are vital to social criticism.

Too relentless a focus on historical heterogeneity, for example, can obscure the transhistorical hierarchical patterns of white, male privilege that have informed the development of Western intellectual, legal, and political traditions.[38] More generally, the deconstruction of dual grids can obscure the dualistic, hierarchical nature of the actualities of power in Western culture. Contemporary feminism, like many other social movements arising in the 1960s, developed out of the recognition that to live in our culture is not (despite powerful social mythology to the contrary) to participate equally in some free play of individual diversity. Rather, one always finds oneself located within structures of dominance and subordination—not least important of which have been those organized around gender. Certainly, the duality of male/female is a discursive formation, a social construction. So, too, is the racial duality of black/white. But, as such, each of these dualities has had profound consequences for the construction of the experience of those who live them.

One of the ways in which these dualities affect people's lives is through the (often unconscious) ideology, imagery, and associations that mediate our perceptions of and relations with each other. Let me provide a concrete, contemporary example here. The fall and winter of 1991–92 brought several dramatic and controversial rape and sexual-harassment cases to the rapt attention of millions of Americans: law professor Anita Hill's allegations of sexual harassment against then-prospective Supreme Court justice Clarence Thomas; Desiree Washington's acquaintance-rape charges against boxer Mike Tyson; and Patricia Bowman's acquaintance-rape case against William Kennedy Smith. Each of these cases was a unique historical event requiring its own specific analysis. Public reactions to each were diverse and often divided by race. (There were often significant differences, as I note in the introduction to this volume, in the way black women and white women perceived and evaluated the actions of Anita Hill.) Nonetheless, I would argue that we can profitably cast a more sweeping glance over all three events, one which reveals the fall and winter of 1991–92 as a cultural moment in which phallocentrism and sexist ideology reared their heads and bared their distinctive teeth in a particularly emphatic way.

Throughout each of the proceedings, the man accused was endowed—by the lawyers, the senators, the media—with personal and social history, with place and importance in the community. The woman concerned was continually portrayed (as Beauvoir has put it) simply as "the Sex," as "Woman," with all the misogynist ideology that attaches to "Woman" when she presents herself as a threat to male security and well-being: she is a vindictive liar, a fantasizer, a scorned neurotic, mentally unbalanced, the engineer of man's fall. It is true that Desiree Washington, whose lawyers cleverly presented her as a child rather than a woman, generally wriggled out of such projections; but Patricia Bowman, who had the most suspect past of the female "accusers" interrogated before us in that year, had them cast at her continually. Of course, these constructions are frequently overlaid and over-determined, in the case of the African American woman, with Jezebel imagery and other stereotypes specific to racist ideology. The strikingly self-contained and professional Anita Hill, however, largely escaped them. She was *not* generally portrayed as a lustful animal (that would have been too great a stretch, even for Arlen Specter). But she *was* continually (contradictorily) portrayed as unbalanced, vindictive, manipulable, deceptive, vengeful, irrational, petulant, hysterical, cold—standard chords in our historical repertoire of misogynist tunes. The governing image suggested by Patricia Williams is not that of Jezebel but that of the Witch:

> Everything she touched inverted itself. She was relentlessly ambitious yet "clinically" reserved, consciously lying while fantasizing truth. Lie detectors broke down and the ashes of "impossible truth" spewed forth from her mouth. She was controlled yet irrational, naive yet knowing, prim yet vengeful—a cool, hot-headed, rational hysteric.[39]

Consider, as well, the way in which the race—and indeed, the humanity—of Hill and Washington were effaced (most frequently by African American men, but by some African American women as well) in the construction of their behavior as purely and simply

a betrayal of the struggle of African American men to combat pernicious stereotypes of black males as oversexed, potential rapists by
nature. Now, there is no denying that such mythology was culturally activated and exploited during these events, particularly
during the Tyson trial. (Was William Kennedy Smith ever publicly
characterized—even by the prosecution—as an instinctual animal?
Mike Tyson was portrayed in this way by prosecution and defense
alike.) The problem with the construction I am discussing is not its
attentiveness to racism but its phallocentric reduction of the struggle
against racism to the struggles of black *males*. The suggestion that
racial justice could simply and *only* be served by the exoneration of
the African American male "accused" constructed the African
American female "accusers" as "outside" the net of racism. In the
face of such constructions, Hill and Washington might well have
asked, à la Sojourner Truth: "And ain't *I* a black?"

They might also have asked: "Don't I count at all?" For when the
"National Committee for Mercy for Mike" spoke of Tyson as an
"African American hero" and a "role model for black youth," they
offered a map of reality on which the experiences of African American women who identified with Desiree Washington's ordeal simply did not appear. They apparently were also oblivious to the fact
that African American women as well as African American men
have been bestialized and hypersexualized in racist ideology, ideology which has played a role throughout history in the construction of the relation of black women to rape. Black women, it has been
imagined, cannot be raped any more than an animal can be raped.
(When Clarence Thomas described his hearings as a "high-tech
lynching," he cynically exploited an analogy that, in the context of
Anita Hill's accusations, submerged the historical realities of African American women's lives; black men were *never* lynched for
abusing or raping black women.)

What was going on here? I believe that for many men (both black
and white), defensive, confused, and angry over the sudden public
exposure and condemnation of sexual behaviors they had believed
to be culturally sanctioned (even expected of them), archetypal
misogynist images (e.g., the Cold, Lying, Castrating Bitch) began
to overwhelm their sense of women as having any identity beyond
that of "the Sex," of "Woman." The actualities of human identity,
as contemporary theorists have pointed out, are indeed plural,

complex, and often ambiguous. But when a highly invested aspect of the self is felt to be in danger, the figures that arise in the threatened imagination may be shaped by cruder formulas, supplied by the stark dualities of racist and sexist ideologies. For those Germans who believed that their racial identity was endangered by a potentially fatal Jewish pollution, the world divided simply into Semite and Aryan. There were no rich Jews and poor Jews, no German Jews and Polish Jews; there was only the Jewish Menace. The perception that "manhood" is under attack may activate similarly dualistic ideologies about the sexes along with their mythologies of Woman as Enemy.

Thus there are contexts within which gender is not accurately theorized as simply one thread in the (undeniably) heterogeneous fabric of women's and men's identities, contexts in which the sexist ideology which is still pervasive in our culture sharply bifurcates that heterogeneity along gender lines. At such moments, women may find themselves discovering that despite their differences they have many things in common by virtue of living in sexist cultures. This is precisely what happened during the Thomas/Hill hearings. Some African American women were enraged at Anita Hill for publicly exposing an African American man—a concern few white women even thought of. But as discussion shifted from the specifics of the case to the general dynamics of sexual harassment and abuse, striking and painful commonalities of experience very frequently emerged, cutting across lines of race, age, and class. My point is not that the Thomas/Hill hearings were "only about gender." Rather, I am arguing that the gender dimension was sufficiently significant to require a separate analysis of its dynamics. The same might be said of the racial dimension. The point is that to analyze either requires that we abstract and generalize across "difference," emphasizing commonality and connection rather than the fragmentations of identity and experience.

I do not agree that such generalizations are methodologically illicit, as Jean Grimshaw has suggested:

> The experience of gender, of being a man or a woman, inflects much if not all of people's lives. . . . But even if one is always a man or a woman, one is never *just* a man or a woman. One is young or old, sick or healthy, married or unmarried, a parent or not a parent, employed or unemployed, middle class or working class, rich or

poor, black or white, and so forth. Gender of course inflects one's experience of these things, so the experience of any one of them may well be radically different according to whether one is a man or a woman. But it may also be radically different according to whether one is, say, black or white or working class or middle class. The relationship between male and female experience is a very complex one. Thus there may in some respects be more similarities between the experience of a working-class woman and a working-class man— the experience of factory labor for example, or of poverty and unemployment—than between a working-class woman and a middle-class woman. But in other respects there may be greater similarities between the middle-class woman and the working-class woman— experiences of domestic labor and child care, of the constraints and requirements that one be "attractive," or "feminine," for example.

Experience does not come neatly in segments, such that it is always possible to abstract what in one's experience is due to "being a woman" from that which is due to "being married," "being middle-class" and so forth.[40]

Grimshaw emphasizes, absolutely on target, that gender never exhibits itself in pure form but always in the context of lives that are shaped by a multiplicity of influences, which cannot be neatly sorted out and which are rarely experienced as discrete and isolatable. This does not mean, however, as Grimshaw goes on to suggest, that abstractions or generalizations about gender are methodologically illicit or perniciously homogenizing of difference. It is true that we will never find the kind of Cartesian neatness, a universe of clear and distinct segments, that Grimshaw requires of such abstraction. Moreover, it is possible to adjust one's methodological tools so that gender commonalities cutting across differences become indiscernible under the finely meshed grid of various interpretations and inflections (or the numerous counterexamples which can always be produced). But what then becomes of social critique? Theoretical criteria such as Grimshaw's, which measure the adequacy of representations in terms of their "justice" to the "extremely variegated nature" of human experience,[41] must find nearly *all* social criticism guilty of methodologically illicit and distorting abstraction. Grimshaw's inflection argument, although designed to display the fragmented nature of gender, in fact deconstructs race, class, and historical coherencies as well. For although race, class, and gender are privileged by current intellectual convention, the inflections that modify experience are in reality endless, and *some* item of difference can always be produced that will shatter any proposed generalization. If generalization is only permitted in the *absence* of multiple inflections or interpretive possibilities, then cultural generalization of any sort—about race, about class, about historical eras—is ruled out. What remains is a universe composed entirely of counterexamples, in which the way men and women see the world is purely as *particular* individuals, shaped by the unique configurations that form that particularity.[42]

The Thomas/Hill hearings proved, to the contrary, that there are contexts in which it is useful to generalize about the limitations of male perspective and the commonalities of women's experiences. *"They just don't get it."* I no longer remember who first uttered these words, but it was quickly picked up by the media as a crystallization and symbol of the growing perception among women that few men seemed to understand the ethical seriousness of sexual harassment or its humiliating and often paralyzing personal dynamics. There *were* men who "got it," of course. "Not getting it" does not come written on the Y chromosome, nor does it issue from some distinctively male cognitive or personality defect. Rather, it is a blindness created by acceptance of and identification with the position and privileges (and insecurities) of being male in a patriarchal culture. (I say "acceptance of" and "identification with" rather than "enjoyment of," because those who *aspire* to, who crave, the male privileges that have been historically denied them can also be blind.)[43] Men who struggle against the limitations of perspective conferred by male position, privilege, and insecurity—who, to borrow Maria Lugones's terms, attempt to "travel" emphatically to the "worlds" of female experience[44]—come to see things very differently.

While acknowledging the mediation of race and class perspective—not to mention party politics—in the Senate committee's questioning of Anita Hill and Clarence Thomas, would any of us want to deny that the limitations of the exclusively male experience helped to shape the discourse of the hearings? Those limitations were even more evident among Thomas's detractors than among his supporters, for his detractors had an *interest* in representing Hill's perspective sympathetically and yet were largely inept in their efforts to do so. They never asked the right questions, and they generally seemed unconvinced by their own pontifications about the seriousness of sexual harassment. In the wake of this spectacle, the media—and thence "the nation"—suddenly woke up to the fact (evident to feminists all along) that the U.S. Senate was virtually an all-male club. The 1992 election brought four new female senators (one of them African American) to Congress. They have not shied away from talking about the importance of bringing "women's perspectives" to their positions, and thus to the different senatorial "culture" they hope to help create.

The transformation of culture, and not merely greater statistical representation of women, must remain the goal of academic feminism as well. In this context, it is disquieting that academic feminists are questioning the integrity of the notion of "female reality" just as we begin to get a foothold in those disciplines that could most radically be transformed by our (historically developed) "otherness" and that have historically been most shielded from it. Foucault constantly reminds us that the routes of individual interest and desire do not always lead where imagined and may often sustain unintended and unwanted configurations of power. Could feminist gender-skepticism be operating in the service of the reproduction of white, male "knowledge/power" (to use Foucault's phrase, which underscores that knowledge is never neutral, but sustains particular power-relations)?

If so, it is, not the result of conspiracy, but a "strategy," as Foucault would say, "without strategists," operating through numerous noncentralized processes: through the pleasure of joining an intellectual community and the social and material rewards of membership; through the excitement of engagement in culturally powerful and dominant theoretical enterprises; through our own exhaustion at maintaining an agnostic stance in the institutions where we work; through intellectual boredom with stale talk about male dominance and female subordination; through our postmodern inclination to embrace the new and the novel; through the genuine insights that new theoretical perspectives offer; through our feminist commitment to the representation of difference; even (most ironically) through our "female" desire to heal wounds made by exclusion and alienation.

More coercively, the demands of "professionalism" and its exacting, "neutral" standards of rigor and scholarship may require us to abandon our "female" ways of knowing and doing. The call to professionalism is especially powerful—almost irresistible—for an academic. In the classical traditions of our culture, "the man of reason" provided the model of such "neutrality." That neutrality feminists have exposed as an illusion and a mystification of its masculinist biases. Today, however, the category of the "professional" functions in much the same way; it may be the distinctively twentieth-century refurbishing of the "view from nowhere."

It is striking—and chilling—to learn how many of the issues confronting professional women today were constructed in virtually the same terms in debates during the 1920s and 1930s, when the social results of the first feminist wave were being realized. Then as now, there was a strong backlash, particularly among professional women, against feminist talk about gender difference. "We're interested in people now—not men and women," declared a Greenwich Village female literary group, proclaiming itself—in 1919!—as "post-feminist."[45] The "New Woman" of the twenties, like her counterpart today, was glamorized for her diversity, equal to that of men: "The essential fact about the New Women is that they differ among themselves, as men do, in work and play, in virtue, in aspiration and in rewards achieved. They are women, not woman," wrote Leta Hollingworth.[46] "The broad unisexual world of activity lies before every human being," declared Miriam Ford.[47]

Professional women in particular shunned and scorned the earlier generation of activist women, who had made themselves a "foreign, irritating body" to prevailing institutions and who attempted to speak for an alternative set of emphatic, relational "female" values.[48] Instead, women were urged to adopt the rationalist, objectivist standards they found in place in the professions they entered, to aspire to "excellence" and "forgetfulness of self" rather than gender consciousness, to develop a "community of interest between themselves and professional men [rather than] between themselves and non-professional women."[49] Professional women saw in the "neutral" standards of objectivity and excellence the means of being accepted as humans, not women. In any case, as Nancy Cott points out, to have mounted a strategy *against* those standards (to expose them as myths, to offer other visions) would have surely "marked them as outsiders."[50]

In a culture that is *in fact* constructed by gender duality, however, one cannot be simply "human." This is no more possible than it is possible that we can "just be people" in a racist culture. (It is striking, too, that one hears this complaint from whites—"why can't we just be people; why does it always have to be 'black' this and 'white' that . . ."—only when *black* consciousness asserts itself.) Our language, intellectual history, and social forms are gendered; there is no escape from this fact and from its consequences on our lives. Some of those consequences may be unintended, may even be fiercely resisted; our deepest desire may be to transcend gender dualities, to have our behavior judged on its merits, not categorized as male or female. But, like it or not, in our present culture our activities *are* coded as male or female and will function as such under the prevailing system of gender-power relations. The adoption of the "professional" standards of academia is no more an activity devoid of gender politics than the current fashion in women's tailored suits and large-shouldered jackets is devoid of gender meaning. One cannot be gender-neutral in this culture.

One might think that poststructuralism, which has historicized and criticized the liberal notion of the abstract "human," would be an ally here. This is partially so. But the poststructuralist critique of liberal humanism is mitigated by its tendency, discussed earlier, to insist on the "correct" destabilization of such general categories of social identity as race,[51] class, and gender. Practically speaking— that is, in the context of the institutions we are trying to transform— the most powerful strategies against liberal humanism have been those that demystify the "human" (and its claims to a "neutral" perspective) *through* general categories of social identity, which give content and force to the notions of social interest, historical location, and cultural perspective. Now, we are being advised that the strongest analyses along such lines—for example, classic feminist explorations of the consequences of female-dominated infant care or of the "male" biases of our disciplines and professions—are to be rejected as resources for understanding history and culture. Most of our institutions have barely begun to absorb the message of modernist social criticism; surely it is too soon to let them off the hook via postmodern heterogeneity and instability. This is not to say that the struggle for institutional transformation will be served by univocal, fixed conceptions of social identity and location. Rather, we need to reserve *practical* spaces both for generalist critique (suitable when gross points need to be made) and for attention to complexity and nuance. We need to be pragmatic, not theoretically pure, if we are to struggle effectively against the inclination of institutions to preserve and defend themselves against deep change.

Of course, it is impossible to predict the cultural meanings one's gestures will take on and the larger formations in which one will find one's activities participating. Nonetheless, history does offer some cautions. The 1920s and 1930s saw a fragmentation and dissipation of feminist consciousness and feminist activism, as women struggled with what Nancy Cott calls "the dilemma of twentieth-century feminism": the tension between the preservation of gender consciousness and identity (as a source of political unity and alternative vision) and the destruction of "gender prescriptions" which limit human choice and possibility.[52] The "postfeminist" consciousness of the twenties and thirties, in pursuit of an ideal world undermined by gender dualities, cut itself adrift from the moorings of gender identity. This was culturally and historically understandable. But we thus, I believe, cut ourselves off from the source of feminism's transformative possibilities—possibilities that then had to be revived and imagined again four decades later. The deconstruction of gender analytics, I fear, may be participating in a similar cultural moment of feminist fragmentation, coming around again.

"Material Girl"

The Effacements of Postmodern Culture

In a culture in which organ transplants, life-extension machinery, microsurgery, and artificial organs have entered everyday medicine, we seem on the verge of practical realization of the seventeenth-century imagination of body as machine. But if we have technically and technologically realized that conception, it can also be argued that metaphysically we have deconstructed it. In the early modern era, machine imagery helped to articulate a totally determined human body whose basic functionings the human being was helpless to alter. The then-dominant metaphors for this body—clocks, watches, collections of springs—imagined a system that is set, wound up, whether by nature or by God the watchmaker, ticking away in predictable, orderly manner, regulated by laws over which the human being has no control. Understanding the system, we can help it to perform efficiently, and we can intervene when it malfunctions. But we cannot radically alter its configuration.

Pursuing this modern, determinist fantasy to its limits, fed by the currents of consumer capitalism, modern ideologies of the self, and their crystallization in the dominance of United States mass culture, Western science and technology have now arrived, paradoxically but predictably (for it was an element, though submerged and illicit, in the mechanist conception all along), at a new, postmodern imagination of human freedom from bodily determination. Gradually and surely, a technology that was first aimed at the replacement of malfunctioning parts has generated an industry and an ideology fueled by fantasies of rearranging, transforming, and correcting, an ideology of limitless improvement and change, defying the historicity, the mortality, and, indeed, the very materiality of the body.

In place of that materiality, we now have what I will call cultural plastic. In place of God the watchmaker, we now have ourselves, the master sculptors of that plastic. This disdain for material limits and the concomitant intoxication with freedom, change, and self-determination are enacted not only on the level of the contemporary technology of the body but in a wide range of contexts, including much of contemporary discourse on the body, both popular and academic. In this essay, looking at a variety of these discursive contexts, I attempt to describe key elements of this paradigm of plasticity and expose some of its effacements—the material and social realities it denies or renders invisible.

PLASTIC BODIES

"Create a masterpiece, sculpt your body into a work of art," urges *Fit* magazine. "You visualize what you want to look like, and then you create that form." "The challenge presents itself: to rearrange things."[1] The precision technology of body-sculpting, once the secret of the Arnold Schwarzeneggers and Rachel McLishes of the professional body-building world, has now become available to anyone who can afford the price of membership in a gym (Figure 39). "I now look at bodies," says John Travolta, after training for the movie *Staying Alive*, "almost like pieces of clay that can be molded."[2] On the medical front, plastic surgery, whose repeated and purely cosmetic employment has been legitimated by Michael Jackson, Cher, and others, has become a fabulously expanding industry, extending its domain from nose jobs, face lifts, tummy tucks, and breast augmentations to collagen-plumped lips and liposuction-shaped ankles, calves, and buttocks (Figure 40). In 1989, 681,000 procedures were done, up 80 percent over 1981; over half of these were performed on patients between the ages of eighteen and thirty-five.[3] The trendy *Details* magazine describes "surgical stretching, tucking and sucking" as "another fabulous [fashion] accessory" and invites readers to share their cosmetic-surgery experiences in their monthly column "Knife-styles of the Rich and Famous." In that column, the transportation of fat from one part of the body to another is described as breezily as changing hats might be:

> Dr. Brown is an artist. He doesn't just pull and tuck and forget about you. . . . He did liposuction on my neck, did the nose job and tight-

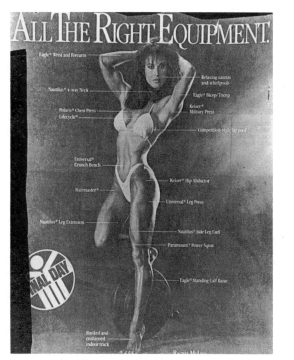

ALL THE RIGHT EQUIPMENT.

FIGURE 39

ened up my forehead to give it a better line. Then he took some fat
from the side of my waist and injected it into my hands. It goes in as
a lump, and then he smooths it out with his hands to where it looks
good. I'll tell you something, the nose and neck made a big change,
but nothing in comparison to how fabulous my hands look. The fat
just smoothed out all the lines, the veins don't stick up anymore, the
skin actually looks soft and great. [But] you have to be careful not to
bang your hands.[4]

Popular culture does not apply any brakes to these fantasies of
rearrangement and self-transformation. Rather, we are constantly
told that we can "choose" our own bodies (Figures 41 and 42). "The
proper diet, the right amount of exercise and you can have, pretty
much, any body you desire," claims Evian. Of course, the rhetoric
of choice and self-determination and the breezy analogies comparing cosmetic surgery to fashion accessorizing are deeply mystifying.
They efface, not only the inequalities of privilege, money, and time
that prohibit most people from indulging in these practices, but the

A Liz Taylor in 1962   . . . and with today's strong new chin   A Michael Jackson, 1977   . . . and reinvented in '90

ON THE CUTTING EDGE

Despite the furor over breast implants, in Hollywood's cult of youth and beauty, the plastic surgeon remains high priest

A "I'd like to look great for as long as I can," says Cher. At age 19 in 1965, she had Sonny–and a more ethnic nose.   A Cher today: a painfully altered state

FIGURE 40

desperation that characterizes the lives of those who do. "I will do anything, *anything*, to make myself look and feel better," says Tina Lizardi (whose "Knife-styles" experience I quoted from above). Medical science has now designated a new category of "polysurgical addicts" (or, in more casual references, "scalpel slaves") who return for operation after operation, in perpetual quest of the elusive yet ruthlessly normalizing goal, the "perfect" body.[5] The dark underside of the practices of body transformation and rearrangement

IF YOU COULD CHOOSE YOUR OWN BODY, WHICH WOULD YOU CHOOSE?

The fact is, you can choose your own body. The proper diet, the right amount of exercise and you can have, pretty much, any body you desire.

It's important to remember, however, that a perfect body isn't just fit on the outside, but fit inside as well.

In other words, balanced.

Evian Natural Spring Water can help maintain this balance. You see, through years and years of filtration deep within the French Alps, Evian is purified as it absorbs a unique balance of calcium, magnesium and other minerals. This naturally pure spring water can be readily absorbed to help cleanse and purify your system. In turn, Evian helps your body run perfectly and efficiently.

So when you decide to have the body you've always wanted, make sure it has the benefit of Evian Natural Spring Water.

EVIAN. THE BALANCE.™

evian
natural spring water

NIKE

THE BODY YOU HAVE IS THE BODY YOU IN-HERITED, BUT **YOU MUST DECIDE WHAT TO DO WITH IT.** YOU MUST DECIDE IF YOU WANT STRENGTH, DECIDE IF YOU WANT AGILITY. YOU MUST DECIDE IF YOU WANT ABSOLUTELY EVERYTHING THAT COMES FROM CROSS-TRAINING, AND ABSOLUTELY ONE SHOE TO DO IT IN. BECAUSE THE NIKE CROSS-TRAINER LOW HAS INHERITED ITS OWN SET OF STRENGTHS, ITS OWN KIND OF RESILIENCE. IT HAS ALSO INHERITED A GOOD DEAL OF CUSHIONING, STABILITY, AND TRUE, INTELLIGENT FIT. SO THANK YOUR MOTHER FOR WHAT YOU HAP-PENED TO BE BORN WITH. BUT THANK YOUR-SELF FOR WHAT YOU ACTUALLY DO WITH IT.

For more information on NIKE Women's products, call 1-800-642-6727. In Canada, call

FIGURES 41 AND 42

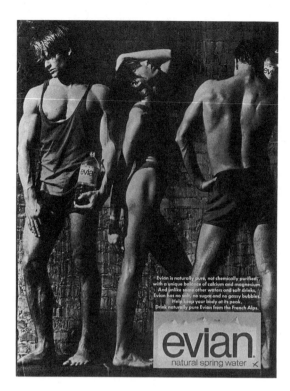

FIGURE 43

reveals botched and sometimes fatal operations, exercise addictions, eating disorders. And of course, despite the claims of the Evian ad, one cannot have *any* body that one wants—for not every body will *do*. The very advertisements whose copy speaks of choice and self-determination visually legislate the effacement of individual and cultural difference and circumscribe our choices (Figure 43).

That we are surrounded by homogenizing and normalizing images—images whose content is far from arbitrary, but is instead suffused with the dominance of gendered, racial, class, and other cultural iconography—seems so obvious as to be almost embarrassing to be arguing here. Yet contemporary understandings of the behaviors I have been describing not only construct the situation very differently but do so in terms that preempt precisely such a critique of cultural imagery. Moreover, they reproduce, on the level of discourse and interpretation, the same conditions that postmodern bodies enact on the level of cultural practice: a construction of life as plastic possibility and weightless choice, undetermined by history, social location, or even individual biography. A 1988 "Donahue" show offers my first illustration.

The show's focus was a series of television commercials for DuraSoft colored contact lenses. In these commercials as they were originally aired, a woman was shown in a dreamlike, romantic fantasy—for example, parachuting slowly and gracefully from the heavens. The male voiceover then described the woman in soft, lush terms: "If I believed in angels, I'd say that's what she was—an angel, dropped from the sky like an answer to a prayer, with eyes as brown as bark." [Significant pause] "No . . . I *don't think so*." [At this point, the tape would be rewound to return us to:] "With eyes as violet as the colors of a child's imagination." The commercial concludes: "DuraSoft colored contact lenses. Get brown eyes a second look" (cf. Figure 44).

The question posed by Phil Donahue: Is this ad racist? Donahue clearly thought there was controversy to be stirred up here, for he stocked his audience full of women of color and white women to discuss the implications of the ad. But Donahue was apparently living in a different decade from most of his audience, who repeatedly declared that there was nothing "wrong" with the ad, and everything "wrong" with any inclinations to "make it a political question." Here are some comments taken from the transcript of the show:

"Why does it have to be a political question? I mean, people perm their hair. It's just because they like the way it looks. It's not something sociological. Maybe black women like the way they look with green contacts. It's to be more attractive. It's not something that makes them—I mean, why do punk rockers have purple hair? Because they feel it makes them feel better." [white woman]

"What's the fuss? When I put on my blue lenses, it makes me feel good. It makes me feel sexy, different, the other woman, so to speak, which is like fun." [black woman]

"I perm my hair, you're wearing make-up, what's the difference?" [white woman]

"I want to be versatile . . . having different looks, being able to change from one look to the other." [black female model]

"We all do the same thing, when we're feeling good we wear new makeup, hairstyles, we buy new clothes. So now it's contact lenses. What difference does it make?" [white woman]

"It goes both ways . . . Bo Derek puts her hair in cornstalks, or corn . . . or whatever that thing is called. White women try to get tan." [white woman]

FIGURE 44

"She's not trying to be white, she's trying to be different." [about a black woman with blue contact lenses]

"It's fashion, women are never happy with themselves."

"I put them in as toys, just for fun, change. Nothing too serious, and I really enjoy them." [black woman][6]

Some points to note here: first, putting on makeup, styling hair, and so forth are conceived of only as free *play*, fun, a matter of creative expression. This they surely are. But they are also experienced by many women as necessary before they will show themselves to the world, even on a quick trip to the corner mailbox. The one comment that hints at women's (by now depressingly well documented) dissatisfaction with their appearance trivializes that dissatisfaction and puts it beyond the pale of cultural critique: "It's fashion." What she means is, "It's *only* fashion," whose whimsical and politically neutral vicissitudes supply endless amusement for women's eternally superficial values. ("Women are never happy with themselves.") If we are never happy with ourselves, it is implied, that is due to our female nature, not to be taken too seriously or made into a political question. Second, the content of fashion, the specific ideals that women are drawn to embody (ideals that vary historically, racially, and along class and other lines) are seen as arbitrary, without meaning; interpretation is neither required nor even appropriate. Rather, all motivation and value come from the interest and allure—the "sexiness"—of change and difference itself. Blue contact lenses for a black woman, it is admitted, make her "other" ("the other woman"). But that "other" is not a racial or cultural "other"; she is sexy because of the piquancy, the novelty, the erotics of putting on a different self. *Any* different self would do, it is implied.

Closely connected to this is the construction of *all* cosmetic changes as the same: perms for the white women, corn rows on Bo Derek, tanning, makeup, changing hairstyles, blue contacts for black women—all are seen as having equal political valance (which is to say, *no* political valance) and the same cultural meaning (which is to say, *no* cultural meaning) in the heterogeneous yet undifferentiated context of the things "all" women do "to be more attractive." The one woman in the audience who offered a different construction of this behavior, who insisted that the styles we aspire to do not simply reflect the free play of fashion or female nature— who went so far, indeed, as to claim that we "are brainwashed to think blond hair and blue eyes is the most beautiful of all," was regarded with hostile silence. Then, a few moments later, someone challenged: "Is there anything *wrong* with blue eyes and blond hair?" The audience enthusiastically applauded this defender of democratic values.

This "conversation"—a paradigmatically postmodern conversation, as I will argue shortly—effaces the same general elements as the rhetoric of body transformation discussed earlier. First, it effaces the inequalities of social position and the historical origins which, for example, render Bo Derek's corn rows and black women's hair-straightening utterly noncommensurate. On the one hand, we have Bo Derek's privilege, not only as so unimpeachably white as to permit an exotic touch of "otherness" with no danger of racial contamination, but her trend-setting position as a famous movie star. Contrasting to this, and mediating a black woman's "choice" to straighten her hair, is a cultural history of racist body-discrimi-nations such as the nineteenth-century comb-test, which allowed admission to churches and clubs only to those blacks who could pass through their hair without snagging a fine-tooth comb hanging outside the door. (A variety of comparable tests—the pine-slab test, the brown bag test—determined whether one's skin was adequately light to pass muster.)[7]

Second, and following from these historical practices, there is a disciplinary reality that is effaced in the construction of all self-transformation as equally arbitrary, all variants of the same trivial game, without differing cultural valance. I use the term *disciplinary* here in the Foucauldian sense, as pointing to practices that do not merely transform but *normalize* the subject. That is, to repeat a point made earlier, not every body will do. A 1989 poll of *Essence* magazine readers revealed that 68 percent of those who responded wear their hair straightened chemically or by hot comb.[8] "Just for fun"? For the kick of being "different"? When we look at the pursuit of beauty as a normalizing discipline, it becomes clear that not all body transformations are the same. The general tyranny of fashion—perpetual, elusive, and instructing the female body in a pedagogy of personal inadequacy and lack—is a powerful discipline for the normalization of *all* women in this culture. But even as we are all normalized to the requirements of appropriate feminine insecurity and preoccupation with appearance, more specific requirements

Hair That Moves

TCB®
No Lye Relaxer
The only no-mix relaxer kit with
the **Reconstructor step** for
beautiful body and shine.
So your hair is so
soft and smooth, it
moves. Use TCB
No Lye Relaxer
and other TCB
products. TCB...
we make you
look good.

FIGURE 45

emerge in different cultural and historical contexts, and for different groups. When Bo Derek put her hair in corn rows, she was engaging in normalizing feminine practice. But when Oprah Winfrey admitted on her show that all her life she has desperately longed to have "hair that swings from side to side" when she shakes her head (Figure 45), she revealed the power of racial as well as gender normalization, normalization not only to "femininity," but to the Caucasian standards of beauty that still dominate on television, in movies, in popular magazines. (When I was a child, I felt the same way about my thick, then curly, "Jewish" hair as Oprah did about hers.) Neither Oprah nor the *Essence* readers nor the many Jewish women (myself included) who ironed their hair in the 1960s have creatively or playfully invented themselves here.

DuraSoft knows this, even if Donahue's audience does not. Since the campaign first began, the company has replaced the orig-

FIGURE 46

inal, upfront magazine advertisement with a more euphemistic variant, from which the word *brown* has been tastefully effaced. (In case it has become too subtle for the average reader, the model now is black—although it should be noted that DuraSoft's failure to appreciate brown eyes also renders the eyes of most of the world not worth "a second look" [Figure 46].) In the television commercial, a comparable "brownwash" was effected; here "eyes as brown as . . ." was retained, but the derogatory nouns—"brown as boots," "brown as bark"—were eliminated. The announcer simply was left speechless: "eyes as brown as . . . brown as . . . ," and then, presumably having been unable to come up with an enticing simile, shifted to "violet." As in the expurgated magazine

Introducing
chestnut
brown
contact
lenses.

A SUBTLE   GET   NOW IN
ENHANCEMENT YOUR EIGHT
FOR   EYES A OTHER
DARK   SECOND STUNNING
EYES.   LOOK. COLORS.

DuraSoft Colors

FIGURE 47

ad, the television commercial ended: "Get *your* eyes a second look."

When I showed my students these ads, many of them were as dismissive as the "Donahue" audience, convinced that I was once again turning innocent images and practices into political issues. I persisted: if racial standards of beauty are not at work here, then why no brown contacts for blue-eyed people? A month later, two of my students triumphantly produced a DuraSoft ad for brown contacts (Figure 47), appearing in *Essence* magazine, and with an advertising campaign directed solely at *already* brown-eyed consumers, offering the promise *not* of "getting blue eyes a second look" by becoming excitingly darker, but of "subtly enhancing"

dark eyes, by making them *lighter* brown. The creators of the
DuraSoft campaign clearly know that not all differences are the
same in our culture, and they continue, albeit in ever more mystified
form, to exploit and perpetuate that fact.[9]

PLASTIC DISCOURSE

The "Donahue" DuraSoft show (indeed, any talk show) provides a
perfect example of what we might call a postmodern conversation.
All sense of history and all ability (or inclination) to sustain cultural
criticism, to make the distinctions and discriminations that would
permit such criticism, have disappeared. Rather, in this conversation, "anything goes"—and any positioned social critique (for example, the woman who, speaking clearly from consciousness of
racial oppression, insisted that the attraction of blond hair and blue
eyes has a cultural meaning significantly different from that of
purple hair) is immediately destabilized. Instead of distinctions,
endless *differences* reign—an undifferentiated pastiche of differences, a grab bag in which no items are assigned any more importance or centrality than any others. Television is, of course, the great
teacher here, our prime modeler of plastic pluralism: if one "Donahue" show features a feminist talking about battered wives, the
next show will feature mistreated husbands. Women who love too
much, the sex habits of priests, disturbed children of psychiatrists,
daughters who have no manners, male strippers, relatives who
haven't spoken in ten years all have their day alongside incest, rape,
and U.S. foreign policy. All are given equal weight by the great
leveler—the frame of the television screen.

This spectacle of difference defeats the ability to sustain coherent
political critique. Everything is the same in its unvalanced difference. ("I perm my hair, you're wearing makeup, what's the difference?") Particulars reign, and generality—which collects, orga-
nizes, and prioritizes, suspending attention to particularity in the
interests of connection, emphasis, and criticism—is suspect. So,
whenever some critically charged generalization was suggested on
Donahue's DuraSoft show, someone else would invariably offer a
counterexample—I have blue eyes, and I'm a black woman; Bo
Derek wears corn rows—to fragment the critique. What is remarkable is that people accept these examples as *refutations* of social

critique. They almost invariably back down, utterly confused as to how to maintain their critical generalization in the face of the destabilizing example. Sometimes they qualify, claiming they meant some people, not all. But of course they meant neither all nor some. They meant *most*—that is, they were trying to make a claim about social or cultural *patterns*—and that is a stance that is increasingly difficult to sustain in a postmodern context, where we are surrounded by endlessly displaced images and are given no orienting context in which to make discriminations.

Those who insist on an orienting context (and who therefore do not permit particulars to reign in all their absolute "difference") are seen as "totalizing," that is, as constructing a falsely coherent and morally coercive universe that marginalizes and effaces the experiences and values of others. ("Is there anything *wrong* with blue eyes and blond hair?") As someone who is frequently interviewed by local television and newspaper reporters, I have often found my feminist arguments framed in this way, as they were in an article on breast-augmentation surgery. After several pages of "expert" recommendations from plastic surgeons, my cautions about the politics of female body transformation (none of them critical of individuals contemplating plastic surgery, all of them of a cultural nature) were briefly quoted by the reporter, who then went on to end the piece with a comment on *my* critique—from the director of communications for the American Society of Plastic and Reconstructive Surgery:

> Those not considering plastic surgery shouldn't be too critical of those who do. It's the hardest thing for people to understand. What's important is if it's a problem to that person. We're all different, but we all want to look better. We're just different in what extent we'll go to. But none of us can say we don't want to look the best we can.[10]

With this tolerant, egalitarian stroke, the media liaison of the most powerful plastic surgery lobby in the country presents herself as the protector of "difference" against the homogenizing and stifling regime of the feminist dictator.

Academics do not usually like to think of themselves as embodying the values and preoccupations of popular culture on the plane of high theory or intellectual discourse. We prefer to see ourselves as the demystifyers of popular discourse, bringers-to-consciousness-and-clarity rather than unconscious reproducers of culture. Despite what we would *like* to believe of ourselves, however, we are always within the society that we criticize, and never so strikingly as at the present postmodern moment. All the elements of what I have here called postmodern conversation—intoxication with individual choice and creative *jouissance*, delight with the piquancy of particularity and mistrust of pattern and seeming coherence, celebration of "difference" along with an absence of critical perspective differentiating and weighing "differences," suspicion of the totalitarian nature of generalization along with a rush to protect difference from its homogenizing abuses—have become recognizable and familiar in much of contemporary intellectual discourse. Within this theoretically self-conscious universe, moreover, these elements are not merely embodied (as in the "Donahue" show's DuraSoft conversation) but explicitly thematized and *celebrated*, as inaugurating new constructions of the self, no longer caught in the mythology of the unified subject, embracing of multiplicity, challenging the dreary and moralizing generalizations about gender, race, and so forth that have so preoccupied liberal and left humanism.

For this celebratory, academic postmodernism, it has become highly unfashionable—and "totalizing"—to talk about the grip of culture on the body. Such a perspective, it is argued, casts active and creative subjects as passive dupes of ideology; it gives too much to dominant ideology, imagining it as seamless and univocal, overlooking both the gaps which are continually allowing for the eruption of "difference" and the polysemous, unstable, open nature of all cultural texts. To talk about the grip of culture on the body (as, for example, in "old" feminist discourse about the objectification and sexualization of the female body) is to fail to acknowledge, as one theorist put it, "the cultural work by which nomadic, fragmented, active subjects confound dominant discourse."[11]

So, for example, contemporary culture critic John Fiske is harshly critical of what he describes as the view of television as a "dominating monster" with "homogenizing power" over the perceptions of viewers. Such a view, he argues, imagines the audience as "powerless and undiscriminating" and overlooks the fact that:

> Pleasure results from a particular relationship between meanings and power. . . . There is no pleasure in being a "cultural dope." . . .
> Pleasure results from the production of meanings of the world and

of self that are felt to serve the interests of the reader rather than those of the dominant. The subordinate may be disempowered, but they are not powerless. There is a power in resisting power, there is a power in maintaining one's social identity in opposition to that proposed by the dominant ideology, there is a power in asserting one's own subcultural values against the dominant ones. There is, in short, a power in being different.[12]

Fiske then goes on to produce numerous examples of how *Dallas*, *Hart to Hart*, and so forth have been read (or so he argues) by various subcultures to make their own "socially pertinent" and empowering meanings out of "the semiotic resources provided by television."

Note, in Fiske's insistent, repetitive invocation of the category of power, a characteristically postmodern flattening of the terrain of power relations, a lack of differentiation between, for example, the power involved in creative *reading* in the isolation of one's own home and the power held by those who control the material production of television shows, or the power involved in public protest and action against the conditions of that production and the power of the dominant meanings—for instance, racist and sexist images and messages—therein produced. For Fiske, of course, there *are* no such dominant meanings, that is, no element whose ability to grip the imagination of the viewer is greater than the viewer's ability to "just say no" through resistant reading of the text. That ethnic and subcultural meaning *may* be wrested from *Dallas* and *Hart to Hart* becomes for Fiske proof that dominating images and messages are only in the minds of those totalitarian critics who would condescendingly "rescue" the disempowered from those forces that are in fact the very medium of their creative freedom and resistance ("the semiotic resources of television").

Fiske's conception of power—a terrain without hills and valleys, where all forces have become "resources"—reflects a very common postmodern misappropriation of Foucault. Fiske conceives of power as in the *possession* of individuals or groups, something they "have"—a conception Foucault takes great pains to criticize—rather than (as in Foucault's reconstruction) a dynamic of noncentralized forces, its dominant historical forms attaining their hegemony, not from magisterial design or decree, but through multiple "processes, of different origin and scattered location," regulating and normalizing the most intimate and minute elements of the construction of time, space, desire, embodiment.[13] This conception of power does *not* entail that there are no dominant positions, social structures, or ideologies emerging from the play of forces; the fact that power is not held by any *one* does not mean that it is equally held by *all*. It is in fact not "held" at all; rather, people and groups are positioned differentially within it. This model is particularly useful for the analysis of male dominance and female subordination, so much of which is reproduced "voluntarily," through our self-normalization to everyday habits of masculinity and femininity. Within such a model, one can acknowledge that women may indeed contribute to the perpetuation of female subordination (for example, by embracing, taking pleasure in, and even feeling empowered by the cultural objectification and sexualization of the female body) without this entailing that they have power in the production and reproduction of sexist culture.

Foucault does insist on the *instability* of modern power relations—that is, he emphasizes that resistance is perpetual and unpredictable, and hegemony precarious. This notion is transformed by Fiske (perhaps under the influence of a more deconstructionist brand of postmodernism) into a notion of resistance as *jouissance*, a creative and pleasurable eruption of cultural "difference" through the "seams" of the text. What this celebration of creative reading as resistance effaces is the arduous and frequently frustrated historical struggle that is required for the subordinated to articulate and assert the value of their "difference" in the face of dominant meanings— meanings which often offer a pedagogy directed at the reinforcement of feelings of inferiority, marginality, ugliness. During the early fifties, when *Brown v. the Board of Education* was wending its way through the courts, as a demonstration of the destructive psychological effects of segregation black children were asked to look at two baby dolls, identical in all respects except color. The children were asked a series of questions: which is the nice doll? which is the bad doll? which doll would you like to play with? The majority of black children, Kenneth Clark reports, attributed the positive characteristics to the white doll, the negative characteristics to the black. When Clark asked one final question, "Which doll is like you?" they looked at him, he says, "as though he were the devil himself" for putting them in that predicament, for forcing them to face the inexorable and hideous logical implications of their situation. Northern children often ran out of the room; southern children tended to answer the question in shamed embarrassment. Clark recalls one little boy who laughed, "Who am I like? That doll! It's a nigger and I'm a nigger!"[14]

Failing to acknowledge the psychological and cultural potency of normalizing imagery can be just as effective in effacing people's experiences of racial oppression as lack of attentiveness to cultural and ethnic differences—a fact postmodern critics sometimes seem to forget. This is not to deny what Fiske calls "the power of being different"; it is, rather, to insist that it is won through ongoing political *struggle* rather than through an act of creative interpretation. Here, once again, although many postmodern academics may claim Foucault as their guiding light, they differ from him in significant and revealing ways. For Foucault, the metaphorical terrain of resistance is explicitly that of the "battle"; the "points of confrontation" may be "innumerable" and "instable," but they involve a serious, often deadly struggle of embodied (that is, historically situated and shaped) forces.[15] Barbara Kruger exemplifies this conception of resistance in a poster that represents the contemporary contest over reproductive control through the metaphor of the body as battleground (Figure 48). Some progressive developers of children's toys have self-consciously entered into struggle with racial and other forms of normalization. The Kenya Doll (Figure 49) comes in three different skin tones ("so your girl is bound to feel pretty and proud") and attempts to create a future in which hair-straightening *will* be merely one decorative option among others. Such products, to my mind, are potentially effective "sites of resistance" precisely because they recognize that the body is a battleground whose self-determination has to be fought for.

The metaphor of the body as battleground, rather than postmodern playground, captures, as well, the *practical* difficulties involved in the political struggle to empower "difference." *Essence* magazine has consciously and strenuously tried to promote diverse images of black strength, beauty, and self-acceptance. Beauty features celebrate the glory of black skin and lush lips; other departments feature interviews with accomplished black women writers, activists, teachers, many of whom display styles of body and dress that challenge the hegemony of white Anglo-Saxon standards. The magazine's advertisers, however, continually play upon and perpetuate consumers' feelings of inadequacy and insecurity over the racial characteristics of their bodies. They insist that, in order to be

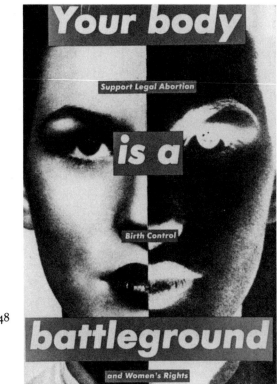

FIGURE 48

beautiful, hair must be straightened and eyes lightened; they almost always employ models with fair skin, Anglo-Saxon features, and "hair that moves," insuring association of their products with fantasies of becoming what the white culture most prizes and rewards.

This ongoing battle over the black woman's body and the power of its "differences" ("differences" which actual black women embody to widely varying degrees, of course) is made manifest in the twentieth-anniversary issue, where a feature celebrating "The Beauty of Black" faced an advertisement visually legislating virtually the opposite (and offering, significantly, "escape") (Figures 50 and 51). This invitation to cognitive dissonance reveals what *Essence* must grapple with, in every issue, as it tries to keep its message of African American self-acceptance clear and dominant, while submitting to economic necessities on which its survival depends. Let me make it clear here that such self-acceptance, not the reverse tyranny that constructs light-skinned and Anglo-featured

Kenya, the doll she'll love for all the right reasons.

CURL IT.

STRAIGHTEN IT.

BRAID IT.

BEAD IT.

Kenya will give your little girl hours of hairstyling fun. She can comb, curl, braid and bead Kenya's beautiful hair, just the way you do hers.

Best of all, Kenya comes in three natural skintones, so your girl is bound to feel pretty and proud. All the reasons why she'll love Kenya.

KENYA
The Beautiful Hairstyling Doll

FIGURE 49

African Americans as "not black enough," is the message *Essence* is trying to convey, against a culture that *denies* "the Beauty of Black" at every turn. This terrain, clearly, is not a playground but a mine-field that constantly threatens to deconstruct "difference" *literally* and not merely literarily.

"MATERIAL GIRL": MADONNA AS POSTMODERN HEROINE

John Fiske's conception of "difference," in the section quoted above, at least imagines resistance as challenging specifiable his-torical forms of dominance. Women, he argues, connect with sub-versive "feminine" values leaking through the patriarchal plot of soap operas; blacks laugh to themselves at the glossy, materialist-cowboy culture of *Dallas*. Such examples suggest a resistance di-rected against *particular* historical forms of power and subjectivity. For some postmodern theorists, however, resistance is imagined as the refusal to embody *any* positioned subjectivity at all; what is celebrated is continual creative escape from location, containment,

The Beauty of
BLACK

Oh, the extraordinary lengths we went to for makeup! Until the 1970's most Black women had limited choices in shades of brown. Those of us who were determined enough mixed brown powders and red rouge with lighter shades to come up with a color that matched our skin tone better. Others added a few drops of red food coloring to warm pale foundations. Whatever we did, it didn't look natural; we usually wound up looking either chalky or too orange. But with the surge of Black pride that swept across the country in the late sixties and early seventies, we began to understand that we didn't have to camouflage or hide our chocolate-colored skin.

The change didn't occur overnight, but soon we could find foundation and powder designed to enhance, not mask, our beauty. In the forefront of the movement to meet the demand for makeup for women of color were such lines as Astarté, Flori Roberts, Posner Custom Blends and Barbara Walden Cosmetics. Joining them with their own product lines were Zuri, Ultra Sheen Cosmetics and, later, Fashion Fair.

Finally, cosmetics that complement our complexions

At long last we aren't forced to resort to kitchen-table chemistry. Today when we visit major department stores, quality chains and drugstores from Watts to Roxbury, we can select from a variety of textures (liquids, creams, mousses, powders) and a multiplicity of colors. If the shades we want don't exist, they can be custom-blended on the spot at makeup counters. And now these products are scientifically tested and can nourish as well as enhance our skin. As never before, we can always put our best and most beautiful faces forward. ▶

NECKLACE/GISELA VON BICKEN. HAIR, JUDY PITTS. MAKEUP, PATRICE POUSSARD FOR TIMOTHY PRIANO, INC. STYLIST, ELAINE WALLACE.

FIGURE 50

A WORD ABOUT
CASUAL CORNER

ESCAPE

Escape to the tropics
in this comfortable
100% cotton jumpsuit.
Chambray blue with
tiny polka dots, $54.
Sizes S, M or L. Hammered silver disc earrings, $14.
Call 1-800-836-7500
for the nearest store
location and to receive
our seasonal catalog.

CASUAL
CORNER.

FIGURE 51

and definition. So, as Susan Rubin Suleiman advises, we must move beyond the valorization of historically suppressed values (for example, those values that have been culturally constructed as belonging to an inferior, female domain and generally expunged from Western science, philosophy, and religion) and toward "endless complication" and a "dizzying accumulation of narratives."[16] She appreciatively (and perhaps misleadingly) invokes Derrida's metaphor of "incalculable choreographies"[17] to capture the dancing, elusive, continually changing subjectivity that she envisions, a subjectivity without gender, without history, without location. From this perspective, the truly resistant female body is, not the body that wages war on feminine sexualization and objectification, but the body that, as Cathy Schwichtenberg has put it, "uses simulation strategically in ways that challenge the stable notion of gender as the edifice of sexual difference . . . [in] an erotic politics in which the female body can be refashioned in the flux of identities that speak in plural styles."[18] For this erotic politics, the new postmodern heroine is Madonna.

This celebration of Madonna as postmodern heroine does not mark the first time Madonna has been portrayed as a subversive culture-figure. Until the early 1990s, however, Madonna's resistance has been interpreted along "body as battleground" lines, as deriving from her refusal to allow herself to be constructed as a passive object of patriarchal desire. John Fiske, for example, argues that this was a large part of Madonna's original appeal to her "wanna-bes"—those hordes of middle-class pre-teeners who mimicked Madonna's moves and costumes. For the "wanna-bes," Madonna demonstrated the possibility of a female heterosexuality that was independent of patriarchal control, a sexuality that defied rather than rejected the male gaze, teasing it with her own gaze, deliberately trashy and vulgar, challenging anyone to call her a whore, and ultimately not giving a damn how she might be judged. Madonna's rebellious sexuality, in this reading, offered itself, not as coming into being through the look of the "other," but as self-defining and in love with, happy with itself—an attitude that is rather difficult for women to achieve in this culture and that helps to explain, as Fiske argues, her enormous appeal for pre-teen girls.[19] "I like the way she handles herself, sort of take it or leave it; she's sexy but she doesn't need men . . . she's kind of there all by herself," says one. "She gives us ideas. It's really women's lib, not being afraid of what guys think," says another.[20]

Madonna herself, significantly and unlike most sex symbols, has never advertised herself as disdainful of feminism or constructed feminists as man-haters. Rather, in a 1985 *Time* interview, she suggests that her lack of inhibition in "being herself" and her "luxuriant" expression of "strong" sexuality constitute her brand of feminist celebration.[21] Some feminist theorists would agree. Molly Hite, for example, argues that "asserting female desire in a culture in which female sexuality is viewed as so inextricably conjoined with passivity" is "transgressive":

> Implied in this strategy is the old paradox of the speaking statue, the created thing that magically begins to create, for when a woman writes—self-consciously from her muted position as a woman and not as an honorary man—about female desire, female sexuality, fe-

male sensuous experience generally, her performance has the effect of giving voice to pure corporeality, of turning a product of the dominant meaning-system into a producer of meanings. A woman, conventionally identified with her body, writes about that identification, and as a consequence, femininity—silent and inert by definition—erupts into patriarchy as an impossible discourse.[22]

Not all feminists would agree with this, of course. For the sake of the contrast I want to draw here, however, let us grant it, and note, as well, that an argument similar to Fiske's can be made concerning Madonna's refusal to be obedient to dominant and normalizing standards of female *beauty*. I am now talking, of course, about Madonna in her more fleshy days. In those days, Madonna saw herself as willfully out of step with the times. "Back in the fifties," she says in the *Time* interview, "women weren't ashamed of their bodies." (The fact that she is dead wrong is not relevant here.) Identifying herself with her construction of that time and what she calls its lack of "suppression" of femininity, she looks down her nose at the "androgynous" clothes of our own time and speaks warmly of her own stomach, "not really flat" but "round and the skin is smooth and I like it." Contrasting herself to anorectics, whom she sees as self-denying and self-hating, completely in the thrall of externally imposed standards of worthiness, Madonna (as she saw herself) stood for self-definition through the assertion of her own (traditionally "female" and now anachronistic) body-type (Figure 52).

Of course, this is no longer Madonna's body type. Shortly after her 1987 marriage to Sean Penn she began a strenuous reducing and exercise program, now runs several miles a day, lifts weights, and has developed, in obedience to dominant contemporary norms, a tight, slender, muscular body (Figure 53). Why did she decide to shape up? "I didn't have a flat stomach anymore," she has said. "I had become well-rounded." Please note the sharp about-face here, from pride to embarrassment. My goal here, however, is not to suggest that Madonna's formerly voluptuous body was a non-alienated, freely expressive body, a "natural" body. While the slender body is the current cultural ideal, the voluptuous female body is a cultural form, too (as are all bodies), and was a coercive ideal in the fifties. My point is that in terms of Madonna's own former lexicon of meanings—in which feminine voluptuousness and the

FIGURE 52

choice to be round in a culture of the lean were clearly connected to spontaneity, self-definition, and defiance of the cultural gaze—the terms set by that gaze have now triumphed. Madonna has been normalized; more precisely, she has self-normalized. Her "wanna-bes" are following suit. Studies suggest that as many as 80 percent of nine-year-old suburban girls (the majority of whom are far from overweight) are making rigorous dieting and exercise the organiz-ing discipline of their lives.[23] They do not require Madonna's ex-ample, of course, to believe that they must be thin to be acceptable. But Madonna clearly no longer provides a model of resistance or "difference" for them.

None of this "materiality"—that is, the obsessive body-praxis that regulates and disciplines Madonna's life and the lives of the young (and not so young) women who emulate her—makes its way into the representation of Madonna as postmodern heroine. In the

madonna: broadway bound

Living proof that exercise does pay off, Madonna shows her shape in revealing clothes that hug every curve. The blazer redefined, opposite page. In navy linen (Maroon), it falls sensuously into a deep décolletage. With delicate white organza cuffs (Hurel). By Christian Lacroix Haute Couture. When you bare a lot of skin, it must be firm and smooth. Crème Cou et Décolleté by Stendhal moisturizes neck and breast area instantly. Daring silhouette, right. The stretch cotton halter with built-in bra in shades of bronze, ends in a peplum skirt, about $1,910. Mauve bicycle pants in stretch cotton with lace trim, about $377. Both by Jean Paul Gaultier. See Fashion Guide for details and stores, next to last page.

141

FIGURE 53

terms of this representation (in both its popular and scholarly instantiations) Madonna is "in control of her image, not trapped by it"; the proof lies in her ironic and chameleon-like approach to the construction of her identity, her ability to "slip in and out of character at will," to defy definition, to keep them guessing.[24] In this coding of things, as in the fantasies of the polysurgical addict (and, as I argue elsewhere in this volume, the eating-disordered woman), *control* and *power*, words that are invoked over and over in discussions of Madonna, have become equivalent to *self-creating*. Madonna's new body has no material history; it conceals its continual struggle to maintain itself, it does not reveal its pain. (Significantly, Madonna's "self-exposé," the documentary *Truth or Dare*, does not include any scenes of Madonna's daily workouts.) It is merely another creative transformation of an ever-elusive subjectivity. "More Dazzling and Determined Not to Stop Changing," as *Cosmopolitan* describes Madonna: ". . . whether in looks or career, this multitalented dazzler will never be trapped in *any* mold!"[25] The plasticity of Madonna's subjectivity is emphasized again and again in the popular press, particularly by Madonna herself. It is how she tells the story of her "power" in the industry: "In pop music, generally, people have one image. You get pigeonholed. I'm lucky enough to be able to change and still be accepted . . . play a part, change characters, looks, attitudes."[26]

Madonna claims that her creative work, too, is meant to escape definition. "Everything I do is meant to have several meanings, to be ambiguous," she says. She resists, however (in true postmodern fashion), the attribution of serious artistic intent; rather (as she told *Cosmo*), she favors irony and ambiguity, "to entertain myself" and (as she told *Vanity Fair*) out of "rebelliousness and a desire to fuck with people."[27] It is the postmodern nature of her music and videos that has most entranced academic critics, whose accolades reproduce in highly theoretical language the notions emphasized in the popular press. Susan McClary writes:

> Madonna's art itself repeatedly deconstructs the traditional notion of the unified subject with finite ego boundaries. Her pieces explore . . . various ways of constituting identities that refuse stability, that remain fluid, that resist definition. This tendency in her work has become increasingly pronounced; for instance, in her recent controversial video "Express Yourself" . . . she slips in and out of every subject position offered within the video's narrative context . . . refusing more than ever to deliver the security of a clear, unambiguous message or an "authentic" self.[28]

Later in the same piece, McClary describes "Open Your Heart to Me," which features Madonna as a porn star in a peep show, as creating "an image of open-ended *jouissance*—an erotic energy that continually escapes containment."[29] Now, many feminist viewers may find this particular video quite disturbing, for a number of reasons. First, unlike many of Madonna's older videos, "Open Your Heart to Me" does not visually emphasize Madonna's subjectivity or desire—as "Lucky Star," for example, did through frequent shots of Madonna's face and eyes, flirting with and controlling the reactions of the viewer. Rather, "Open Your Heart to Me" places the viewer in the position of the voyeur by presenting Madonna's body as object, now perfectly taut and tightly managed for display. To be sure, we do not identify with the slimy men, drooling over Madonna's performance, who are depicted in the video; but, as E. Ann Kaplan has pointed out, the way men view women *in* the filmic world is only one species of objectifying gaze. There is also the viewer's gaze, which may be encouraged by the director to be either more or less objectifying.[30] In "Open Your Heart to Me," as in virtually all rock videos, the female body is offered to the viewer purely as a spectacle, an object of sight, a visual commodity to be consumed. Madonna's weight loss and dazzling shaping-up job make the spectacle of her body all the more compelling; we are riveted to her body, fascinated by it. Many men and women may experience the primary reality of the video as the elicitation of desire *for* that perfect body; women, however, may also be gripped by the desire (very likely impossible to achieve) to *become* that perfect body.

These elements can be effaced, of course, by a deliberate abstraction of the video from the cultural context in which it is historically embedded—the continuing containment, sexualization, and objectification of the female body—and in which the viewer is implicated as well and instead treating the video as a purely formal text. Taken as such, "Open Your Heart to Me" presents itself as what E. Ann Kaplan calls a "postmodern video": it refuses to "take a clear position vis-à-vis its images" and similarly refuses a "clear position for the spectator within the filmic world . . . leaving him/her decentered, confused."[31] McClary's reading of "Open Your Heart to Me" emphasizes precisely these postmodern elements, insisting on the ambiguous and unstable nature of the relationships depicted in the narrative of the video, and the frequent elements of parody and play. "The usual power relationship between the voyeuristic male gaze and object" is "destabilized," she claims, by the portrayal of the male patrons of the porno house as leering and pathetic. At the same time, the portrayal of Madonna as porno queen–object is deconstructed, McClary argues, by the end of the video, which has Madonna changing her clothes to those of a little boy and tripping off playfully, leaving the manager of the house sputtering behind her. McClary reads this as "escape to androgyny," which "refuses essentialist gender categories and turns sexual identity into a kind of play." As for the gaze of the viewer, she admits that it is "risky" to "invoke the image of porn queen in order to perform its deconstruction," but concludes that the deconstruction is successful: "In this video, Madonna confronts the most pernicious of her stereotypes and attempts to channel it into a very different realm: a realm where the feminine object need not be the object of the patriarchal gaze, where its energy can motivate play and nonsexual pleasure."[32]

I would argue, however, that despite the video's evasions of clear or fixed meaning there *is* a dominant position in this video: it is that of the objectifying gaze. One is not *really* decentered and confused by this video, despite the "ambiguities" it formally contains. Indeed, the video's postmodern conceits, I would suggest, facilitate rather than deconstruct the presentation of Madonna's body as an object on display. For in the absence of a coherent critical position telling us how to read the images, the individual images themselves become preeminent, hypnotic, fixating. Indeed, I would say that ultimately this video is entirely about Madonna's body, the narrative context virtually irrelevant, an excuse to showcase the physical achievements of the star, a video centerfold. On this level, any parodic or destabilizing element appears as cynically, mechanically tacked on, in bad faith, a way of claiming trendy status for what is really just cheesecake—or, perhaps, soft-core pornography.

Indeed, it may be worse than that. If the playful "tag" ending of "Open Your Heart to Me" is successful in deconstructing the notion that the objectification, the sexualization of women's bodies is a serious business, then Madonna's *jouissance* may be "fucking with" her youthful viewer's perceptions in a dangerous way. Judging from the proliferation of rock and rap lyrics celebrating the rape, abuse, and humiliation of women, the message—not Madonna's responsibility alone, of course, but hers among others, surely—is getting through. The artists who perform these misogynist songs also claim to be speaking playfully, tongue-in-cheek, and to be daring and resistant transgressors of cultural structures that contain and define. Ice T, whose rap lyrics gleefully describe the gang rape of a woman—with a flashlight, to "make her tits light up"—claims that he is only "telling it like it is" among black street youth (he compares himself to Richard Wright), and he scoffs at feminist humorlessness, implying, as well, that it is racist and repressive for white feminists to try to deny him his indigenous "style." The fact that Richard Wright embedded his depiction of Bigger Thomas within a critique of the racist culture that shaped him, and that *Native Son* is meant to be a *tragedy*, was not, apparently, noticed in Ice T's postmodern reading of the book, whose critical point of view he utterly ignores. Nor does he seem concerned about what appears to be a growing fad—not only among street gangs, but in fraternity houses as well—for gang rape, often with an unconscious woman, and surrounded by male spectators. (Some of the terms popularly used to describe these rapes include "beaching"—the woman being likened to a "beached whale"—and "spectoring," to emphasize how integral a role the onlookers play.)

My argument here is a plea, not for censorship, but for recognition of the social contexts and consequences of images from popular culture, consequences that are frequently effaced in postmodern and other celebrations of "resistant" elements in these images. To turn back to Madonna and the liberating postmodern subjectivity that McClary and others claim she is offering: the notion that one can play a porno house by night and regain one's androgynous innocence by day does not seem to me to be a refusal of essentialist categories about gender, but rather a new inscription of mind/body dualism. What the body does is immaterial, so long as the imagination is free. This abstract, unsituated, disembodied freedom, I have argued in this essay, glorifies itself only through the effacement of the material praxis of people's lives, the normalizing power of cultural images, and the continuing social realities of dominance and subordination.

Postmodern Subjects, Postmodern Bodies, Postmodern Resistance

The *postmodern* has been described and redescribed with so many different points of departure that the whole discussion is by now its own most exemplary definition. Every discipline has its own theories, key figures, watershed events. In architecture—one of the most concrete and historically influential instances—postmodernism arose as a response to modern*ism*, with its faith in social amelioration through technological innovation and systematic design. The buildings that resulted from this ideology were often cold and unlivable, and sometimes flimsy; as they began in the late 1960s and 1970s to deteriorate and collapse, the "death" of modernist architecture was declared.[1] In philosophy and literary theory, at the other extreme, it is usually modern*ity* that we diagnose as being "post," and its correspondingly more abstract (and highly debatable) "deaths"—of Man, of the Subject, of the Author—that we take as proclaiming the end of the ideology of a historical *era* and not just an artistic movement within it.

As modernity is described as beginning (and ending, according to some) at very different historical junctures and for very different reasons, the kaleidoscope of the postmodern shifts from discipline to discipline (sometimes revealing inventively postmodern configurations). One of my colleagues begins her course on postmodernism with the Holocaust, as delivering an unhealable wound to Enlightenment notions of human perfectibility and rationality. Other, more epistemologically oriented philosophers characterize the postmodern largely in terms of breakdown of belief in scientific truth and objectivity. Many tie this epistemological fragmentation to the collapse of the hegemony of Western culture; others see the "information explosion" as key. If you view (as I do) the progress of consumer capitalism as central, then the amoral and ceaseless proliferation of products and images will figure strongly in your story of the postmodern. There are those academics in literature and philosophy who, conflating theory with all of culture, identify the postmodern solely in terms of particular poststructuralist authors and the schools of thought they have spawned. And then, too, sitting atop these various notions of the postmodern condition, there is tremendous disagreement over whether that condition is cause for celebration or depression.

"Post," too, is a slippery notion. Insofar as modernity, whatever else it is, conceives of itself as breaking with the past and inaugurating the "new," then any movement or condition which describes itself as "postmodern" is something of a redundancy. On certain understandings of modernity, the heralding of a "postmodern age" is symptomatic of modernity's endless infatuation with innovation, with wiping the slate clean and beginning afresh. For a modern, to be "post" is de rigueur, and today it is academically fashionable as well, with its evocation of cutting edge, avant-garde sophistication attractively combined with the suggestion of politically informed opposition. And sometimes, the appellation *postmodern* appears to be used simply to advertise or indicate work or attitudes that are believed to manifest such qualities, to mark membership in an exclusive club of the brilliant and subversive. In this way, the spirit of being "post" completely overwhelms any substantive understanding of modernity, and *postmodern* comes to mean, as Charles Jencks points out, "anything resisting or deconstructing common assumptions of culture."[2] This oppositional spirit is reflected in the Foucauldian buzz words which liken our professional activity to daring epistemological guerrilla warfare: intervention, contestation, resistance, subversion, interrogation, and so forth.

Membership, as the commercial says, has its privileges. It can replace the need for ongoing critical self-reflection with delusions of purity—delusions that are particularly galling (and self-contradictory) when they claim to be "post" hierarchical thinking. I once heard a well-known speaker go on at some length about the dangers and distortions of oppositional constructs, congratulating contemporary academics on having "gone beyond" all that, but reminding the (academic) audience of the hopelessly retrograde world "outside" that continues to think in dualistic terms. "We" cannot become complacent, so long as "they" remain in the cave. Dualism, apparently, is easier to "go beyond" in theory than in practice. The bad faith of such theoretical hubris is also evident in much academic writing, where the division between the enlightened (averring, of course, to be thoroughly "postenlightenment") and "the others" is continually reinforced by the obscure, exclusive power-language which has become virtually an obligatory club uniform in much poststructuralist prose.

Is the postmodern merely a stylish, self-promoting, have-it-any-way-you-like fancy of contemporary intellectuals? Despite what I have said above, I don't think so. A good deal of the linguistic paraphernalia of academic postmodernism, for all its pretentiousness, has its origins in important insights and ideas that ought not to be dismissed out of annoyance with the elitism and insularity that are, after all, hardly new to academia. Heterogeneity, discontinuity, displacement, destabilization: these terms may be items of postmodern academic accessorizing, but they also point to real elements of contemporary experience. "Something *is* happening" (to borrow Jane Flax's phrase); an array of cultural alterations *have* made significant changes in the conditions of life, changes which need to be named, described, and understood.

Three books by feminist authors can help us to map the postmodern. None of these books is exclusively about postmodernism. Jane Flax, in *Thinking Fragments: Psychoanalysis, Feminism, Postmodernism in the Contemporary West*, considers postmodern philosophy as one of three "modes of contemporary Western thought" which she brings into conversation with each other (the others are psychoanalysis and feminism). Bell hooks, in *Yearning: Race, Gender and Cultural Politics*, devotes one essay explicitly to "Postmodern Blackness" and comments on various aspects of postmodernism in several other essays in a wide-ranging collection of cultural criticism. Judith Butler, in *Gender Trouble: Feminism and the Subversion of Identity*, critiques several theorists often described as postmodern, but her book is less a commentary on postmodernism than itself a postmodern approach to gender.[3] These books are very different—in style, in content, in concerns, in language, in their relation to the postmodern. Yet all seem (in varying ways) "inside" the contemporary condition—embodying it as well as commenting on it—as much academic writing is not.

To illustrate this point, let me contrast the mood of Jane Flax's opening section (evocatively titled "Something Is Happening") with a few lines from a letter I received soliciting contributions for a collection on postmodernism. "Where are our historical surveys and our critical judgments to dwell," the prospective editors ask, "after the disruption of the framework of historical periods and of the assurance of the critic/intellectual? We don't want to give post-modernity its place in the Academy; we know that the academy is a modernist project." Here, with apparently no consciousness of bad faith, the editors fashionably invoke the loss of stable historical frameworks and crises of authority, and in the very next sentence manage to retain their *own* authority neatly and unequivocally to locate the academy as a "modernist" project!

That attitude is not unique; many academic writers pronounce solemnly about the "groundlessness" of the postmodern while demonstrating no evidence that the ground has been shaken for them personally or professionally at all. Jane Flax, contrastingly, is disconcerted, troubled, and personally challenged by the prospect of trying to "do knowledge" in conditions of epistemological frag-mentation and foundationlessness. "What meanings can writing have," she asks, "when every proposition and theory seems ques-tionable, one's own identity is uncertain, and the status of the intellectual is conceived alternatively as hopelessly enmeshed in oppressive knowledge/power relations or utterly irrelevant to the workings of the technical-rational bureaucratic state?"[4] I take Flax's question to be asked fully in good faith. Throughout her book she struggles not only with the project of constructing new sources of meaning out of the partialness of others' theories (a task at which she is superb, providing detailed examinations of Freud, Lacan, and Winnicott, as well as equally incisive general discussions of femi-nism and postmodernism) but with her *own* "authority" as well. Scrupulously monitoring any impulse to speak from magisterial heights, Flax wins both my admiration and my affection, and also at times frustrates me. For there are insights of great importance in this book, which deserve to be showcased more than Flax's qualified "No Conclusions" (the title of the last section of her book) approach allows.

For example, as a practicing psychotherapist, Flax has an excel-lent grasp of the fantasies of omnipotence and control that drive philosophy and the characteristic "blind spots" that result. Not since John Dewey's has there been such a penetrating critique of the philosopher's "overestimation of the power of thinking and its centrality to human life" and of the narcissistic reduction of history to the story of philosophy. Flax extends this critique to Derrida, Rorty, Lyotard, and (less accurately, I believe) to Foucault: "Under the cover of the 'displacement' of philosophy, a traditional activity continues: an inquiry into the conditions of possibility, meaning, and limitations of our *knowledge* via a critique of reason and philosophy."[5] She emphasizes that this "mentalist, de-eroticized" conception of the subject of history as philosophy is gendered (she earlier offers a similar critique of Lacanian psychoanalysis). If the story were written from the perspective of women's experiences "the dramatic episodes might not be the three deaths [of Man, of history, of metaphysics], but rather an ongoing series of struggles: to give birth and to avoid giving birth; to be represented or to avoid being misrepresented; to be concretely in time and to have one's activities order time and conceptions of history; not to exist as the eternal, 'feminine,' 'other' or 'mysterious' life source."[6] Other feminists have, of course, criticized Western philosophy's privileging of reason. What is most impressive and timely about Flax's discussion is how skillfully she brings poststructuralist thought—which advertises itself as the antagonist of the "phallogocentrism" of past philosophy—under this critique. As such, poststructuralist thought presents itself not simply as a "fragment" of partial truth with which Flax is "conversing" (her chosen metaphors) but also as an important illustration within an *argument* Flax is making (extremely persuasively, perhaps despite herself), an argument about persistent and resilient *continuities* within Western culture. The Great White Father (who also has a class identity, as Dewey first pointed out) just keeps on returning, even amid the seeming ruptures of postmodern culture.

My divided reaction to Flax's postmodern hesitation to present her book as (at least in part) an argument is exemplary, perhaps, of the love-hate relationship that many of us who are trying to develop insights and perspectives out of marginalized experience have with the postmodern fragmentation of knowledge. When I was in college and graduate school in philosophy, feminists were in the vanguard of the challenge to the ahistorical, eternalizing notions of Truth and Reason that have ever been dear to our discipline. Our iconoclasm was not merely an intellectual fascination (and it certainly was not then in academic style), but was painfully grounded in our historical experience of *knowing* other truths than the Philosopher's Timeless Ones and continually having them dismissed. I do not remember becoming "converted to" historicism, contextualism, pluralism, or "the social construction of reality." Rather, that had always been the way I (and many other academic feminists) saw things. In no little part, our intellectual perspective had been shaped by the more politically focused feminist challenge to cultural consciousness that began in the late sixties and that had raised for so many of us the startling idea that the organization and deployment of gender as we knew it (not to mention "Man" and "Woman") were human constructions rather than eternal forms.

When historicism and contextual considerations began to be seen as philosophically legitimate (rather than mushy thinking, a position many philosophers still take), not only did we feel intellectually vindicated, but it also seemed as though the moment might be at hand when the significance and vitality of those "other truths" (the truths made available through non-European cultural traditions, through gendered experience, through histories of subordination) would be culturally recognized. Not for an instant did I think of any of the emerging knowledges as new candidates for the throne of Timeless Truth, but neither did I see the only choice as being that between an imperial monarchy and epistemological anarchy. In my eyes, historicism was an ally against arrogant perception and insular thinking, fostering a healthy suspicion of the "givenness" of our realities, and *not* a foreclosure on meaning, judgments, or distinctions. So much for the "love" part of the relationship.

The "hate" part has to do with the disconcerting swiftness with which the toppling of the Timeless Truths of Western thought gave way to the postmodern fragmentation of culture, with its "stylish nihilism" (as bell hooks calls it in her trenchant review of *Sammy and Rosie Get Laid*)[7] and its never-ending proliferation of images and options. Within this climate, feminist knowledge and the knowledges born of racial experience and consciousness were allotted the historical equivalent of approximately ten minutes to stake a claim on the conscience of our culture before the processes of their deconstruction—not only by academic theory, but also in the popular and aesthetic imagination—began. The author was suddenly dead in the academy, just as we began to write for it; and just as we began to locate and describe the systemic racism and sexism of our culture, we found our accounts reduced to nothing more than talk-show topics, on a par with every other complaint and disorder of the moment. At the same time as this postmodern deconstruction was occurring, moreover, charges of left-wing totalitarianism were emerging from other quarters, fragmenting our efforts in more backward-yearning ways.

Both Flax and hooks, while eschewing essentialist notions of race and gender, are suspicious of any undermining of the authority of our experience just at that cultural moment when we might begin to "re-member ourselves" and "to make ourselves subject" (Flax's and hooks's respective formulations). "There is a radical difference," hooks points out, "between a repudiation of the idea that there is a black 'essence' and recognition of the way black identity has been specifically constituted in the experience of exile and struggle."[8] Similarly, Flax criticizes postmodern deconstructions of subjectivity and urges that feminists continue to seek "location and participation" in the retelling and reconstruction of women's "differentiated yet collective experience." "What memories of history," she asks, "will our daughters have if we do not find ways to speak of and practice [the sense of 'we']?"[9]

At the same time, both Flax and hooks take very seriously what poststructuralist writers have called the "decentering" of the subject—*not*, however, as a methodological or theoretical dogma (according to which any articulation of identity, of the "we," is a totalizing fiction) but as part of the lived experience of acting, thinking, writing in fragmenting times. For neither of them is this decentering wholly positive (as it may be for those who spin it out abstractly, "in theory"); in human communities it has often meant homelessness, dislocation from history, a sense of political and intellectual vertigo and paralysis, and the replacement of lost human bonds by the individual search for stimulation and material gratification. Hooks's essays in *Yearning* (see especially "Postmodern Blackness," "The Politics of Radical Black Subjectivity," "Chitlin' Circuit," and "Homeplace") are especially instructive in their exploration of the consequences of postmodern fragmentation for African American identity and culture.

The decentering of the self is, however, also viewed by hooks as offering opportunities: for "new and varied forms of bonding" among people, for artistic and intellectual engagement with popular culture, and for creating transformative subjectivities that express and exhibit the multiple aspects of identity, the different locations from which we see and think.[10] She urges African American intellectuals and artists to embody in their work and presence all the complexity and variety of the cultural traditions that have shaped them. Only through such embodiment—by means of which elements of identity developed "at the margins" are brought to the "center"—can the hegemony of existing cultural styles of subjectivity be challenged. Her perfectly chosen example is a talk by Cornel West:

> Though highly intellectual and theoretical in content, his manner of presentation was akin to a sermon mode popular in black communities, where such a style indicates depth and seriousness. In the context of white institutions, particularly universities, that mode of address is questionable precisely because it moves people. Style is equated in such a setting with a lack of substance. West not only transformed social space, legitimating an aspect of black experience in a context which rarely recognizes the values of black culture, he was also able to include non-scholarly members of the audience. His style of presentation required of the audience a shift in paradigms; a marginal aspect of black cultural identity was centralized. To understand what was happening, individuals had to assume a different literary standpoint.[11]

Hooks's discussion was extremely meaningful to me. I once lost a prestigious job because (as I was informed later by one of the members of the committee) I "moved my body around so much" during my presentation. I know this was not the only time that my expressive style—part Jewish, part "feminine"—disqualified me as a serious philosopher; it was simply the one time that I was informed of it. Reconstructing subjectivity is risky, as hooks points out. When we give expression in academic settings to those aspects of our identity forged in marginality, we may be seen as "spectacle." Yet, as she argues (and I fully agree), this is a risk we must run, not only in the interests of our own "right to subjectivity" but also as the means by which culture is *transformed* and not simply reproduced with different players in the same game. Every time we *are* taken seriously it means that an entrenched paradigm has been shaken; every time that I am taken seriously, for example, by those in my profession or by my students, it means that the deeply sedimented image of "the philosopher"—not simply as white and male, but as demonstrating his rigor through detachment, superiority, "cool" reason—has been upset.

Both hooks and Flax self-consciously and deliberately inhabit a variety of locations—none of them taken on in the interests of textual play, all of them rooted in aspects of their own histories, professions, politics—in their books. They do not attempt to reconcile these locations, but simply allow them to speak in turn, each a different center of "authority." In this "polyphonic vocality" (as hooks describes it)[12] these books are acutely postmodern. But because the insights that emerge are grounded in experience, the result is neither chaotic nor fanciful; rather, the security and elegance of theoretical unity are replaced by the different satisfaction of having sometimes incommensurable realities (that is, real life) described with precision, intelligence, and honesty.

For instance, as a therapist Flax is soberly aware of the terror that *literally* decentered selves endure, as well as of the limitations of postmodern "textual indeterminacy" as a principle for helping actual human beings; as a philosopher, however, she is appreciative of these notions for inviting "ambivalence, ambiguity and multiplicity" into our theorizing.[13] Criticizing the poststructuralist discourse on "difference," hooks is stunningly on target concerning white theorists' continuing reading of black writers *only* for race issues (as representatives of the claims of "otherness") while they leave whiteness unproblematized, unexamined, constructed as no race at all. A shift of perspective, however, finds her hopeful that the "contemporary engagement with issues of 'otherness and difference' . . . indicates that there is a growing body of work that can provide and promote critical dialogue and debate across boundaries of class, race and gender."[14] This assessment is only contradictory in the abstract; in the context of academic communities, the concern for "difference" *has* functioned in a complex variety of ways, some stifling, some liberating. Throughout, hooks's *Yearning* exhibits a feeling for the complexity and multiplicity of cultural phenomena—from poststructuralist theory, to relations between white and black feminists, to film representations of race and gender, to the much-publicized rape of a jogger in Central Park—that I have not found in any other contemporary work of criticism:

> To fully understand the multiple meanings of [the Central Park rape], it must be approached from an analytical standpoint that considers the impact of sexism and racism. Beginning there enables many of us to empathize with both the victim and the victimizers. If one reads *The Demon Lover* and thinks about this crime, one can see it as part of a continuum of male violence against women, of rape and terror as weapons of male domination—yet another horrific and brutal expression of patriarchal socialization. And if one considers this case by combining a feminist analysis of race and masculinity, one sees that since male power within patriarchy is relative, men from poorer groups and men of color are not able to reap the material and social rewards for their participation in patriarchy. In fact they often suffer from blindly and passively acting out a myth of masculinity that is life-threatening. Sexist thinking blinds them to this reality. They become victims of the patriarchy. No one can truly believe that the young black males involved in the Central Park incident were not engaged in a suicidal ritual enactment of a dangerous masculinity that will ultimately threaten their lives, their well being.
>   If one reads again Michael Dyson's piece "The Plight of Black Men" . . . it is easy to understand why young black males are despairing and nihilistic. And it is rather naive to think that if they do not value their own lives, they will value the lives of others. Is it really so difficult for folks to see the connection between the constant pornographic glorification of male violence against women that is represented, enacted and condoned daily in the culture and in the Central Park crime? Does racism create and maintain this blindspot or does it allow black people and particularly black men to become the scapegoats, embodying society's evils?[15]

I have quoted this section at some length because as I write about hooks's appreciation of multiplicity I am aware of how empty that word—reverentially intoned over and over in contemporary writing—now sounds. Despite the constant lip service paid to multiplicity, we have few models of thinkers who are genuine "'world'-travellers" (as Maria Lugones calls them).[16] Many people *theorize* about multiplicity, and deconstructionist readings *seek* it from texts—often guided by *jouissance* alone rather than a hunger for understanding. But becoming a world-travelling thinker cannot, in my opinion, be accomplished by sight-seeing, textual or cultural.

Nor does it require extensive coverage of "foreign" territory. As Lugones describes it, it has fundamentally to do with the desire and ability to explore reality "wearing the other's shoes." This means recognizing, wherever one goes, that the other's perspective *is* fully realized, not a bit of exotic "difference" to be incorporated within one's own world. The world-travelling thinker thus must be prepared, not only to "appreciate" the foreign, but also to recognize and nurture those places where worlds meet. And the world-travelling thinker will always be ready to abandon familiar territory when human understanding and communication seem to require it. It is in these senses that *Yearning*, in its complex and expanding understandings of race and gender politics, is beyond dualism not merely theoretically but also in intellectual practice, and so models the best of postmodern multiplicity for us.

Flax and hooks, with their concerns about knowledge, voice, and intellectual and political perspective, do not devote much discussion to the body as a carrier of culture, postmodern or otherwise. But there are many who do see the body—both as a living cultural form and as a subject of scholarly theorizing—as a significant register of the fact that we are living in fragmented times. Our cultural attitudes toward the body are full of dissonances, expressive of the contradictions of our society. On the one hand, sex has become deadly; on the other hand, it continues to be advertised as the preeminent source of ecstasy, power, and self-fulfillment. Both on MTV and on daytime soaps, sobering messages about AIDS are broadcast back-to-back with video images of mindless abandon; the abandon—which by definition precludes attentiveness to such "practical" considerations as condoms—is depicted as the essence and proof of erotic charge. At one extreme, our culture seems newly recaptivated by biological determinism. Although the Human Genome Project has had its critics, excitement over progress it has made in interpreting the entirety of the human genetic blueprint has been rekindled in 1992. Even as I write this, a friend has just come into the room, showing me a full page in the *New York Times* entitled "Blueprint for a Human" and illustrated both with a photo of a newborn and with the latest, most complete chromosomal maps devised by the project. Daily, newspaper articles appear declaring genetic and chemical bases for physical and psychological disorders of all sorts, including many—such as anorexia nervosa and bulimia—for which the evidence for cultural origins seems overwhelming. At the other extreme, it is being just as unequivocally declared that "Bodies are not born. They are in fact made by culture."[17]

For many scholars, this commitment to cultural constructionism has gone far beyond notions that the biological body never *presents* itself to us in innocent or "natural" form but is always historically and politically "inscribed" and shaped (a position I adhere to), to the much more radical position that the very notion of the biological body is itself a fiction. Popular culture has its own versions of this thesis, as we alter our bodies without regard for biological consequences, recklessly making them over through yo-yo dieting and plastic surgery and eagerly embracing any technology that challenges our various biological clocks. Arguably, we are more in touch with our bodies than ever before. But at the same time, they have become alienated products, texts of our own creative making, from which we maintain a strange and ironic detachment.

Turning back to more scholarly contexts, arguably (as I suggest in the introduction to this volume) a major paradigm shift has occurred over the past hundred years. Formerly, the body was dominantly conceptualized as a fixed, unitary, primarily physiological reality. Today, more and more scholars have come to regard the body as a historical, plural, culturally mediated form. To the degree that such a shift has occurred, feminism (as I have argued) has contributed much to it, to the corollary development of a "political" understanding of the body, and to a new suspicion of the category of "nature" and its accompanying ideologies concerning women's "species role." To feminism's recognition of the body as a cultural form and "site" of "disciplinary power" poststructuralist thought has contributed two additional elements. First, in its more Foucauldian manifestations, poststructuralism has encouraged recognition of the fact that prevailing configurations of power, no matter how dominant, are never seamless but are always spawning new forms of subjectivity, new contexts for resistance to and transformation of existing relations. Second, in its more Derridean manifestations, poststructuralism has encouraged us to recognize that the body is not only materially acculturated (for example, as it conforms to social norms and habitual practices of "femininity" and "masculinity"),[18] but also mediated by language: by metaphors (for instance, microbes as "invading," egg as "waiting" for sperm) and semantical grids (such binary oppositions as male/female, inner/ outer) that organize and animate our perception and experience. We thus have no direct, innocent, or unconstructed knowledge of our bodies; rather, we are always reading our bodies according to various interpretive schemes.

These are important insights, which have deepened, enriched, and complicated contemporary feminist understandings of the politics of the body; Judith Butler's *Gender Trouble* is a striking example. Butler's aim is both to provoke "gender trouble" in the mind of the reader—by "denaturalizing" the categories of gender and of the "natural" itself—and to suggest how "gender trouble" is *culturally* stirred up through "subversive bodily acts" that exhibit the artificiality of gender. The latter aspect, although it was for me the most intriguing part of Butler's book, actually gets the shortest shrift when it comes to detailed elaboration and illustration. The greater part of Butler's considerable philosophical energy and expertise is devoted to a "genealogical" critique of gender (for Butler this means an exploration of gender categories as the *effect* of discourse rather than the "natural" ground of identity) through examination of the work of Freud, Lacan, Irigaray, Kristeva, and Wittig. Her strategy is to expose their concealed assumptions naturalizing heterosexuality and/or maternity, while also teasing out the elements of their work that problematize such assumptions.

The genealogical critique is the deconstructive aspect of Butler's work. The "constructive" aspect is her theory of gender, which has two parts: an analysis of gender as "performance" and an argument for parody as the most effective strategy for subverting the fixed "binary frame" of gender. Sociologists may recognize in Butler's "performative theory" a poststructuralist, feminist reincarnation of Erving Goffman's innovative and persuasive performative theory of identity.[19] For Butler, as for Goffman, our identities, gendered and otherwise, do not express some authentic "core" self but are the dramatic *effect* (rather than the cause) of our performances. These we learn how to "fabricate" in the same way we learn how to manipulate a language: through imitation and gradual command of public, cultural idioms (for instance, the corporeal gestures of gender). Within this framework, the illusion of an "interior and organizing gender core" is itself a "fantasy instituted and inscribed on the surface of bodies" through our performances.[20] That illusion, moreover (and here Butler provides a significant dimension missing in Goffman) effectively protects the institution of reproductive heterosexuality from scrutiny and critique *as* an institution, continually regulating rather than merely reflecting our sexuality.

Whether or not one is willing to go so postmodern as to deny *all* interior determinations of identity, the performative approach is enormously insightful (and pedagogically useful) as a framework for exploring the ongoing, interactive, imitative processes by means of which the self, gender (I would add race as well), and their illusions of authenticity are constructed. What cultural gestures are involved in the performance of masculinity, femininity, heterosexuality, homosexuality, maternity, paternity, whiteness, blackness? How is authenticity "fabricated" and conveyed? How is the "binary frame" (of race as well as gender) enacted and regulated? These questions can be concretely explored by students through examination of the everyday artifacts of culture such as advertisements and commercials and through critical reflection on their own interactions with each other. By experiencing the "strangeness" of examining themselves and their culture as fabricated out of specific lexicons of publicly available gestures, and by recognizing the degree to which their selves are created in public interaction, they find that the given is thrown into fresh critical relief and that productive "trouble" has been made for entrenched assumptions about what is "natural" and what is "unnatural."

I also found Butler's intricate and deft exposure of various theorists' hidden commitments to "heterosexual matrices" and maternal essences to be brilliant—particularly her incisive critique of Kristeva's heterosexism. Butler is superb at the detection and deconstruction of naturalist assumptions; even Foucault is shown to have concealed commitments to the notion of a "true body beyond the law." Her own antibiologism is, indeed, far more relentless and programmatic than Foucault's. Primarily a cultural historian, he was notoriously resistant to identifying with any theoretical position. For Butler, contrastingly, there *is* one correct, unimpeachable position: it is that any conception of the "natural" is a dangerous "illusion" of which we must be "cured."[21] The "cure" is to "recast" all biological claims within the "more encompassing framework" that sees discourse as foundational and the body as thoroughly "text." Thus, Kristeva's postulation of a "maternal body prior to discourse" is described as "fundamentally inverted" and must be "reversed"[22]—that is, must be shown to be the product of language: "[Kristeva's] argument makes clear that maternal drives constitute those primary processes that language invariably represses or sublimates. But perhaps her argument could be recast within an *even more encompassing framework*: What cultural configuration of language, indeed, of discourse, generates the trope of a pre-discursive libidinal multiplicity, and for what purposes?"[23]

Here, in my opinion, Butler shifts from performing edifying genealogical therapy on entrenched assumptions to offering discursive or linguistic foundationalism as the highest critical court, the clarifying, demystifying and liberating Truth. The notion of discursive foundationalism as "cure" suggests that the textualization of the body is itself a privileged theoretical turn immune from cultural suspicion and critique. I would argue, against this, that both naturalist and textualizing notions of the body are culturally situated (the latter in postmodern culture), and that both are thus equally amenable to being historically utilized as coercive instruments of power. Some historical eras clearly have been dominated by biologistic paradigms, paradigms which have serviced and continue to service heterosexist and sexist ideology. But does it follow from this that "biology" is ipso facto and in all contexts merely the discursive "product" of heterosexist and sexist regimes? Or that a textualist view of the body necessarily escapes those regimes?

Note that Butler does not so much *argue* against Kristeva's notion of the biological maternal as *consume* it within the "more encompassing framework" of discourse. Butler's world is one in which language swallows everything up, voraciously, a theoretical pasta-machine through which the categories of competing frameworks are pressed and reprocessed as "tropes." In this linguistic foundationalism, Butler is very much more the Derridean than the Foucaudian, even though Foucauldian language and ideas dominate in the book. Within Foucault's understanding of the ways in which the body is "produced" through specific historical practices, "discourse" is not foundational but is, rather, one of the many interrelated modes by which power is made manifest. Equally, if not more, important for him are the institutional and everyday *practices* by means of which our experience of the body is organized: institutionalized monitoring, "normalizing" examinations, the spatial and temporal organization of schools and prisons, the "confessional" mode between physicians and patients, teachers and students, and so forth. Correlatively, determining whether a particular act or stance is resistant or subversive requires examination of its practical, historical, institutional reverberations. For Foucault, such determinations can never simply be read from the textual surface of the body. Contrastingly, Butler's analyses of how gender is constituted and subverted take the body as just such a text whose meanings can be analyzed in abstraction from experience, history, material practice, and context.

Butler's theory of parody as subversion is a striking example. This theory is an extremely interesting suggestion of the consequences, for a theory of resistance, of the thoroughly linguistic and performative nature of the gendered body as she has described it. As was discussed earlier, there are for Butler no "natural" resources (for instance, no polymorphous sexuality or androgyny that exists prior to our genderization) to inform struggle against the system of gender. What *can* occur (and what *does* continually occur, Butler suggests) is that the "natural" or "essential" nature of gender is challenged (and thus the system destabilized) from within the resources of the system itself, through parody of it—for example, drag: "In imitating gender, drag implicitly reveals the imitative structure of gender itself—as well as its contingency."[24] Butler thus offers a theory of subversion that equally honors the role of marginalized sexualities *and* what for many thinkers are hallmarks of postmodern art: the use of obvious artifice, quotation marks, irony, and parody to subvert established conventions.

This is ingenious and exciting, and it sounds right—in theory. And so long as we regard the body in drag as an abstract, unsituated linguistic structure, as pure text, we may be convinced by Butler's claim that the gender system is continually being playfully destabilized and subverted from within. But subversion of cultural assumptions (despite the claims of some deconstructionists) is not something that happens *in* a text or *to* a text. It is an event that takes place (or doesn't) in the reading of the text, and Butler does not explore this. She does not locate the text in question (the body in drag) in cultural context (are we watching the individual in a gay club or on the "Donahue" show?), does not consider the possibly different responses of various readers (male or female, young or old, gay or straight?) or the various anxieties that might complicate their readings, does not differentiate between women in male attire and men in female drag (two very different cultural forms, I would argue), and does not consult (or at least does not report on) a single human being's *actual* reaction either to seeing or to enacting drag. On what basis, then, does she conclude that drag "effectively mocks . . . the notion of a true gender identity" and "displaces the entire enactment of gender significations from the discourse of truth and falsity"?[25]

Attempting to give this abstract text some "body" through my own (admittedly limited) intuitions, drag performances (and cross-dressing and "the sexual stylization of butch/femme identities,"[26] also mentioned by Butler) seem far less destabilizing of the "binary frame" of gender than those identities that present themselves not as parodying either masculinity or femininity but as thoroughly ambiguous with regard to gender. (Only rarely do we interpret bodies as sexually ambiguous, for—as Suzanne Kessler and Wendy McKenna have argued, and as Holly Devor's interviews with female "gender-blenders" indicate—our readings are overdetermined for *maleness*, that is, it only takes a few male cues for bodies to be interpreted as male.)[27] Ambiguity *is* unsettling and challenging. Somehow I managed to see *M. Butterfly* without foreknowledge that the role of Butterfly was played by a man. When the actor slowly removed his clothes and gradually slipped out of his female "presentation of self," I was quite shaken. But—and this is crucial with respect to Butler's argument—my disequilibrium was the result, *not* of my having been made parodically aware of the gap between illusion and "reality," but because precisely in the absence of that awareness, I watched "femininity" segue into "masculinity" without a clear and distinct boundary to mark the transformation. In that transitional space, gender reality was shaken for me, not because I realized that gender is an artifice (I knew that before I went to the play) but because the familiar dualities (the "binary frame") had been forced to yield to an unclear and uncharted continuum.

Turning now to the "author" side of the text, what does Butler make of the fact that highly dualist gender ontologies frequently prevail in the worldviews of drag performers? Drag star Chili Pepper, speaking on the "Donahue" show, said without irony that he felt drag queens could help teach women how to be "real women." According to Esther Newman, such attitudes are far from unusual;

many female impersonators "see masculinity and femininity as *the* polar modes of existence."[28] So, too, do many transsexuals. Jan Morris, who eventually had a sex-change operation, has written of "that inner factor" which he identified in himself (when still physically male) as "femaleness," of gender as the "essentialness of oneself"; she approvingly quotes C. S. Lewis's description of gender as "reality, a more fundamental reality than sex."[29] Lesbian butch and femme identities, too, are frequently read by heterosexuals as proof of how irresistible masculine and feminine roles are—an irresistibility they then go on to attribute to the "naturalness" of heterosexuality. How culturally subversive can these forms be if they are so readily interpreted as proof of the foundational nature of gender, the essential reality of the "binary frame"?

I want to make clear that my criticism of the abstract nature of Butler's argument does not entail a denial of the fact that subversive elements are continually at work (or at play) in our culture. My point is that subversion is contextual, historical, and, above all, social. No matter how exciting the destabilizing potential of texts, bodily or otherwise, whether those texts are subversive or recuperative or both or neither cannot be determined in abstraction from actual social practice. In "'Material Girl,'" I criticized Susan McClary's reading of Madonna's music video "Open Your Heart to Me" for romanticizing what McClary sees as the playful, parodic, subversive aspects of that text at the expense of effacement of the grimmer *social* reality of how young men and women are actually responding to the images of music videos. Assessing Butler's work is more complicated, for it has a dual identity. With her keen feminist understanding of how historically normalizing and defining the institutions of phallocentrism and heterosexism are, Butler is strongly attuned to the social world that her parodic bodily "texts" (they are people, after all, not literature) live in. The Derridean/Foucauldian agenda of *Gender Trouble*, however, leads in another direction. Butler's texts become signifiers without context, and her analysis begins to exhibit along with McClary's a characteristically postmodern inclination to emphasize and celebrate resistance, the creative agency of individuals, and the instabilities of current power-relations rather than their recuperative tendencies.

What is wrong with such a celebration? I want to point to several problems here. Let me first acknowledge, however, that no culture is static or seamless. Resistance and transformation are indeed continual and creative, and subversive responses are possible under even the most oppressive circumstances. This all seems obvious from history. What Foucault himself recognized and his more postmodern followers sometimes forget is that resistance and transformation *are* historical processes. Instead, intoxicated with the interpretive and creative *possibilities* of cultural analysis, they neglect to ask themselves what is actually going on in the culture around them. Here, the influence of deconstructionism is apparent. I agree with Foucault that where there is power there is also resistance. For Foucault this was a statement of social dynamics, not a formula for reading texts. Analyses and interpretations that go against the grain of dominant readings of literature are powerful to the degree that they excite the intellect and imagination of the reader; the actuality and effectiveness of social resistance, however, can be determined only by examining historical situations. These vary, and therefore so too does the degree to which resistance can legitimately be emphasized in cultural analysis. Failure to recognize this can result in theorizing potentially subversive but still highly culturally contained forms of subjectivity as though they were on an equal footing with historically dominant forms, romanticizing the degree of cultural challenge that is occurring, and thus diverting focus from continued patterns of exclusion, subordination, normalization.

Here, I will shift focus from *Gender Trouble* to consider resistance in the context of other issues raised throughout this book. Just how helpful, for example, is an emphasis on creative agency in describing the relation of women and their bodies to the image industry of post-industrial capitalism, a context in which addictive bingeing and purging, exercise compulsions, and "polysurgical addictions" are flourishing? Do we have a multi-million-dollar industry in corrective surgery because people are asserting their racial and ethnic identities in resistance to prevailing norms, or because they are so vulnerable to the power of those norms? My own resistance to being swept up in a celebratory postmodernism is due, in part, to the fact that the particular power-terrain I have been examining in this book does not offer much cause for celebration.

Admittedly, relentlessly focusing on cultural normalization can be depressing. It is exciting and hope-inspiring to believe, rather, that "resistance is everywhere." Moreover, as I have discovered from the many presentations I have given about our contemporary obsessions with slenderness, youth, and physical perfection, people may feel deeply threatened when their own behaviors are situated within normalizing cultures. They want, understandably, to be able to pursue happiness on the terms of the culture they live in (terms to which we all submit to one degree or another in various areas of our lives). But they also want to feel that they are self-determining agents, and some want to be reassured that their choices are "politically correct," as well. It thus becomes very important that they believe their own choices to be individual, freely motivated, "for themselves." Consider, for example, the way seventeen-year-old actress Sara Gilbert describes her decision to have her nose "fixed," shortly after her television mom Roseanne Arnold had hers done (because it was too wide, as she told Oprah Winfrey!): "I think it's important to be attractive to yourself. Your body just kind of gets in the way of what you try to do. So if you're concentrating that much energy on your body, then just change it so you can move on and deal with the intellectual."[30]

Actually, Gilbert's is a pretty reasonable argument. What is lurking unexpressed, however, is acknowledgment of the cultural norms which made Gilbert feel unattractive with the nose she had, as well as the cultural premium on looks which had her "concentrating" on her body all the time. Such elements, as we have seen in this book, are continually mystified in commercial constructions of body alteration as self-determination and creative self-fashioning. ("The body you have is the body you inherited, but you must decide what to do with it," instructs Nike, offering glamorous shots of lean, muscled athletes to help us "decide.") Some of these ads go so far as to present the normalized body as the body of cultural resistance. "I Believe" is the theme of a recent series of Reebok commercials, each of which features muscled, energetic women declaring their feminist rebellion as they exercise: "I believe that babe is a four-letter word," "I believe in baying at the moon," "I believe that sweat *is* sexy." The last declaration—which "answers" the man in a "Secret" deodorant commercial who claims that "a woman just isn't sexy when she sweats"—not only rebels against gender ideology but suggests resistance to the world of commercials itself (nice trick for a commercial!).

Figures 54 and 55 present magazine advertisements from the "I Believe" series. In each, a lean, highly toned, and stylishly attractive young exerciser declares her invulnerability to traditional insecurities of women, resistance to gender expectations, and confidence in her own power of self-determination. "I believe a man who wants something soft and cuddly to hold should buy a teddy bear" reads the copy in Figure 54. The suggestion is that this woman's own desire to be hard and ripped, rather than her need to appeal to men, has determined the type of body she is working out to achieve. The man who doesn't like it can look somewhere else for someone to hold, she implies. But just how many men in 1992—at least of this young woman's generation—find the "soft and cuddly" an erotic or aesthetic ideal? My male students (as well as my female students) almost literally swooned over Linda Hamilton's fierce expression and taut body in *Terminator II*. By creating the impression that Sandra Dee is still what men want,[31] Reebok is able to identify its product with female resistance to cultural norms of beauty while actually reinforcing those norms.

The copy in Figure 55 reads: "I believe if you look at yourself and see what is right instead of what is wrong, that is the true mark of a healthy individual." Now, those convinced that "resistance is everywhere" might see this ad (along with the one discussed above) as offering a transgressive, subversive model of femininity: a woman who is strong, fit, and (unlike most women) *not* insecure about her body. What this reading neglects is that we have a visual message here as well: the model's body *itself*—probably the most potent "representation" in the ad—is precisely the sort of perfected icon that women compare themselves to and of course see "what is wrong." The ad thus puts "real" women in a painful double bind. On the one hand, it encourages them to view themselves as defective; on the other hand, it chastises them for their insecurities. The offered resolution to this bind, of course, is to buy Reebok and become like the woman in the ad.

One might argue that an adequate analysis of advertisements such as those I have been discussing would take into account both their resistant elements and their normalizing messages. This is an appealingly postmodern solution, which acknowledges the heterogeneous and unstable meanings of the texts. (After all, as was

FIGURE 54

discussed in the introduction to this book, weight-training and exercise often do have socially empowering results for women.) I have no problem granting this, so long as the normalizing thrust of these ads vis-à-vis the politics of appearance is not obscured. We need to recognize, in connection with this, that the most obvious symbols of resistance in these ads are included by advertisers in the profoundest of cynical bad faith; they pretend to reject the sexualization of women ("I believe that 'babe' is a four-letter word") and value female assertiveness ("Coloring my hair with Nice and Easy made me feel more powerful!") while attempting to convince women who *fail* to embody dominant ideals of (slender, youthful) beauty that they need to bring themselves into line. To resist *this* normalizing directive is *truly* to go against the grain of our culture, not merely in textual "play," but at great personal risk—as the many women who have been sexually rejected for being "too fat" and fired from their jobs for looking "too old" know all too well. Sub-

I believe

if you look at yourself
and see what is right
instead of what is wrong,
that is the true mark
of a healthy individual.

FIGURE 55

version of dominant cultural forms, as bell hooks has said, "happens much more easily in the realm of 'texts' than in the world of human interaction . . . in which such moves challenge, disrupt, threaten, where repression is real."[32]

The pleasure and power of "difference," I would once again insist against postmodern theorists, is hard-won; it does not bloom freely, insistently nudging its way through the cracks of dominant forms. Sexism, heterosexism, racism, and ageism, while they do not determine human values and choices, while they do not deprive us of agency, remain strongly normalizing within our culture. The commercial texts that I have been examining, in contrast, participate in the illusion (which they share with other postmodern texts) that our "differences" are already flourishing in the culture as it is, that we are already self-determining, already empowered to look in the mirror and see what is right instead of what is wrong. The fact is, we are *not* empowered in this way by our culture; indeed, we are continually being taught to see the body that reflects back to us in exactly the opposite way—as wrong, defective, "a caricature, a swollen shadow, a stupid clown" (to invoke some phrases from the poem with which I opened this book). To begin to see differently requires, in the nineties even more than in the sixties, that people come together and explore what the culture continually presents to them as their individual choices (or—as in the case of anorexia and bulimia—their "pathology") as instead culturally situated and culturally shared. Such acknowledgment, to my mind, must remain central to a feminist politics of the body.

Notes

INTRODUCTION

Portions of this essay grew out of a talk, entitled "Feminism Reconceives the Body," that I delivered for the Women's Studies Inaugural Lecture Series at Bates College. I thank Edward Lee for invaluable comments, suggestions, and encouragement throughout the process of writing this introduction.

1. For elaboration, see Susan Bordo, *The Flight to Objectivity* (Albany: State University of New York Press, 1987).

2. At first glance it may seem as though in our culture the body, far from being imagined as a drag on self-realization, is promoted as a central route *to* such self-realization. Certainly, the training, toning, slimming, and sculpting of the body are frequently depicted in this way: as a current Bally Fitness Center commercial insists, "You don't just shape your body. You shape your life." However, as I argue in several essays in this collection, such images and associations are actually an appeal to the *will* (to "will power" and "control") and encourage an adversarial relationship to the body.

3. Simone de Beauvoir, *The Second Sex* (New York: Alfred A. Knopf, 1957), p. 146.

4. Dorothy Dinnerstein, *The Mermaid and the Minotaur: Sexual Arrangements and Human Malaise* (New York: Harper and Row, 1976), p. 133.

5. Timothy Beneke, *Men on Rape: What They Have to Say About Sexual Violence* (New York: St. Martin's Press, 1982), p. 43 (emphasis in original).

6. My quotation marks indicate my view that not only the ideology but also the very concept of "race" is a cultural construction. From this point on in the book, however, I will omit the quotation marks. I will also frequently employ the racial constructions "black" and "white" (rather than ethnic or national designations of identity), despite their problematic nature. For example, when describing the content of racist ideology, ethnic or national descriptions would be incorrect and misleading. The racial categorization of human beings is a racist invention, but it is an invention that has shaped and bent human history and experience; racial terms are still necessary, in order to describe that experience accurately.

7. Quoted in Sander Gilman, *Difference and Pathology* (Ithaca: Cornell University Press, 1985), p. 85.

8. Beverly Guy-Sheftall, "The Body Politic: Black Women and Sexuality," talk given at Bates College, 1991.

9. For discussions of the specific themes mentioned in this introduction concerning the treatment of African American women under slavery, see especially Angela Davis, *Women, Race, and Class* (New York: Vintage, 1983), and Barbara Omolade, "Hearts of Darkness," in Ann Snitow, Christine Stansell, and Sharon Thompson, eds., *Powers of Desire: The Politics of Sexuality* (New York: Monthly Review Press, 1983).

10. Aristotle, *The Basic Works of Aristotle*, ed. Richard McKeon (New York: Random House, 1941), *On the Generation of Animals*, trans. Arthur Platt, 729a 25–30, p. 676.

11. Hegel, *The Philosophy of Right*, trans. with notes by T. M. Knox (London: Oxford University Press, 1967), pp. 263–64.

12. Alan Guttmacher, *Pregnancy, Birth, and Family Planning*, rev. ed. (New York: Signet, 1987), pp. 20–22.

13. See, for example, Catharine Gallagher and Thomas Laqueur, eds., issue called "Sexuality and the Social Body in the Nineteenth Century," *Representations* 14 (Spring 1986); Sander Gilman, "AIDS and Syphilis: The Iconography of Disease," *October* 43 (Winter 1987): 87–108; Mary Jacobus, Evelyn Fox Keller, and Sally Shuttleworth, eds., *Body/Politics: Women and the Discourses of Science* (New York: Routledge, 1990); Kathleen Kete, "La Rage and the Bourgeoisie: The Cultural Context of Rabies in the French Nineteenth Century," *Representations* 22 (Spring 1988): 89–107; Thomas Laqueur, *Making Sex: Body and Gender from the Greeks to Freud* (Cambridge: Harvard University Press, 1990); Emily Martin, *The Woman in the Body: A Cultural Analysis of Reproduction* (Boston: Beacon Press, 1987); Margaret Miles, *Carnal Knowing: Female Nakedness and Religious Meaning in the Christian West* (Boston: Beacon, 1989); Susan Suleiman, ed., *The Female Body in Western Culture* (Cambridge: Harvard University Press, 1986); Simon Watney, "Aids, 'Africa,' and Race," *Differences* (Winter 1989): 83–86.

14. Don Hanlon Johnson, "The Body: Which One? Whose?" *Whole Earth Review* (Summer 1989): 4–8.

15. Linda Zirelli, "Rememoration or War? French Feminist Narrative and the Politics of Self-Representation," *Differences* (Spring 1991): 2–3.

16. Michel Foucault, *Discipline and Punish* (New York: Vintage, 1979); *The History of Sexuality*. Vol. 1: *An Introduction* (New York: Vintage, 1980).

17. Mary Wollstonecraft, "A Vindication of the Rights of Woman," in Alice Rossi, ed., *The Feminist Papers* (Boston: Northeastern University Press, 1988), pp. 55–57.

18. Reproduced in Nancy Cott, *The Grounding of Modern Feminism* (New Haven: Yale University Press, 1987), p. 12.

19. Pat Mainardi, "The Politics of Housework," in Robin Morgan, ed., *Sisterhood Is Powerful* (New York: Vintage, 1970), pp. 447–54.

20. Williamette Bridge Liberation News Service, "Exercises for Men," *The Radical Therapist* (Dec.–Jan. 1971).

21. See Morgan, *Sisterhood Is Powerful*, pp. 521–23, for this document.

22. Amy Collins, "Abreast of the Bra," *Lear's* 4, no. 4 (June 1991): 80.

23. Kathy Davis, "Remaking the She-Devil: A Critical Look at Feminist Approaches to Beauty," in *Hypatia* 6, no. 2 (Summer 1991): 23 (emphasis mine).

24. Andrea Dworkin, *Woman-Hating* (New York: Dutton, 1974), pp. 113–14 (emphasis in original).

25. Among the "classics": Susan Brownmiller, *Against Our Will* (New York: Bantam, 1975); Mary Daly, *Gyn-Ecology* (Boston: Beacon, 1978); Davis, *Women, Race, and Class*; Dworkin, *Woman-Hating*; Germaine Greer, *The Female Eunuch* (New York: McGraw-Hill, 1970); Susan Griffin, *Rape: The Power of Consciousness* (New York: Harper and Row, 1979), and *Woman and Nature* (New York: Harper and Row, 1978); Adrienne Rich, "Compulsory Heterosexuality and Lesbian Existence," *Signs* 5, no. 4 (1980): 631–60. Also see the anthologies collected by Morgan, *Sisterhood Is Powerful*, and Vivian Gornick and Barbara Moran, *Woman in Sexist Society* (New York: Mentor, 1971).

26. Omolade, "Hearts of Darkness," p. 354.

27. Susan Brownmiller, *Femininity* (New York: Ballantine, 1984).

28. Foucault, *Discipline and Punish*, p. 138.

29. Michel Foucault, "The Eye of Power," in his *Power/Knowledge*, ed. and trans. C. Gordo (New York: Pantheon, 1977), p. 155.

30. Even in the politics of appearance, of course, external coercion may figure in—for example, when women are threatened with loss of their jobs unless they lose weight, or are fired for looking too old.

31. See in particular Michel Foucault, "The Subject and Power," interview in Hubert Dreyfus and Paul Rabinow, *Michel Foucault: Beyond Structuralism and Hermeneutics* (Chicago: University of Chicago Press, 1983).

32. See, for example, Harry Brod, *A Mensch Among Men: Explorations in Jewish Masculinity* (Freedom, Calif.: The Crossing Press, 1988); Michael Kimmel and Michael Messner, eds., *Men's Lives*, 2d ed. (New York: Macmillan, 1992); Michael Kimmel, ed., *Men Confront Pornography* (New York: Meridian, 1991); Richard Majors and Janet Mancini Billson, *Cool Pose: The Dilemmas of Black Manhood in America* (New York: Lexington Books, 1991); Brian Pronger, *The Arena of Masculinity: Sports, Homosexuality, and the Meaning of Sex* (New York: St. Martin's Press, 1990).

33. Diane Johnson, "Something for the Boys," *New York Review of Books* (Jan. 16, 1992): 13.

34. The phrase "cultural dope" comes from Anthony Giddens. Giddens stresses that "every competent actor has a wide-ranging, yet intimate and subtle, knowledge of the society of which he or she is a member" (*New Rules of Sociological Method* [New York: Basic Books, 1976], p. 73). Giddens, however, does *not* take this to mean—as many "postmodern" writers have— that we are free agents with regard to culture, which, on the contrary, he

regards as strongly recursive, reproductive, and "socializing." Giddens's point is that this socialization is not done behind people's backs, but involves their active participation.

35. Sandra Bartky, *Femininity and Domination* (New York: Routledge, 1990); Wendy Chapkis, *Beauty Secrets* (Boston: South End Press, 1986); Rita Freedman, *Beauty Bound* (London: Columbus Books, 1986); Frigga Haug, ed., *Female Sexualization: A Collective Work of Memory* (London: Verso, 1987); Robin Lakoff and Raquel Scherr, *Face Value: The Politics of Beauty* (Boston: Routledge and Kegan Paul, 1984); and Naomi Wolf, *Beauty Secrets* (New York: William Morrow, 1991). Wolf's book has received a good deal of media attention and shows some promise of stirring up a new generation of young women about such issues. See also Kathryn Pauly Morgan, "Women and the Knife: Cosmetic Surgery and the Colonization of Women's Bodies," in *Hypatia* 6, no. 3 (Fall 1991): 25–53; and Iris Marion Young, "Breasted Experience," in her *Throwing Like a Girl and Other Essays in Feminist Philosophy and Social Theory* (Bloomington: Indiana University Press, 1990), pp. 189–209.

36. Joan Jacobs Brumberg, *Fasting Girls: The Emergence of Anorexia Nervosa as a Modern Disease* (Cambridge: Harvard University Press, 1988).

37. Susie Orbach, *Hunger Strike: The Anorectic's Struggle as a Metaphor for Our Age* (New York: W. W. Norton, 1986); Kim Chernin, *The Obsession: Reflections on the Tyranny of Slenderness* (New York: Harper and Row, 1981), and *The Hungry Self: Women, Eating, and Identity* (New York: Harper and Row, 1985).

38. Richard Mohr, *Gay Ideas: Outing and Other Controversies* (Boston: Beacon Press, 1992), p. 142.

39. Emily Martin, *The Woman in the Body*, pp. 128–35.

40. Joan Peters, "Mittelschnerz: A Lady's Complaint upon Reaching the Age of 44," *Michigan Quarterly Review* (Fall 1991): 685–93. Peters ends her piece with a plea for us to "fuse" these "divided camps" which have "chopped us each into ineffectual bits" (p. 692).

41. Ann Snitow, "A Gender Diary," in Marianne Hirsch and Evelyn Fox Keller, eds., *Conflicts in Feminism* (New York: Routledge, 1990), p. 9.

42. Sherman Silber, *How to Get Pregnant with the New Technology* (New York: Wagner, 1991), p. 375. In fact, such protocols involve tremendous commitment of time and expense, as well as subjection of the body to numerous invasive procedures and powerful drugs: a two-week-long series of injections to stimulate ovulation in the donor, replace the necessary hormones in the recipient, and synchronize the cycles of donor and recipient, numerous ultra-sounds and blood tests, the surgical procedures of follicle aspiration and gamete intra-fallopian transfer from donor to recipient, and continued hormonal supplements and monitoring for three months for the recipient. All this, Silber assures his readers, is "really not that difficult for the patient" (p. 276).

43. Susan Faludi, *Backlash: The Undeclared War Against American Women* (New York: Crown, 1991).

WHOSE BODY IS THIS?

This essay grew out of a shorter piece, "Eating Disorders: The Feminist Challenge to the Concept of Pathology," which was written for Drew Leder, ed., *The Body in Medical Thought and Practice* (Dordrecht, Holland: Kluwer Press, 1992). Early versions, under the original name, were delivered at Le Moyne College and at the University of Missouri at Columbia. I thank all those who commented on those versions.

1. Kim Chernin, *The Obsession: Reflections on the Tyranny of Slenderness* (New York: Harper and Row, 1981); see also her *The Hungry Self: Women, Eating, and Identity* (New York: Harper and Row, 1985).

2. Rachel Calam and Peter Slade, "Sexual Experience and Eating Problems in Female Undergraduates," *International Journal of Eating Disorders* 8 (1989): 392–97; Alexander McFarlane et al., "Posttraumatic Bulimia and Anorexia Nervosa," *International Journal of Eating Disorders* 7 (1988): 705–8; Justin Schechter et al., "Sexual Assault and Anorexia Nervosa," *International Journal of Eating Disorders* 6 (1987): 313–16.

3. Catherine Steiner-Adair, "The Body Politic: Normal Female Adolescent Development and Eating Disorders," Ph.D. dissertation, Harvard University Graduate School of Education, 1987.

4. Susie Orbach's analysis is presented in detail in *Hunger Strike: The Anorectic's Struggle as a Metaphor for Our Age* (New York: W. W. Norton, 1986). Orbach is also co-founder of the Women's Therapy Center Institute in New York and the Women's Therapy Centre in London, which have developed techniques of treatment grounded in object relations and feminist theory.

5. See in particular Marlene Boskind White and William White, "Bulimarexia: A Historical-Sociocultural Perspective," in Kelly Brownell and John Foreyt, eds., *Handbook of Eating Disorders* (New York: Basic Books, 1986), pp. 353–66; Lisa Fabian, "Body Image and Eating Disturbance in Young Females," *International Journal of Eating Disorders* 8 (1989): 63–74; D. Greenfeld et al., "Eating Behavior in an Adolescent Population," *International Journal of Eating Disorders* 6 (1987): 99–111; Robert Klesges et al., "Self-Help Dieting Strategies in College Males and Females," *International Journal of Eating Disorders* 6 (1987): 409–17; Debbie Vanderheyden et al., "Critical Variables Associated with Binging and Bulimia in a University Population: A Factor Analytic Study," *International Journal of Eating Disorders* 7 (1988): 321–29.

6. See, as paradigmatic of this approach, Paul Garfinkel and Allan Kaplan, "Anorexia Nervosa: Diagnostic Conceptualizations," in Brownell and Foreyt, *Handbook of Eating Disorders*, pp. 266–82; Harrison Pope and James Hudson, "Is Bulimia Nervosa a Heterogeneous Disorder?" *International Journal of Eating Disorders* 7 (1988): 155–66.

7. Craig Johnson and Mary Connors, *The Etiology and Treatment of Bulimia Nervosa: A Biopsychosocial Perspective* (New York: Basic Books, 1987).

8. H. G. Pope et al., "Is Bulimia a Heterogeneous Disorder?" *International Journal of Eating Disorders* 7, no. 2:158.

9. Joan Jacobs Brumberg, *Fasting Girls: The Emergence of Anorexia Nervosa as a Modern Disease* (Cambridge: Harvard University Press, 1988); S. Lee et al., "Anorexia Nervosa in Hong Kong: Why Not More in Chinese?" *British Journal of Psychiatry* 154 (1989): 683–88; Orbach, *Hunger Strike*. See also "Reading the Slender Body," in this volume.

10. Brumberg, *Fasting Girls*, pp. 41–125.

11. D. J. Ben-Tovim et al., "Bulimia: Symptom and Syndromes in an Urban Population," *Australia and New Zealand Journal of Psychiatry* 23:73–80; A. Crisp et al., "How Common Is Anorexia Nervosa?" *British Journal of Psychiatry* 128 (1976): 549–54; D. Jones et al., "Epidemiology of Anorexia Nervosa in Monroe County, New York: 1960–1976," *Psychosomatic Medicine* 42 (1980): 551–58; Marianne Rosenzweig and Jean Spruil, "Twenty Years After Twiggy: A Retrospective Investigation of Bulimic-Like Behaviors," *International Journal of Eating Disorders* 6 (1987): 59–65.

12. Present-day clinicians may still occasionally (or more than occasionally) see symptoms like those the nineteenth century diagnosed as "hysterical." The tendency to produce such a diagnosis, however, has greatly diminished. The woman who spends her days sleeping, daydreaming, dissociating, languishing in bed, is far more likely today to be diagnosed as suffering from depressive disorder than from hysteria or neurasthenia. Contemporary clinical descriptions of the personality profile of anorectics are often remarkably similar to those nineteenth-century medicine constructed as the "hysterical personality"—and, indeed, anorexic behavior was then almost always seen as an hysterical symptom. Today, however, anorexia is associated with other rubrics of disorder: affective, perceptual, narcissistic, depressive.

13. Kelly Brownell and John Foreyt, "The Eating Disorders: Summary and Integration," in Brownell and Foreyt, *Handbook of Eating Disorders*, p. 508.

14. Brownell and Foreyt, "The Eating Disorders," p. 507.

15. Harrison Pope and James Hudson, *New Hope for Binge Eaters* (New York: Harper and Row, 1985).

16. Paul Garfinkel and David Garner, *Anorexia Nervosa: A Multidimensional Perspective* (New York: Brunner/Mazel, 1982), p. 159.

17. Ira Sacker and Marc Zimmer, *Dying to Be Thin* (New York: Warner, 1987), p. 50.

18. Vanderheyden et al., "Critical Variables Associated with Binging and Bulimia"; Vanderheyden et al., "Very Low Calorie Diets and Obesity Surgery After 5 Years," *International Obesity Newsletter* 3, no. 5 (May 1989): 33–38; Brett Silverstein et al., "Possible Causes of the Thin Standard of Bodily Attractiveness for Women," *International Journal of Eating Disorders* 5 (1986): 907–16.

19. Hilde Bruch, *Eating Disorders* (New York: Basic Books, 1973), p. 89; Hilde Bruch, "Perceptual and Conceptual Disturbances in Anorexia Nervosa," *Psychosomatic Medicine* 24 (1962): 187–94.

20. Roberta Marks, "Anorexia and Bulimia: Eating Habits That Can Kill," *RN* (Jan. 1984): 44 (emphasis mine).

21. "Feeling Fat in a Thin Society," *Glamour* (Feb. 1984): 198–201, 251–52.

22. Kevin Thompson, "Larger Than Life," *Psychology Today* (April 1986): 39–44. Also see Sandra Birtchnell et al., "Body Image Distortion in Non-Eating Disordered Women," *International Journal of Eating Disorders* 6 (1987): 385–91.

23. Linnea Lindholm and G. Terrence Wilson, "Body Image Assessment in Patients with Bulimia Nervosa and Normal Controls," *International Journal of Eating Disorders* 7 (1988): 527–39; A. Whitehouse et al., "Body Size Estimation," *British Journal of Psychiatry* 149 (1986): 98–103; M. Willmuth et al., "Body Size Distortion in Bulimia Nervosa," *International Journal of Eating Disorders* 4 (1985): 71–78.

24. Thompson, "Larger Than Life," p. 42; Thomas Cash et al., "The Great American Shape-Up," *Psychology Today* (April 1986): 30–37; D. Goleman, "Dislike of Own Body Found Common Among Women," *New York Times*, March 19, 1985; Dalma Heyn, "Why We're Never Satisfied with Our Bodies," in *McCall's* (May 1982); Klesges et al., "Self-Help Dieting Strategies."

25. In 1991 an article finally appeared in the *International Journal of Eating Disorders* questioning the value of the concept of Body Image Disturbance and acknowledging that "it has generated little meaningful research despite the attention it has attracted in the last 16 years . . . , creates confusion both in the mind of the public and in our own . . . [and] suggests progress when there is none. It is certainly sad to abandon a term that seemed such a conceptual breakthrough at first sight, but we believe that it is time to move on to new ideas." (George Hsu and Theresa Sobkiewicz, "Body Image Disturbance: Time to Abandon the Concept for Eating Disorders?" *International Journal of Eating Disorders* 10, no. 1 [Jan. 1991]: 28.) I applaud Hsu and Sobkiewicz for being willing to "move on," but I find their suggestion limited, in that they seem to expect to discover in the new research on "body attitudes and feelings" the distinctive "pathology" that is lacking in the concept of Body Image Disturbance.

26. See Garfinkel and Garner, *Anorexia Nervosa*; Craig Johnson and Darryl Pure, "Assessment of Bulimia: A Multidimensional Model," in Brownell and Foreyt, *Handbook of Eating Disorders*, pp. 406–49; Reinhold Laessle et al., "Cognitive Correlates of Depression in Patients with Eating Disorders," *International Journal of Eating Disorders* 7 (1988): 681–86; Deborah Thompson et al., "The Heterogeneity of Bulimic Symptomatology: Cognitive and Behavioral Dimensions," *International Journal of Eating Disorders* 6 (1987): 215–34.

27. Garfinkel and Garner, *Anorexia Nervosa*, p. 159.

28. W. Stewart Agras and Betty Kirkley, "Bulimia: Theories of Etiology", in Brownell and Foreyt, *Handbook of Eating Disorders*, pp. 367–78; F. M. Berg, "Starvation Stages in Weight-loss Patients Similar to Famine Victims," *International Obesity Newsletter* 3 (April 1989): 27.

29. "Semi-Starvation Diets Gain in Popularity," *International Obesity Newsletter* 3 (April 1989): 25, 28–30.

30. Vanderheyden et al., "Very Low Calorie Diets and Obesity Surgery."

31. *Time* (April 18, 1988): 89.

32. "Girls, at 7, Think Thin, Study Finds," *New York Times*, Feb. 11, 1988; Jeffrey Zaslow, "Fat or Not, 4th Grade Girls Diet Lest They Be Teased or Unloved," *Wall Street Journal*, Feb. 11, 1986, p. 28.

33. Brumberg, *Fasting Girls*.

34. A. Anderson and A. Hay, "Racial and Socioeconomic Influences in Anorexia Nervosa and Bulimia," *International Journal of Eating Disorders* 4 (1985): 479–87.

35. Steiner-Adair, "The Body Politic"; Christine Tinko et al., "Femininity/Masculinity and Disordered Eating in Women: How Are They Related?" *International Journal of Eating Disorders* 6 (1987): 710–11.

36. Garfinkel and Garner, *Anorexia Nervosa*, pp. 102–3; Simon Gowers and John McMahon, "Social Class and Prognosis in Anorexia Nervosa," *International Journal of Eating Disorders* 8 (1989): 105–9; Janet Gross and James Rosen, "Bulimia in Adolescents: Prevalence and Psychosocial Correlates," *International Journal of Eating Disorders* 7 (1988): 51–61.

37. James Gray et al., "The Prevalence of Bulimia in a Black College Population," *International Journal of Eating Disorders* 6 (1987): 733–40; L. K. George Hsu, "Are the Eating Disorders Becoming More Common Among Blacks?" *International Journal of Eating Disorders* 6 (1987): 113–24.

38. Retha Powers, "Fat Is a Black Women's Issue," *Essence* (Oct. 1989): 75–78, 134–36. See also Georgiana Arnold, "Fat War," *Essence* (July 1990): 52–53, 104–5; Kathleen Hiebert et al., "Comparison of Outcome in Hispanic and Caucasian Patients with Anorexia Nervosa," *International Journal of Eating Disorders* 7 (1988): 693–96; Lionel Rosen et al., "Prevalence of Pathogenic Weight-control Behaviors Among Native American Women and Girls," *International Journal of Eating Disorders* 7 (1988): 807–11.

39. Mary Mohler, "A New Look at Anorexia," *Ladies Home Journal* (April 1986).

40. See note 2, above.

41. See Dalma Heyn's interview with Steven Levenkron: "Body Hate," *Ms.* (July 1989): 35–36.

42. Michael Strober, "Anorexia Nervosa: History and Psychological Concepts," in Brownell and Foreyt, *Handbook of Eating Disorders*, p. 241.

43. Brumberg, *Fasting Girls*, p. 3.

44. It is tempting to conclude that Brumberg simply does not understand what metaphor and analogy are or grasp notions such as *unconscious* process or the fact that our bodies may carry meanings unintended or only dimly understood by the subject. But Brumberg's attitude is all the more perplexing when later, borrowing heavily from the feminist theory she criticizes, she argues that the food refusal of Victorian anorectics should be interpreted as a symbolic "voice," "a silent and potent form" of rebellion against family expectations, emotional repression, and lack of autonomy (*Fasting Girls*, p. 140).

45. Brumberg, *Fasting Girls*, pp. 35–37. Revealingly, this example of schizophrenia was taken nearly word for word by Brumberg from an article by an author who was advocating forced feeding of anorectics: Eliot Goldner, "Treatment Refusal in Anorexia Nervosa," *International Journal of Eating Disorders* 8, no. 3 (May 1989): 301.

46. *Newsday* (Feb. 12, 1984): 2.

47. Brumberg, *Fasting Girls*, p. 14; Garfinkel and Kaplan, "Anorexia Nervosa: Diagnostic Conceptualizations," pp. 270–71; Gina Kolata, "Bulimia Epidemic Fears May Be a False Alarm," *New York Times*, Aug. 25, 1988, p. B6; Susan Squire, "If You Think a Woman Can Never Be Too Thin . . . ," *Mademoiselle* (Oct. 1984): 180–81, 252–54.

48. Here, even those who *have* incorporated elements of the feminist critique need to go still further in the direction of systemic, political understanding. In the absence of such understanding, influential findings such as Steiner-Adair's can easily be interpreted as suggesting that women's eating problems are the result of our "trying to be like men" and not developing our nurturing, empathic inclinations as nature intended. Analyzed systemically, the superwoman syndrome reveals, on the contrary, how little alteration of fundamental relations has taken place. Women who participate in the professional sphere and who are obliged, while in that sphere, to embody its masculinist styles and values are not thereby permitted to abandon their "femininity." Rather, at the end of the public workday they must return to their already full-time careers as devoted wives and mothers and to the "feminine" styles and values demanded by these roles ("The Second Shift," as Arlie Hochschild calls it, in Arlie Hochschild with Anne Maching, *The Second Shift: Working Parents and the Revolution at Home* [New York: Viking, 1989]). The superwoman syndrome reveals that whatever else women are "permitted" to do in this culture, they are still required to do "their" work.

49. Weir Mitchell quoted in Elaine Showalter, *The Female Malady: Women, Madness and English Culture, 1830–1980* (New York: Pantheon, 1985), p. 130; Hilde Bruch, *The Golden Cage: The Enigma of Anorexia Nervosa* (New York: Vintage, 1979).

50. Bruch, *The Golden Cage*, p. ix.

51. Rudolph Bell, *Holy Anorexia* (Chicago: University of Chicago Press, 1985).

52. Brumberg, *Fasting Girls*, p. 46.

53. Jennifer Woods, "I Was Starving Myself to Death," *Mademoiselle* (May 1981).

54. Brumberg, *Fasting Girls*, p. 7 (emphasis mine).

ARE MOTHERS PERSONS?

This essay could not have been written without the generous help of Katherine Bartlett and Susan Behuniak-Long, who provided me with court cases, articles, and incisive advice about the legal issues discussed, as well as crucial encouragement as I embarked on the study of a discourse unfamiliar to me. Earlier versions, under different titles, were delivered at the eighteenth annual Scholar and the Feminist Conference, the State University of New York at Binghamton, McGill University, Carleton University, and the Syracuse Consortium for the Cultural Foundations of Medicine. As the paper went through various drafts, many people provided useful criticisms, suggestions, and material; in particular, I want to thank Lynne Arnault, Robert Bogdan, Jack Carlson, Ynestra King, Ted Koditschek, Edward Lee, Paul Mattick, and John Wilcox.

1. Union Pacific Railway v. Botsford, 141 U.S. 250, 251 (1891).

2. Gilbert Ryle, *The Concept of Mind* (New York: Barnes and Noble, 1949), passim.

3. Stephen Wermiel, "Legal Beat: Bone Marrow Test," *Wall Street Journal*, Oct. 1, 1990, p. 16.

4. McFall v. Shimp, No 78–17711 (C.P. Allegheny County, Pa., July 16, 1978), quoted in Lawrence J. Nelson, Brian P. Buggy, and Carol Weil, "Forced Medical Treatment of Pregnant Women: 'Compelling Each to Live as Seems Good to the Rest,'" *Hastings Law Journal* 37 (May 1986): 255. Many newspaper commentaries that appeared before the Illinois decision (cf. note 3, above) emphatically echoed such sentiments, insisting that "one person's right to life stops where another person's body starts" (Lynn Baker, "Are We Safe in Our Own Skins?" *New York Times*, Aug. 21, 1990, p. 27) and declaring the father's efforts to have the twins forced to become donors "a potentially dangerous precedent for allowing bodily invasions without the consent of the donor" (editorial, *New York Times*, Aug. 29, 1990, p. 20).

5. Nelson et al., "Forced Medical Treatment," p. 723.

6. McFall v. Shimp, quoted in Nelson et al., "Forced Medical Treatment," p. 755.

7. 342 U.S. 165 (1952), quoted in Nancy Rhoden, "The Judge in the Delivery Room: The Emergence of Court-Ordered Cesareans," *California Law Review* 74 (1986): 1983.

8. Other bodily invasions that have been constitutionally permitted are compulsory vaccinations and nonconsensual treatment of institutionalized persons. The former have been permitted because they serve a broad public interest and are required of all members of the society reciprocally. The history of nonconsensual treatment of institutionalized persons (one aspect of which—sterilization abuse—will be discussed briefly later in this essay) is a scandal in itself. Those who have been deemed "mentally defective" or "mentally ill" clearly represent another major category of persons whose rights to bodily integrity and informed consent have regularly been ignored and effaced. It is outside the scope of this essay to discuss that effacement except insofar as it intersects with the specific themes developed here, but this limited treatment should not be understood as minimizing its relevance or importance.

9. Schmerber v. California, 384 U.S. 757 (1966).

10. Winston, Sheriff, et al. v. Lee, 470 U.S. 753 (1985).

11. Even the subjectivity of persons in persistent vegetative states is respected; determination of the wishes of such patients is always one of the central issues raised in decisions involving termination of their life support (e.g., the Nancy Cruzan and Helga Wanglie cases). And our cultural horror of unconsented-to bodily intrusion extends, as well, to *dead* bodies; cadavers are legally protected against the unconsented-to use of their organs and tissues, even when their use could save the lives of others. Here, respect is extended to the "subjectivity" of corpses far beyond the value placed on those *living* beings who could be benefited if a purely mechanistic, depersonalizing attitude toward body parts prevailed.

12. Rust v. Sullivan, 59 USLW 4451 (1991).

13. Philip R. Reilly, *The Surgical Solution* (Baltimore: Johns Hopkins University Press, 1991), p. xiii.

14. Angela Davis, *Women, Race, and Class* (New York: Vintage, 1983), pp. 215–21.

15. Reilly, *The Surgical Solution*, pp. 94–95.

16. Walker v. Pierce, 560 F.2d 609 (1977). Pierce won the case, but with an extremely strong dissent from one of the circuit court judges, who argued that beyond doubt Dr. Pierce's policy pertaining to sterilization was based on economic factors instead of the health of his Medicaid patients.

17. Veronika Kolder et al., "Court-Ordered Obstetrical Interventions," *New England Journal of Medicine* 316, no. 19 (May 7, 1987): 1192.

18. In re: A. C. Appellant, 523 2d 611 (1987).

19. These procedures, moreover, may turn out not to have been essential to the life of the fetus. In Jefferson v. Griffin Spaulding Hospital Authority (GA 86, 274 S.E. 2d 457 1981), Mrs. Jefferson, suffering from placenta previa, was ordered to undergo a cesarean. The order was never enforced, and she wound up uneventfully delivering a healthy child vaginally.

20. Taft v. Taft, 446 N.E. 2d 395 (Mass. 1983).

21. Performed when there is high risk of third-trimester miscarriage due to weakness of the cervix (often described as "incompetent cervix"), cerclage involves suturing the cervix closed in order to maintain the pregnancy.

22. So the District of Columbia Court of Appeals described it, in overturning the circuit court's decision on Angela Carder (too late, unfortunately, to affect Carder, but extremely meaningful nonetheless, as I will shortly discuss).

23. Tamar Lewin, "Court Acting to Force Care of the Unborn," *New York Times*, Nov. 28, 1988, p. 1.

24. See Nelson et al., "Forced Medical Treatment," and Rhoden, "Judge in the Delivery Room," and also Janet Gallagher, "Prenatal Invasions and Interventions: What's Wrong with Fetal Rights," *Harvard Women's Law Journal* 10 (1987): 9–58.

Some judges *have* attempted to offer a legal rationalization for such contradictions. The dissenting judge in the District of Columbia Court of Appeals overturn of the A.C. ruling, for example, argued that the third-trimester pregnant woman belongs to a "unique category of persons," by virtue of her having "undertaken to bear another human being" and having carried it to viability, and thus having "placed herself" in a special class of persons, those upon whom another's life is totally dependent. Against such arguments, it might reasonably be asked why such a commitment, if indeed it can be said to exist, ends with the birth of the child, and why it does not apply as well to the father of the child. That it does not so apply, legally, is manifest in the decisions that have consistently refused to order parents to donate marrow and organs to their children (even when their lives are "totally dependent" on the donation). I suspect, too, that the element of voluntarily "undertaking" the preservation of the life of another would hold no legal water against broken commitments to donate organs or marrow or to take blood tests. Finally, the question remains: Does the undertaking to care for another entail a commitment to do so *at all costs*?

25. Nelson et al., "Forced Medical Treatment," p. 714.

26. This construction seems to be in the background of the many frequent misapplications of Roe v. Wade, arguing in favor of forced cesareans on the basis of the "state's interest in protecting the life of the fetus." The Roe decision does indeed acknowledge that this interest increases as pregnancy advances. However, it emphasizes that it is never to supersede that of the life and health of the mother, right up to term. Rather, as American College of Obstetricians and Gynecologists v. Thornberg made clear, "the woman's life and health must always prevail over the fetus's life and health when they conflict" (737 F. 2d 283 [1984], quoted in Nelson et al., "Forced Medical Treatment," p. 744). The slippage from state interest in fetal life (which Roe grants) to the elevation of that interest above the preservation of maternal health (which neither Roe nor its progeny accept) converts the protection of fetal life into a doctrine of maternal self-sacrifice. (For an interesting discussion of the misapplications of Roe, see Susan Behuniak-Long, "Reproductive Issues and the Applicability of *Roe v. Wade*: Limits and Essence," in *Biomedical Technology and Public Policy*, ed. Robert Black and Miriam Mills [New York: Greenwood Press, 1990].)

27. Walker v. Pierce.

28. District of Columbia Court of Appeals No. 87-609 In Re: A.C., April 26, 1990, p. 1142.

29. Kolder et al., "Court-Ordered Obstetrical Interventions."

30. See, for example, Robertson, "The Right to Procreate and In Utero Fetal Therapy," *Journal of Legal Medicine* 333 (1982): 351–61.

31. What is most chilling about these cases is how rarely they occasion real moral controversy, and how casually newspapers describe the procedures in terms that utterly dehumanize the mother. In Syracuse this year, a brain-dead woman who had suffered a brain aneurysm was kept alive for more than seven weeks until her baby could be delivered by cesarean

section. The family, acting in proxy, claimed certitude that this would have been her wish. My point here is not to challenge their interpretation. It is striking, however, that *no one* did. In the local newspaper the case was reported purely as a technological achievement, with no suggestion that there might be any sort of ethical conflict involved. Throughout the piece the brain-dead woman was described simply as a *body*: "Aubry said the woman's body probably would go into labor on its own"; "It would be better to deliver before the mother really deteriorates"; etc. (Amber Smith, "Brain-dead Pregnant Woman Kept Alive So Her Baby Could Be Born," *Syracuse Herald-American*, Nov. 3, 1991, p. 1.) My strong suspicion is that even if the family had made their case without reference to the woman's wishes, their request would still have been viewed as morally unproblematic.

Compare this to the highly publicized controversy occasioned in 1989 when Martin Klein (acting in concert with his wife's family) sought a court order appointing him guardian of comatose Nancy Klein, in order to authorize an abortion for her (an abortion doctors deemed necessary to the recovery of the seventeen-weeks-pregnant woman, and after which she did indeed regain consciousness). In the face of *that* family's claim, right-to-life activists created a national furor and initiated legal proceedings (which ultimately failed) to stay Klein's court order ("Court OKs Abortion for Comatose Woman," *Syracuse Herald Journal*, Feb. 11, 1989, pp. A1–A4). Later that year, a father easily won an order—passionately contested by his wife's family—to sustain his brain-dead pregnant wife's life for seven and a half weeks; she was disconnected from the life-support system immediately after the delivery. In that case, unlike the more recent one, the woman's wishes were not even an issue for the father's case; his claim was argued simply on the basis of *his* desire that the baby be born. I am not suggesting that he had no moral argument. What I *am* pointing out are the dramatic inconsistencies in our moral responses to proxy actions and interpretations affecting the lives of the comatose and the brain-dead. Because the fetal-incubator construction is so normative within cultural attitudes, treating a pregnant comatose woman as mere body simply does not rouse the moral qualms that other such cases do (see also note 11, above).

32. *Guidelines for Legislation on Life-Sustaining Treatment*, National Conference of Catholic Bishops Administrative Committee, November 10, 1984, as reported in "New York State's Health Care Proxy Law: A Catholic Perspective," pamphlet produced by New York State Catholic Conference, Albany, n.d.

33. Nelson et al., "Forced Medical Treatment," pp. 756–57.

34. Eileen McNamara, "Fetal Endangerment Cases on the Rise," *Boston Globe*, Oct. 3, 1989, p. 1.

35. Ellen Goodman, "Pregnant and Prosecuted," *Finger Lakes Times*, Feb. 9, 1990.

36. Robb London, "Two Waiters Lose Jobs for Liquor Warning to Woman," *New York Times*, Saturday, March 30, 1991, p. 7.

37. Cal Thomas, "Watch What You Say to a Pregnant Woman," *Syracuse Herald Journal*, April 18, 1981.

38. Rhoden, "Judge in the Delivery Room," p. 1959.

39. "Two Waiters Lose Jobs," p. 7.

40. Often waiting lists for drug treatment programs are as much as six months long, and a 1989 New York City survey found that of the existing seventy-eight treatment centers, 54 percent did not accept pregnant woman and 87 percent would not treat pregnant women on Medicaid addicted to crack cocaine ("Fetal Endangerment Cases on the Rise").

41. Katha Pollitt, "Fetal Rights: A New Assault on Feminism," *The Nation* (March 26, 1990): 410.

42. Robert Pear, "The Hard Thing About Cutting Infant Mortality Is Educating Mothers," *New York Times*, Sunday, Aug. 12, 1990, p. 5.

43. Discussed in Pollitt, "Fetal Rights," p. 415, a "duty of care" has been proposed by fetal rights advocates as ethically justifying the obstetrical and life-style interventions they argue for.

44. Quoted in Gallagher, "Prenatal Invasions," p. 58.

45. Michael Harrison, "Unborn: Historical Perspective of the Fetus as Patient," *Pharos* (Winter 1982): 19–24, quoted in Ruth Hubbard, *The Politics of Women's Biology* (New Brunswick: Rutgers University Press, 1990), pp. 175–76.

46. Hubbard, *The Politics of Women's Biology*, p. 176.

47. See Rosalind Petchesky, "Fetal Images: The Power of Visual Culture in the Politics of Reproduction," in Michelle Stanworth, ed., *Reproductive Technologies* (Minneapolis: University of Minnesota Press, 1987), pp. 57–80, for an extremely insightful and balanced discussion of this issue.

48. "A lot of doctors," says George Annas, "identify more with the fetus than with a woman who is different from them" (quoted in Lewin, "Courts Acting," p. B10). Especially interesting about this identification is its apparently greater significance than, for example, *racial* "differences" between fetus and doctor, which pale (so to speak) beside deep psychic sources of sympathy with the fetus's state of helpless dependence on the mother.

49. Stefan Semchyshyn and Carol Colman, *How to Prevent Miscarriage and Other Crises of Pregnancy* (New York: Macmillan, 1989), p. 5.

50. I hasten to emphasize here that this criticism is not directed against women who choose to take such risks, but toward the discourse that effaces or minimizes those risks.

51. See Nelson et al., "Forced Medical Treatment," pp. 732–45, for an excellent discussion of these changes.

52. Dietrich v. Inhabitants of Northhampton, 138 Mass. 14 (1884).

53. W. Prosser, quoted in Nelson et al., "Forced Medical Treatment," p. 733.

54. 65 F. Supp. 138 (D.D.C. 1946).

55. 31 N.J. 353, 157 A.2d 497 (1960), quoted in Nelson et al., "Forced Medical Treatment," p. 734.

56. And this is not to mention the disparity between the respect afforded fetuses and grown women: in Minnesota, the same state that has ordered numerous medical procedures sanctioning the unconsented-to invasion of living women's bodies, a law went into effect in 1990 requiring hospitals and clinics to bury or cremate already dead fetuses, to preserve their "dignity" ("Law Says Cremate or Bury Fetuses," *Syracuse Herald Journal,* Oct. 1, 1990, p. 2.

57. Terence Monmaney and Kate Robinson, "Doesn't a Man Have Any Say?" *Newsweek* (May 23, 1988): 74–75.

58. "Big Win for Pro-Lifers: Pennsylvania Passes Strictest State Abortion Law," *Finger Lakes Times,* Nov. 15, 1989.

59. Peggy Orenstein, "Does Father Know Best?" *Vogue* (April 1989): 314.

60. Aeschylus, *Oresteia,* trans. and intro. by Richard Lattimore (Chicago: University of Chicago Press, 1953), quote from *The Eumenides,* p. 158.

61. James Hillman, *The Myth of Analysis: Three Essays in Archetypal Psychology* (New York: Harper and Row, 1978), p. 218.

62. See the introduction to this volume for a discussion of these representations.

63. Aristotle, *The Basic Works of Aristotle,* ed. Richard McKeon (New York: Random House, 1941), *On the Generation of Animals,* trans. Arthur Platt, 729a 25, p. 676.

64. To be fair, there was another version of preformation and emboîtement (the "ovist" version), according to which God placed the animalcules in the woman's womb when she was created. This version, however, was far less widely accepted than the official animalculist version. In any case, in both versions the woman functions as container.

65. Quoted in Brian Easlea, *Witch-hunting, Magic and the New Philosophy* (Atlantic Highlands, N.J.: Humanities Press, 1980), p. 148.

66. 428 U.S. 52 (1976), quoted in Patricia Hennessey, "On the Rise: Men Make Claims in Abortion Suits," *Conscience* 9, no. 4 (July–Aug. 1988): 4.

67. Transcript of "Nightline" show "Abortion Rights," July 22, 1988, Journal Graphics, New York, N.Y.

68. "Embryo's Rights Upheld," *Syracuse Herald Journal,* Sept. 21, 1989, p. A12.

69. "Doesn't a Man Have Any Say?" p. 74.

70. In the Matter of the Unborn Child "H," No. 84CO1 8804 JP 185 (1988), quoted in Hennessey, "On the Rise," p. 4.

71. It could be argued that what is required is to bring the social and legal system into line with the treatment of pregnant women, not the other way around. That is, *everyone* (not only pregnant women) should be required to be Good Samaritans toward those who require our aid. It is beyond the scope of this essay to evaluate such an ideal beyond suggesting that those for whom such a transformation is genuinely the goal (and is not merely being paid lip-service to, with the covert goal of justifying current inequities) need to demonstrate their good faith by requiring some social care and

sacrifice from sources other than pregnant women. A good place to start would be with a national health system that would give poor, pregnant women the care *they* need.

72. The phrases in quotes are from bell hooks's discussion of the reclamation of "black subjectivity," a discussion that is applicable as well to the reclamation of other marginalized and desubjectified identities, including women's reproductive identities: "Contemporary African-American resistance struggle must be rooted in a process of decolonialization that continually opposes re-inscribing notions of 'authentic' black identity. This critique should not be made synonymous with a dismissal of the struggle of oppressed and exploited people to make ourselves subject. Nor should it deny that in certain circumstances this experience affords us a privileged critical location from which to speak. This is not a re-inscription of modernist master narratives of authority which privilege some voices by denying voice to others. Part of our struggling for radical black subjectivity is the quest to find ways to construct self and identity that are oppositional and liberatory. The unwillingness to critique essentialism on the part of many African-Americans is rooted in the fear that it will cause folks to lose sight of the specific history and experience of African-Americans and the unique sensibilities and culture that arise from that experience. An adequate response to this concern is to critique essentialism while emphasizing the significance of 'the authority of experience.' There is a radical difference between a repudiation of the idea that there is a black 'essence' and recognition of the way black identity has been specifically constituted in the experience of exile and struggle." (*Yearning* [Boston: South End Press, 1990], pp. 28–29.)

73. Emily Martin, *The Woman in the Body* (Boston: Beacon Press, 1989), pp. 139–65.

74. Davis, *Women, Race, and Class*, pp. 20–21.

75. Iris Young, "Pregnant Embodiment: Subjectivity and Alienation," *Journal of Medicine and Philosophy* 9 (Jan. 1984): 45–62.

76. I used to argue that this issue should be avoided, insisting that the fetus's status is not simply *there*, "in nature," awaiting an accurate reading, but is a matter of human decision, shaped according to the conventions of particular communities. I still believe all this. But I no longer believe that such meta-considerations remove the responsibility to participate in the public process of shaping those conventions. We retreat into the disembodied haven of meta-discourse only at great risk. For whether or not we choose to engage in the process, cultural determinations and imaginations of the fetus are being made, and currently they have begun to endow the fetus not merely with human status but (as I have shown in this essay) with superhuman status.

77. As Nancy Miller insists: "[T]he postmodernist decision that the Author is dead . . . does not necessarily work for women and prematurely forecloses the question of identity for them. Because women have not had the same historical relation of identity to origin, institution, production,

that men have had, women have not, I think, (collectively) felt burdened by too much Self, Ego, Cogito, etc. Because the female subject has juridically been excluded from the polis, and hence decentered, 'disoriginated,' deinstitutionalized, etc., her relation to integrity and textuality, desire and authority, is structurally different." ("Changing the Subject," in Teresa de Lauretis, ed., *Feminist Studies, Critical Studies* [Bloomington: Indiana University Press, 1986], p. 106.)

HUNGER AS IDEOLOGY

This essay grew out of a shorter piece, "How Television Teaches Women to Hate Their Hungers," in *Mirror Images* (Newsletter of Anorexia Bulimia Support, Syracuse, N.Y.) 4, no. 1 (1986): 8–9. An earlier version was delivered at the 1990 meetings of the New York State Sociological Association, and some of the analysis has been presented in various talks at Le Moyne and other colleges and community organizations. I owe thanks to all my students who supplied examples.

1. Journalist Beatrice Fairfax, quoted in Lois Banner, *American Beauty* (Chicago: University of Chicago Press, 1984), p. 136.

2. "Starvation Stages in Weight-loss Patients Similar to Famine Victims," *International Obesity Newsletter* 3 (April 1989).

3. Jean Baudrillard, *Simulations* (New York: Semiotext(e), 1983), pp. 1–3; quotation is on p. 2.

4. Geneen Roth, *Feeding the Hungry Heart* (New York: New American Library, 1982), p. 15.

5. See Helena Mitchie, *The Flesh Made Word* (New York: Oxford University Press, 1987), for an extremely interesting discussion of this taboo in Victorian literature.

6. Quoted from *Godey's* by Joan Jacobs Brumberg, *Fasting Girls* (Cambridge: Harvard University Press, 1988), p. 179.

7. Mitchie, *The Flesh Made Word*, p. 15. Not surprisingly, red meat came under especial suspicion as a source of erotic inflammation. As was typical for the era, such anxieties were rigorously scientized: for example, in terms of the heat-producing capacities of red meat and its effects on the development of the sexual organs and menstrual flow. But, clearly, an irresistible associational overdetermination—meat as the beast, the raw, the primitive, the masculine—was the true inflammatory agent here. These associations survive today, put to commercial use by the American Beef Association, whose television ads feature James Garner and Cybil Shepard promoting "Beef: Real Food for Real People." Here the nineteenth-century link between meat aversion, delicacy, and refinement is exploited, this time in favor of the meat-eater, whose down-to-earth gutsiness is implicitly contrasted to the prissiness of the weak-blooded vegetarian.

8. Mrs. H. O. Ward, *The Young Lady's Friend* (Philadelphia: Porter and Coates, 1880), p. 162, quoted in Mitchie, *The Flesh Made Word*, pp. 16–17.

9. Quoted in Mitchie, *The Flesh Made Word*, p. 193.

10. Bram Dijkstra, *Idols of Perversity* (New York: Oxford University Press, 1986), pp. 30–31.

11. *Malleus Malificarum* quoted in Brian Easlea, *Witch-Hunting, Magic, and the New Philosophy* (Atlantic Highlands, N.J.: Humanities Press, 1980), p. 8; Hall and Oates, "Man-Eater."

12. Women were thus warned that "gluttonous habits of life" would degrade their physical appearance and ruin their marriageability. "Gross eaters" could develop thick skin, broken blood vessels on the nose, cracked lips, and an unattractively "superanimal" facial expression (Brumberg, *Fasting Girls*, p. 179). Of course, the degree to which actual women were able to enact any part of these idealized and idolized constructions was highly variable (as it always is); but *all* women, of all classes and races, felt their effects as the normalizing measuring rods against which their own adequacy was judged (and, usually, found wanting).

13. Caroline Walker Bynum, *Holy Feast and Holy Fast: The Religious Significance of Food to Medieval Women* (Berkeley: University of California Press, 1987), p. 191.

14. *Syracuse Herald-American*, May 8, 1988, p. D1.

15. Charles Butler, *The American Lady*, quoted in Dijkstra, *Idols of Perversity*, p. 18. Margery Spring Rice noted this same pattern of self-sacrifice among British working-class housewives in the 1930s. Faced with the task of feeding a family on an inadequate budget and cooking in cramped conditions, the housewife, according to Rice, often "takes one comparatively easy way out by eating much less than any other member of her family." She gives a multitude of examples from social workers' records, including "'Her food is quite insufficient owing to the claims of the family'"; "'She is . . . a good mother spending most of the housekeeping money on suitable food for the children and often goes without proper food for herself'"; "'Mrs. A . . . gives her family of eight children an excellent diet . . . but cannot eat herself as she is so exhausted by the time she has prepared the family meals'"; and, interestingly, "'the children look well fed and one cannot help believing that Mrs. F. is starving herself unnecessarily'" (*Working-Class Wives: Their Health and Conditions* [London: Virago, 1989; orig. pub. 1939], pp. 157, 160, 162, 167).

16. Elias Canetti, *Crowds and Power* (New York: Viking, 1962), p. 221.

17. John Berger, *Ways of Seeing* (London: Penguin, 1977).

18. bell hooks, *Yearning* (Boston: South End Press, 1990), p. 42.

19. Marcia Millman, *Such a Pretty Face: Being Fat in America* (New York: Norton, 1980), p. 106.

20. John Schneider and W. Stewart Agras, "Bulimia in Males: A Matched Comparison with Females," *International Journal of Eating Disorders* 6, no. 2 (March 1987): 235–42.

ANOREXIA NERVOSA

This essay was presented as a public lecture at Le Moyne College, was subsequently presented at D'Youville College and Bennington College, and was originally published in the *Philosophical Forum* 17, no. 2 (Winter 1985). I wish to thank all those in the audiences at Le Moyne, D'Youville, and Bennington who commented on my presentations, and Lynne Arnault, Nancy Fraser, and Mario Moussa for their systematic and penetrating criticisms and suggestions for the *Forum* version. In addition, I owe a large initial debt to my students, particularly Christy Ferguson, Vivian Conger, and Nancy Monaghan, for their observations and insights.

1. Jules Henry, *Culture Against Man* (New York: Alfred A. Knopf, 1963).

2. When I wrote this piece in 1983, the term *anorexia* was commonly used by clinicians to designate a general class of eating disorders within which intake-restricting (or abstinent) anorexia and bulimia-anorexia (characterized by alternating bouts of gorging and starving and/or gorging and vomiting) are distinct subtypes (see Hilde Bruch, *The Golden Cage: The Enigma of Anorexia Nervosa* [New York: Vintage, 1979], p. 10; Steven Levenkron, *Treating and Overcoming Anorexia Nervosa* [New York: Warner Books, 1982], p. 6; R. L. Palmer, *Anorexia Nervosa* [Middlesex: Penguin, 1980], pp. 14, 23–24; Paul Garfinkel and David Garner, *Anorexia Nervosa: A Multidimensional Perspective* [New York: Brunner/Mazel, 1982], p. 4). Since then, as the clinical tendency has been increasingly to emphasize the differences rather than the commonalities between the eating disorders, bulimia has come to occupy its own separate classificatory niche. In the present piece I concentrate largely on those images, concerns, and attitudes shared by anorexia and bulimia. Where a difference seems significant for the themes of this essay, I will indicate the relevant difference in a footnote rather than overcomplicate the main argument of the text. This procedure is not to be taken as belittling the importance of such differences, some of which I discuss in "Reading the Slender Body."

3. Although throughout history scattered references can be found to patients who sound as though they may have been suffering from self-starvation, the first medical description of anorexia as a discrete syndrome was made by W. W. Gull in an 1868 address at Oxford (at the time he called the syndrome, in keeping with the medical taxonomy of the time, *hysteric apepsia*). Six years later, Gull began to use the term *anorexia nervosa*; at the same time, E. D. Lesegue independently described the disorder (Garfinkel and Garner, *Anorexia Nervosa*, pp. 58–59). Evidence points to a minor "outbreak" of anorexia nervosa around this time (see Joan Jacobs Brumberg, *Fasting Girls* [Cambridge: Harvard University Press, 1988]), a historical occurrence that went unnoticed by twentieth-century clinicians until renewed interest in the disorder was prompted by its reemergence and striking increase over the past twenty years (see note 11 of "Whose Body Is This?" for sources that document this increase). At the time I wrote the present piece, I was not aware of the extent of anorexia nervosa in the second half of the nineteenth century.

4. Ludwig Binswanger, "The Case of Ellen West," in Rollo May, ed., *Existence* (New York: Simon and Schuster, 1958), p. 288. He was wrong, of course. The symptom was not new, and we now know that Ellen West was

not the only young woman of her era to suffer from anorexia. But the fact that Binswanger was unaware of other cases is certainly suggestive of its infrequency, especially relative to our own time.

5. Hilde Bruch, *Eating Disorders* (New York: Basic Books, 1973), p. 4.

6. Levenkron, *Treating and Overcoming Anorexia Nervosa*, p. 1; Susan Squire, "Is the Binge-Purge Cycle Catching?" *Ms.* (Oct. 1983).

7. Dinitia Smith, "The New Puritans," *New York Magazine* (June 11, 1984): 28.

8. Kim Chernin, *The Obsession: Reflections on the Tyranny of Slenderness* (New York: Harper and Row, 1981), pp. 63, 62.

9. Garfinkel and Garner, *Anorexia Nervosa*, p. xi. Anorectics characteristically suffer from a number of physiological disturbances, including amenorrhea (cessation of menstruation) and abnormal hypothalamic function (see Garfinkel and Garner, *Anorexia Nervosa*, pp. 58–89, for an extensive discussion of these and other physiological disorders associated with anorexia; also Eugene Garfield, "Anorexia Nervosa: The Enigma of Self-Starvation," *Current Contents* [Aug. 6, 1984]: 8–9). Researchers are divided, with arguments on both sides, as to whether hypothalamic dysfunction may be a primary cause of the disease or whether these characteristic neuroendocrine disorders are the result of weight loss, caloric deprivation, and emotional stress. The same debate rages over abnormal vasopressin levels discovered in anorectics, touted in tabloids all over the United States as the "explanation" for anorexia and key to its cure. Apart from such debates over a biochemical predisposition to anorexia, research continues to explore the possible role of biochemistry in the self-perpetuating nature of the disease, and the relation of the physiological effects of starvation to particular experiential symptoms such as the anorectic's preoccupation with food (see Bruch, *The Golden Cage*, pp. 7–12; Garfinkel and Garner, *Anorexia Nervosa*, pp. 10–14).

10. Initially, anorexia was found to predominate among upper-class white families. There is, however, widespread evidence that this is now rapidly changing (as we might expect; no one in America is immune from the power of popular imagery). The disorder, it has been found, is becoming more equally distributed, touching populations (e.g., blacks and East Indians) previously unaffected, and all socioeconomic levels (Garfinkel and Garner, *Anorexia Nervosa*, pp. 102–3). There remains, however, an overwhelming disproportion of women to men (Garfinkel and Garner, *Anorexia Nervosa*, pp. 112–13).

11. Chernin's *The Obsession*, whose remarkable insights inspired my interest in anorexia, remains *the* outstanding exception to the lack of cultural understanding of eating disorders.

12. Chernin, *The Obsession*, pp. 36–37. My use of the expression "our culture" may seem overly homogenizing here, disrespectful of differences among ethnic groups, socioeconomic groups, subcultures within American society, and so forth. It must be stressed here that I am discussing ideology and images whose power is *precisely* the power to homogenize culture. Even

in pre-mass-media cultures we see this phenomenon: the nineteenth-century ideal of the "perfect lady" tyrannized even those classes who could not afford to realize it. With television, of course, a massive deployment of images becomes possible, and there is no escape from the mass shaping of our fantasy lives. Although they may start among the wealthy elite ("A woman can never be too rich or too thin"), media-promoted ideas of femininity and masculinity quickly and perniciously spread their influence over everyone who owns a TV or can afford a junk magazine or is aware of billboards. Changes in the incidence of anorexia among lower-income groups (see note 10, above) bear out this point.

13. Christopher Lasch, *The Culture of Narcissism* (New York: Warner Books, 1979), p. 88.

14. I choose these three primarily because they are where my exploration of the imagery, language, and metaphor produced by anorexic women led me. Delivering earlier versions of this essay at colleges and conferences, I discovered that one of the commonest responses of members of the audiences was the proffering of further axes; the paper presented itself less as a statement about the ultimate meaning or causes of a phenomenon than as an invitation to continue my "unpacking" of anorexia as a crystallizing formation. Yet the particular axes chosen have more than a purely autobiographical rationale. The dualist axes serve to identify and articulate the basic body imagery of anorexia. The control axis is an exploration of the question "Why now?" The gender/power axis continues this exploration but focuses on the question "Why women?" The sequence of axes takes us from the most general, most historically diffuse structure of continuity—the dualist experience of self—to ever narrower, more specified arenas of comparison and connection. At first the connections are made without regard to historical context, drawing on diverse historical sources to exploit their familiar coherence in an effort to sculpt the shape of the anorexic experience. In this section, too, I want to suggest that the Greco-Christian tradition provides a particularly fertile soil for the development of anorexia. Then I turn to the much more specific context of American fads and fantasies in the 1980s, considering the contemporary scene largely in terms of popular culture (and therefore through the "fiction" of homogeneity), without regard for gender difference. In this section the connections drawn point to a historical experience of self common to both men and women. Finally, my focus shifts to consider, not what connects anorexia to other general cultural phenomena, but what presents itself as a rupture from them, and what forces us to confront how ultimately opaque the current epidemic of eating disorders remains unless it is linked to the particular situation of women.

The reader will notice that the axes are linked thematically as well as through their convergence in anorexia: the obsession with control is linked with dualism, and the gender/power dynamics discussed implicitly deal with the issue of control (of the feminine) as well.

15. Michel Foucault, *The History of Sexuality*. Vol. 1: *An Introduction* (New York: Vintage, 1980), p. 155.

16. Foucault, *History of Sexuality*, pp. 47–48.

17. Hubert L. Dreyfus and Paul Rabinow, *Michel Foucault: Beyond Structuralism and Hermeneutics* (Chicago: University of Chicago Press, 1983), p. 112.

18. Foucault, *History of Sexuality*, p. 95.

19. Michel Foucault, *Discipline and Punish* (New York: Vintage, 1979), p. 26.

20. Plato, *Phaedo*, in *The Dialogues of Plato*, ed. and trans. Benjamin Jowett, 4th ed., rev. (Oxford: Clarendon Press, 1953), 83d.

21. St. Augustine, *The Confessions*, trans. R. S. Pine-Coffin (Middlesex: Penguin, 1961), p. 164.

22. *Phaedo* 81d.

23. *Phaedo* 66c. For Descartes on the body as a hindrance to knowledge, see *Conversations with Burman* (Oxford: Clarendon Press, 1976), p. 8, and *Passions of the Soul* in *Philosophical Works of Descartes*, 2 vols., trans. Elizabeth S. Haldane and G. R. T. Ross (Cambridge: Cambridge University Press, 1969), vol. 1, p. 353.

24. *Phaedo* 80a.

25. Indeed, the Cartesian "Rules for the Direction of the Mind," as carried out in the *Meditations* especially, are actually rules for the transcendence of the body—its passions, its senses, the residue of "infantile prejudices" of judgment lingering from that earlier time when we were "immersed" in body and bodily sensations.

26. Alan Watts, *Nature, Man, and Woman* (New York: Vintage, 1970), p. 145.

27. Bruch, *Eating Disorders*, p. 84.

28. Chernin, *The Obsession*, p. 8.

29. Entry in student journal, 1984.

30. Bruch, *The Golden Cage*, p. 4.

31. Binswanger, "The Case of Ellen West," p. 253.

32. Bruch, *Eating Disorders*, p. 253.

33. Levenkron, *Treating and Overcoming Anorexia Nervosa*, p. 6.

34. Bruch, *Eating Disorders*, p. 270; Augustine, *Confessions*, p. 164.

35. Bruch, *Eating Disorders*, p. 50.

36. Bruch, *Eating Disorders*, p. 254.

37. Entry in student journal, 1984.

38. Bruch, *Eating Disorders*, p. 279.

39. Aimee Liu, *Solitaire* (New York: Harper and Row, 1979), p. 141.

40. Jennifer Woods, "I Was Starving Myself to Death," *Mademoiselle* (May 1981): 200.

41. Binswanger, "The Case of Ellen West," p. 251 (emphasis added).

42. Why they should emerge with such clarity in the twentieth century and through the voice of the anorectic is a question answered, in part, by the following two axes.

43. Augustine, *Confessions*, p. 165; Liu, *Solitaire*, p. 109.

44. Binswanger, "The Case of Ellen West," p. 343.

45. Entry in student journal, 1983.

46. Woods, "I Was Starving Myself to Death," p. 242.

47. Liu, *Solitaire*, p. 109.

48. "I equated gaining weight with happiness, contentment, then slothfulness, then atrophy, then death." (From case notes of Binnie Klein, M.S.W., to whom I am grateful for having provided parts of a transcript of her work with an anorexic patient.) See also Binswanger, "The Case of Ellen West," p. 343.

49. Klein, case notes.

50. Cherry Boone O'Neill, *Starving for Attention* (New York: Dell, 1982), p. 131.

51. O'Neill, *Starving for Attention*, p. 49.

52. Liu, *Solitaire*, p. 101.

53. Levenkron, *Treating and Overcoming Anorexia Nervosa*, p. 122.

54. Since the writing of this piece, evidence has accrued suggesting that sexual abuse may be an element in the histories of many eating-disordered women (see note 2 in "Whose Body Is This?").

55. Bruch, *The Golden Cage*, p. 73. The same is not true of bulimic anorectics, who tend to be sexually active (Garfinkel and Garner, *Anorexia Nervosa*, p. 41). Bulimic anorectics, as seems symbolized by the binge-purge cycle itself, stand in a somewhat more ambivalent relationship to their hungers than do abstinent anorectics. See "Reading the Slender Body," in this volume, for a discussion of the cultural dynamics of the binge-purge cycle.

56. Bruch, *The Golden Cage*, p. 33.

57. Liu, *Solitaire*, p. 36.

58. Liu, *Solitaire*, p. 46. In one study of female anorectics, 88 percent of the subjects questioned reported that they lost weight because they "liked the feeling of will power and self-control" (G. R. Leon, "Anorexia Nervosa: The Question of Treatment Emphasis," in M. Rosenbaum, C. M. Franks, and Y. Jaffe, eds., *Perspectives on Behavior Therapy in the Eighties* [New York: Springer, 1983], pp. 363–77).

59. Bruch, *Eating Disorders*, p. 95.

60. Liu, *Solitaire*, p. 123.

61. Bruch, *The Golden Cage*, p. 65 (emphasis added).

62. Smith, "The New Puritans," p. 24 (emphasis added).

63. Entry in student journal, 1984.

64. Entry in·student journal, 1984.

65. Trix Rosen, *Strong and Sexy* (New York: Putnam, 1983), p. 108.

66. Rosen, *Strong and Sexy*, pp. 62, 14, 47, 48.

67. Smith, "The New Puritans," pp. 27, 26.

68. Rosen, *Strong and Sexy*, pp. 61–62.

69. Rosen, *Strong and Sexy*, pp. 72, 61. This fantasy is not limited to female body-builders. John Travolta describes his experience training for *Staying Alive*: "[It] taught me incredible things about the body . . . how it can be reshaped so you can make yourself over entirely, creating an entirely

new you. I now look at bodies almost like pieces of clay that can be molded." ("Travolta: 'You Really Can Make Yourself Over,'" *Syracuse Herald-American*, Jan. 13, 1985.)

70. Smith, "The New Puritans," p. 29.

71. Durk Pearson and Sandy Shaw, *Life Extension* (New York: Warner, 1982), p. 15.

72. Chernin, *The Obsession*, p. 47.

73. Smith, "The New Puritans," p. 24.

74. Sidney Journard and Paul Secord, "Body Cathexis and the Ideal Female Figure," *Journal of Abnormal and Social Psychology* 50: 243–46; Orland Wooley, Susan Wooley, and Sue Dyrenforth, "Obesity and Women—A Neglected Feminist Topic," *Women's Studies Institute Quarterly* 2 (1979): 81–92. Student journals and informal conversations with women students have certainly borne this out.

75. "Feeling Fat in a Thin Society," *Glamour* (Feb. 1984): 198.

76. The same trend is obvious when the measurements of Miss America winners are compared over the past fifty years (see Garfinkel and Garner, *Anorexia Nervosa*, p. 107). Some evidence has indicated that this tide is turning and that a more solid, muscular, athletic style is emerging as the latest fashion tyranny.

77. Entry in student journal, 1984.

78. Bruch, *The Golden Cage*, p. 58.

79. This is one striking difference between the abstinent anorectic and the bulimic anorectic: in the binge-and-vomit cycle, the hungering female self refuses to be annihilated, is in constant protest. And, in general, the rejection of femininity discussed here is *not* typical of bulimics, who tend to strive for a more "female"-looking body as well.

80. Entry in student journal, 1983.

81. O'Neill, *Starving for Attention*, p. 53.

82. Entry in student journal, 1983.

83. Bruch, *The Golden Cage*, p. 72; Bruch, *Eating Disorders*, p. 277. Others have fantasies of androgyny: "I want to go to a party and for everyone to look at me and for no one to know whether I was the most beautiful slender woman or handsome young man" (as reported by therapist April Benson, panel discussion, "New Perspectives on Female Development," third annual conference of the Center for the Study of Anorexia and Bulimia, New York, 1984).

84. Levenkron, *Treating and Overcoming Anorexia Nervosa*, p. 28.

85. See, for example, Levenkron's case studies in *Treating and Overcoming Anorexia Nervosa*, esp. pp. 45, 103; O'Neill, *Starving for Attention*, p. 107; Susie Orbach, *Fat Is a Feminist Issue* (New York: Berkley, 1978), pp. 174–75.

86. Liu, *Solitaire*, p. 79.

87. Bruch, *The Golden Cage*, p. 65.

88. Klein, case study.

89. Chernin, *The Obsession*, pp. 102–3; Robert Seidenberg and Karen DeCrow, *Women Who Marry Houses: Panic and Protest in Agoraphobia* (New York: McGraw-Hill, 1983), pp. 88–97; Bruch, *The Golden Cage*, p. 58; Orbach, *Fat Is a Feminist Issue*, pp. 169–70. See also my discussions of the protest thesis in "Whose Body Is This?" and "The Body and the Reproduction of Femininity" in this volume.

90. Bruch, *The Golden Cage*, pp. 27–28.

91. Bruch, *The Golden Cage*, p. 12.

92. Binswanger, "The Case of Ellen West," p. 243.

93. At the time I wrote this essay, I was unaware of the fact that eating disorders were frequently an element of the symptomatology of nineteenth-century "hysteria"—a fact that strongly supports my interpretation here.

94. See, among many other works on this subject, Barbara Ehrenreich and Dierdre English, *For Her Own Good* (Garden City: Doubleday, 1979), pp. 1–29.

95. See Martha Vicinus, "Introduction: The Perfect Victorian Woman," in Martha Vicinus, ed., *Suffer and Be Still: Women in the Victorian Age* (Bloomington: Indiana University Press, 1972), pp. x–xi.

96. Ernest Jones, *Sigmund Freud: Life and Work* (London: Hogarth Press, 1956), vol. 1, p. 193.

97. On the nineteenth-century epidemic of female invalidism and hysteria, see Ehrenreich and English, *For Her Own Good*; Carroll Smith-Rosenberg, "The Hysterical Woman: Sex Roles and Conflict in Nineteenth-Century America," *Social Research* 39, no. 4 (Winter 1972): 652–78; Ann Douglas Wood, "The 'Fashionable Diseases': Women's Complaints and Their Treatment in Nineteenth Century America," *Journal of Interdisciplinary History* 4 (Summer 1973).

98. Ehrenreich and English, *For Her Own Good*, p. 2.

99. Ehrenreich and English, *For Her Own Good*, p. 102.

100. Sigmund Freud and Josef Breuer, *Studies on Hysteria* (New York: Avon, 1966), p. 311.

101. Freud and Breuer, *Studies on Hysteria*, p. 141; see also p. 202.

102. See especially pp. 76 ("Anna O."), 277, 284.

103. Marjorie Rosen, *Popcorn Venus* (New York: Avon, 1973); Lois Banner, *American Beauty* (Chicago: University of Chicago Press, 1983), pp. 283–85. Christian Dior's enormously popular full skirts and cinch-waists, as Banner points out, are strikingly reminiscent of Victorian modes of dress.

104. Liu, *Solitaire*, p. 141.

105. Binswanger, "The Case of Ellen West," p. 257.

106. This is one of the central themes I develop in "The Body and the Reproduction of Femininity," the next essay in this volume.

107. Dorothy Parker, *Here Lies: The Collected Stories of Dorothy Parker* (New York: Literary Guild of America, 1939), p. 48.

108. D. H. Lawrence, *Sons and Lovers* (New York: Viking, 1958), p. 257.

109. This experience of oneself as "too much" may be more or less emphatic, depending on such variables as race, religion, socioeconomic class, and sexual orientation. Luise Eichenbaum and Susie Orbach (*Understanding Women: A Feminist Psychoanalytic Approach* [New York: Basic Books, 1983]) emphasize, however, how frequently their clinic patients, nonanorexic as well as anorexic, "talk about their needs with contempt, humiliation, and shame. They feel exposed and childish, greedy and insatiable" (p. 49). Eichenbaum and Orbach trace such feelings, moreover, to infantile experiences that are characteristic of all female development, given a division of labor within which women are the emotional nurturers and physical caretakers of family life. Briefly (and this sketch cannot begin to do justice to their rich and complex analysis): mothers unwittingly communicate to their daughters that feminine needs are excessive and bad and that they must be contained. The mother does this out of a sense that her daughter will have to learn the lesson in order to become properly socialized into the traditional female role of caring for others—of feeding others, rather than feeding the self—and also because of an unconscious identification with her daughter, who reminds the mother of the "hungry, needy little girl" in herself, denied and repressed through the mother's *own* "education" in being female: "Mother comes to be frightened by her daughter's free expression of her needs, and unconsciously acts toward her infant daughter in the same way she acts internally toward the little-girl part of herself. In some ways the little daughter becomes an external representation of that part of herself which she has come to dislike and deny. The complex emotions that result from her own deprivation through childhood and adult life are both directed inward in the struggle to negate the little-girl part of herself and projected outward onto her daughter" (p. 44). Despite a real desire to be totally responsive to her daughter's emotional needs, the mother's own anxiety limits her capacity to respond. The contradictory messages she sends out convey to the little girl "the idea that to get love and approval she must show a particular side of herself. She must hide her emotional cravings, her disappointments and her angers, her fighting spirit. . . . She comes to feel that there must be something wrong with who she really is, which in turn must mean that there is something wrong with what she needs and what she wants. . . . This soon translates into feeling unworthy and hesitant about pursuing her impulses" (pp. 48–49). Once she has grown up, of course, these feelings are reinforced by cultural ideology, further social training in femininity, and the likelihood that the men in her life will regard her as "too much" as well, having been schooled by their own training in masculine detachment and autonomy.

(With boys, who do not stir up such intense identification in the mother and who, moreover, she knows will grow up into a world that will meet their emotional needs [that is, the son will eventually grow up to be looked after by his future wife, who will be well trained in the feminine arts of care], mothers feel much less ambivalent about the satisfaction of needs and behave much more consistently in their nurturing. Boys therefore grow up, according to Eichenbaum and Orbach, with an experience of their needs as legitimate, appropriate, worthy of fulfillment.)

The male experience of the woman as "too much" has been developmentally explored, as well, in Dorothy Dinnerstein's ground-breaking *The Mermaid and the Minotaur: Sexual Arrangements and Human Malaise* (New York: Harper and Row, 1976). Dinnerstein argues that it is the woman's capacity to call up memories of helpless infancy, primitive wishes of "unqualified access" to the mother's body, and "the terrifying erotic independence of every baby's mother" (p. 62) that is responsible for the male fear of what he experiences as "the uncontrollable erotic rhythms" of the woman. Female impulses, a reminder of the autonomy of the mother, always appear on some level as a threatening limitation to his own. This gives rise to a "deep fantasy resentment" of female impulsivity (p. 59) and, on the cultural level, "archetypal nightmare visions of the insatiable female" (p. 62).

110. Quoted in Brian Easlea, *Witch-Hunting, Magic, and the New Philosophy* (Atlantic Highlands, N.J.: Humanities Press, 1980), p. 242 (emphasis added).

111. Quoted in Easlea, *Witch-Hunting*, p. 242 (emphasis added).

112. See Peggy Reeve Sanday, *Female Power and Male Dominance* (Cambridge: Cambridge University Press, 1981), pp. 172–84.

113. Quoted in Easlea, *Witch-Hunting*, p. 8.

114. Peter Gay, *The Bourgeois Experience: Victoria to Freud*. Vol. 1: *Education of the Senses* (New York: Oxford University Press, 1984), pp. 197–201, 207.

115. Chernin, *The Obsession*, p. 38.

116. Ehrenreich and English, *For Her Own Good*, p. 124.

117. See Jeffrey Masson's controversial *The Assault on Truth: Freud's Suppression of the Seduction Theory* (Toronto: Farrar Straus Giroux, 1984) for a fascinating discussion of how this operation (which, because Fliess failed to remove half a meter of gauze from the patient's nasal cavity, nearly killed her) may have figured in the development of Freud's ideas on hysteria. Whether or not one agrees fully with Masson's interpretation of the events, his account casts light on important dimensions of the nineteenth-century treatment of female disorders and raises questions about the origins and fundamental assumptions of psychoanalytic theory that go beyond any debate about Freud's motivations. The quotations cited in this essay can be found on p. 76; Masson discusses the Eckstein case on pp. 55–106.

118. Banner, *American Beauty*, pp. 86–105. It is significant that these efforts failed in large part because of their association with the women's rights movement. Trousers like those proposed by Amelia Bloomer were considered a particular badge of depravity and aggressiveness, the *New York Herald* predicting that women who wore bloomers would end up in "lunatic asylums or perchance in the state prison" (p. 96).

119. Banner, *American Beauty*, pp. 149–50.

120. Amaury deRiencourt, *Sex and Power in History* (New York: David McKay, 1974), p. 319. The metaphorical dimension here is as striking as the functional, and it is a characteristic feature of female fashion: the dominant styles always decree, to one degree or another, that women *should not take up too much space*, that the territory we occupy should be limited. This is as true of cinch-belts as it is of foot-binding.

121. Quoted in deRiencourt, *Sex and Power in History*, p. 319.

122. Kathryn Weibel, *Mirror, Mirror: Images of Women Reflected in Popular Culture* (New York: Anchor, 1977), p. 194.

123. Christy Ferguson, "Images of the Body: Victorian England," philosophy research project, Le Moyne College, 1983.

124. Quoted in E. M. Sigsworth and T. J. Wyke, "A Study of Victorian Prostitution and Venereal Disease," in Vicinus, ed., *Suffer and Be Still*, p. 82.

125. See Kate Millett, "The Debate over Women: Ruskin vs. Mill," and Helene E. Roberts, "Marriage, Redundancy, or Sin: The Painter's View of Women in the First Twenty-Five Years of Victoria's Reign," both in Vicinus, ed., *Suffer and Be Still*.

126. Gay, *The Bourgeois Experience*, p. 197; Millett, "Debate over Women," in Vicinus, ed., *Suffer and Be Still*, p. 123.

127. Vicinus, "Introduction," p. x.

128. Lasch, *The Culture of Narcissism*, p. 343 (emphasis added).

129. Chernin, *The Obsession*, p. 148.

130. Charles Gaines and George Butler, "Iron Sisters," *Psychology Today* (Nov. 1983): 67.

THE BODY AND THE REPRODUCTION OF FEMININITY

Early versions of this essay, under various titles, were delivered at the philosophy department of the State University of New York at Stony Brook, the University of Massachusetts conference on Histories of Sexuality, and the twenty-first annual conference for the Society of Phenomenology and Existential Philosophy. I thank all those who commented and provided encouragement on those occasions. The essay was revised and originally published in Alison Jaggar and Susan Bordo, eds., *Gender/Body/Knowledge: Feminist Reconstructions of Being and Knowing* (New Brunswick: Rutgers University Press, 1989).

1. Mary Douglas, *Natural Symbols* (New York: Pantheon, 1982), and *Purity and Danger* (London: Routledge and Kegan Paul, 1966).

2. Pierre Bourdieu, *Outline of a Theory of Practice* (Cambridge: Cambridge University Press, 1977), p. 94 (emphasis in original).

3. On docility, see Michel Foucault, *Discipline and Punish* (New York: Vintage, 1979), pp. 135–69. For a Foucauldian analysis of feminine practice, see Sandra Bartky, "Foucault, Femininity, and the Modernization of Patriarchal Power," in her *Femininity and Domination* (New York: Routledge, 1990); see also Susan Brownmiller, *Femininity* (New York: Ballantine, 1984).

4. During the late 1970s and 1980s, male concern over appearance undeniably increased. Study after study confirms, however, that there is still a large gender gap in this area. Research conducted at the University of Pennsylvania in 1985 found men to be generally satisfied with their appearance, often, in fact, "distorting their perceptions [of themselves] in a positive, self-aggrandizing way" ("Dislike of Own Bodies Found Common Among Women," *New York Times*, March 19, 1985, p. C1). Women, however, were found to exhibit extreme negative assessments and distortions of body perception. Other studies have suggested that women are judged more harshly than men when they deviate from dominant social standards of attractiveness. Thomas Cash et al., in "The Great American Shape-Up," *Psychology Today* (April 1986), p. 34, report that although the situation for men has changed, the situation for women has more than proportionally worsened. Citing results from 30,000 responses to a 1985 survey of perceptions of body image and comparing similar responses to a 1972 questionnaire, they report that the 1985 respondents were considerably more dissatisfied with their bodies than the 1972 respondents, and they note a marked intensification of concern among men. Among the 1985 group, the group most dissatisfied of all with their appearance, however, were teenage women. Women today constitute by far the largest number of consumers of diet products, attenders of spas and diet centers, and subjects of intestinal by-pass and other fat-reduction operations.

5. Michel Foucault, *The History of Sexuality.* Vol. 1: *An Introduction* (New York: Vintage, 1980), pp. 136, 94.

6. On the gendered and historical nature of these disorders: the number of female to male hysterics has been estimated at anywhere from 2:1 to 4:1, and as many as 80 percent of all agoraphobics are female (Annette Brodsky and Rachel Hare-Mustin, *Women and Psychotherapy* [New York: Guilford Press, 1980], pp. 116, 122). Although more cases of male eating disorders have been reported in the late eighties and early nineties, it is estimated that close to 90 percent of all anorectics are female (Paul Garfinkel and David Garner, *Anorexia Nervosa: A Multidimensional Perspective* [New York: Brunner/Mazel, 1982], pp. 112–13). For a sophisticated account of female psychopathology, with particular attention to nineteenth-century disorders but, unfortunately, little mention of agoraphobia or eating disorders, see Elaine Showalter, *The Female Malady: Women, Madness and English Culture, 1830–1980* (New York: Pantheon, 1985). For a discussion of social and gender issues in agoraphobia, see Robert Seidenberg and Karen DeCrow, *Women Who Marry Houses: Panic and Protest in Agoraphobia* (New York: McGraw-Hill, 1983). On the history of anorexia nervosa, see Joan Jacobs Brumberg, *Fasting Girls: The Emergence of Anorexia Nervosa as a Modern Disease* (Cambridge: Harvard University Press, 1988).

7. In constructing such a paradigm I do not pretend to do justice to any of these disorders in its individual complexity. My aim is to chart some points of intersection, to describe some similar patterns, as they emerge through a particular reading of the phenomenon—a political reading, if you will.

8. Showalter, *The Female Malady*, pp. 128–29.

9. On the epidemic of hysteria and neurasthenia, see Showalter, *The Female Malady*; Carroll Smith-Rosenberg, "The Hysterical Woman: Sex Roles and Role Conflict in Nineteenth-Century America," in her *Disorderly Conduct: Visions of Gender in Victorian America* (Oxford: Oxford University Press, 1985).

10. Martha Vicinus, "Introduction: The Perfect Victorian Lady," in Martha Vicinus, *Suffer and Be Still: Women in the Victorian Age* (Bloomington: Indiana University Press, 1972), pp. x–xi.

11. See Carol Nadelson and Malkah Notman, *The Female Patient* (New York: Plenum, 1982), p. 5; E. M. Sigsworth and T. J. Wyke, "A Study of Victorian Prostitution and Venereal Disease," in Vicinus, *Suffer and Be Still*, p. 82. For more general discussions, see Peter Gay, *The Bourgeois Experience: Victoria to Freud*. Vol. 1: *Education of the Senses* (New York: Oxford University Press, 1984), esp. pp. 109–68; Showalter, *The Female Malady*, esp. pp. 121–44. The delicate lady, an ideal that had very strong class connotations (as does slenderness today), is not the only conception of femininity to be found in Victorian cultures. But it was arguably the single most powerful ideological representation of femininity in that era, affecting women of all classes, including those without the material means to realize the ideal fully. See Helena Mitchie, *The Flesh Made Word* (New York: Oxford, 1987), for discussions of the control of female appetite and Victorian constructions of femininity.

12. Smith-Rosenberg, *Disorderly Conduct*, p. 203.

13. Showalter, *The Female Malady*, p. 129.

14. Erving Goffman, *The Presentation of the Self in Everyday Life* (Garden City, N.J.: Anchor Doubleday, 1959).

15. Betty Friedan, *The Feminine Mystique* (New York: Dell, 1962), p. 36. The theme song of one such show ran, in part, "I married Joan . . . What a girl . . . what a whirl . . . what a life! I married Joan . . . What a mind . . . love is blind . . . what a wife!"

16. See I. G. Fodor, "The Phobic Syndrome in Women," in V. Franks and V. Burtle, eds., *Women in Therapy* (New York: Brunner/Mazel, 1974), p. 119; see also Kathleen Brehony, "Women and Agoraphobia," in Violet Franks and Esther Rothblum, eds., *The Stereotyping of Women* (New York: Springer, 1983).

17. In Jonathan Culler, *Roland Barthes* (New York: Oxford University Press, 1983), p. 74.

18. For other interpretive perspectives on the slenderness ideal, see "Reading the Slender Body" in this volume; Kim Chernin, *The Obsession: Reflections on the Tyranny of Slenderness* (New York: Harper and Row, 1981); Susie Orbach, *Hunger Strike: The Anorectic's Struggle as a Metaphor for Our Age* (New York: W. W. Norton, 1985).

19. See "Hunger as Ideology," in this volume, for a discussion of how this construction of femininity is reproduced in contemporary commercials and advertisements concerning food, eating, and cooking.

20. Aimee Liu, *Solitaire* (New York: Harper and Row, 1979), p. 123.

21. Striking, in connection with this, is Catherine Steiner-Adair's 1984 study of high-school women, which reveals a dramatic association between problems with food and body image and emulation of the cool, professionally "together" and gorgeous superwoman. On the basis of a series of interviews, the high schoolers were classified into two groups: one expressed skepticism over the superwoman ideal, the other thoroughly aspired to it. Later administrations of diagnostic tests revealed that 94 percent of the pro-superwoman group fell into the eating-disordered range of the scale. Of the other group, 100 percent fell into the noneating-disordered range. Media images notwithstanding, young women today appear to sense, either consciously or through their bodies, the impossibility of simultaneously meeting the demands of two spheres whose values have been historically defined in utter opposition to each other.

22. See "Anorexia Nervosa" in this volume.

23. Dianne Hunter, "Hysteria, Psychoanalysis and Feminism," in Shirley Garner, Claire Kahane, and Madelon Sprenger, eds., *The (M)Other Tongue* (Ithaca: Cornell University Press, 1985), p. 114.

24. Catherine Clément and Hélène Cixous, *The Newly Born Woman*, trans. Betsy Wing (Minneapolis: University of Minnesota Press, 1986), p. 42.

25. Clément and Cixous, *The Newly Born Woman*, p. 95.

26. Seidenberg and DeCrow, *Women Who Marry Houses*, p. 31.

27. Smith-Rosenberg, *Disorderly Conduct*, p. 208.

28. Orbach, *Hunger Strike*, p. 102. When we look into the many autobiographies and case studies of hysterics, anorectics, and agoraphobics, we find that these are indeed the sorts of women one might expect to be frustrated by the constraints of a specified female role. Sigmund Freud and Joseph Breuer, in *Studies on Hysteria* (New York: Avon, 1966), and Freud, in the later *Dora: An Analysis of a Case of Hysteria* (New York: Macmillan, 1963), constantly remark on the ambitiousness, independence, intellectual ability, and creative strivings of their patients. We know, moreover, that many women who later became leading social activists and feminists of the nineteenth century were among those who fell ill with hysteria and neurasthenia. It has become a virtual cliché that the typical anorectic is a perfectionist, driven to excel in all areas of her life. Though less prominently, a similar theme runs throughout the literature on agoraphobia.

One must keep in mind that in drawing on case studies, one is relying on the perceptions of other acculturated individuals. One suspects, for example, that the popular portrait of the anorectic as a relentless overachiever may be colored by the lingering or perhaps resurgent Victorianism of our culture's attitudes toward ambitious women. One does not escape this hermeneutic problem by turning to autobiography. But in autobiography one is at least dealing with social constructions and attitudes that animate the subject's own psychic reality. In this regard the autobiographical literature on anorexia, drawn on in a variety of places in this volume, is strikingly full of anxiety about the domestic world and other themes that suggest deep rebellion against traditional notions of femininity.

29. Kim Chernin, *The Hungry Self: Women, Eating, and Identity* (New York: Harper and Row, 1985), esp. pp. 41–93.

30. Mark Poster, *Foucault, Marxism, and History* (Cambridge: Polity Press, 1984), p. 28.

31. Liu, *Solitaire*, p. 99.

32. Brett Silverstein, "Possible Causes of the Thin Standard of Bodily Attractiveness for Women," *International Journal of Eating Disorders* 5 (1986): 907–16.

33. Showalter, *The Female Malady*, p. 48.

34. Smith-Rosenberg, *Disorderly Conduct*, p. 207.

35. Orbach, *Hunger Strike*, p. 103.

36. Brownmiller, *Femininity*, p. 14.

37. Toril Moi, "Representations of Patriarchy: Sex and Epistemology in Freud's *Dora*," in Charles Bernheimer and Claire Kahane, eds., *In Dora's Case: Freud—Hysteria—Feminism* (New York: Columbia University Press, 1985), p. 192.

38. Foucault, *Discipline and Punish*, p. 136.

39. Foucault, *Discipline and Punish*, p. 136.

40. A focus on the politics of sexualization and objectification remains central to the anti-pornography movement (e.g., in the work of Andrea Dworkin, Catherine MacKinnon). Feminists exploring the politics of appearance include Sandra Bartky, Susan Brownmiller, Wendy Chapkis, Kim Chernin, and Susie Orbach. And a developing feminist interest in the work of Michel Foucault has begun to produce a poststructuralist feminism oriented toward practice; see, for example, Irene Diamond and Lee Quinby, *Feminism and Foucault: Reflections on Resistance* (Boston: Northeastern University Press, 1988).

41. See, for example, Susan Suleiman, ed., *The Female Body in Western Culture* (Cambridge: Harvard University Press, 1986).

42. Mitchie, *The Flesh Made Word*, p. 13.

43. Mitchie, *The Flesh Made Word*, p. 149.

READING THE SLENDER BODY

This piece originally appeared in Mary Jacobus, Evelyn Fox Keller, and Sally Shuttleworth, eds., *Body/Politics: Women and the Discourses of Science* (New York: Routledge, 1989). I wish to thank Mary Jacobus, Sally Shuttleworth, and Mario Moussa for comments and editorial suggestions on the original version.

1. See Keith Walden, "The Road to Fat City: An Interpretation of the Development of Weight Consciousness in Western Society," *Historical Reflections* 12, no. 3 (1985): 331–73.

2. See Michel Foucault, *The Use of Pleasure* (New York: Random House, 1986).

3. See Rudolph Bell, *Holy Anorexia* (Chicago: University of Chicago Press, 1985); and Caroline Walker Bynum, *Holy Feast and Holy Fast: The Religious Significance of Food to Medieval Women* (Berkeley: University of California Press, 1987), pp. 31–48.

4. See Kim Chernin, *The Obsession: Reflections on the Tyranny of Slenderness* (New York: Harper and Row, 1981).

5. See Thomas Cash, Barbara Winstead, and Louis Janda, "The Great American Shape-up," *Psychology Today* (April 1986); and "Dieting: The Losing Game," *Time* (Jan. 20, 1986), among numerous other general reports. Concerning women's preoccupation in particular, see note 24 below.

6. See Mary Douglas, *Natural Symbols* (New York: Pantheon, 1982); and her *Purity and Danger* (London: Routledge and Kegan Paul, 1966).

7. This approach presupposes, of course, that popular cultural images *have* meaning and are not merely arbitrary formations spawned by the whimsy of fashion, the vicissitudes of Madison Avenue, or the logic of post-industrial capitalism, within which (as has been argued, by Fredric Jameson and others) the attraction of a product or image derives solely from pure differentiation, from its cultural positioning, its suggestion of the novel or new. Within such a postmodern logic, Gail Faurschou argues, "Fashion has become the commodity 'par excellence.' It is fed by all of capitalism's incessant, frantic, reproductive passion and power. Fashion *is* the logic of planned obsolescence—not just the necessity for market survival, but the cycle of desire itself, the endless process through which the body is decoded and recoded, in order to define and inhabit the newest territorialized spaces of capital's expansion." ("Fashion and the Cultural Logic of Postmodernity," *Canadian Journal of Political and Social Theory* 11, no. 1–2 [1987]: 72.) While I don't disagree with Faurschou's general characterization of fashion here, the heralding of an absolute historical break, after which images have become completely empty of history, substance, and symbolic determination, seems itself an embodiment, rather than a demystifier, of the compulsively innovative logic of postmodernity. More important to the argument of this piece, a postmodern logic cannot explain the cultural hold of the slenderness ideal, long after its novelty has worn off. Many times, in fact, the principle of the new has made tentative, but ultimately nominal, gestures toward the end of the reign of thinness, announcing a "softer," "curvier" look, and so forth. How many women have picked up magazines whose covers declared such a turn, only to find that the images within remained essentially continuous with prevailing norms? Large breasts may be making a comeback, but they are attached to extremely thin, often athletic bodies. Here, I would suggest, there are constraints on the pure logic of postmodernity—constraints that this essay tries to explore.

8. See Robert Crawford, "A Cultural Account of 'Health'—Self-Control, Release, and the Social Body," in John McKinlay, ed., *Issues in the Political Economy of Health Care* (New York: Methuen, 1985), pp. 60–103.

9. Ira Sacker and Marc Zimmer, *Dying to Be Thin* (New York: Warner, 1987), p. 57.

10. Dalma Heyn, "Body Vision?" *Mademoiselle* (April 1987): 213.

11. See Lois Banner, *American Beauty* (Chicago: University of Chicago Press, 1983), p. 232.

12. Banner, *American Beauty*, pp. 53–55.

13. See Walden, "Road to Fat City," pp. 334–35, 353.

14. I thank Mario Moussa for this point, and for the Heather Locklear quotation.

15. Sacker and Zimmer, *Dying to Be Thin*, pp. 149–50.

16. Foucault, *The Use of Pleasure*, pp. 64–70.

17. See Douglas, *Purity and Danger*, pp. 114–28.

18. See Crawford, "A Cultural Account of 'Health.'"

19. John Farquhar, Stanford University Medical Center, quoted in "Dieting: The Losing Game," *Time* (Feb. 20, 1986): 57.

20. See Marcia Millman, *Such a Pretty Face: Being Fat in America* (New York: Norton, 1980), esp. pp. 65–79.

21. Millman, *Such a Pretty Face*, p. 77.

22. Sacker and Zimmer, *Dying to Be Thin*, p. 32.

23. These quotations are taken from transcripts of the "Donahue" show, provided by Multimedia Entertainment, Cincinnati, Ohio.

24. The discrepancy emerges very early. "We don't expect boys to be that handsome," says a nine-year-old girl in the California study cited above. "But boys expect girls to be perfect and beautiful. And skinny." A male classmate agrees: "Fat girls aren't like regular girls," he says. Many of my female students have described in their journals the pressure their boyfriends put on them to stay or get slim. These men have plenty of social support for such demands. Sylvester Stallone told Cornelia Guest that he like his woman "anorexic"; she immediately lost twenty-four pounds (*Time* [April 18, 1988]: 89). But few men want their women to go that far. Actress Valerie Bertinelli reports (*Syracuse Post-Standard*) how her husband, Eddie Van Halen, "helps keep her in shape": "When I get too heavy, he says, 'Honey, lose weight.' Then when I get too thin, he says, 'I don't like making love with you, you've got to gain some weight.'"

25. The most famous of such studies, by now replicated many times, appeared in *Glamour* (Feb. 1984): a poll of 33,000 women revealed that 75 percent considered themselves "too fat," while only 25 percent of them were above Metropolitan Life Insurance standards, and 30 percent were *below*. ("Feeling Fat in a Thin Society," p. 198). See also Kevin Thompson, "Larger Than Life," *Psychology Today* (April 1986); Dalma Heyn, "Why We're Never Satisfied with Our Bodies," *McCall's* (May 1982); Daniel Goleman, "Dislike of Own Body Found Common Among Women," *New York Times*, March 19, 1985.

26. On cultural associations of male with mind and female with matter, see, for instance, Dorothy Dinnerstein, *The Mermaid and the Minotaur: Sexual Arrangements and Human Malaise* (New York: Harper and Row, 1976); Genevieve Lloyd, *The Man of Reason* (Minneapolis: University of Minnesota

Press, 1984); and Luce Irigaray, *Speculum of the Other Woman* (Ithaca: Cornell University Press, 1985).

27. Bram Dijkstra, *Idols of Perversity* (New York: Oxford University Press, 1986), p. 29.

28. "Mutable Beauty," *Saturday Night* (Feb. 1, 1892): 9.

29. Mary Jacobus and Sally Shuttleworth (personal communication), pointing to the sometimes boyish figure of the "new woman" of late Victorian literature, have suggested to me the appropriateness of this interpretation for the late Victorian era; I have, however, chosen to argue the point only with respect to the current context.

30. Dinnerstein, *The Mermaid and the Minotaur*, pp. 28–34. See Chernin, *The Obsession*, for an exploration of the connection between early infant experience and attitudes toward the fleshy female body.

31. Historian LeeAnn Whites has pointed out to me how perverse this body symbolism seems when we remember what a pregnant and nursing body is actually like. The hourglass figure is really more correctly a symbolic advertisement to men of the woman's reproductive, domestic *sphere* than a representation of her reproductive *body*.

32. See Banner, *American Beauty*, pp. 283–85.

33. It is no accident, I believe, that Dolly Parton, now down to one hundred pounds and truly looking as though she might snap in two in a strong wind, opened her new show with a statement of its implicitly anti-feminist premise: "I'll bust my butt to please you!" (Surely she already has?) Her television presence is now recessive, beseeching, desiring only to serve; clearly, her packagers are exploiting the cultural resonances of her diminished physicality. Parton, of course, is no androgynous body-type. Rather, like Vanna White of "Wheel of Fortune" (who also lost a great deal of weight at one point in her career and is obsessive about staying thin), she has tremendous appeal to those longing for a more traditional femininity in an era when women's public presence and power have greatly increased. Parton's and White's large breasts evoke a nurturing, maternal sexuality. But after weight-reduction regimens set to anorexic standards, those breasts now adorn bodies that are vulnerably thin, with fragile, spindly arms and legs like those of young colts. Parton and White suggest the pleasures of nurturant female sexuality without any encounter with its powers and dangers.

34. *The Waist Land: Eating Disorders in America*, 1985, Gannett Corporation, MTI Teleprograms. The analysis presented here becomes more complicated with bulimia, in which the hungering "female" self refuses to be annihilated, and feminine ideals are typically not rejected but embraced.

FEMINISM, POSTMODERNISM, AND GENDER SKEPTICISM

A version of this essay originally appeared in Linda Nicholson, ed., *Feminism/Postmodernism* (New York: Routledge, 1989); most of it has been reprinted here virtually unchanged. However, the last section of the essay has been substantially expanded to include a discussion of the dramatic and highly publicized Thomas hearings (and to a lesser extent the Tyson and Kennedy Smith trials) of the fall and winter of 1991–92; these events seemed to me to illustrate strikingly some of the central points made in the original essay. Parts of this discussion originally appeared in Susan Bordo, "'Maleness' Revisited," *Hypatia* 7, no. 3 (Summer 1992): 197–207. The ideas of "Feminism, Postmodernism, and Gender Skepticism" were brewing in my mind for a long time before I actually set pen to paper, and thus they have been affected by many conversations, in particular those in which I engaged while a visiting scholar in Alison Jaggar's seminar at Douglass College in 1985 (and especially my talks with Alison Jaggar and Ynestra King), those that occurred while I was a Rockefeller Humanist-in-Residence at the Duke University/University of North Carolina Center for Research on Women in 1987–88, and those that have continuously taken place with Lynne Arnault and LeeAnn Whites. For comments on earlier drafts, I thank Patrick Keane, Ted Koditschek, Edward Lee, Mario Moussa, Linda Nicholson, Jean O'Barr, Linda Robertson, Bruce Shefrin, Lynne Tirrell, Jane Tompkins, and Mary Wyer.

1. Jean Grimshaw, *Philosophy and Feminist Thinking* (Minneapolis: University of Minnesota Press, 1986).

2. Susan Suleiman, "(Re)Writing the Body: The Politics and Poetics of Female Eroticism," in *The Female Body in Western Culture*, ed. Susan Suleiman (Cambridge: Harvard University Press, 1986), p. 24.

3. This is not to say that I disdain the insights of poststructuralist thought. My criticism here is addressed to certain programmatic uses of those insights. Much poststructuralist thought (the work of Foucault in particular) is better understood, I would argue, as offering interpretive *tools* and *historical* critique rather than theoretical frameworks for wholesale adoption.

4. My discussion here is focused on the emergence of gender analytics in North America. The story if told in the context of France and England would be different in many ways.

5. Carol Gilligan, *In a Different Voice* (Cambridge: Harvard University Press, 1982). It must be noted, however, that Gilligan does *not* view the different "voices" she describes as essentially or only related to gender. She "discovers" them in her clinical work exploring gender difference, but the chief aim of her book, as she describes it, is to "highlight a distinction between two modes of thought" that have been culturally reproduced along (but not only along) gender lines (p. 2).

6. Dorothy Dinnerstein, *The Mermaid and the Minotaur: Sexual Arrangements and Human Malaise* (New York: Harper and Row, 1976); Nancy Chodorow, *The Reproduction of Mothering: Psychoanalysis and the Sociology of Gender* (Berkeley: University of California Press, 1978); Gilligan, *In a Different Voice*.

7. Thomas Nagel, *The View from Nowhere* (Oxford: Oxford University Press, 1986).

8. Minnie Bruce Pratt, "Identity: Skin Blood Heart," in Elly Bulkin, Minnie Bruce Pratt, and Barbara Smith, *Yours in Struggle: Three Feminist Perspectives on Anti-Semitism and Racism* (Brooklyn: Long Haul Press, 1984), p. 18.

9. At the 1988 Eastern meetings of the American Philosophical Association in Washington, D.C., I presented a paper discussing some consequences of the fact that the classical philosophical canon has been dominated by white, privileged males. But these men have also, as was pointed out to me afterward by Bat-Ami Bar On, overwhelmingly been Christian. Although I am Jewish myself, I had not taken this into account, and I had to think long and hard about what *that* exclusion of mine meant. I was grateful to be enabled, by Ami's insight, to do so. This is, of course, the way we learn; it is not a process that should be freighted (as it often is nowadays) with the constant anxiety of "exposure" and political discreditation.

10. Barbara Christian, "The Race for Theory," *Feminist Studies* 14, no. 1 (1988): 67–69.

11. Grimshaw's *Philosophy and Feminist Thinking* is an example of work by a feminist who expresses these theoretical concerns through the categories and traditional formulations of problems of the Anglo-American analytic style of philosophizing rather than those of Continental poststructuralist thought.

12. Nancy Fraser and Linda Nicholson, "Social Criticism Without Philosophy: An Encounter Between Feminism and Postmodernism," in Nicholson, ed., *Feminism/Postmodernism*, p. 35.

13. Fraser and Nicholson, "Social Criticism Without Philosophy," p. 29.

14. Donna Haraway, "A Manifesto for Cyborgs: Science, Technology, and Socialist Feminism in the 1980s," in Nicholson, ed., *Feminism/Postmodernism*.

15. Fraser and Nicholson, "Social Criticism Without Philosophy," p. 35.

16. Friedrich Nietzsche, *On the Genealogy of Morals* (New York: Vintage, 1969), p. 119.

17. Michel Foucault, "On the Genealogy of Ethics," interview with Foucault in Hubert Dreyfus and Paul Rabinow, *Michel Foucault: Beyond Structuralism and Hermeneutics* (Chicago: University of Chicago Press, 1983), p. 232.

18. The Fraser and Nicholson article, which exhibits a strong, historically informed appreciation of past feminist theory, is fairly balanced in its critique. In contrast, other travels through the same literature have sometimes taken the form of a sort of demolition derby of previous feminist thought—portrayed in reductive, ahistorical, caricatured, and downright distorted terms and presented, from the enlightened perspective of advanced feminist method, as hopelessly inadequate.

19. Susan Bordo, *The Flight to Objectivity: Essays on Cartesianism and Culture* (Albany: State University of New York Press, 1987), pp. 114–18.

20. Haraway, "A Manifesto for Cyborgs," p. 199.

21. See Christian, "The Race for Theory," for an extended discussion of such dynamics and the way they sustain the exclusion of the literatures and critical styles of peoples of color.

22. Suleiman, "(Re)Writing the Body," p. 24.

23. Haraway, "A Manifesto for Cyborgs," p. 219.

24. Jacques Derrida and Christie V. McDonald, "Choreographies," *Diacritics* 12, no. 2 (1982): 76.

25. Drucilla Cornell and Adam Thurschwell, "Feminism, Negativity, Intersubjectivity," in Seyla Benhabib and Drucilla Cornell, eds., *Feminism as Critique* (Minneapolis: University of Minnesota Press, 1987), pp. 143–62.

26. Suleiman, "(Re)Writing the Body," p. 24.

27. Haraway, "A Manifesto for Cyborgs," pp. 205, 223.

28. Carroll Smith-Rosenberg, *Disorderly Conduct: Visions of Gender in Victorian America* (Oxford: Oxford University Press, 1985), p. 291.

29. Haraway, "A Manifesto for Cyborgs," p. 191.

30. Haraway elides these implications by adopting a constant and deliberate ambiguity about the nature of the body she is describing: It is both "personal" and "collective." Her call for "polyvocality" seems at times to be directed toward feminist culture as a collectivity; at others, toward individual feminists. The image she ends her piece with, of a "powerful infidel heteroglossia" to replace the old feminist dream of a "common language," sounds like a cultural image—until we come to the next line, which equates this image with that of "a feminist speaking in tongues." I suggest that this ambiguity, although playful and deliberate, nonetheless reveals a tension between her imagination of the cyborg as liberatory "political myth" and a lingering "epistemologism" which presents the cyborg as a model of "correct" perspective on reality. I applaud the former and have problems with the latter.

31. Friedrich Nietzsche, *The Will to Power*, ed. and trans. Walter Kaufmann (New York: Vintage, 1968), p. 272.

32. Haraway, "A Manifesto for Cyborgs," p. 216.

33. Grimshaw, *Philosophy and Feminist Thinking*, p. 73.

34. In speaking of "the practice of reproduction" I have in mind, not only pregnancy and birth, but menstruation, menopause, nursing, weaning, and spontaneous and induced abortion. I do not deny, of course, that all of these have been constructed and culturally valued in diverse ways. But does that diversity utterly invalidate any abstraction of significant points of general contrast between female and male bodily realities? The question, it seems to me, is to be approached through concrete exploration, not decided by theoretical fiat.

35. Coppélia Kahn, "Excavating 'Those Dim Minoan Regions': Maternal Subtexts in Patriarchal Culture," *Diacritics* 12, no. 3 (1982): 33.

36. "On Separation from and Connection to Others: Women's Mothering and the Idea of a Female Ethic," keynote address, tenth annual conference of the Canadian Society for Women in Philosophy, University of Guelph, September, 1987.

37. "Philosophy, Psychoanalysis, and Feminism," University of North Carolina Women's Studies lecture series, Chapel Hill, October, 1987.

38. I discuss this point in detail with respect to the history of philosophy in "Feminist Skepticism and the 'Maleness' of Philosophy," in Elizabeth Harvey and Kathleen Okruhlik, eds., *Women and Reason* (Ann Arbor: University of Michigan Press, 1992).

39. Patricia Williams, "The Bread and Circus Literacy Test," *Ms.* 2, no. 4 (Jan.–Feb. 1992): p. 37.

40. Grimshaw, *Philosophy and Feminist Thinking*, pp. 84–85.

41. Grimshaw, *Philosophy and Feminist Thinking*, p. 102.

42. Lynne Arnault makes a similar point in "The Uncertain Future of Feminist Standpoint Epistemology" (unpublished paper).

43. Bell hooks is particularly insightful about sexism as "a political stance mediating racial domination, enabling white men and black men to share a common sensibility about sex roles and the importance of male domination. Clearly both groups have equated freedom with manhood, and manhood with the right of men to have indiscriminate access to the bodies of women." She goes on to analyze this sexualization of male freedom and self-determination as a myth of masculinity that is dangerous and "life-threatening" not only to women but to the young men who "blindly and passively" enact it. (*Yearning* [Boston: South End Press, 1990], p. 59.)

44. Maria Lugones, "Playfulness, 'World'-Travelling, and Loving Perception," *Hypatia* 2, no. 2 (1987): 3–20.

45. Nancy Cott, *The Grounding of Modern Feminism* (New Haven: Yale University Press, 1987), p. 282.

46. Cott, *The Grounding of Modern Feminism*, p. 277.

47. Cott, *The Grounding of Modern Feminism*, p. 281.

48. Cott, *The Grounding of Modern Feminism*, p. 231.

49. Cott, *The Grounding of Modern Feminism*, pp. 232, 237.

50. Cott, *The Grounding of Modern Feminism*, p. 235.

51. Such destabilization is not equivalent to recognition that the very notion of "race" is a cultural construction. One can acknowledge the latter (as I do), yet insist that when the context calls for it we remain able to talk in general terms about the social and historical consequences of being marked as a certain "race."

52. Cott, *The Grounding of Modern Feminism*, p. 239.

"MATERIAL GIRL"

Earlier versions of this essay were delivered at the 1988 meetings of the Society for Phenomenology and Existentialist Philosophy, Duke University, Syracuse University, the 1990 meetings of the Popular Culture Association, the State University of New York at Binghamton's 1990 Conference on Feminism and Cultural Studies: Theory, History, Experience, and Sienna College. I thank all those who offered comments on those occasions, and Cynthia Willett and Cathy Schwichtenberg for reading an earlier written draft and making suggestions on it. This version was originally published in *Michigan Quarterly Review* (Fall 1990), and is here reprinted with some revisions and several new illustrations.

1. Quoted in Trix Rosen, *Strong and Sexy* (New York: Putnam, 1983), pp. 72, 61.

2. "Travolta: 'You Really Can Make Yourself Over,'" *Syracuse Herald-American*, Jan. 13, 1985.

3. "Popular Plastic Surgery," *Cosmopolitan* (May 1990): 96.

4. Tina Lizardi and Martha Frankel, "Hand Job," *Details* (Feb. 1990): 38.

5. Jennet Conant, Jeanne Gordon, and Jennifer Donovan, "Scalpel Slaves Just Can't Quit," *Newsweek* (Jan. 11, 1988): 58–59.

6. "Donahue" transcript 05257, n.d., Multimedia Entertainment, Cincinnati, Ohio.

7. Dahleen Glanton, "Racism Within a Race," *Syracuse Herald-American*, Sept. 19, 1989.

8. *Essence* reader opinion poll (June 1989): 71.

9. Since this essay first appeared, DuraSoft has altered its campaign once more, renaming the lenses "Complements" and emphasizing how "natural" and subtle they are. "No one will know you're wearing them," they assure. One ad for "Complements" features identical black twins, one with brown eyes and one wearing blue lenses, as if to show that DuraSoft finds nothing "wrong" with brown eyes. The issue, rather, is self-determination: "Choosing your very own eye color is now the most natural thing in the world."

10. Linda Bien, "Building a Better Bust," *Syracuse Herald-American*, March 4, 1990.

11. This was said by Janice Radway in an oral presentation of her work, Duke University, Spring, 1989.

12. John Fiske, *Television Culture* (New York: Methuen, 1987), p. 19.

13. Michel Foucault, *Discipline and Punish* (New York: Vintage, 1979), p. 138.

14. Related in Bill Moyers, "A Walk Through the Twentieth Century: The Second American Revolution," PBS Boston.

15. Foucault, *Discipline and Punish*, pp. 26–27.

16. Susan Rubin Suleiman, "(Re)Writing the Body: The Politics and Poetics of Female Eroticism," in Susan Rubin Suleiman, ed., *The Female Body in Western Culture* (Cambridge: Harvard University Press, 1986), p. 24.

17. Jacques Derrida and Christie V. McDonald, "Choreographies," *Diacritics* 12, no. 2 (1982): 76.

18. Cathy Schwichtenberg, "Postmodern Feminism and Madonna: Toward an Erotic Politics of the Female Body," paper presented at the University of Utah Humanities Center, National Conference on Rewriting the

(Post)Modern: (Post)Colonialism/Feminism/Late Capitalism, March 30–31, 1990.

19. John Fiske, "British Cultural Studies and Television," in Robert C. Allen, ed., *Channels of Discourse* (Chapel Hill: University of North Carolina Press, 1987), pp. 254–90.

20. Quoted in John Skow, "Madonna Rocks the Land," *Time* (May 27, 1985): 77.

21. Skow, "Madonna Rocks the Land," p. 81.

22. Molly Hite, "Writing—and Reading—the Body: Female Sexuality and Recent Feminist Fiction," in *Feminist Studies* 14, no. 1 (Spring 1988): 121–22.

23. "Fat or Not, 4th Grade Girls Diet Lest They Be Teased or Unloved," *Wall Street Journal*, Feb. 11, 1986.

24. Catherine Texier, "Have Women Surrendered in MTV's Battle of the Sexes?" *New York Times*, April 22, 1990, p. 31.

25. *Cosmopolitan* (July 1987): cover.

26. David Ansen, "Magnificent Maverick," *Cosmopolitan* (May 1990): 311.

27. Ansen, "Magnificent Maverick," p. 311; Kevin Sessums, "White Heat," *Vanity Fair* (April 1990): 208.

28. Susan McClary, "Living to Tell: Madonna's Resurrection of the Fleshy," *Genders*, no. 7 (Spring 1990): 2.

29. McClary, "Living to Tell," p. 12.

30. E. Ann Kaplan, "Is the Gaze Male?" in Ann Snitow, Christine Stansell, and Sharon Thompson, eds., *Powers of Desire: The Politics of Sexuality* (New York: Monthly Review Press, 1983), pp. 309–27.

31. E. Ann Kaplan, *Rocking Around the Clock: Music Television, Postmodernism and Consumer Culture* (New York: Methuen, 1987), p. 63.

32. McClary, "Living to Tell," p. 13.

POSTMODERN SUBJECTS, POSTMODERN BODIES,
POSTMODERN RESISTANCE

A version of this essay containing only reviews of the books and my introductory comments on postmodernism, appeared as a review essay in *Feminist Studies* 18, no. 1 (Winter 1992). The essay as it is printed here contains anecdotal material and new cultural analysis that did not appear in the review essay, and some of the book reviews themselves have been revised. I thank Edward Lee for his insights into modernity and postmodernity and his invaluable criticisms of earlier drafts of the essay. Thanks also to Linda Alcoff, Lynne Arnault, and the editors of *Feminist Studies* for their suggestions.

1. Charles Jencks, *What Is Post-Modernism?* 3d ed. (London: St. Martin's Press, 1989), p. 16.

2. Jencks, *What Is Post-Modernism?* p. 30.

3. Jane Flax, *Thinking Fragments* (Berkeley: University of California Press, 1990), p. 3; bell hooks, *Yearning* (Boston: South End Press, 1990); Judith Butler, *Gender Trouble* (New York: Routledge, 1990).

4. Flax, *Thinking Fragments*, p. 5.

5. Flax, *Thinking Fragments*, p. 194.

6. Flax, *Thinking Fragments*, p. 226.

7. hooks, *Yearning*, p. 155

8. hooks, "Postmodern Blackness," in *Yearning*, p. 29.

9. Flax, *Thinking Fragments*, p. 221.

10. hooks, *Yearning*, p. 31.

11. hooks, *Yearning*, pp. 21–22.

12. hooks, *Yearning*, p. 229.

13. Flax, *Thinking Fragments*, pp. 219, 183.

14. hooks, *Yearning*, p. 111.

15. hooks, *Yearning*, p. 63.

16. Maria Lugones, "Playfulness, 'World'-Travelling, and Loving Perception," *Hypatia* 2, no. 2 (Summer 1987): 3–20.

17. Domna Stanton, quoted in Scott Heller, "The Human Body and Changing Cultural Conceptions of It Draw Attention of Humanities and Social-Science Scholars," *Chronicle of Higher Education* (June 12, 1991): A4.

18. See the introduction to this volume for clarification of my use of the term *material* here.

19. Erving Goffman, *The Presentation of Self in Everyday Life* (Garden City, N.J.: Anchor Doubleday, 1959). Goffman also explores the specifically gendered dimension of the presentation of self in *Gender Advertisements* (New York: Harper and Row, 1976).

20. Butler, *Gender Trouble*, p. 136.

21. Butler, *Gender Trouble*, p. 93.

22. Butler, *Gender Trouble*, p. 92.

23. Butler, *Gender Trouble*, p. 91 (emphasis mine).

24. Butler, *Gender Trouble*, p. 137.

25. Butler, *Gender Trouble*, p. 137.

26. Butler, *Gender Trouble*, p. 137.

27. Suzanne Kessler and Wendy McKenna, *Gender: An Ethnomethodological Approach* (Chicago: University of Chicago Press, 1978); Holly Devor, *Gender Blending: Confronting the Limits of Duality* (Bloomington: Indiana University Press, 1989).

28. Esther Newman, *Mother Camp: Female Impersonators in America* (New York: Prentice-Hall, 1972), p. 127.

29. Jan Morris, *Conundrum* (New York: New American Library, 1974), pp. 25–26.

30. "People" column, *Syracuse Herald Journal*, Sept. 4, 1992, p. A3.

31. Even Sandra Dee, in her day, did not believe that she was what men wanted. In 1992, looking extremely thin, she revealed that she had struggled with food and body-image problems throughout her career and had in fact been anorexic for much of her adult life.

32. Hooks, *Yearning*, p. 22.

Index

Abortion, 71–97; and fathers' rights, 88–93; rights, 90, 93–94, 313n.313. *See also* Fetuses; Pregnant women

Academics, 259–60, 280, 285; feminist, 232–33, 240–42, 281–85; postmodern, 240, 260, 263, 278–83

Accused, 29

Active spirit: vs. passive body, 11–15, 90; and reproductive rights, 90

Acton, William, 162, 169

Addams, Jane, 158

Advertisements, 100–10, 296–98; African Americans targeted by, 100–102, 124–25, 257–58, 263–64; Crystal Light, 139; dieting-related, 99–112 passim, 126, 129, 199; DuraSoft contact lenses, 251, 255–58, 340n.9; food-related, 99–134 passim, 199; gender difference represented in, 118, 119–21, 128–29; gender duality in, 14; gender represented nontraditionally in, 131–34; ideal woman of, 164; with muscles, 193–95, 296; and plastic bodies, 247–50, 251; and sex, 287; Virginia Slims, 100–102, 103; women's strengths in, 207–9

Affirmative action, 28

African Americans, 9–11; and abortion rights, 95; advertisements targeted for, 100–103, 124–25, 257–58, 263–64; and beauty, 63, 251–58, 263–65; body-discriminations, 254; and body image, 63, 100–102, 103; children's view of black and white dolls, 262–63; cosmetic changes, 253, 254, 257–58, 264; diet and exercise for, 63, 103; and Hill/Thomas hearings, 9, 11, 235–36, 237; hooks and, 124, 283–84, 285, 286, 316n.72, 339n.43; Jezebel, 235; men, 9, 11, 125, 235–36, 237, 286; models, 25; postmodern deconstruction and, 283–84; racist ideology and, 9–11, 79–80; sermon mode, 42, 284; in servitude,

9–11, 22, 124; subjectivity, 316n.72; women, 9–11, 22, 63, 100–102, 103, 124–25, 235–36, 264

Age: of anorectics, 156; of cosmetic surgery patients, 246

Aging, 4–5, 25–26, 104, 153

Agoraphobia, 159, 167–84 passim, 331n.28; and femininity, 168, 170, 174–75, 179–80; and gender, 167, 329n.6; and power, 179–80; as protest, 175, 176

AIDS, 287

Alterity: and critical imagination, 41

Amenorrhoea, anorectics and, 207, 320n.9

American Civil Liberties Union, 80

American Medical Association, 80

American Philosophical Association, 337n.9

American Society of Plastic and Reconstructive Surgery, 259

Anatomy of Melancholy (Burton), 161

Andes Candies, 129, 130

Androgyny, 206; eating disorders and, 141, 148, 174, 324n.83; Madonna and, 269, 274

Anglo-Americans. *See* Whites

"Animalcules," 90, 315n.64

Animality: of body, 2–3, 4, 144; and muscles, 193; racism and, 9–11, 236

Annas, George, 80, 314n.48

Anorexia mirabilia, 68–69

Anorexia nervosa, 8, 15, 35, 45–47, 137, 139–64, 167–84 passim, 319–28; ambivalent cultural attitudes toward, 201–2; "axes of continuity," 142, 144–64, 321n.14; and BIDS, 5, 55–56, 57; boyfriends influencing, 64, 154–55, 334n.24; and breasts / bodily bulges, 46, 141, 159, 178, 188–89, 207–9; vs. bulimia, 323n.55, 324n.79; consumer culture and, 201–2; and control, 59, 142–54 passim, 171–72,

343

Compositor:	Braun-Brumfield, Inc.
Text:	10/13 Palatino
Display:	Palatino
Printer:	Thomson-Shore, Inc.
Binder:	Thomson-Shore, Inc.